minor cosmopolitan

minor cosmopolitan
Thinking Art, Politics, and the Universe Together Otherwise

Edited by Zairong Xiang

DIAPHANES

Funded by the Deutsche Forschungsgemeinschaft (DFG, German Research Foundation) – 265331351/RTG 2130
minor cosmopolitanisms

Preface

More than a year has passed since the *minor cosmopolitan weekend*, which I curated together with the DFG Research Training Group (RTG) minor cosmopolitanisms, was held at the Haus der Kulturen der Welt in December 2018. A warm breeze was just felt on the streets of Berlin.

This was February 2020. The recent memories of braving the northern wind to line up for Berlinale screenings suddenly seemed unreal or misremembered. "It's not that bad, come on!," a filmmaker from Montreal told us Berliners the other day at a dinner table, as we casually talked about how awful the Berlin winter can be. And he was right; it's not that bad at all. It's awful. Climate change has accelerated to the extent that some predict the end of the world will come much sooner than previously imagined. Even just one year ago, when we brought scholars, artists, activists, filmmakers, musicians, dancers, curators, and journalists from around the world to Berlin for a long minor cosmopolitan weekend, the ecological question, although present, was not given a dedicated slot in the program. Yet ecological crisis is markedly cosmopolitan—if by "cosmopolitan" we mean, minimally, ways of thinking and living based on an assumption that the world is immensely connected and, therefore, like it or not, we (must) live and think together. This immense connection has been hailed in cosmopolitanisms big and small, major and minor, often as an ideal to be realized.

Cosmopolitanism is a theory about how to live together. The earliest formulation of cosmopolitanism in the West is usually traced back to as early as the fourth century BCE in ancient Greece and specifically to Diogenes, who famously said that he was a "citizen of the world—*kosmopolitês,*" an idea later picked up, among others, by Immanuel Kant, the German philosopher who proposed a philosophy of a world of "perpetual peace." When cosmopolitanism first emerged as a political idea for modernity in the European Enlightenment, the project embraced the liberal promises of a globalizing economy, yet remained oblivious to, and even complicit with, capitalism, slavery and colonialism. It centered on the male, bourgeois, and white liberal subject, without regard for the ongoing disenfranchisement, dehumanization, and extermination of its "Others."

In the wake of rapid globalization at the dawn of the twenty-first century, academics, politicians and other pundits were already declaring cosmopolitanism to be no longer just a philosophical ideal, but a real, existing fact, because across the globe, they argued, people were increasingly thinking and feeling beyond the nation, considering themselves citizens of the world. Not much remains of this euphoria today. "If you think you are a citizen of the world, you are a citizen of nowhere," argued Teresa May, the former prime minister of the UK, enthusiastically, at the height of the Brexit debate. Fast forward, as the UK has already cut itself off from Europe, Europe is also fencing itself ever more, to the extent that its growingly aggressive, violent and indeed murderous border regimes have brought their armies to the Euro-Turkish border. Fortress Europe hides its favorite flags of democracy, freedom and human rights—the West constantly chooses itself as these values' unquestionable bearer—behind live ammunition, directed at human beings in dire need of refuge from war-torn countries. The cosmopolitan ideal of imagining humanity as *One Happy Family* was burnt to ashes on the Greek island of Lesvos, not very far away from the birthplace of cosmopolitanism—at least according to the frequently reiterated European origin story.

Another month has passed since I wrote the previous three paragraphs. A pandemic is devastating the world. This is March 2020. A new coronavirus (Covid-19) seems to have become the true citizen of the world. Literally, physically, a *minor* one, it appears to have realized the cosmopolitan ideal, albeit of a morbid kind. It possesses no passport and yet is able to travel across artificial borders much more easily and efficiently than any human being. It even seems, at first sight, to offer everyone an equal opportunity to get infected. Perhaps we didn't realize the cosmopolitan premise of the bounded nature of humanity until it was too late. It was only after the virus arrived in Europe and US America that we read words of universalism and pledges for "global solidarity" (a very cosmopolitan idea indeed) from politicians, pundits and philosophers. Judith Butler wrote on March 30th, 2020: "The virus does not discriminate. We could say that it treats us equally, puts us equally at risk of falling ill, losing someone close, living in a world of imminent threat. By the way it moves and strikes, the virus demonstrates that the human community is equally precarious."[1]

These statements of viral non-exceptionalism are, of course, extremely convoluted. No, the virus does not nod to the liberal premise of equal access. It does not affect everyone equally. Butler rightly points out how "radical inequality" has been exacerbated, but it is not only the superstructures of evil ("nationalism, white supremacy, violence against women, queer, and trans people, and capitalist exploitation"[2]) that do the work. The pandemic reveals the utter failure of the Eurocentric liberal subject. While most middle-class households could afford to "self-quarantine" and "home-office," many cannot. While many individuals in the Berlin conclave of "the free world" actively resist quarantine measures by claiming their "personal liberty" to gather in cafes, in big crowds, in "corona-parties,"—to the point that the German chancellor, Angela Merkel, had to hold a public speech to remind the population that every life counts and that "Niemand ist verzichtbar" (no one is dispensable)—many workers, mainly from under-privileged classes and with a migrant background, are overworking, stocking food and toilet paper to keep up with the euphoria of panic buying that has turned the "rational" human individual into a hamster. Meanwhile, the verzichtbar refugees continue to be disposed of at the border as unmournable life waiting to die—unless, of course, they are medical workers (we've seen in the past weeks that those who have been kept in perpetual bureaucratic limbo are suddenly asked to contribute their medical knowledge and join forces to combat the pandemic), or can fill in for seasonal agricultural workers stuck in their home countries.[3]

Although most contributions were written before the Covid-19 pandemic, the book *minor cosmopolitan: Thinking Art, Politics and the Universe Together Otherwise*, which emerged from the *minor cosmopolitan weekend*, is edited against this historic background: one of a rapidly collapsing world-as-we-know-it, as the global ecological crisis worsens, fascism returns, the repression of disenfranchised groups on a global scale persists, the "refugee crisis" inundates the mediascape, and the coronavirus joins forces with neoliberal capitalism to kill the most vulnerable. *minor cosmopolitan* invites scholars, activists, and artists to face the trouble, with the questions raised, but not properly resolved, by cosmopolitanisms.
It challenges the underlying premises of major cosmopolitanism without letting go of the unfulfilled emancipatory potential of the concept at large. It rethinks cosmopolitanisms in the plural, and it traces multiple origins and trajectories of cosmopolitan thought across the globe.

minor cosmopolitan takes the "ism" out of "cosmopolitanism," for *ism*, even in its pluralized version, seems to be premised on a false division between theory and practice (a trademark of eurocentrism), which in turn saturates a colonial north-south, east-west division for which we are paying a deadly price. The dizzying multiplicity and complexity we are confronted with in today's world require us to be suspicious of any conceptual totality and monopoly that could claim a theory, and therefore an *ism*, for all. Importantly, the disproportionate power of a little suffix, like the tiny *ism*, teaches us that we need to use all small words, like "minor," with care and attention.

This small change—from *ism*, to no *ism*—engenders a big question: how do we think about, and with, but also most importantly learn from, the minor cosmopolitan afforded by the richness of the diverse practices, theories and ways of being in the world that already exist across history, and across cultural and linguistic boundaries? Without subsuming these exciting complexities under one singular notion, the book is designed to blend together critical inquiries, activism, and art, to explore and enact the myriad ways of being and thinking together, emphatically other-wise.

In order to reflect and accommodate the diversity and therefore richness of issues, genres, and creativities of our contributions, the book is designed to defy the single genre—be it "edited volume," "conference proceedings" or "exhibition catalogue." Theoretical, artistic, and literary contributions are placed side by side. Different approaches, concerns, and spelling conventions are interwoven with each other without synthesis.

The book is loosely constructed in five parts. **Entering the (minor) Cosmos**, scholar Arjun Appadurai opens our journey through the minor cosmopolitan with a succinct reflection on a small object that possesses big capacities: the passport, which cosmopolitan travels in today's world cannot do without. Artist Marina Camargo's reflections on the visualization of time and space, a flat-media rendering of her installation *Mikrokosmos* commissioned for the *minor cosmopolitan weekend*, brings our *polis* of Berlin into the cosmos. The universe is immense and immensely empty. Philosopher Sundar Sarrukai takes the cosmic dimension visualized in Camargo's work to the macro and therefore micro extremes—the minor cosmopolitan is here theorized, with the help of Buddhism, as first and foremost a question of how to understand "emptiness, negation and absence." The meditation on zero and one-ness is poetically enriched by writer Mario Bellatin, his grandma's canary, and the perch inside its birdcage, in a piece that was recited by the author during the *minor cosmopolitan weekend*, and which can be listened to on the website accompanying this book.

Poleis addresses concrete questions raised by the city. Scholar James Miller poses the question of planetary porosity through a timely reflection on the global pandemic caused by the Covid-19 coronavirus, which has brought megacities to total lockdown. Performer Liad Hussein Kantorowicz's love letter to her deceased partner Timi (Tim Stüttgen) tenderly speaks to and yet forcefully protests against a Berlin that is rapidly dying because of gentrification. Former graphic novelist Sarnath Banerjee maintains our gaze on Berlin, where objects, places, and people are woven into uncanny experiences. He asks, but does not answer, "how cosmopolitan is Berlin, really?" Moving one step eastwards from Berlin to Hungary, Romania, and "a Bohemia by the sea," we encounter a cartographic and indeed ontological question of Europe's very (self)-definition. Scholar Lucy Gasser takes us on a literary quest through Other Europes, guided by three writers from the European canon, non-canon, and non-European non-canon.

Who Sustains the Flourishing of the World? It has become newly evident, in the current pandemic of Covid-19, that the essential work that sustains the functioning of the world is carried out by marginalized groups with the most precarious working conditions. Convened by the research collective In Front of the Factory (Rosa Barotsi, Saima Akhtar, Clio Nicastro), the third part of the book takes the "minor" in the minor cosmopolitan to mean the precarity of labor practices historically associated with women's work, in the context of global neoliberalism and its accompanying discursive and institutional approaches to (gendered) precarity. In the first piece of the section, the collective invites us to look at visual representations that emerge from women's work and labor organization. Filmmaker and geographer Mary Jirmanus Saba and filmmaker, activist, and scholar Vivian Price subsequently guide us through their respective works to discuss questions of gender, race, labor, activism, and environmental justice.

What minor cosmopolitan(isms) also asks us to think otherwise is a collective future that is more just and liveable. Imagining a better future whilst overlooking historical realities as well as socio-economic and cultural specificities, however, often risks becoming complicit with major power structures. **Ambiguous Utopias** looks at literary and artistic practices and movements that have imagined a world otherwise: historian and curator Tom Holert traces surrealism and its ambiguous relation to its non-European "peripheries," which include not only the European-colonized but also the peripheral colonial power of Japan. Holert extends his rich historiography to a recent film: *Le Moulin* (2015), by Taiwanese director Huang Ya-Li, about a Taiwanese surrealist poetry society under Japanese colonial rule. Huang, together with Sing Song-Yong and Iwaya Kunio, curated the exhibition *Synchronic Constellation: Le Moulin and its Time*; a selection of images from that exhibition are featured at the end of Holert's essay. From surrealism to science fiction: scholar James Burton's essay theorizes the critical power of science fiction, exemplified by the works of Ursula Le Guin, Clifford Simak and Octavia Butler, which are able to negotiate some dazzling contradictions—minor and cosmopolitan being one of them. Poet and scholar Hinemoana Baker's reflections, punctuated with poetry in Māori, German and English, want to trigger "more questions," as she puts it, when indigeneity and cosmopolitanism are put together, as when someone with Māori roots navigates the world as a global citizen.

Some of Baker's poems can be listened to on our website. These spoken words lead us to the topic of sound, which occupies the next section of the book: **Voicing the minor Cosmopolitan** opens up to less explored questions of the minor cosmopolitan endeavor of thinking together and thinking otherwise. Scholar Irene Hilden and artist Anaïs Héraud-Louisadat discuss their respective works on, or inspired by, Humboldt University's sound archive (Lautarchiv)—an acoustic witness to, not only the under-discussed German colonial history, but also the racializing scientific practices of the early twentieth century. The complex relationship between colonial sound recording and techno-capitalism is further explored by artist Liu Chuang in his 3-channel video and accompanying text that establishes (in)visible and (in)audible connections from seemingly unrelated events: bitcoin mining operations and hydroelectric plants in Zomia, iPhone touch technology and (colonial) anthropology of sound, twentieth-century electronic devices and the astronaut. Some of the *shanzhai* (counterfeit or hodgepodge bricolage) electronic equipment invoked in Liu's video might have been used by the underground rock bands featured in curator Dong Bingfeng's exhibition, which invokes the short-lived but historically significant underground music scene in the industrial Northeast of China. Situated in the context of the 1990s, with the torrential transformation of Chinese society on the one hand and a precarious and in fact absent institutional (infra)structure on the other, Dong's essay explores the rock scene's stories of self-organization and strategies of anti-institutionalization. Sound artist and scholar Julian Henriques, in conversation with me, invites us to learn from marginalized and colonized cosmopolitans their survival strategies, which he calls, borrowing from the Rastafarian vocabulary, a *politrick*, as practiced in Reggae music, street sound-technology (not unrelated to *shanzhai* bricolage), and the tradition of trickery with its bewitching mumbo-jumbo puns. Ranging from the painful history of enslavement in the black Atlantic to the playful global resonance of Reggae music, Henriques ends the conversation with a magic (mis)spell: *cosmopolitricks*, which continue to tease the self-importance of major, ocularcentric, rational, eurocentric, colonial cosmopolitanism.

Neither a long weekend nor a book could exhaust the myriad ways of minor cosmopolitan theories and practices. While graphic artist Nik Neves' drawings and filmmaker Camila Gonzatto's photoessay in the **Intermezzo** of the book give us an impression of the *minor cosmopolitan weekend*, in the hope of continuing the conversation beyond the constraints of the event and this publication, the book features an open section, **Constellations**, in lieu of a conclusion. It invites contributions of short glossary entries that will be posted on the website accompanying the book. The constellation series of concepts included here are written by the first generation of young researchers (Mariya Nikolova, Heinrich Wilke, Anouk Madörin, Sara Morais dos Santos Bruss, Jens Temmen, Anna von Rath) of the DFG Research Training Group minor cosmopolitanisms.

Zairong Xiang
Berlin, April 9th 2020

1 Judith Butler, "Capitalism Has its Limits," *Verso Books Blog*, 30 March 2020, https://www.versobooks.com/blogs/4603-capitalism-has-its-limits.

2 Judith Butler, "Capitalism Has its Limits."

3 Benjamin Bathke, "Over 150,000 refugees could work on farms to fill labor gap: German government," *InfoMigrants*, 27 March 2020, https://www.infomigrants.net/en/post/23713/over-150-000-refugees-could-work-on-farms-to-fill-labor-gap-german-government; Tobias Buck, Olaf Storbeck and Judith Evans, "Germany lifts coronavirus ban on seasonal workers," *Financial Times*, 2 April 2020, https://www.ft.com/content/871b6d39-4497-49c5-856c-549cb42e67ce.

Website

This publication is supported by multimedia content that can be found on its website. To access it, enter:
www.uni-potsdam.de/minorcosmopolitanweekend/index.php/book/

The texts that have supporting content online are marked with the icon 🌐.

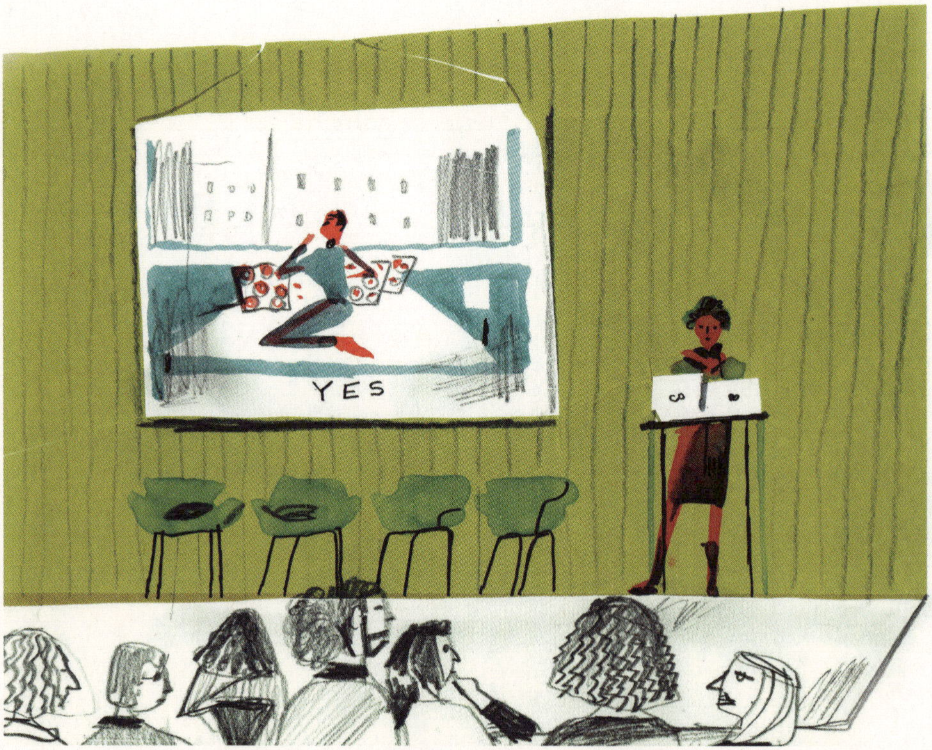

From Mary Jirmanus Saba's presentation during the panel "Film, Women's Work & Labour Organizing," *minor cosmopolitan weekend*. Illustration by Nik Neves. Find out more in the book and on the website.

01

ENTERING THE minor COSMOS

OS ENTERING THE minor COSMOS ENTERING THE mino
ERING THE minor COSMOS ENTERING THE minor COS
HE minor COSMOS ENTERING THE minor COSMOS EN-
inor COSMOS ENTERING THE minor COSMOS ENTERING
OSMOS ENTERING THE minor COSMOS ENTERING THE
OS ENTERING THE minor COSMOS ENTERING THE mino
ERING THE minor COSMOS ENTERING THE minor COS
HE minor COSMOS ENTERING THE minor COSMOS EN-
inor COSMOS ENTERING THE minor COSMOS ENTERING
OSMOS ENTERING THE minor COSMOS ENTERING THE
OS ENTERING THE minor COSMOS ENTERING THE mino
ERING THE minor COSMOS ENTERING THE minor COS
HE minor COSMOS ENTERING THE minor COSMOS EN-
inor COSMOS ENTERING THE minor COSMOS ENTERING
OSMOS ENTERING THE minor COSMOS ENTERING THE
OS ENTERING THE minor COSMOS ENTERING THE mino
NTERING THE minor COSMOS ENTERING THE minor COS

Arjun Appadurai

17 The Passport

I focus here, briefly, on a small object with big capacities. Passports are not only small, they are also virtually identical in size due to the growing standardization of immigration rules, of scanning machines, and of visa needs across the world. Their small size disguises the fact that they are containers for something large, namely the nation-state of which the passport holder is a citizen. Thus, the small passport is a container and a condensation of the always bigger nation which issues it. Furthermore, the issuance of a passport makes even the smallest nation equal to the biggest and most powerful. This illusion of formal equality is the cornerstone of the international regime of the nation-state and the mutual recognition which is its most important precondition.

Passports signify citizenship but not all citizens have or need passports, because passports are typically used to travel (whether for students, tourists, refugees or job-seekers). But without the passport, citizens cannot usually exit their nations. So, the small passport is also something larger, a prison, or the nation seen as a prison. The passport is, in this respect, a tool of incarceration and immobilization, as it also is, for example, for guest workers in authoritarian states, such as Filipino, Indian, Pakistani and Indonesian domestic workers in the Gulf, whose employers confiscate their passports, thus turning them into slaves in the labor market.

At the other end, the passport is a screen and a sieve, allowing some to enter and others not. In this case, the passport is tied to another small object, which is the visa, usually stamped or attached to the passport. This most powerful cousin of the passport is much harder to get for most people who want to travel from poorer places to richer ones. The visa is the secret master of the passport, although it appears to be a servant or supplement. Without the right visas, the passport means nothing. It is, in some ways, an empty object.

The passport, from the point of view of both the nation which introduces it and the one which inspects it at the border, is also a leaky object, in spite of its smooth and closed exterior. It admits exceptions, abuses, fakes and frauds. It is always an object of suspicion. For the citizen in his own home country, the object of suspicion is both the document and the holder, both of which may be disguising some criminal intention or market. For the inspecting immigration officer, not only are the document and its owner objects of suspicion (because both one or the other could be fakes), but the issuing nation is also an object of suspicion, as a suspected home of drugs, arms, criminals or terrorists. Thus, the passport is leaky from every point of view, because it is the site or surface of that epistemology of suspicion which the system of nation-states seeks always to deny, but which is its primary weakness. Not all citizens deserve passports (in the paranoid view of the nation-state) and not all nation-states issue legitimate passports, according to those who inspect passports at borders. The passport is an effort to contain the nation and eliminate suspicion, but since the nation and its borders are always leaky, the passport is mostly an effective container of suspicion, but a leaky container of national citizenship.

So, what about the relationship of this small object to mobility? Well, the passport is as important a means of producing mobility as it is of producing immobility. In fact, visas are the tools of mobility whereas passports are mostly the tools of immobility, whether at or within the borders of the nation-state. There is one exception to this rule, and that is for rich individuals who wish to flee the tax regimes of their own countries and buy passports in countries which seek wealthy citizens for their economies and do not mind selling their passports in this market. The latest surprising member of this club is Singapore, which has promised a certain form of virtual citizenship to all those who invest in their new brand of national cryptocurrency. For these people, the purchased passport is the same as a visa for their new national domicile.

Like all objects, the legibility of the passport comes from its membership in a set. This set is a series of sacred national objects, which includes the flag, the postage stamp, coins and currency, the national anthem and national monuments. The passport is among the humbler of these objects, but it is special, insofar as it is unique for each citizen although it is given to many citizens. It is a site of national identification but not a site of national identity, and thus not sacred in quite the way the flag or the national anthem are sacred. It is leaky but it is strangely secular.

For refugees, migrants, and asylum-seekers in privileged states, like Germany, the struggle to get a passport is hard and arduous, and getting it is a big victory. Thus, this small object can mean a lot. The tragic sublime of the passport is that it is a precious object for many who seek to move to a better life, but, in fact, it materializes the leaky, suspicious, and obsolete idea of the nation-state, and thus it is the currency of entry into a political form which runs against the inexorable logic of globalization.

This short essay was delivered as a lecture at the *minor cosmopolitan weekend*, held at the Haus der Kulturen der Welt in Berlin, on December 6-8, 2018. I am grateful to the organizers and especially to Zairong Xiang for inviting me.

Sundar Sarukkai

Empty Objects

20

I will begin with an extract from the *minor cosmopolitan weekend* blurb:

> Around the turn of the millennium, academics and politicians predicted that the world would grow together as one and that people would become less bound by national affiliations. Almost twenty years later, there is little left of this vision. This is not such a surprise when we consider that the cosmopolitan ideal (as articulated during the European Enlightenment) wholeheartedly embraced the promises of a globalising economy, yet has remained oblivious to, and even complicit with, capitalist exploitation, slavery, and colonialism. Yet should we abandon the cosmopolitan idea because of this corrupt history? Or should it rather be reviewed and rethought in the face of rising nationalism? What are alternative traditions and practices of the cosmopolitan from across the globe?[1]

There are many points of interest in this quotation, but I will only deal with two words—"as one." What exactly could this innocent phrase really mean? In what follows, I want to reflect freely on this idea and although, in order to do this, I draw on other cultural intellectual resources, I want them to be understood as a practice of cosmopolitanism and not of nationalism!

First of all, we begin with the assumption that there are already many nations, many cultures and many people. Becoming one, in this respect, means for them to come together as one—through legal and economic agreements—and/or become one *as* nation, culture, and people. But obviously becoming one people, one culture, is not desirable: after all, cultures today are hot commodities that sell based on their difference and multiplicity. We would still like to have Chinese and Indian food and not reduce them to a oneness with German food! We can thus see minor cosmopolitanism as an expression of keeping the distinctness of nations and cultures, while still seeing them as "one" in some sense.

The theme of one among the many is much discussed in various philosophical traditions and has been referred to as the one-many problem. There are a number of ways to understand this "puzzle" of the one and the many. Most simply, "one" thing always seems to be made up of many qualities and, at the same time, one quality is present across many entities. We can immediately see how this relates to the idea of universals and particulars. This is one way to understand the meaning of "one." But there are others, such as the idea of one itself as a quality, one as unity, one as defined by a boundary, one as indistinguishable, etc. Oneness is also the core concept of the philosophical traditions of non-duality, such as advaita, an influential school in Indian philosophical traditions.

How can we make many different things one? The most common way is to erase the individualities of each—the boundaries which characterise the individualities. It is easiest to create oneness through erasure of differences, and more generally through erasure. The challenge of minor cosmopolitanism is to create an idea of one while keeping the individualities of the many intact—this I would like to see as the basic difference between cosmopolitanism and minor cosmopolitanisms.

Erasure is the most common way of understanding how to create one out of the many. Not just erasure of differences, but also erasure of qualities, erasure of undesirable elements, erasure of difficult metaphysical entities, and so on. Erasure is important because it is a dominant way by which we understand the notion of oneness and unity.

A simple model we can use to understand the one-many is that of an object. An object has many qualities (properties) and these qualities are distinct entities—colour and shape are different kinds of "entities," but they come together in one object. An object has identity and is individuated in some way. But even with all these diverse qualities, it is nevertheless one object—it presents itself as a form of unity which brings together completely different kinds of qualities. Bringing together cultures and nations should be much easier!

The human body and the nature of sensation is another example of unity that unifies diversity. The body is not only a model of the one which brings together many organs and other biological parts, but it also "unifies" completely different kinds of entities, like the mind, consciousness, self and its physical parts. We could look at the body as a model of cosmopolitanism if we like, and see how models of cosmopolitanism can actually draw upon different theories of the body.

How does a body unify its diverse elements? There are two dominant ways: one, unity coming from the *working together* of the elements of the body and two, from the sense of identity derived through *belonging together*, related to ideas of unity, oneness, continuity and so on. A machine is one machine even when it has many parts, because all of them work together. All the parts are also needed to make the machine work as one. But belonging together is not necessarily like this. When extended to human systems, such as a society, this becomes a major issue, since elements which do not work with the other elements are still an important part of the oneness of that society. For example, babies and old people may not participate in the working of the society but they contribute to a great sense of belonging together in one. Another problem that arises from attaching the idea of oneness in societies to that of working together (and other metaphors of the machine) is that of agency. The idea of human, a single unified human being, is deeply present in the notion of action and in the agency of an individual. In the case of machines, the question of agency becomes reduced to that of humans who run machines. In the case of human bodies, the question of agency is deeply related to metaphysical assumptions about entities such as the mind, soul or the self. The hypothesis of the mind as the agent behind actions of the body implies that this model is inherently hierarchical and is not really working towards the ideal of the cosmopolitan. One also derives notions of identity through experience of oneness, mineness and so on. But this approach needs to postulate entities like the self and the soul to ground this oneness. If we want to believe that all the bodily experiences I have are indeed happening to "me," then I need a self to stand for this identity of "me."

Thus, the price for imagining the oneness of the body is quite high! It needs the postulation of terms like mind, self, and the soul, which are, by definition, not the body and in most traditions placed hierarchically higher than the body. Moreover, these entities, which define the oneness of the diverse body, cannot be like the body. Thus, we have the many traditions of philosophy that struggle to understand the nature of mind, self and the soul since they cannot be like the body. To summarize these points in a simple manner, we could say that any attempt to create a sense of oneness out of a diverse collection is to invoke something outside the system which can *ground* the claims of unity. If we extend this argument to societies, then we can see the reason why entities like the abstract nation (which cannot be like the individual humans of which it is composed) is necessary to create a sense of oneness among a diverse group of people.

There is a common cognitive process by which we isolate such origins that create experiences of oneness. This cognitive process is closely related to the way we understand the nature of an object. An object is a paradigm of unity and it seems obvious that an object is "one thing." But how can it so easily be "one thing"? After all, it is made up of many qualities, such as colour, shape, size and so on. These are all different kinds of qualities. Yet, we are easily able to assimilate the differences of the qualities into one coherent, integral object, "thing." The first problem is that there might actually be nothing corresponding to the "object"—that is, the very idea of an object may be nothing more than a word that stands for the unity of properties. But it is impossible for us to talk about an entity without using object-oriented language. When I see an apple, I talk about its red colour, its interesting shape or its sweet taste. Where is the object in these descriptions? We are only describing properties that we experience, and one might say that we never experience an object per se. This question of whether it is possible to know an object in-itself has been an important one in many traditions of philosophy. Here, I am interested in understanding this process in order to inquire into the nature of what any object can be.

One way to make sense of the idea of the object is to understand the nature of change. It is the idea of change and difference that creates the urgency of the idea of a unified object. Consider the simple example of a green leaf which changes colour to brown. Even though the colour has changed, we think that it is a change of the same leaf. What does this sameness amount to? The change of green to brown can also be imagined in this manner: we could imagine stripping away the colour green from an object and adding the colour brown to it. In this common way of understanding change, we are presuming that the "leaf" (as an object) remains the same while we change its colour. But what really is the object "leaf" once colour is stripped away from it? Similarly, we could then strip away other properties, like shape and size. Does the object remain invariant under all these changes? What really is the "object" that remains after all its qualities have been removed? Can that which remains at the end even be called an "object"? For example, if we strip away all the qualities of a person including gender, age, weight, height, class, caste and so on, what are we left with? Are we left with the most important essence of the individual? The arguments about self or the soul are based on such an essentialist view. The self or the soul cannot be like other qualities of the individual nor can they be material like the body. This is the most basic conundrum of understanding change and identity, whether of objects, individuals or societies. The substantivist position in philosophy is one answer to this question. It postulates the substance as a substratum in which qualities of the object inhere. Thus, the complex of the qualities which inhere in a substance is the object. However, the substance in itself does not have any qualities and thus is not perceptible in any manner. Those who do not subscribe to this substance ontology offer other options, such as trope theory.[2]

Empty Object

In the spirit of minor cosmopolitanism, I want to relook at this question of objects and their relationship to qualities through an alternative approach, a different conceptual schema. Independently of theories of substance or tropes, the basic point that I want to consider is the nature of the "object" that remains after all the qualities have been extracted away from it. This final state is not a quality but has the potential to hold all qualities—as in substance theories. Or one could argue that there is nothing left when qualities are removed from what is perceived at first to be an object—more akin to the trope theories. There is a conceptual term that captures both these points and that is the notion of an "empty object." The final state of an empty object is both a state which is by itself without quality and one that is actually "empty." I want to argue here that any notion of oneness and unity—whether of physical objects or cultures—seems to be based on this notion of the empty object.

But what about cultural oneness? How can different cultures come together in some sense as one? It seems to happen in a similar way to that discussed above. The process of stripping away properties in order to discover that which is left behind leads to a notion of emptiness defined through reduction and absence. It is also the process by which you get zero by subtracting away one part of a number ad infinitum. So, emptiness, in a colloquial sense, is defined as that which has nothing within it, including no properties. This cognitive mechanism is very much a part of colonial discourse, where European civilization gets to be seen as that where the qualities of the colonized are absent. So, also, in the discourse of Race: black defined in terms of the removal of all other forms of light. Black is, strictly speaking, not another colour (which always has to do with light) but something else (as in a black hole, which destroys light). Black is the residue of that which is left when all the positive qualities of light are removed. This leads to an important consequence: following what I mentioned above, we could look upon black as the basic substratum on which any quality of light can reside. Other colours can only be instantiated in blackness. Black is not a colour like the other colours and is also not a colour that absorbs all other colours. Perception of black may be a perception of absence. As Eugene Thacker notes, "Black is at once the foundation of all colour and, in its absence or emptiness, it is also what undermines the substantiality of all colour."[3]

The consequences of explicitly invoking the idea of blackness are that (1) an "empty object" is necessary to define the very idea of object and in particular to make sense of the unity/oneness that makes an object what it is, and (2) this emptiness may not actually be empty—it is only empty of qualities that are removed, but it could truly exhibit the fullness of absence. This ontology of emptiness as the ground for all existence can be found in the philosophy of set theory and extensions of it by writers like Alain Badiou in contemporary times. The basic argument in philosophy of set theory is that the ontology of numbers can be reduced to the ontology of sets, which in turn needs nothing more than an ontology of empty sets.[4] However, there is yet another discourse of emptiness, which we can access from Indian philosophical traditions.

This is where a major intellectual shift occurs in understanding emptiness and absence. Some of the most seminal ideas on these topics come from Indian philosophical traditions, primarily the Buddhist and Nyāya philosophical schools. (It might not be a surprise therefore that the concept of zero was "discovered" in ancient India.) Both emptiness and absence are extremely important categories for these schools respectively: Emptiness for the Buddhists and Absence for Nyāya.

I want to use these concepts to highlight a larger point about differences in cultures, and the difficulty of transcending such differences in a project such as cosmopolitanism. These differences are deeply held metaphysical positions and the importance of the concepts of emptiness and absence for Indian philosophies illustrate this well. In western philosophy, the approach to the theme of negation, absence, and emptiness is quite limited. We can see the marker of this in theories of empty space held by the Greeks and the Indian schools of thought. Empty space was a big problem for the Greeks, but for the Indians, it was the starting point. Infinite, empty space is not only one of the most important notions for Indian philosophies, it is also a starting point of those philosophies.

Emptiness, perhaps surprisingly, shares many important attributes with oneness. In fact, emptiness is the paradigmatic example of something which can only be "one." We can have two apples, many apples, but in our common understanding of emptiness we tend to believe that there is only one emptiness, only one kind of emptiness. Emptiness is universal in that sense. There are no parts of emptiness; we cannot say that one region of emptiness is different from another region. Emptiness is actually a good model of ideal unity, ideal oneness. In many of these characteristics, emptiness seems to share all the qualities of space, although when we use the term "empty space," emptiness functions as a specific quality of that space and not of space in general. The major difference is that objects are seen to exist "in" space and empty space is primarily a characterisation of a space without any objects. However, in the case of emptiness, we cannot say that objects exist "in" emptiness because the mere presence of an object destroys the emptiness.

What does this have to do with cosmopolitanism and minor cosmopolitanisms? I am proposing here that a rich cultural meaning of emptiness is necessary for minor cosmopolitanism, since the hierarchy of cultures which destroys oneness among diverse cultures is itself based on particular acts of negation. Consider the colonial discourse, a classic instance of a discourse which creates a hierarchy of cultures as an important goal. Typically, a colonial discourse will begin by description of the colonized through negative terms. Again typically, the negative terms will be the negation of the most important qualities of the colonizer. Thus, the European colonizers describe the colonized as not having any of the valued qualities of European cultures. They describe Indian culture as not having the capacity for reason, for logic, for mathematics, for philosophy, for art, even for "religion," as defined by the Germans and others. The natives are then described as not having a sense of time and space, not keeping to their word, not being moral and so on. Negation of this kind—i.e. describing qualities as not-logical, not-moral etc.—, is the best way to create artificial hierarchies among different groups.

However, this technique is based on a simplistic understanding of negation. First of all, the removal of qualities does not really decrease something, since negation is always an excess. To say somebody is kind has different implications to saying that person is not-kind. Attributes, as positive qualities, are referential, in general. We know what the word "kind" means in a specific sense. We can describe other qualities of being kind. Not-kind, like not-red, is not positive, in that there is no referent which seems to be accessible. The meaning of not-red consists of a variety of other "positive" terms such as green, blue, violet and so on. Thus, if one asked the meaning of not-red, then we could have a very large number of terms that stand for "not-red." The aim of colonial discourse is to show how the colonized do not have the qualities of the colonizer, but it is not really about finding out what other ("positive") qualities characterise the colonized. This is true of hierarchy in general; we can note this in patriarchal discourses about women or in "upper" caste descriptions of the "lower" castes. So also for racism, since the term black, which is by itself not a colour like the other colours, is defined through absence of other light-forms. For racism, it is important to think of black as another colour, although black is really the absence of colours. The "negative" qualities associated with black are generated through negation, through its role as not-something. So it also becomes attached to negative power and savagery. Even the physical description of the world doesn't escape this connotation, as in the use of the term Black Hole!

For western philosophy, western thought, as most powerfully articulated by Kant, neo-Kantians, and from Hegel to Heidegger, was not only considered superior to Asian and African thought. It went so far as to deny the capacity of philosophy to these cultures.[5] Similar claims in colonial discourse were not just about the difference of knowledge about mathematics, science or logic between the colonial ruler and the colonized, but they were more about the colonized lacking the capacity to engage with these subjects. In certain classical Indian traditions, there are very similar claims of exclusion of certain communities who are viewed as not having the capacity to learn and do philosophy (or the sciences). In today's India, we still hear such claims about the incapacity of certain groups to be part of mainstream schooling or of elite educational institutions. In all these cases, the origin of hegemony lies in the creation of an independent essence, which serves to exclude. For example, philosophy and mathematics will be defined so as to keep out the possibility of other cultures "possessing" them. This is only possible because of the essentialization of certain characteristics of these disciplines. Such acts lead to a hegemony of one culture over another, and that is the greatest obstacle to reaching oneness in the cosmopolitan sense.

Thus, hierarchies which negate the possibility of oneness are not just a reflection of a difference, but an active construction of what cannot be known or what cannot be done by the hegemonized. This leads to the most important characteristic of hegemony: that it can only be understood negatively. This is what happens in discourses of race or caste, as I will briefly illustrate below. Thus, hegemony is not really a relation of comparison, but a relation based on denial. We can find hegemony at work wherever we find denial and a negative ontology in place. This is so in the claims of western knowledge systems over the Asian and African, or the scientific over the humanities, or, in caste discourse within Indian knowledge systems, in the practice of untouchability, and so on.

But denial of capabilities alone is not enough, since it will always be legitimized by converting it into a fact of incapacity. The power of hegemony lies in the fact that the denial that is its central mark is a denial not only of actuality but also of possibility. Thus, it is not that Indian philosophy is not philosophy (or that Gandhi and Ambedkar cannot be seen as philosophers): it cannot be philosophy or aspire to the status of philosophy. Similarly, the practice of untouchability is hegemonic because it is really about the impossibility of escaping untouchability, that is, the hegemonic is actually a statement of the impossibility of getting out of that state. In the case of untouchability, this impossibility is inscribed through hereditary norms. We can multiply these instances in hundreds of cases. If we understand hegemony through this framework, then we can see that hegemony is ultimately the impossibility of imagination, of finding ways of imagining the other to be like me, to know and to act like I do. The social aspect of hegemony is merely the social process by which the impossible is forced to remain impossible. We know we are in the force of hegemony when we try to break the impossible, but find it impossible to do so. Thus the face of hegemony is most centrally located within the discourse of the negative, of the double impossibility, and in the act of negation.

Ironically, a particular form of reason functions at the core of maintaining the status of the impossible. Philosophy, as a discipline, has been a participant in this, along with scientific reason. The problem is not of philosophy and science as disciplines, but of a particular common element in both of them—the privilege given to essences. A study of scientific description of objects and phenomena clearly exhibits the centrality of the idea of independent essences as an operating principle of scientific knowledge and method. And most philosophical systems draw extensively upon the idea of essence in their analysis of the world, language, the nature of humans, etc.

Thus, the use of negation, in this sense, negates the possibility of cosmopolitanism. One could claim that, in a true sense of the term, cosmopolitanism has to be based on the conceptual world of emptiness, which creates the possibility of universal equivalence without qualities that can be used for hierarchies and hegemony. However, it might also be argued that this universal sense of emptiness is quite unusable, since it is too broad and too vague. But such a conclusion would be too hasty, since there are complex approaches to emptiness and one can draw upon different theories of emptiness to discover the possibility of grounding cosmopolitanisms.

Emptiness and Cosmopolitanism

Emptiness itself can be understood in many interesting ways. To grasp this, we can begin with the recognition that there are at least two ways of creating oneness—by inclusion and by exclusion. In the first case, we can include everything and create oneness; or, as in the case of exclusion, we can keep eliminating qualities till we have another kind of oneness. A jigsaw puzzle is a good example of oneness created through addition. Thousands of pieces which are so different can be put together in a way that creates a sense of a whole—of one picture. This is done not by erasing qualities but by finding links between them, in such a way that the whole mass of individual pieces functions as one picture. Although it is a way of creating oneness through addition, this analogy also requires a pre-given order. Pieces that don't fit might be discarded in the attempt to choose only those parts that can function together. This is a model similar to how nationalism works in most countries. The other method, through exclusion, is what we discussed earlier—removing one quality after another and reaching a substratum which is the ground for all qualities. The substratum is itself without quality and is truly a space of absence.

Is there really any fundamental difference between the oneness created through addition (presence) and that created through absence? The former appears to be "full" and the latter completely "empty." However, emptiness is not complete absence. On the contrary, emptiness can be seen as a "fullness of absence," as it is a collection of many kinds of absences that create emptiness.

Thus, if the absence of something is viewed as a property in itself, as something real, then emptiness is not really empty—it is actually the *fullness of absence*. I am tempted to add, here, that one can see a relation between these statements and the notions of zero and infinity in mathematics, and, more importantly, the relation between zero and infinity. Infinity is the oneness created through inclusion of everything and zero is the oneness that is left after the exclusion of everything. Both infinity and zero are paradigms of sameness—if you remove a part of infinity from infinity, you still get infinity, and so also for zero. (That is, infinity − infinity = infinity and 0 − 0 = 0, a result that is not true for anything else.) If zero is the absence after removal, then infinity's relation with zero (most commonly—although not mathematically accurate—expressed by the inverse relation between zero and infinity, i.e. infinity as one divided by zero) illustrates another important facet of the relation between fullness and emptiness.

Accumulating absences is like accumulating presences, if we accept the reality of absences and negative terms. So, one way to understand the *plenitude* of emptiness is to equate it to the fullness of absences. For such a position, we need to consider the possibility that both absences and emptiness are "real," ontologically meaningful terms.

Two philosophical traditions that take such a position are the Nyāya school, often called the realist and logical school of Indian philosophy—regarding absences—and the Buddhist school— regarding the ontological primacy of emptiness. For the Nyāya tradition, absences are not only real but are also perceptible. Their philosophical complexity is, to a great extent, driven by an attempt to ascribe meaningful ontology to absences. As a first step, they classify absences into different kinds and explore in what sense absences could be real.

For the Buddhists, emptiness is probably their most important concept. It goes back to questions of identity and whether essence captures the identity of objects and phenomena. But emptiness is not something which cannot be characterised by other terms. The best example that I can offer here is the monumental philosophical work produced by the famous Buddhist philosopher Nāgārjuna (second century), the author of *Műlamādhyamakakărika*.

Műlamādhyamakakărika is the foundational text of the "middle path" doctrine of Buddhist philosophy, and primarily argues against the tenability of independent essences. Through a critical evaluation of most fundamental concepts, including motion, time, space, self, etc., Nāgārjuna demolishes the possibility of any commitment to independent, real essences that can characterise things, humans and phenomena. To do this, he uses the critical logical formulation of the early Buddhists, the *catuskoti*. This logical analysis is as much an analysis of the negative, of making sense of terms like not-A, and of the act of denial in general.

The book consists of twenty-seven chapters in verse, dealing with a single-minded attack on essences. Nāgārjuna argues against the idea that things and phenomena are empty of essence.[6] To sustain this formulation, he has to develop ways of articulating emptiness, an emptiness which cannot have any essence to characterise it. The basic philosophical insight from this critical tradition of Buddhist thought is "that every entity depends for its existence on causes and conditions, upon its parts, upon the wholes to which it belongs, and for its identity on nominal and conceptual imputation and conventions." Commentators of this text point out that the conceptualization of emptiness in Nāgārjuna is a middle path between accepting phenomena and essences as real and having independent existence (reificationism) and its opposite (nihilism), which sees empirical phenomena as entirely false. Nāgārjuna's methodology in this text is to show that both these positions lead to inconsistency and become contradictory by their own assumptions and logic.

Developing on Nāgārjuna, one of the most prominent Buddhist scholars, Candrakīrti (seventh century), gives a typology of sixteen types of emptiness. The sixteen types described by Candrakirti include the following: emptiness of the outer, emptiness of the inner, emptiness of the beginningless and endless, emptiness of emptiness, emptiness of the essential nature of non-entities, emptiness of all phenomena, and so on. Candrakīrti gives us a way to understand the complexity of emptiness in a manner that is original and striking, and one which I believe has relevance to more complex formulations of the idea of oneness in minor cosmopolitanism since, as we saw above, it involves an interesting relation between oneness and emptiness.

As mentioned previously, the most important idea for the Buddhist school associated with Nāgārjuna and Candrakīrti is that there are no completely independent essences of anything, including emptiness, and everything is mutually interdependent. This will be true of oneness, too. Oneness, therefore, cannot be defined through independence (defined by objects, essences) but through necessary interdependence. Such a view has immediate implications for the idea of cosmopolitanism and the capacity to have genuine oneness across cultures. Following this view, we can say that any quality of any community is mutually interdependent and hence it is impossible to establish hierarchies between individuals, groups or cultures. The obstacles to any notion of cosmopolitanism are the hierarchies based on the essences of these qualities. Thus, one way to reach towards an ideal cosmopolitanism in its truest sense is to either get rid of essences, or get rid of the hierarchy inherent in them. To do that, we need a theoretical approach such as that of the Buddhist philosophical tradition described here. This also means that we need to incorporate new ways of thinking about emptiness, negation and absence. I believe that this approach is absolutely necessary if we want to really understand minor cosmopolitanism in its truest sense.

1 *minor cosmopolitan weekend*, https://www.uni-potsdam.de/minorcosmopolitanweekend/.

2 See Michael Loux, *Metaphysics: A Contemporary Introduction* (London: Routledge, 1997).

3 Eugene Thacker, "Black on Black," *The Public Domain Review*, April 9, 2015, https://publicdomainreview.org/2015/04/09/black-on-black/.

4 See Mary Tiles, *Philosophy of Set Theory* (London: Blackwell, 1989).

5 See Peter Park, *Africa, Asia and the History of Philosophy* (New York: SUNY Press, 2014). See also Michael Adas, *Machines as the Measure of Men* (Ithaca: Cornell University Press, 1989).

6 Quoted in the Introduction by Tsong Khapa, *Ocean of Reasoning*, trans. G.N. Samten and J. L. Garfield (Oxford: Oxford University Press, 2006).

Marina Camargo

Notes on the Representation of Time and Space

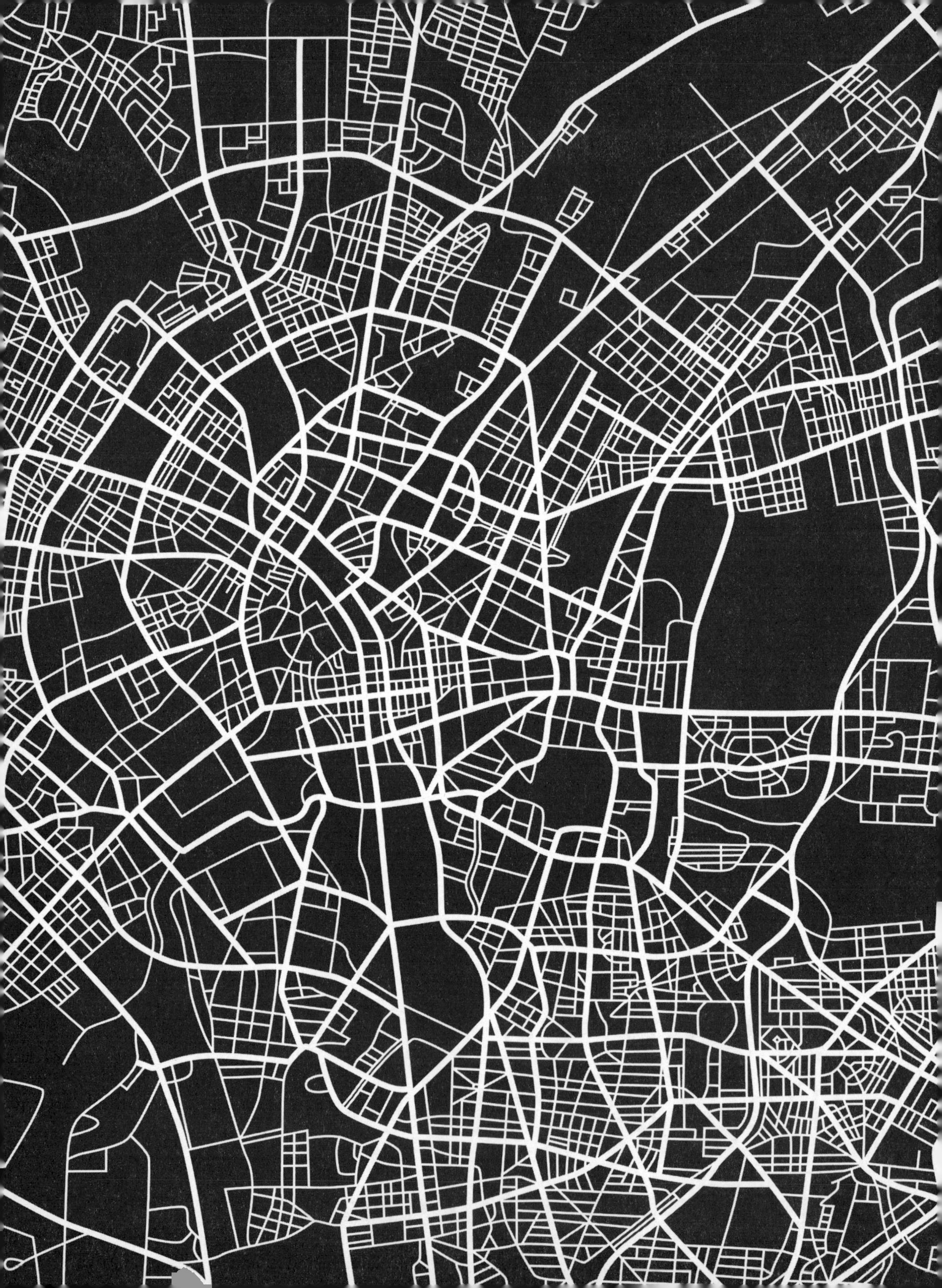

Script has thus become, like language, an archive of nonsensuous similarities, of nonsensuous correspondences.

Walter Benjamin,
"Doctrine of the Similar"

The star is always a kind of ruin. That its light is never identical to itself, is never revealed as such, means that it is always inhabited by a certain distance or darkness.

Eduardo Cadava,
Words of Light: Theses on the Photography of History

Space determines the context where things take place, influencing the facts. At the same time, the facts can alter the space where they happen, in a connection of mutual affection. Likewise, there is always a specific moment when things occur: time is a constant vector in every action, deed or historical fact. How could time and space be visualised?

We can see a starry sky as a marker of time: the position of stars in space allows the construction of specific moments in time. When looking at a starry sky we are looking at a kind of time chart. The time we see through the configuration of the stars in the sky is obviously an abstraction: what we see is a partial image of a universe, which, in reality, is formed by traces of light from stars in movement.

Nonetheless, a starry sky shows us a specific moment of time and a specific position in space, making it possible to situate the geographical point and moment in time of our looking (where and when).

By tracing connections between the physical space of the city and that of the universe, what we perceive is determined by the reduced virtual space of a graphic representation, where the local dimension is brought closer to global space.

The map of the city

To look at the structure of a city you need distance: once inside the city, understanding of its structure is lost. On a map drawing, we can see all those layers formed on a surface reduced to a collection of lines—as if all the temporal and spatial dimensions have been projected onto a single surface, forming a flat image based on a complex organism.

A map of a city is a kind of plan view of fragments, different stories and sedimentations of time occurring in space. Rather than a linear narrative, it is a transformation of a complex topography into the two-dimensional form of a drawing. There are no cities in a map drawing: there is a representation of urban space in which only one of the many layers can be seen.

Thinking with the stars

A map of the stars is a charting of the position of various celestial bodies in the universe. It is also a map that records disappearances: each spot of light that we see indicates a past moment that reaches our eyes after some delay and with the simplified appearance of a bright spot in the sky.

To consider[1] that the stars indicate a specific moment in time is to think about stars in their own temporal dimension. A map of constellations is a map of time. If every star is a kind of ruin of its own existence, we are witnesses of these vestiges shining through time and the darkness of the universe.

Maps of disappearances

Maps of cities are formed of a series of constructions, destructions, appearances, and reconstructions. Star maps indicate the position of celestial bodies from our visible perspective. The nature of these two types of maps is quite different: the lines on the map of a city can be followed, that is to say, it is possible to get lost in those streets that we see as lines; the spots that mark the position of stars indicate specific moments in time, despite being registers of disappearances more than anything. Physical space reveals layers of past time, but it does so by shaping the evidence according to layers of those overlapping times that transform space. The dimension of time is more abstract for human perception: we attempt to grasp the temporal dimension through its relationship with space, through our circulation and presence in places (nonetheless, the temporal dimension is greater than the measure of life).

Looking to the sky

Looking at the constellations and using them to *read* time positions us as one point in the universe. Our position forms a triangulation in relation to the visible universe: so we exist in relation to that image of the universe. But the universe does not depend on our gaze. What we are looking at is a fragmented charting of past time.

How can time be visualised?

Over the course of a century, it is possible to witness the constant transformations of a starry sky: by observing the movements of spots of light, evidence of the passing of time. Stars represent[2] the past and the present. The drawing of constellations as a map is the writing down of time.

The star map can be a way of visualising the temporal dimension, as a drawing in space. Like the letters of the alphabet, here the dots and lines on a flat surface demonstrate the basic principles of graphic representation.

When we *read* the constellations, are we then establishing a kind of language in relation to the universe? Might maps be considered as a kind of language?

One possible view for a microcosmos

In the video installation *Mikrokosmos*, the drawing of constellations can be seen in slow circular movements across eighteen maps of the sky over Berlin (each map represents one day of the year, throughout the twenty-first century, until the moment when the video is shown). These star maps can be seen on one screen arranged in front of another, which shows the map of Berlin.[3] One part of the city map can be seen at each moment, as a kind of fragmented record of the space in which we live.

We move between two moving images, between a representation of past and present time (shown in the star-map constellations) and of the space we move through and experience. We move between graphic representations of space and time, between a possible visualisation of the space we occupy (micro), and the dimension of the universe as a measure of time (macro).

The representations of space and time are abstractions that create another reality which is neither spatial nor temporal—although it exists in time and space. In the video installation, the virtual nature of the relationship established between the two representations suggests a kind of metaphor for our actual position: we live in the space between city and sky, between urban map and map of the constellations, where perceptions of time and space are mutually formed and transformed.

This text was originally written in English and Portuguese by the author; the translation from Portuguese to English was done by Nick Rands.

---

1 The etymology of the word "consider" suggests a way of thinking with the stars (con + sider - sidus [with + heavenly body]: considerare (Latin) or considerer (French)).

---

2 "To represent a star, then, ... is to bring to the light of history what, not waiting for the day, cannot be brought to light. This is why the reading of stars involves the destruction of stars." Eduardo Cadava, *Words of Light : Theses on The Photography of History* (Princeton: Princeton University Press, 1997), 30.

---

3 Marina Camargo's video installation *Mikrokosmos* was shown at *minor cosmopolitan weekend*, Haus der Kulturen der Welt (Berlin), in December 2018.

El palito de la jaula del pájaro de la abuela*

*The Perch in Grandma's Birdcage

Zen and the infinite. For many years I saw my grandma's canary standing on the only perch in its cage. Such was the bird's condition in life. To spend much of the day on that perch. In addition to eating birdseed and drinking water, its other activities included singing from time to time and bathing in the receptacle placed in its cage for that purpose. For twenty years, I saw the bird perched there. Atop the stick that crossed the cage and provided it with a point of view. I remember it from when I was a boy until I abandoned those lands forever. I never heard about the bird again. I don't know how many years of life it had or if it's still alive. What I do know for certain is that during the years I saw the canary, a series of events took place that at the time were crucial to those around it. Births, deaths, illnesses that befell the humans who passed by the cage. Marriages, divorces, natural disasters that took many people's lives. Some days were luminous, often of an unusual transparency, and others were grey, cold, damp. Around the perch in that cage, the canary also saw a series of human passions flare up. Tears that couldn't be contained, fits of laughter, or of desperation. But the bird was always impassive, unswerving in its routine. It seemed to find the events in its surroundings insignificant. I imagine it perceived that day had changed into night when, at exactly the same hour each time, its cage was covered with a blanket. One took great care when turning on a light during the nocturnal hours while the bird slept. Cases were known of canaries that had suffered a fatal heart attack when suddenly flooded with the light of a bulb turned on without warning at midnight. It was only years later, during circumstances I don't feel the need to go into, but will nevertheless say occurred somewhat involuntarily, that I discovered that the canary's unswerving presence on its perch hadn't been a banal matter. The cage and the bird inside it hadn't merely played a decorative role nor one removed from the infinite number of events that occurred over so many years in that kitchen. While I was deepening not only my understanding but my experience of the idea of Oneness, the fundamental principle of all

Lo Zen y lo infinito. Durante muchos años vi al canario de mi abuela posarse en el único palito con el que contaba su jaula. Era su condición de vida. Permanecer de pie buena parte del día en ese palito. Aparte de comer alpiste y de tomar agua, otras de sus actividades era cantar de vez en cuando y bañarse en la vasija colocada dentro de la jaula para tal fin. Fueron veinte los años que vi al canario posado allí. En aquel travesaño que le servía de punto de vista. Lo recuerdo desde que era un niño hasta que abandoné esas tierras para siempre. Nunca más volví a saber del pájaro. Ignoro la cantidad de años que alcanzó a vivir o si sigue con vida todavía. De lo que estoy seguro es de que durante los años que lo vi ocurrieron una serie de acontecimientos cruciales en ese momento para el entorno. Nacimientos, muertes, enfermedades de seres que rondaban aquella jaula. Matrimonios, divorcios desastres naturales que se llevaron muchas vidas de la población. Algunos fueron dias luminosos, de una transparencia muchas veces inusitada, y también jornadas grises, frías, húmedas. Alrededor del palito de esa jaula el canario vio también desatarse una serie de pasiones humanas. Llantos descontrolados, ataques de risa o de desesperación. Sin embargo, el ave continuó siempre impasible, cumpliendo de manera inalterable con su rutina. Parecía serle intrascendente lo que ocurría alrededor. Supongo que notaba el cambio del día a la noche cuando a una hora exacta cubrían la jaula con una manta. veces notaba que cambiaba la hora en la que cada noche cubrían la jaula con una manta para que pasara las noches en la mejor de las condiciones posibles. Se era muy cuidadoso en las horas nocturnas de encender la luz mientras el ave dormía. Se sabía de casos de canarios que habían sufrido algún ataque mortal de corazón al verse de pronto inundado por el repentino encendido de un foco a medianoche. Sólo años después, cuando por circunstancias que no creo importante describir pero que, sin embargo puedo decir qué sucedieron de manera un tanto involuntaria, descubrí que la presencia inalterable del canario en su palito no había sido un tema banal. Esa jaula y el

mystical experience, that everything is nothing but a single whole, I understood that the perch was the necessary perspective from which to become enraptured by the miracle of creation. If everything is nothing but an indivisible whole, then we don't have the means necessary to escape it in order to then contemplate the Oneness we seek. My grandma's canary was lucky to have that point of view from the moment it first sang in her kitchen. Not I. And I'm searching for it. For a different perspective before which to be enraptured, not by it, but rather by its serving as a reference point to behold the whole.
Until now, my intentions, my discoveries, and my searches have led to my acceptance of Oneness as it's so magnificently described by the mystic Ibn al-Arabi in his infinite Treatise on Unity, which was written in the solitude of Murcia when the Iberian Peninsula was an active site of thought. Ibn al-Arabi doesn't reveal whether he found other eyes before which to find rapture. The Indian saint Nizamuddin did experience this state of trance upon offering the poet through whom he was able to see the universe the most impressive gift of all time: If, in the future, someone comes in pilgrimage to my grave, I'll exhort them to first pay a visit to that of the poet. Don't anyone ask who he was or where his verses can be found; he is simply the man who made it possible for Nizamuddin, who speaks now, to see the whole that reality always presents behind a veil. This reason is more than sufficient to make visiting him an obligation for pilgrims.
And this is now my obligation, to linger in my own writing, as though before the grave of a mystic poet, so I'm able to admire the whole as did the canary that spent much of the day atop the perch in my grandma's birdcage.

Translated from Spanish by Sarah Moses

pájaro dentro no habían jugado meramente un rol decorativo o ajeno a la infinidad de sucesos que ocurrieron durante todos esos años en aquella cocina. Mientras me adentraba no sólo a entender sino a experimentar la Idea de la Unicidad, el principio fundamental de toda experiencia mística, Todo no es más que Todo, entendí que aquel palito era el punto de observación necesario desde el cual extasiarse con el milagro de la creación. Si todo no es más que un todo indivisible, pues no contamos con un recurso necesario para escapar de ese todo y contemplar entonces recién la Unicidad añorada.
El canario de mi abuela tuvo la suerte de contar con ese punto de vista desde que llegó a cantar a esa cocina. Yo no. Y lo ando buscando. Esa otra mirada ante la cual extasiarme para extasiarme no con esa mirada sino teniéndola como punto de referencia para admirar el todo. Hasta ahora mis intenciones, mis descubrimientos y mis búsquedas me han llevado a aceptar la Unicidad, tal como la describe tan magníficamente el místico Ibn Al Arábi en su infinito Tratado de la Unidad, que escribió en la soledad de Murcia cuando la península ibérica formaba parte activa del pensamiento. Ibn al Arabi no revela si halló otros ojos frente a los cuales hallar el extasis.
Si logró experimentar el trance del santo de la India, Nizamuddin, al ofrendar al poeta a través del cual logró ver el universo el regalo más impresionante de todos los tiempos: a las generaciones futuras exhortaré que si alguien del futuro viene en peregrinación a mi tumba tendrá que pasar primero por la del poeta. Nadie pregunte quién, dónde están sus versos, sencillamente es quien hizo posible que Nizamudin, quien les habla en este momento, pudiese ver el Todo que la realidad nos presenta siempre en forma velada, ese es motivo más que suficiente para hacerlo una obligación para el peregrino.
Y esa es ahora mi obligación, detenerme ante mi propia escritura, como si de la tumba de un poeta místico se tratara, para poder admirar el Todo de la misma manera como lo lograba el canario posado buena parte del día en el palito de la jaula de mi abuela.

P
O
L
E
I
S

02

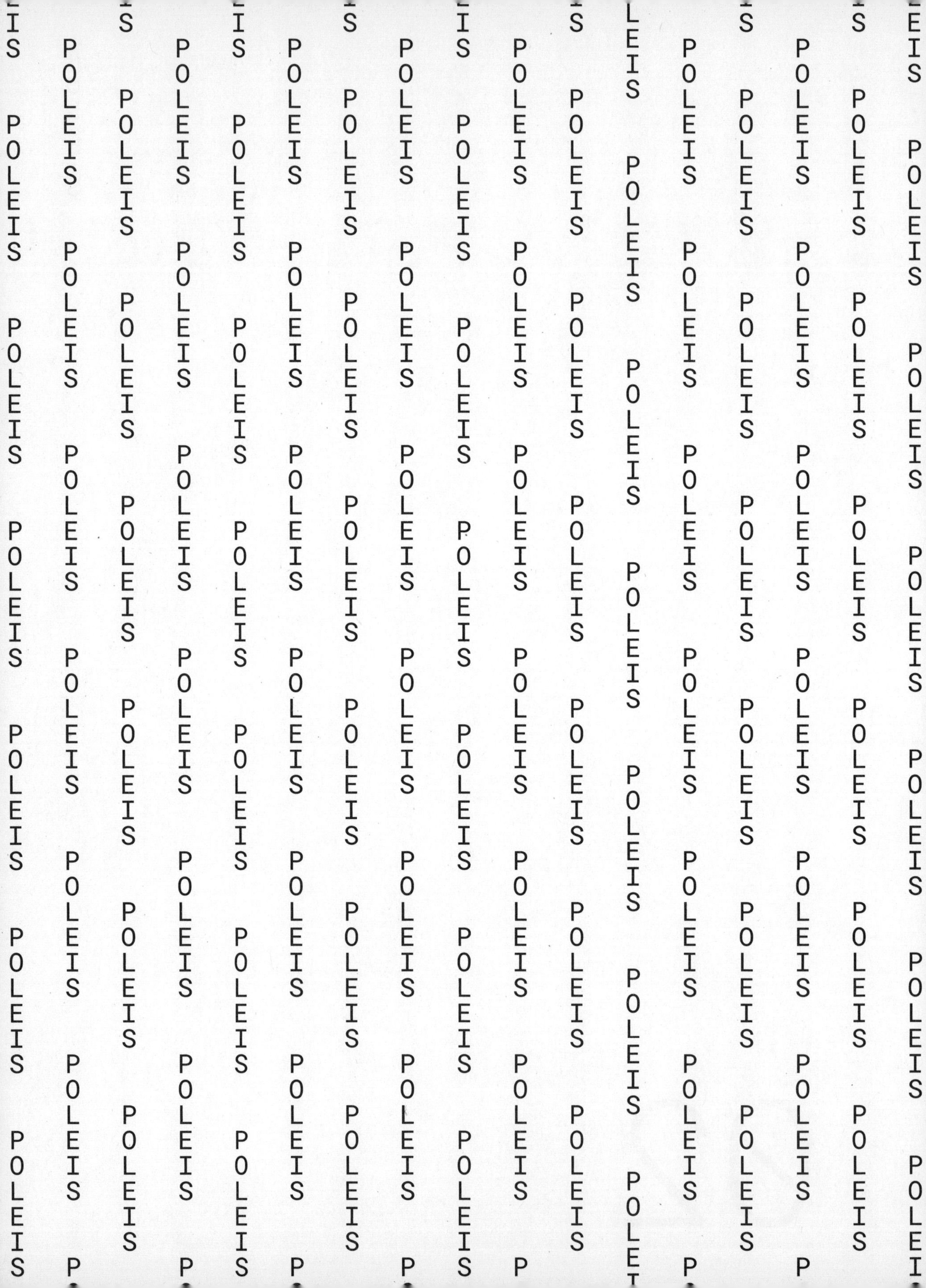
POLEIS

James Miller

Porosity and Planetarity: On (minor) Cosmopolitan Virality

March 23, 2020

Per tema di morir negai la vita
(For fear of death, I denied life)

Luigi Tansillo, *Lagrime di San Pietro*

I

One of the chief conceits of the modern era, according to Charles Taylor's *The Secular Age*, is that we moderns imagine that we are "buffered" from the world, rather than open to it.[1] The characteristic of porosity, or openness, is one that we imagine was shared by pre-modern people who feared that their bodies were susceptible to attacks from all manner of demons or other supernatural forces. The age of COVID-19, however, reveals, in the celebrated words of Bruno Latour, that we have "never been modern." Despite the physical barriers erected between states and the shutting down of global air travel, bodies across the world have become, not only victims of the novel coronavirus, but also innocent, asymptomatic carriers of it. The question that this raises is whether the present condition of global virality can be helpfully considered under the rubric of "minor cosmopolitanism."

A "minor" cosmopolitanism can be understood as a form of cosmopolitanism that is subdominant, that is to say, not thematized front and center in common perceptions of cosmopolitanism and globality. Commonly, we might understand cosmopolitanism in terms of urbanity and civilization, a world of interconnected humanity that aspires to some utopian ideal of planetary citizenship. Such "major cosmopolitanisms," however, have always been inflected by subdominant forms of cosmopolitanism: refugee camps; transnational sex traffickers; the global drugs trade; offshore tax havens for the rich. The novel coronavirus reveals another form of minor cosmopolitanism that depends on two conditions for its existence: planetarity and porosity. Our bodies are porous bodies constantly ingesting, transpiring and excreting, exchanging fluids, energies, and, yes, viruses with the world around. Our bodies are also planetary bodies, capable of exchanging these materials and energies with humans and other animals nearby and far away.

In order to think through some of the implications of such a "minor cosmopolitanism" I find it helpful to return to some so-called "premodern" anthropologies, ones that emerged not in a time of "buffered selves" but as elements of a world view where the porosity of our bodies was taken for granted.

A classic example of a premodern "porous" imagination can be seen in the famous parable of Jesus healing the Gerasene madman. Here is the story as is told in Mark's gospel.

> They came to the other side of the sea, to the
> country of the Gerasenes. 2 And when he had stepped
> out of the boat, immediately a man out of the
> tombs with an unclean spirit met him. 3 He lived
> among the tombs; and no one could restrain him any
> more, even with a chain; 4 for he had often been
> restrained with shackles and chains, but the chains
> he wrenched apart, and the shackles he broke in
> pieces; and no one had the strength to subdue him.
> 5 Night and day among the tombs and on the moun-
> tains he was always howling and bruising himself
> with stones. 6 When he saw Jesus from a distance,
> he ran and bowed down before him; 7 and he shouted
> at the top of his voice, "What have you to do with
> me, Jesus, Son of the Most High God? I adjure you
> by God, do not torment me." 8 For he had said to
> him, "Come out of the man, you unclean spirit!"
> 9 Then Jesus asked him, "What is your name?" He
> replied, "My name is Legion; for we are many."
> 10 He begged him earnestly not to send them out of
> the country. 11 Now there on the hillside a great
> herd of swine was feeding; 12 and the unclean spir-
> its begged him, "Send us into the swine; let us
> enter them." 13 So he gave them permission. And the
> unclean spirits came out and entered the swine; and
> the herd, numbering about two thousand, rushed down
> the steep bank into the sea, and were drowned in
> the sea. (Mark 5:1-13, NRSV)

According to the story, the madman had been quarantined in the tombs, among the dead outside the city. He had been restrained with chains presumably to prevent his attempts to harm himself, but also to keep him at a distance because he had been possessed by an "unclean spirit." Seeing him, Jesus commanded the spirit to leave and instead enter the herd of pigs who were feeding nearby. The pigs drowned, but the man was saved and returned to the city to tell everyone what had happened to him.

This story trades on the important anthropological concept of purity. In the Israelite religion, people were obliged to follow laws of purity that dictated what things were clean and unclean. The laws further dictated that, should you come into contact with something that was unclean, then you too would be deemed unclean, and would have to go through a process of ritual purification before re-entering society.

In this story, Jesus acts to transfer the unclean spirit of the man to the pigs, who, under Jewish law, were deemed to be unclean animals anyway. Note that the uncleanliness cannot go away, it can only be transferred to someone else.

How are we to understand this story in light of our present planetary preoccupation with virality?

The urban residents of Decapolis, seeing that the man was infected with an unclean spirit had, in effect, quarantined him outside the city among the tombs. The unclean man was thus forced to live in an unclean space (dead bodies were also deemed to be unclean), an existence that was half alive and half dead. His salvation came when Jesus approached the unclean space, and transferred the man's uncleanliness to the unclean pigs.

This ancient narrative of cleanliness, contagion, virality, quarantine and cross-species infection is surely a story for our times.

A constant trope in the media has been that of the Chinese practice of consuming animals that are unfamiliar in the Western diet. Alain Badiou, for example, shamelessly wrote in the *Verso Books Blog* (March 20, 2020):

> Chinese markets are known for their dangerous dirtiness, and for their irrepressible taste for the open-air sale of all kinds of living animals, stacked on top of one another. Whence the fact that at a certain moment the virus found itself present, in an animal form itself inherited from bats, in a very dense popular milieu, and in conditions of rudimentary hygiene.[2]

This racist and inflammatory rhetoric about the "rudimentary hygiene" of "Chinese markets" trades on classic tropes of purity in two senses. Firstly, from the Western point of view, civet cats, bats and other animals are deemed "unclean" in the sense that Westerners would never normally eat those animals. Secondly, they are deemed "unclean" in that they are kept in live (or wet) markets and slaughtered in front of the consumer. The first issue, that of which animals are seen as fit for human consumption, is easily dismissed as a cultural prejudice: witness the horror of British people at the French traditions of eating horses or frogs. The second kind of "uncleanness" attributed to the Chinese wet markets is hidden in modern society through the process of intensive agriculture and factory slaughter. Meat in Western supermarkets arrives conveniently packaged in polystyrene foam and wrapped in plastic.

The ancient Israelite religion dictated that animals must be slaughtered by specialists and in precise ways, not right in front of us by the vendor: such an action would bring uncleanliness to the consumer. In this sense, our modern industrial abattoirs repeat the same cultural trope, and our modern social imaginary demands that we are buffered from the realities of animal blood. No "true modern" wishes to see an animal slaughtered in front of them. Such an act would be repulsive, even disgusting, as it evidently is to Badiou, and therefore so-called civilized Europeans slaughter their animals in secret. In "modern society," we keep our distance from the impurity of slaughter, refusing to be tainted by the witnessing of death produced in front of us.

II

When Taylor argues that we moderns live in a buffered "social imaginary," this condition of modernity is both "social" and "imaginary." It is social in that it is widely shared within society and is seen as a shared cultural norm. If only one person were to think in a certain way, then they would be regarded as strange, to say the least. But if many people share an "imaginary" then it functions like a worldview, giving value and character to shared human experience, confirming and strengthening, through numbers, our perception of reality.

The social imaginary, however, is imaginary in the sense that it is an illusion. We can no more isolate ourselves from the world than we can refuse to breathe the air around us. But it is also imaginary in the sense that it is in an ideal to which we aspire. We moderns yearn to be authentic to ourselves, to be, in effect, free from the social and economic conditions that shape our society and culture, to have the agency to do with our lives what we will, and "to thine own self be true."[3]

This sense of self, as an autonomous rational individual free from the chains of historical, social, or economic circumstance has been roundly critiqued, but still persists in our social imagination. Marx critiqued this from the perspective of the philosophy of history, famously arguing that "men make their own history but they do not make it just as they please; they do not make it under circumstances chosen by themselves, but under circumstances directly encountered and inherited from the past."[4] Yes, we do have agency, the ability to shape our own narratives and identities, but these agencies are ones that are precisely "encountered and inherited" from history. Our agency is, so to speak, encoded in our social-historical DNA, an inheritance from the past that not only gives shape to the specific character of our agency, but also one that seeks to reproduce itself.

One *locus classicus* of the buffered self can be found in the famous story of Robinson Crusoe, the story of a hero shipwrecked on a desert island. This figure of the lone adult male in pristine nature can be understood as the ultimate description of the authentic human: a man alone with himself, surrounded by natural fecundity. As Judith Butler has noted in a recent lecture, "in other words, the individual who is introduced to us as the first moment of the human, the outbreak of the human onto the world, is posited as if he were never a child, was never provided for, never depended upon parents or kinship relations, or social institutions in order to survive and grow and presumably learn."[5] In this fantasy of independence and primal authenticity, the man is who he is because of himself alone, and never because of the prior social-historical conditions into which he was born and raised. He is the model of a "self-made man," an oxymoron if ever there were one. Butler's point, of course, is that the story of Robinson Crusoe is one that begins with the erasure of women, and relationality in general. His identity is one that depends on no mother or family to support him. He is like Adam in the Garden of Eden, but without the recognition that his existence depends on something prior.

III

Today we have another reason to doubt the social imaginary of the buffered self: not history, not gender, but virus.

The virus is a part of nature that is often described as both living and not living. It is living in that it contains nucleic acids (RNA and DNA) and seeks to replicate itself. It is not living in that it cannot do so in and of itself. For a virus to replicate, it must invade a truly "living" cell and reprogram that cell with its own viral DNA. In this regard, viruses can be said to lead "a kind of borrowed life."[6] This quotation comes from an article that goes on to make a distinction between viral life, organic life, and non-living things: a virus is a kind of parasite that depends on the metabolism of the host to reproduce. Organic life possesses metabolism and reproductive capacities; non-organic matter, like a rock, is clearly not alive.

I find myself at odds with this description of what it means to be alive and not-alive. The argument for the virus's not being alive is that it depends on another body in order to live and reproduce. This seems to suggest that a characteristic of being alive is being independent from other living beings. Does this not repeat the fallacy that Butler observed in the story of Robinson Crusoe? Surely all living beings, including human beings, depend on other living things for their existence, at least their food, water and air. To be alive, far from being independent from other living beings, is more accurately the condition of dependency. Yet it is a dependency that, in our modern social imaginary, we conveniently overlook.

IV

One of the greatest shifts in Western ethical thinking in the past century has been the recognition that relationship is not something individuals freely contract with each other (the classic liberal view), but rather the shared condition that enables individuals to be individuals in the first place. This shift is exemplified in the famous statement of Marx, quoted earlier, that it is the inheritance of historical conditions that both constrains but also grounds our ability to make choices in the present.

A similarly relational view has also been long argued by Confucian ethicists who see filiality as the essence of identity. The Confucian view is based on the notion that life is given by parents. When parents see their child, their natural condition is to love, protect and nurture it. Similarly, when children see their parents, their natural condition is to love their parents, to look to them for guidance and protection. The foundation of all morality, all relationship, is the natural biological state of affection that arises between parents and their children. Without this there can be no morality. As we grow older, this affective relationship is steadily broadened so that we learn to love our extended family, our friends, and strangers. But the origin of this lies with our parents.

The famous Ming dynasty intellectual Wang Yangming (1472-1529) wrote in his *Inquiry on the Great Learning*: "the great man regards Heaven and earth and the myriad things as one body. He regards the world as one family and the country as one person. As to those who make a distinction between objects and distinguish between the self and others, they are small men." In his view, humans "form one body" with others and therefore have the capacity for commiseration: to feel the suffering of another. This "inability to bear the suffering" of others extends easily to other humans. Even in our cold, calculating modern world, Wang would argue, although we may express indifference to the plight of homeless people on the street, we do so only by suppressing an innate feeling of sympathy for them.

Wang further argued that this feeling of commiseration extends not only to human beings but to other species. We naturally cannot bear to see the suffering of other animals: that we slaughter animals in abattoirs far away from the social gaze only proves his point. More radically, he argued that the great man, "when he sees tiles and stones shattered and crushed, ... cannot help a feeling of regret."[7] And this was from a successful army general who doubtless had witnessed a great deal of death and destruction in his own career.

If the capacity to feel regret at a thing's destruction is a determining factor in whether we consider something to be living, then I am sure Wang Yangming would argue, contrary to *Scientific American* magazine, that rocks are alive. In his worldview, our capacity to feel the suffering of animals, plants, and even rocks, is due to the fact that we "form one body" with them, that we have some shared genetic inheritance. Not that rocks possess DNA, but that in his universe, everything that comes into being does so from the cosmic dance of yin and yang. The rhythm of life beats through the heart of the cosmos, humans, animals, trees, and rocks.

I wonder what he would think about viruses.

V

The relatively new science of astrobiology is an interdisciplinary effort that attempts to unite astronomy, the study of the universe beyond our planetary home, with biology, the study of living organisms. Three important questions have emerged in astrobiology: (1) Is the earth alive? (2) How should we detect life on other planets? and (3) How does the 4.5 billion-year history of the earth relate to the 13.7 billion-year history of the universe? One finding stands out for me in all of this research: it takes a planet to create a life. To put it another way, life cannot emerge in places that are less complex than planets. It takes the complex interactions between what goes on under the molten surface of the earth, the thin layer of crust above it, and the even thinner layer of gas that surrounds the earth for life to emerge. And when it does so, life further interacts with the atmosphere, and the atmosphere changes radically as a result. This is why astrobiologists search for life on distant exoplanets by scanning the composition of their atmospheres. So far as we know, only large planets have the size and complexity to enable the interactivity of life to emerge.

The story of the emergence of life on earth is also the story of the history of the universe. As David Grinspoon puts it:

> Out of the Big Bang came a dense fog of racing, swarming particles. As the universe expanded and cooled, they clumped into small atoms of hydrogen. Gravity pulled these together into stars, where they fused into a wider diversity of atomic elements. Stars burned and exploded, spewing their guts into vast, diffuse clouds of dust enriched with heavier, chemically reactive elements, where simple molecules formed. Gravity again gathered those clouds into new stars, and planets. On some of these planets, more complex molecules formed.[8]

Then on at least one planet, the story kept going, and a whole new saga started in some dirty, warm ponds where organic molecules experimented on themselves.

A dirty pond. Self-experimenting molecules. Hardly the pristine categories of the Garden of Eden or the island of Robinson Crusoe. More like the fecund breeding ground for a novel coronavirus.

Viruses work by managing to enter cells they are not supposed to enter. Some, through a process known as endocytosis, trick the cell into allowing them in through the cell membrane. In effect they take advantage of the natural porosity of the membrane which, just like the skin on our body, purposely allows limited interaction between the interior and exterior. If a cell had a solid wall instead of a porous membrane, then it could not do its work.

Not only is planetarity a condition of life. So also is porosity.

VI

We are planetary beings, and we are porous beings. What do these two conditions say about our existence, our ethics and our society?

To be a planetary being is to recognize and accept that without the complexity and deep history of our planet, we could not be alive at all. It is to recognize our ultimate dependence on the air, water and material life that teems on our planet and to live with that recognition as the foundation of our ethics. To be alive is to be in relation with the myriad vital processes that emerge, transform and decay all around us. It is also to recognize that no other life is possible. As much as we might imagine creating a home for ourselves on another planet or in a starship, such a life would be diminished in proportion to the diminishment of the environment. We may survive for a long time on the memories of our home world, but without the fresh scent of life in the air, our capacity for imagination, creativity and thought would be severely diminished. Consequently, our ethics must be based on the recognition that the best of all possible social-political worlds cannot take place except in the context of the best of all possible ecological worlds. As long as we damage the planetary foundation for human life, we limit our capacity for justice and equity in the political realm.

To be a porous being is to recognize and accept that our skin is not only a wall that protects our inner body from the outer environment, but it is also a membrane that enables us to interact with our environment. To be alive is to have a porous skin, and a body with orifices. Through these we are in a continuous process of exchange of energy, breath and food with the world around us. It is also to recognize that no life other than porous life is possible. As much as we build walls and enclaves for ourselves, we also depend on interaction with the world outside for our life and livelihood. While some people may be able to survive as hermits living on their own for a long time, our basic character is to be social beings, and our sociality is a condition for our happiness and wellbeing. Consequently, our ethics must be based on the recognition that the best of all possible worlds cannot take place except under the condition of porosity. To be porous means to accept the vulnerability that comes from the possibility of being hurt, whether by viruses who trick our cells to reproduce their own DNA, or by lovers who may one day reject us. To be alive is to be vulnerable, and it is our shared vulnerability and our mutual “inability to bear” the sufferings of others, rather than our invincibility, that makes us truly human.

One should not die just from fear of life.

1 Charles Taylor, *The Secular Age* (Cambridge, MA: Harvard University Press, 2007).

2 Alain Badiou, "On the Epidemic Situation," *Verso Books Blog*, March 20, 2020, https://www.versobooks.com/blogs/4608-on-the-epidemic-situation.

3 It is an irony of modernity that we have largely forgotten that, when Polonius utters these immortal words in Shakespeare's *Hamlet,* they are intended as the vacuous platitudes of a self-important nobody. Instead they have become the cornerstone of our modern sense of self.

4 Karl Marx, *The Eighteenth Brumaire of Louis Bonaparte,* 1852, https://www.marxists.org/archive/marx/works/1852/18th-brumaire/ch01.htm.

5 Judith Butler, "Non-violence, Grievability, and the Critique of Individualism," (lecture, Meiji University, December 11, 2018).

6 Luis P. Villareal, "Are Viruses Alive," *Scientific American*, August 8, 2008, https://www.scientificamerican.com/article/are-viruses-alive-2004/.

7 Wang, Yangming, *The Philosophical Letters of Wang Yang-ming*, trans. Julia Ching (Canberra: Australia National University Press, 1972), 272.

8 David Grinspoon, *Earth in Human Hands* (New York: Grand Central Publishing, 2016), 228.

Liad Hussein Kantorowicz

When You Died, the City Died with You

Dear Timi,

It's summer. Barbie Deinhoff's. Berlin. 2010. You, standing on a small makeshift stage, hosting a fundraising event for a short queer film. *Cruel Sluts*. Do you remember? It was the first time I saw you perform. Makeup smeared on your face. A rose. You stuck a rose up your ass, upside down. Its head is dangling between your legs. You're naked. You keep turning around, as though off-handedly. Showing your ass with the upside-down rose in it to the crowd. Everyone laughs. You're kinda brilliant, and I love you. Do you remember?

When you died, the city died with you.

Flowers were never particularly important to you. They're only important to me when they help me remember. Every year on your birthday I buy flowers and walk with them around the neighborhood. I look at the places where our relationship lived in Berlin, and watch them disappear. In my mind, I re-create our joined memories when I stand there. I look at the places we would inhabit from the outside, like a thief staring at a house they're planning to rob. I stand there, and in my heart I tell you what happened to the place since you left. I throw some flower petals there in memory of our love, and continue walking to my next destination.

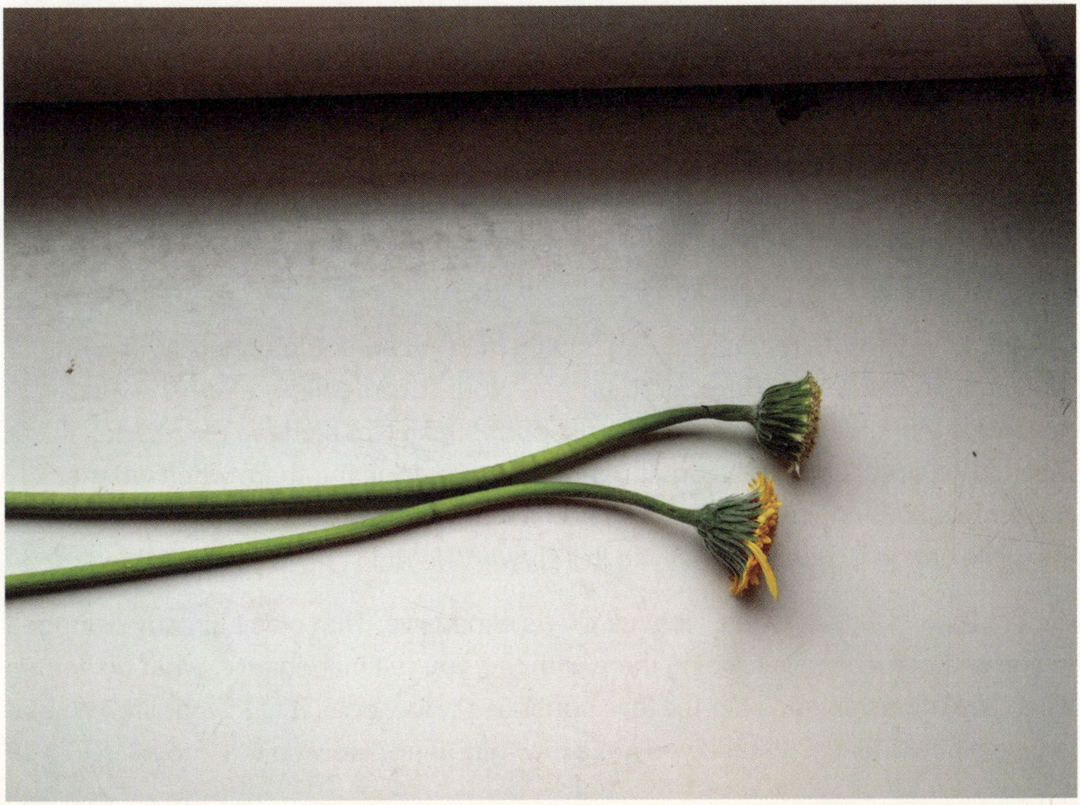

You said: "Berlin is 3 Bs: Basso, Barbie's, and Berghain." Do you remember? All three were conveniently located close to your house. Basso. An open, free art space. You loved this place. When I moved to Berlin, I didn't understand what a "free art space" meant. Where I come from, nothing is free. There's rent to pay. There's an entry fee. How could performance events just happen for free? You took me to my first-ever no-burlesque performance event there. You were trying to give me a sense of what "art" and "culture" are. I came from the gutter of queer subculture. I was doing trash-inspired lip-sync-and-striptease shows. The performance was dramatic, but too slow. I later learned that it's called "durational." Basso had a side entrance from an ugly parking lot where the sun never shined. You starred in a short feminist porn movie that was filmed there. It was called *To Rape Tim*. It had women stripping you of your clothes and fucking you, and bringing some joy of life into that gray lifeless parking lot. Basso had a publication, which brought together some fantastic artists and creative minds, I guess. You published texts there. They were brilliant and you were proud. I couldn't read them. They were in German.

Basso shut down to the public around the time of your death.

When you died, the city died with you.

I wonder: if I write to you, if I channel our love, will I get any of it back? Our love wasn't about "the couple." Three and a half tumultuous years, which we spent loving each other and assessing and re-reassessing if and how to be together. There was a constant that pulled us together, that provided the foundation for our drama, that gave a tone and a color to our love, that we loved and that loved us back: Berlin. Our love was a threesome. Our love didn't happen in a void. It's not like it could have happened anywhere. Berlin. Our love didn't have a place. Our love was a place. The place where we stopped trying to escape.

Cuno's. Your favorite restaurant. Best sushi in Kreuzberg. Pictures of Wong Kar-Wai films on the lamps. Do you remember? Your favorite filmmaker. The best avocados in their rolls. Never a 50%-discount sushi. Not a cheap place. Me feeling like a real adult at an adult restaurant. You took me there when we met. November, 2007. A sort-of date. You had a girlfriend. I ordered pho. I cried with joy while eating it. Back then, I lived in Tel Aviv. We didn't have pho in Tel Aviv.

We didn't go to Cuno's often. Not cuz it was expensive. That place already belonged to you and someone else. Going there with me, you felt inadequate. What do you do when a relationship ends but the love continues? How does it fit in your life? What if you stay best friends? What if you get a new girlfriend? How do I fit into it?

It wasn't easy. Until you found a place for us both. Polyamory. Non-traditional relationship structures. We needed to learn how to do it. Beyond proclamations and theoretical allegiance. And then we chilled. For a while. Our regular booth. A cute waitress that knew us.

Cuno's was closed for over a year. Official-looking papers glued to its doors. I didn't understand what was written. It was in bureau-deutsch.

Eventually some east-Asian restaurant opened there.

Eventually I went in.

You'd hate it.

When you died, the city died with you. It's a slow death, it's still in the process of happening.

My memory is shitty. I need to be in the place, to stand in it, I need to see it, in order to remember. Our love is here, but the city is dying. The city is slowly turning into something that I don't recognize. Places get erased, and with them, so is the memory of us. The city is dying and I feel like I am losing us, I'm losing my memories.

There used to be a spaeti at Schlesisches Tor. I don't remember its name. Do you remember? A small place, selling foodstuffs, owned by some Kreuzberger Turks. On Sundays, the owner's twenty-some-year-old son would work at the shop. He'd have this disgruntled look on his face, sitting behind the counter. On Sundays, you'd go there and buy some olives and tomatoes, if you hadn't gotten your food shopping done during the week. On Saturday night, after finishing my 10-hour bar shift at Barbie's, I'd come over and sleep at your place. On Sunday, my body would be exhausted, torn from too many hours on my feet. You'd go to the store across the street and get me sunflower seeds. The good kind. I got you addicted. You took me to see Ai Weiwei's artwork *Sunflower Seeds*. It's a room-size mountain of sunflower seeds made of porcelain. On Sundays, we'd spend the day on your couch, smoking joints and watching movies. We'd eat sunflower seeds and pile the shells high on your glass coffee table. Sometimes the sunflower seed shells would become a huge mountain that covered the table. We would laugh and say that it's art, and that we're clearly on our way to becoming successful artists, just like Ai Weiwei. Were we on our way?

Your death was a choice. I know it wasn't a choice to break up with me. It was you, breaking up with the world. It was you, breaking up with Berlin.

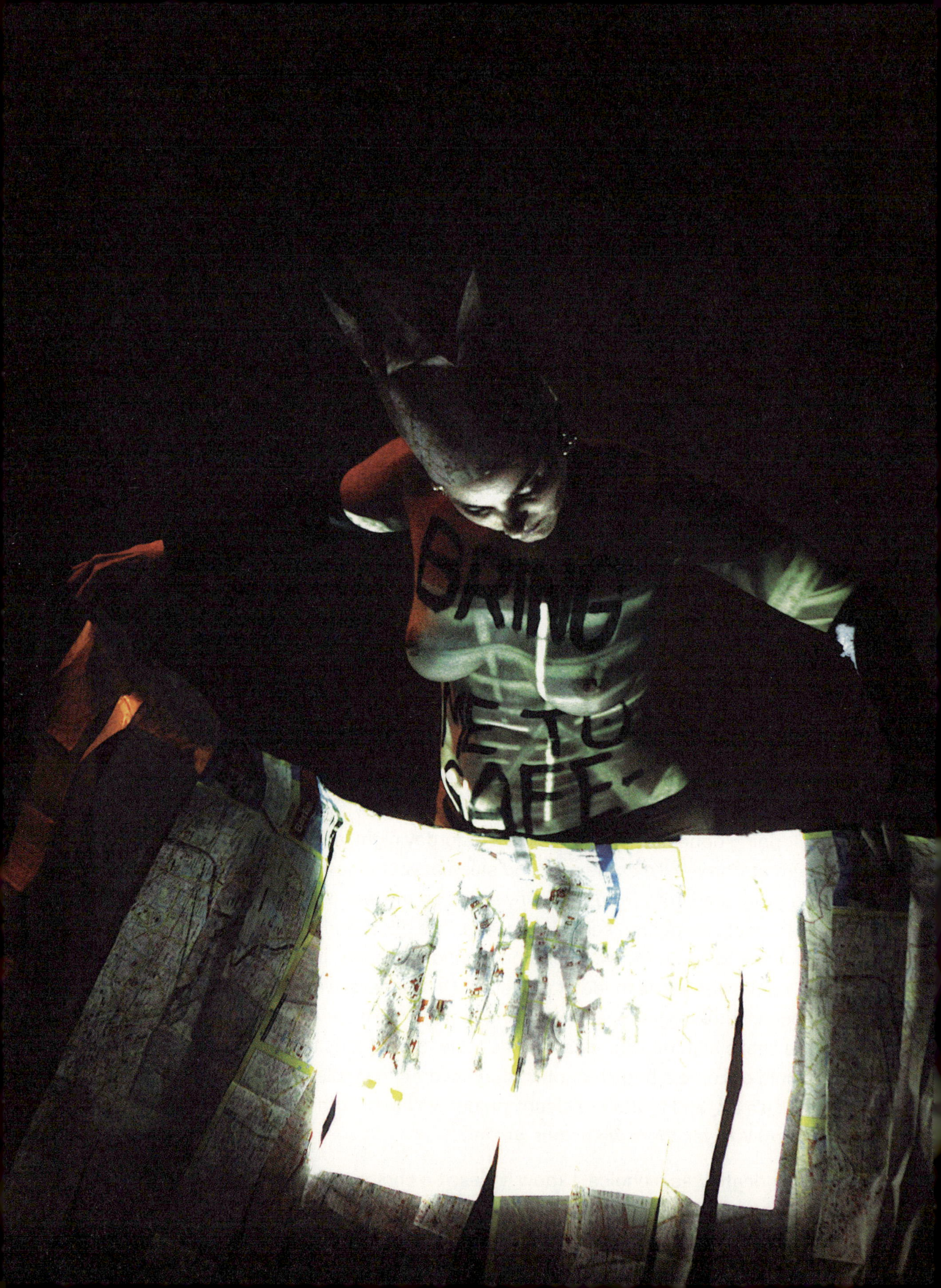
BRING

So often while walking by our houses, I would look at the changing landscape around them. So often I thought: how would you react to these changes if you were still alive? So often I thought: if you were still alive, your heart would be breaking. Look at what has become of this city. If you were alive now, you surely wouldn't be able to withstand it.

When you died, the city died with you. Your death was a choice, and you could choose to leave this city. Unlike you, I don't have anywhere else to go.

Josi's strip club. The first strip club-brothel I worked in. A few blocks from your house. Do you remember it? You had a period when you were obsessed with coke and strip clubs. Before I moved to Berlin. You even wrote some text about it, and about the dark side of masculinity and addiction. You'd frequent the place. You made some lonely sex worker fall in love with you. You introduced me to the place. I started working there in 2010. I would dance on the bar for dollars. I was the only non-European. The rest were Romanian women who all came from one village, and a fat Turkish owner. I brought my German language book to work. I did my German homework while sitting at the bar. At six a.m. I'd take off my stripper shoes. My feet hurt so much, they'd be in the shape of Barbie doll feet and refuse to straighten. I'd jump on my bike, speed cycle to your house, and go to sleep in your arms. Police raids on brothels weren't so popular then. I worked illegally. "If the cops show up, tell them it's your first day, and that you didn't have time to get a tax number yet." That's what the boss said. Six weeks later, the police knocked. I was rushed out of the back door. I jumped on my bike. I speed-cycled to your house and into your arms in the middle of the night. I was scared I'd get deported. I wasn't allowed to return to work there.

After that, the Media-Spree Project took over. The club shut down. A hipster dance bar opened in its place. "Josis." They thought that advertising the club as a former brothel would make it seem cool. The place didn't last though. There's a german restaurant there now. "Richard." Upscale and vanilla-looking. That place isn't even hipster.

Some months after you died, I was determined to find new places in the city. I felt like Berlin shrunk. It wrapped itself around me. It was chaining me to memories of you, and of Kreuzberg, and of our threesome love. I'm sorry to tell you, but the memory of you was some heavy shit to carry. I wanted new neighborhoods, new avenues, new memories, new ways of knowing the city, away and outside of our love. And now, everything has turned itself around.

Photo on previous page: Corinna Sauer

Now I find that I want to visit Berlin again. Yet I live in Berlin. In fact, I live in the same house, and same street, and same neighborhood as when we were together. When I say that I wanna visit Berlin, it's not about a movement in space. I wanna to go to another time, to a Berlin that no longer exists.

To me, this feels like what happens when a couple breaks from a third side, in an attempt to salvage something from the relationship. Do I need to de-territorialize my love?

Dear Timi,

It's November 12th, 2013. Six months after you died, almost to the day. I wrote: "Six months ago today. I'm standing, but not very stable. When I was 24, people were making bets on whether or not I'd make it to 30. Today I know that I'll outlive them all." I outlived your death. Albeit being deeply destabilized by it. My friend Chandra told me: "Stability is a balancing act that's slightly overrated. Trees bend and sway with the forces of nature. Sometimes things shift and break off, but newer things grow in their place with greater strength and flexibility where needed. People who survive and move on are always inspiring."

I was always jealous of you. You had your parents' house to go to, the house where you grew up. I was a perpetual migrant. My family and belongings are scattered all over the world, and none of them are in the house I grew up in. I only

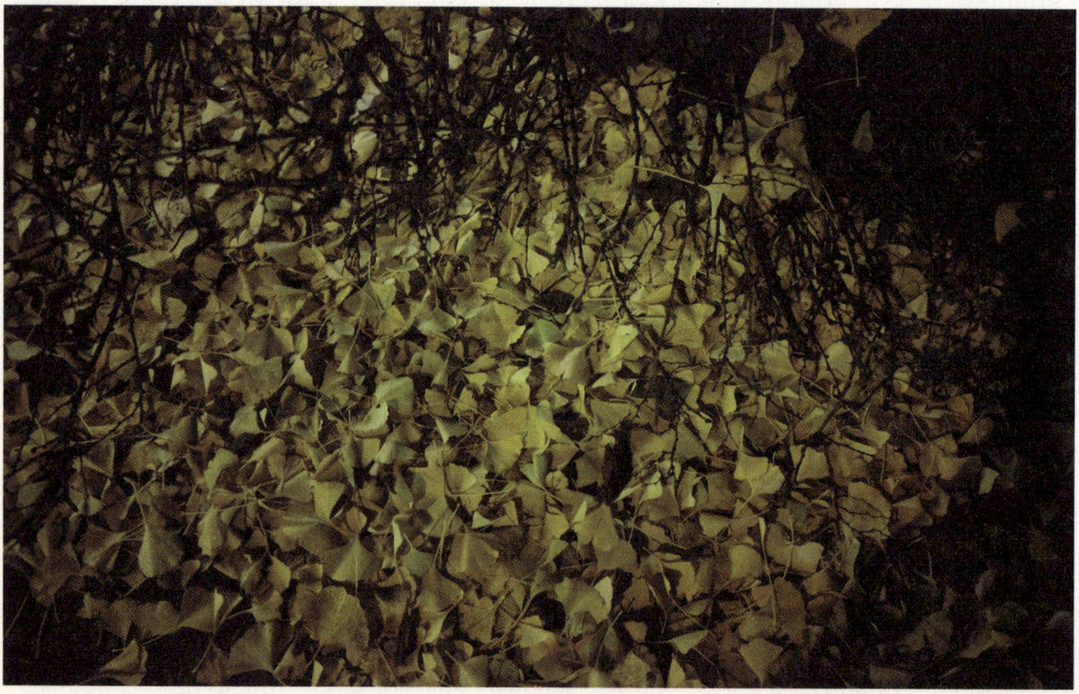

have memories. Are people like trees? What happens when people migrate? What happens when they leave behind their surroundings and friends, and everything they've known? What happens when they start life in a new place, uprooted from the old? Can they be like trees? Can they bend with the forces of change? Can they grow new strengths and new love to replace the parts that broke off?

What happens to people who flee from war? What happens when war doesn't end? What happens when people wanna go home and they can't? They can only live their home in their memories. They look at the places they would inhabit from the outside. Like thieves staring at a house they're planning to rob. When they want to go home, do they want to go to another time?

Barbie Deinhoff's. Your favorite bar. The first bar you took me to in Berlin. Do you remember? Someone stole my wallet the first time I was there with you. The walls were painted dirty pink. Old furniture that reeked of smoke. A swing that hung above the bar. People would climb up and swing from it. People snorting drugs in the dirty toilet. Queer performances every week. From the avant-guard to lo-fi trash. A makeshift stage from beer crates and wood. I performed there too. I did a striptease-lipsync to a song called "War is Good." The queer community would gather there to drink. You knew everyone. I got to know everyone through you. The owner loved you. Then she loved me. And then I got a job there. I was the only femme behind the bar. You'd come there in the evening to visit me, bring a book, sit at the bar and read. You're the only person I knew who would read books at a bar. You said that we can't make out at the bar. It's a queer space. We have to respect it. Back then I didn't get you. Where I come from, queer spaces were for everyone.

I continued working there after you died. It was hard. Every time I was there, pictures of you that hung on the wall were staring at me. The entire place mourned you. Being there was mourning you. But it got easier. Eventually I'd go to someone else's house to sleep when my shift was over. The owner had multiple nightlife-related burnouts. The queer performances stopped. The swing on the bar got taken down. The street got popular for weekend party-tourists. They would overtake the bar on weekends. The prices went up. The place stayed busy. But it stopped being queer. People stopped telling their friends to come hang out there during their DJ sets. I stopped working there. Then I stopped hanging out there. For me, it's not tragic. I found other bars to hang out in. I don't have to beat a dead horse. The place exists but its spirit is depleted.

I really think that if you lived here now, you wouldn't go there anymore.

When you died, the city died with you.

When bombs fall on a city, it isn't only homes and the places of the everyday that get destroyed and erased. People have to flee. Their daily routine gets destroyed. With it, all the social fabric, the human connections, and the personal networks that make the topography of a city, and that tie people to each other and to the place—all of that turns into dust. It's more than just a loss of one's home and material things. Urbicide is about the killing of a city. People are closely connected to their places, since it is the fabric that connects them to their community, their culture, sometimes their language. It is where their sense of self comes to life. People who lived in one city for most of their lives, or even for many years—their notion of self depends on their everyday routes, their connections and interactions with the people that surround them. Their knowledge of a place and its community is a part of them. It is their culture. What happens when that entire social fabric is suddenly gone? Can you sever your belonging to a place, like cutting a limb with cancer, and recreate your existing knowledge of self from scratch in a new place? Can you do it as a community?

There's a link between place and memory, and those are connected to identity, to a sense of self. Once culture cannot be lived in a physical place, it relies on memory. And eradication of that memory is, in the end, an eradication of existence.

I'm thinking of Yarmouk. It was the largest unofficial Palestinian refugee camp in Syria. Basically a tight-knit neighborhood. 110,000 Palestinian refugees who created their lives with one another. Because the Palestinians in Yarmouk were already refugees, for many of them, life in the camp is all they ever knew. On the grounds of the camp they re-created together the notion of what it means to be Palestinian, a joint living memory of the villages in Palestine they came from. There were no trees in Yarmouk. During the ongoing Syrian civil war, in 2014, the camp became besieged. Fighting took place there and 200 people were killed. By 2015, ISIS took over the camp. Most of its residents had to flee Syria. Yarmouk lost its topographical identity. People lost their home. Once they were no longer in Yarmouk, did they stop being "the Palestinians from Yarmouk"? Did the fact that they were no longer living in the camp make the "Yarmouk" part of who they are less present in their identity and lives? I don't think so.

Berlin is not Yarmouk. Kreuzberg is alive and prospering with tourists and hipster bars and vegan Vietnamese restaurants. But its residents have been getting priced out and kicked out. And that too, is topographical violence, though it occurs at a slower pace than as a result of war. It's interesting to me that Berlin now houses at least two types of victims of urbicide: those dispossessed of their homes due to war who arrived in Berlin, and those who are dispossessed of their homes in neighborhoods like Kreuzberg and Neukölln, as a result of gentrification.

Historically, Kreuzberg was at the end of West Berlin, the abandoned far edges of the universe. It was a Turkish neighborhood, because Turkish migrants were only allowed to live in the far edges of the universe, where no one wanted to live. But they put community and bakeries and small men's clubs and playgrounds and leftie social centers—and life—into Kreuzberg. Kreuzberg is the land that took part in defining what it means to be a Turkish migrant in Berlin. Some spent their lives and their days and their livelihoods in this neighborhood. What happens to their collective memory? What happens to their everyday once they have to move? Do they stop being Kreuzbergers? Do they come back and visit? Do they also stand and stare at places they grew up in, or buildings that were a part of their history? What if they can no longer recognize what has become of them?

In order to stay Kreuzbergers, they have to live it with other people. Their sense of self depends on a communal re-creation. In case of territorial dispossession, they would need to de-territorialize their identity. Their memory is a tool to collectively recreate their sense of self, a tool to resist the changing of the time that forces displacement and the erasure of the self. When I speak to the you that is Timi and to the you that is the audience, and share with you my memories of Berlin, it is my humble way to resist. I insist on keeping something from the changing of the time, from the erasure of this city. It is with you that my memories and my sense of self can come to life.

When you died, the city died with you.

And then, there is your house. A big room. Walls covered with small pictures of all the queer events you went to. Business cards and invitations from all the queer artists and thinkers you knew. Your huge record collection. Your room was our refuge from the world, the place where we could be with each other, away from the Berlin stress bla. And yet, you felt haunted by it. The street-level windows made you feel exposed to the world when you weren't well. The ubahn passing right at your window. Its sound—a reminder of the passing of time. Of the never-stopping pace of the city outside. You wanted to move. You were trying to leave this place. You were looking for other apartments. It's not so easy when new rental contracts are expensive, and free apartments are sparse. I made it even harder. I didn't want you to move far. I wanted our houses to stay close to each other. How would our lives look if we lived in different parts of the city? How much time would we spend on public transport? Would we see each other? But there were no more apartments around us. You were trapped by your apartment. Your time was running out. You never found a new place in your lifetime. You stayed close to me in your death.

I thought I'd never be able to walk by your house again without crying. That I'd never be able to go to that ubahn station. Every time I'd see the blinds on your window, I'd remember me throwing small rocks at it at 4 a.m., after my work shift ended. Waking you up so you'd let me in. Walking by this house, having no place in it, it broke my heart. When you died, I took all the pictures and business cards from your walls. I compiled them in a folder. A mobile, wall-less version of your house. So I wouldn't need to go to your room to feel your presence. We gave the apartment to a friend of a friend. I never visited her, never again saw the place from the inside. But I would stand in front of your street-level windows. Looking at the light inside. Looking for a sense of adequacy. Five years later, and look what happened to every storefront business on your block. The pizza place, the upscale coffee place, the cafe with the mismatched furniture that I went to after the last time I saw you. They're all erased. There's a bio Italian ice cream place right next to your house. Some guy took me there on a date. We sat on the foot-steps of your house and ate ice cream. I said nothing, then I ran away and never talked to him again. Sometimes I still stop when I walk by, try to look inside when the light is on. But I can no longer picture you there.

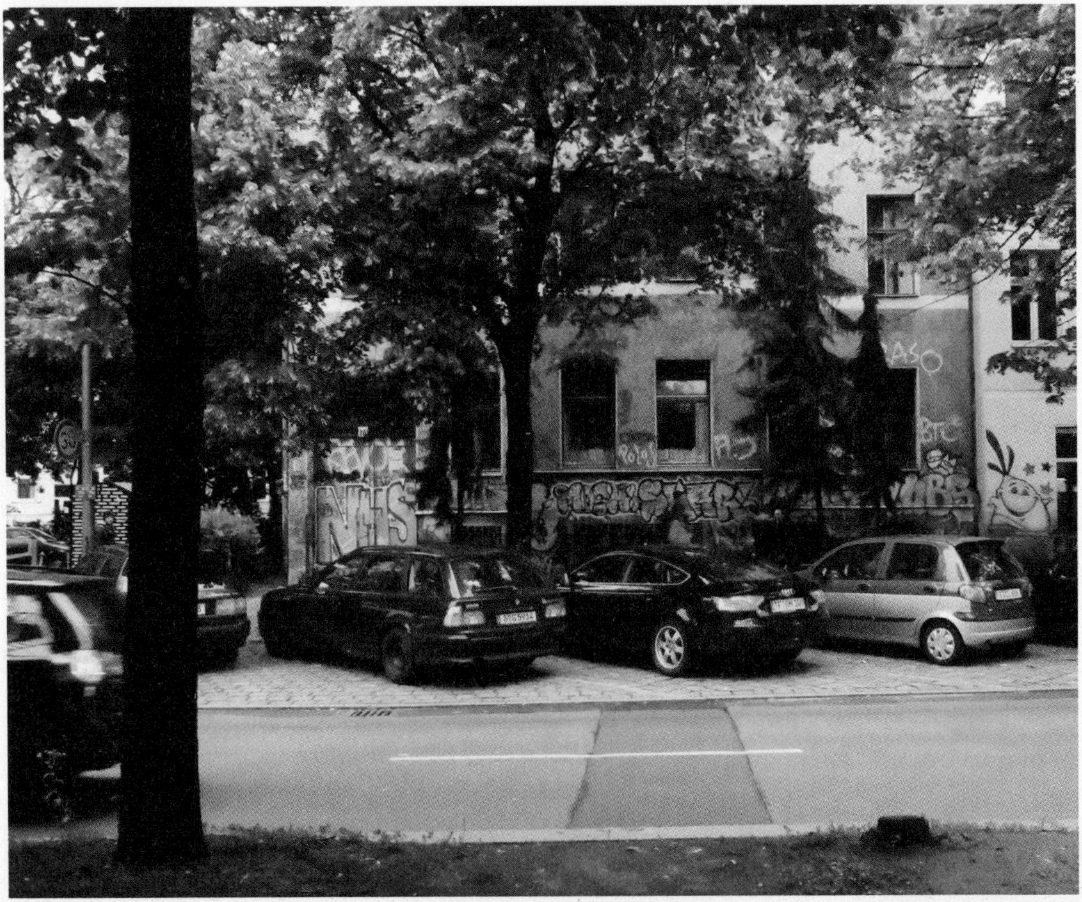

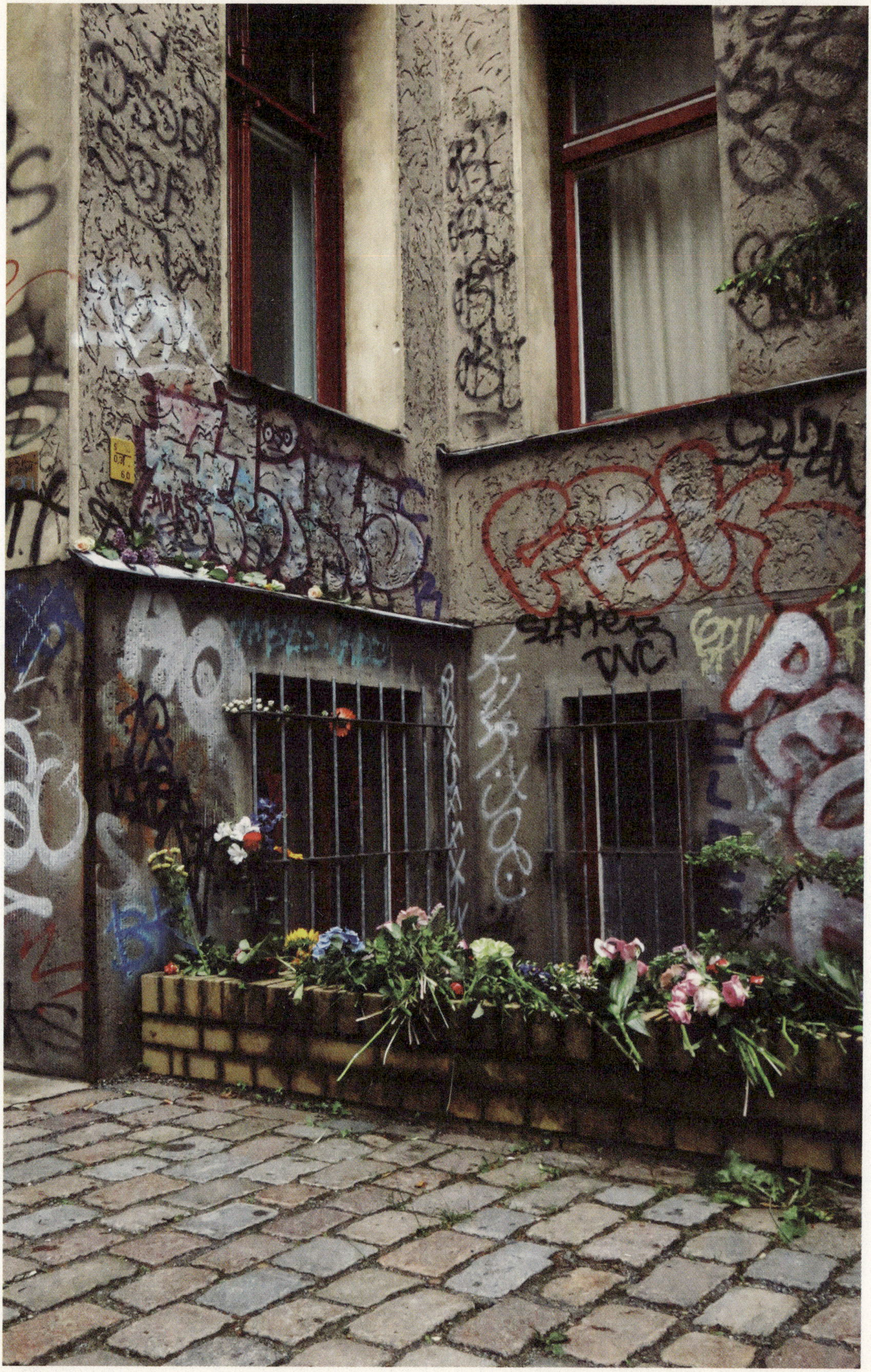

When you died, the city died with you.

The city changes so fast. It erases its people, its buildings, its memories. But trees tend to outlast these. They outlast the lifespans and presence of people who inhabit them.

When you died we got you a tree, to remember you by. A ginkgo tree. Its leaves are shaped like a Spanish fan when it's open. Ginkgo is said to have attributes that increase memory. For me, the tree played a doubly symbolic role. A means to remember you by, and a means to improve my own memory, dwindling, bruised and battered by the loss of you.

The tree was placed on a balcony, in the same place where you ended your life. It was waiting for us to find a place to plant it. And the waiting took weeks. No matter how hard we tried, we couldn't find a place in Berlin that would house your tree. We asked some city-appointed gardener if we could plant it on a piece of land by the river. We were immediately refused. My roommate approached the authorities presiding over Görlitzer Park. They said: no. The authorities said that ginkgo trees are difficult to handle, and dangerous for the park. They won't allow it. Berlin seemed to be full of regulations, city ordinances, application processes—big and small laws controlling the public space. Excuses as to why not to house a tree in your memory in this city.

We devised every tree-planting idea imaginable: guerrilla gardening in parks without permission. Planting it in huge buckets on the street. In inner courtyards of the building of a friend's apartment. Each plan had its faults. What if the clandestine tree was uprooted by city officials? Or stolen from the street? What if we moved, or got kicked out of the apartment we rent? And the building and courtyard where your tree is planted were no longer accessible? Losing you was hard enough. We couldn't risk losing your memory tree. Meanwhile, the tree grew and grew across that balcony. But Berlin had no stable place for it. It's as though the city refused to inhabit the memory of you after your death, the way it refused to inhabit you when you were alive.

We eventually planted the Timi-tree in the front yard of a Schrebergarten house of a friend. Past the Berlin city limits. It's been five years. The tree stayed small. Its branches never kept stretching after it left that balcony. I imagine that, without Berlin, it just couldn't continue to grow. Just like you, when you took yourself from Berlin and this world. It's too far and unfamiliar to visit, so I've made friends with every single ginkgo tree in Berlin. There are twenty-five of them in this city that I know of. I know where each one of them lives. They're city trees, their roots firmly placed in the grey soil. They're like my children. I visit them regularly. My love for you lives in them.

Sarnath Banerjee

I Don't Feel Postcolonial When I Wake up Every Morning in Delhi (No One Here Does)

When Peter Carey returned to his native Australia after a prolonged period in the US, he felt that he could not write an Australian novel anymore, neither could he be wholly American. He realised that he had effectively lost his place. Former graphic novelist Sarnath Banerjee talks about his anxieties of how being easily understood by European Institutions can make him lose his local relevance. How looking for cosmopolitanism in Europe can be an act of serial defeat. And how having lived in Europe for eight years makes him feel that he has lost his place. He uses the example of *Enchanted Geographies*, a series he did on uncanny experiences in Berlin. The series ran for eighteen episodes in a national newspaper in India, after which the author ran out of stories.

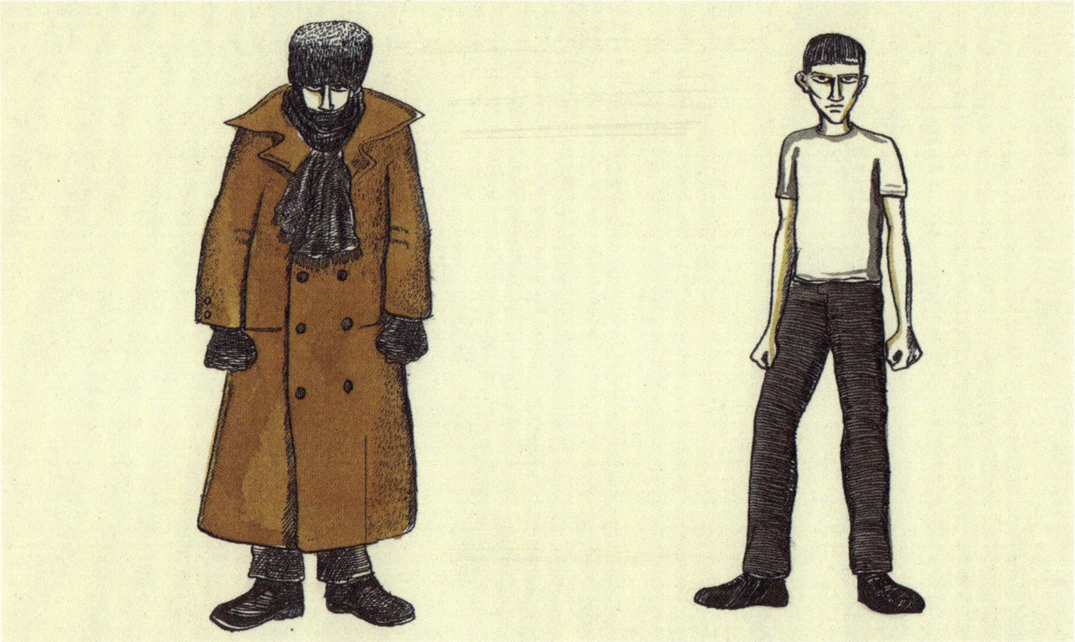

Growing up in the third world, there was a never-ending stream of western writers explaining Indian societies with their characteristic confidence. Many were well-researched and produced valuable understanding. Something that only an outsider can bring. Banerjee feels Europe has done poorly when it comes to incorporating outsiders' perspectives. When a culture is hyper-understood in its own terms there is a danger of devolution. There are very few examples of a third world subject looking into European society. Whether it is because of a lack of confidence among foreign writers when it comes to commenting on an extremely self-actualised society; or Europe's inability to trust outsider voices to comment on their society, when they themselves can do it so well, remains a topic of debate.

Of course, there is migrant writing—colliding or coexisting with the west, fitting or failing, conflict and trauma. There is Diaspora writing about identity and the decolonial condition. But clear chronicling of the west by non-western authors is rare. All literature coming from the Global South need not be migrant literature. Curators from the Global South need not be cultural sherpas, and all south Asians need not identify themselves as postcolonial subjects.

My ex-wife is Pakistani and I am Indian; after living in the subcontinent for four years we finally gave up. The geo-politics of the region eventually caught up with us. We moved out of south Asia eight years ago and made Berlin our home. Leaving Delhi meant not only leaving home but also leaving the very culture from which we derived our imagination. Dislocated from context, we tried to make sense of our new circumstances. German life is rich and pleasant, but initially I found German culture fundamentally different from south Asian—whether it is politics, society, humour, food, topics of conversation or lifestyle choices, they were different and sometimes counter-intuitive for south Asians.

It was good for me. Prolonged exposure to one's familiar surroundings can make one impervious to multi-dimensionality of thought. Cultural vulnerability primes the mind to open up to tantalising prospects. In Delhi, you sometimes meet a category of intellectuals, unchallenged by peers, who are, as a friend observed, "scuba diving within their shallow intellectual puddle."

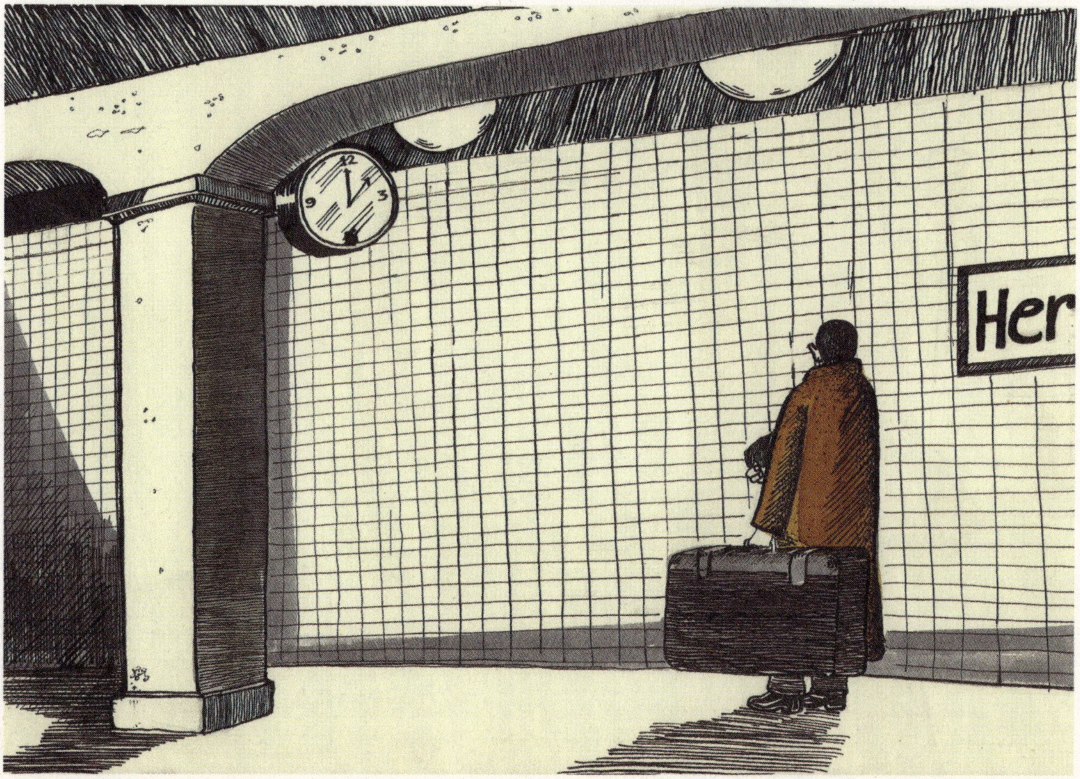

The choice left for me was to either embrace contemporary German culture whole-heartedly or else wilfully hold on to my own context and look at society from my unique vantage point—that of an outsider. The fact that you could also fuse them harmoniously did not occur to me as a possibility at the time.

Particularities of cultures and how one defines "the local" has always been my artistic concern, but it got amplified when I moved here. I devised a project called *Enchanted Geographies*, which looked at Berlin from the point of view of an outsider from the third world. I have always looked at society as an insider; the idea of looking at it as an outsider excited me.

Cosmopolitanism

My protagonist intricately weaves together a dinge-welt, a world of objects, which, although ordinary, achieves meaning and significance in its oblique reading. The surreal narratives create an inventory of objects, places and people. My character, Brighu, a solemn investigator of futile things, sets out on the footsteps of Fernando Pessoa in Lisbon, Charles Baudelaire in Paris, Harun Al-Rashid in ancient Baghdad, and Raymond Roussel to create a personal terra obscura.

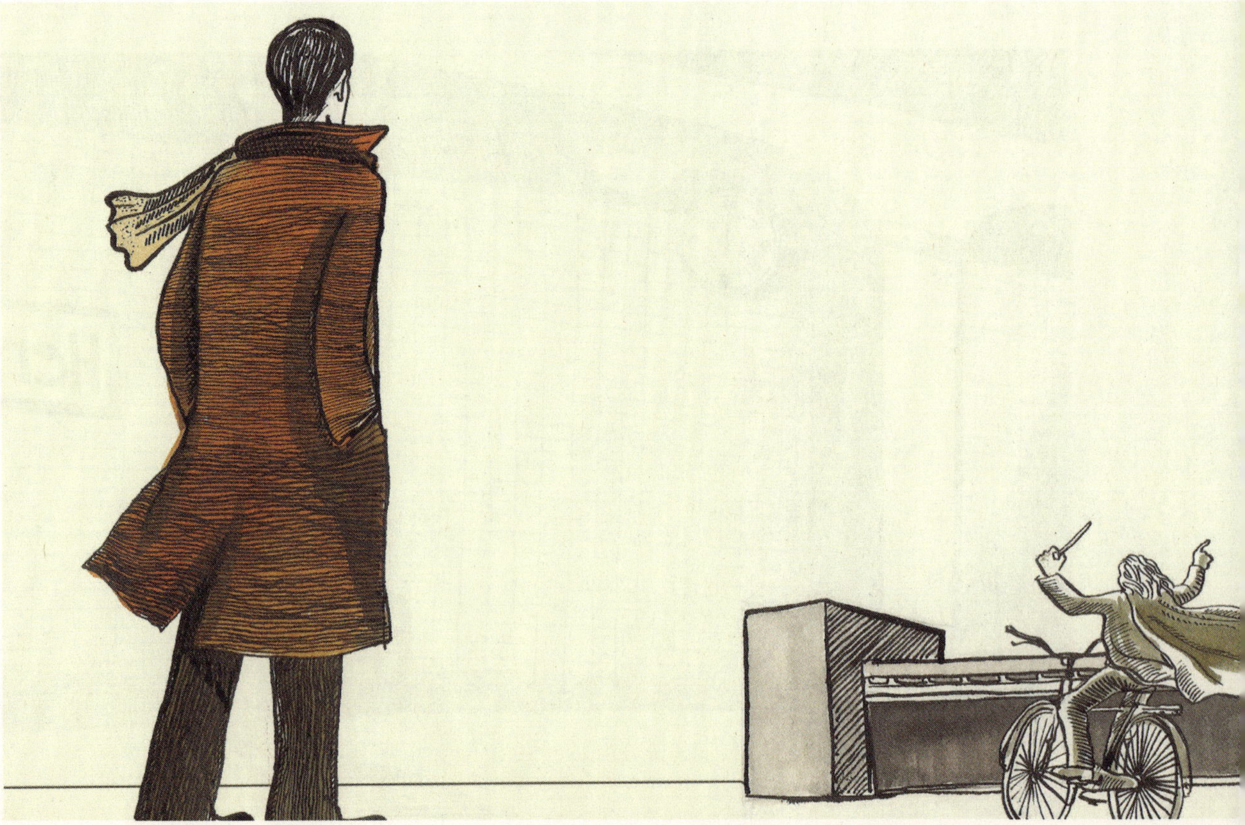

The narrative was structured around the idea of Denkbilder (thought figures)—of miniature image and text portraits. Brighu's impressions are tainted by false memories, generalisations, rumours and hearsay. Nostalgia for things that never happened. Speculated history. Fabrication. Although local, the narrative had a faraway quality, as it awkwardly tried to pose some questions:

How cosmopolitan is Berlin, really? Does a large group of international artists, curators or a nomadic group of lifestyle seekers make a city cosmopolitan?

I have always had a suspicion about writers who translate very well between cultures. In my opinion, to search for any grand notion of cosmopolitanism in Europe is to expose oneself to the possibility of serial defeat; the natural narcissism of dominant cultures will always come in the way. This tendency towards self-reference is increasingly becoming common in India as it aggressively flexes its muscles in the region.

Enchanted Geographies wasn't published anywhere in Germany but ran for eighteen episodes in a national newspaper in India. After that, the author ran out of stories about Berlin.

All drawings courtesy of the author

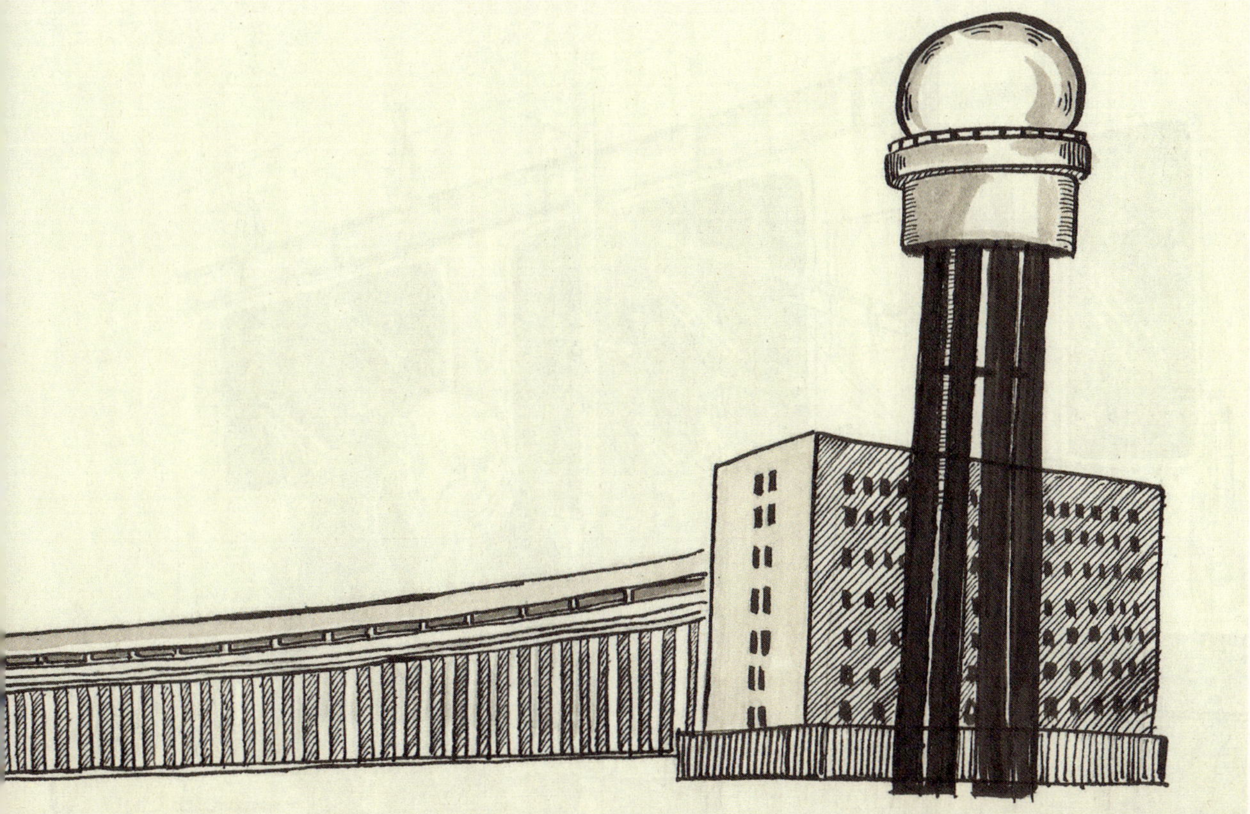

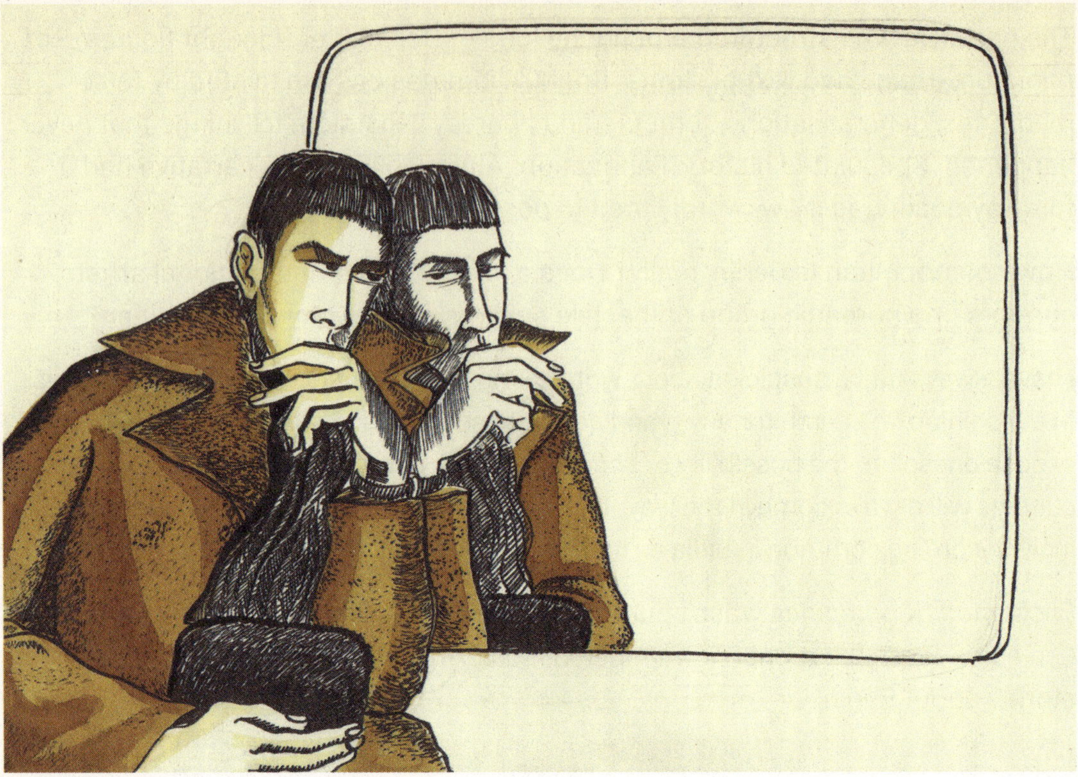

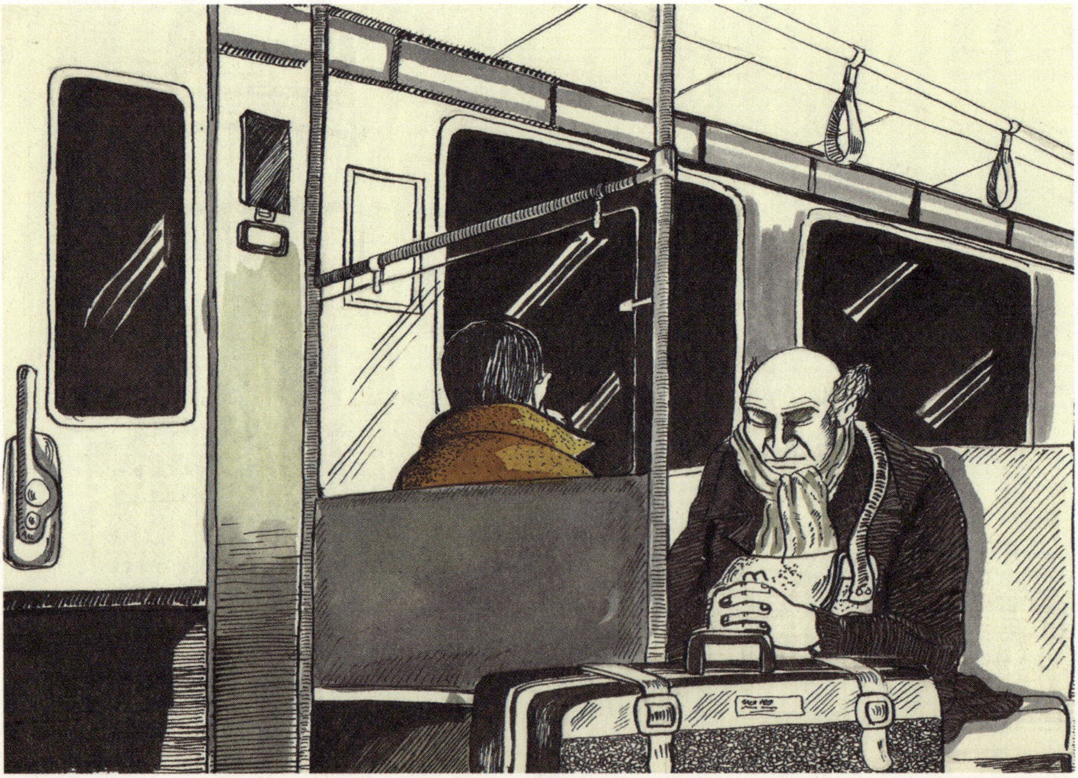

Lucy Gasser

Other Europes, Past and Future

I invite you on a journey to some Other Europes. The itinerary of our excursion, should you choose to accept, moves through Hungary and Romania, to a Bohemia by the sea, and on outward to Eurasia. Literary mappings provide the means of orientation and transportation. The trip begins with British author Bram Stoker, hops over to Czech novelist Libuşe Moníková, and leaps on to South African writer Alex La Guma; it travels from the European literary canon, via the European non-canon, to the non-European non-canon, to see what happens when the maps of these imagined Europes are folded into each other, overlaid and rearranged. It seeks to enunciate how the marginal(ised) can be made productively, momentarily central; and to illustrate how old centres can be shuffled into the margins.

Literature is always making and mapping a world, whether explicitly or implicitly: when a work of literature imagines a Europe, it also imagines a world in which that Europe takes up a position. While the spatial dimension of mapping as a guiding metaphor is clear, it also entails less visible temporal facets. The Mercator world map, which facilitated the navigation required for the fruition of various colonial endeavours, also set the ground for an overstatement of the size of the northern hemisphere and the centrality of western Europe. So too the Greenwich Meridian in London constructed an axis for time that assured Great Britain's centrality as a point of origin: the locus from whence being *ahead* or *behind the times* was to be measured. This, in turn, has had consequences for both how pasts are structured, and how the aspirational is projected onto imagined futures. Thus were European colonies in the global South taught to understand their *backwardness*, and that desirable futures were to be found in the *advanced* North, in narratives that served imperial interests of exploitation and subjugation.

Today, these colonial pasts and their varied ramifications are far from dead. For so many migrants seeking a liveable life, Europe still appears to hold the promise of a better future. When confronted with the murderous responses to this from nationalist resurgences across the continent, there is perhaps cause to cultivate a capacity to re-imagine this erstwhile centre; reason to seek out resources for rethinking Europes in the plural, for opening out a closed and exclusionary Fortress Europe, and for reconfiguring dated notions of its centrality in the world.

Literature, that analogue means of shaping cultural imaginaries, might yet have resources to offer in doing this imaginative work. A work of literature invents for itself the arrangement, the coordinates, and the axes that determine its possible worlds, the worlds it renders imaginable, and their normative content. It can inflect how we think about Europe; how we embark on imaginative journeys through it; how we imagine and relate to its pasts; and how we locate aspirations to envision possible futures, planetary and local.

We begin with Stoker, and the British canon, to articulate divisions within Europe: to foster, as we move outward from and beyond its restrictive boundaries, a nuanced grasp of Europe's internal margins and marginalisations; its gradients of Europeanness. We embark for an imaginary kingdom of Bohemia by the Sea for its collaborative energy, for its contestation of stories of western superiority, for its creative negotiation with imagined pasts, and for its animating hopefulness. We travel on outward-bound, from Kaunas to the Siberian taiga through a snowstorm, to dissolve, at least momentarily, the borders of Europe; to think about Tajik astronomy and Tanzanian mountains; to relocate aspirational futures and to concoct alternative logics of time.

Map in hand, our itinerary starts with Dracula. In Bram Stoker's *Dracula*, published in 1897 and firmly established in the British literary canon, Jonathan Harker ventures out on a perilous journey East. He notes, in Budapest, "the impression I had was that we were leaving the West and entering the East."[1] His perceived move eastward is accompanied by the observation that "the further East you go the more unpunctual are the trains."[2] Dracula's castle, in turn, is situated "in the extreme East of the country" which, in his view, is "one of the wildest and least known portions of Europe."[3] Stoker's setting is Transylvania, in Romania, a part of Europe he never visited himself. It is here that Jonathan Harker will encounter the diabolical evils of a creature it seems—in the novel's world—could only be born in the non-west; a character supposedly loosely based on the historical figure of Vlad the Impaler, who in fact ruled over the slightly less spooky landscapes of Wallachia, to the south.

For many, today, Europe as a whole is represented by the European Union. Romania's positioning as a literal periphery of the EU—it is, with Finland, the most easterly of the member states—is accompanied by its (continued) discursive articulation as questionably European. While the religious dominance of the Orthodox Christian faith, and a history of Ottoman rule in some of its territory, often serve as substantiation for its casting as emphatically *eastern* Europe, Romanians oftentimes emphasise the Latin roots of their language, and from the mid-nineteenth century fostered an understanding of themselves as having a deep affinity to France and all things French: Bucharest garlanded as the Paris of the Balkans.

Dracula is an early exemplar of how western Europe has produced eastern Europe as Other to itself: a distant lawless cousin, somehow unknown and somewhat dangerous. Divisions of the Cold War did little to alter such ascribed demarcations. Western Europe's wilful self-styling as the cradle of civilisation and the inventor of social justice and progressive politics has also benefitted from using this Other

Europe as its foil: a screen onto which to project that which is incompatible with its self-imaging. The political institutions in this Other Europe are presented as less stable and reliable; its conflicts as bloodier; its commodities as not quite up to scratch; and its emigrants as not entirely desirable. Such designations are accompanied by temporal markers too: Harker's unpunctual trains serve as synecdoche for an ascribed *belatedness* of eastern Europe, a construction that buttresses western Europe's development of itself as intrinsically *progressive*. Not all Europeans, it seems, are equal; nor are all construed as equally European.

The itinerary moves on to Bohemia: specifically, to William Shakespeare's Bohemia-by-the-sea. In *A Winter's Tale*, Shakespeare famously though unaccountably made Bohemia a "desert country by the sea": an imaginative-geographical move which has been multiply appropriated. Bohemia by the Sea, or *Böhmen am Meer*, is a recurring motif in German(-language) literature and arts, which has come to stand for a dreamed utopia of sorts: from Ingeborg Bachmann's 1964 much-celebrated poem; to Hans Magnus Enzensberger's essentially hopeful epilogue carrying the same title in *Ach Europa!* (1987); Volker Braun's play staged in Berlin in 1989-1990; and Anselm Kiefer's 1995 painting.

Czech-born writer Libuşe Moníková took the suggestion of Bohemia's coastline as imaginatively generative: asserting the artist's right to redefine geography, and herself inventing her own "ideal Europe." She imaginatively participates in a project of re-mapping Europe by shifting the borders of her map of the continent after the fall of the Iron Curtain (and before the dissolution of Czechoslovakia):

> In my daily perusal of the map I shift the borders of Bohemia frequently: sometimes according to the historical template of Greater Bohemia; sometimes according to Shakespeare, who knew—Bohemia lies by the sea. It would always be wise to consider the suggestions of poets, instead of leaving the dividing of the world to politicians, who don't read.[4]

For Moníková, the borders of Europe are malleable: sometimes historical, sometimes poetic; mostly moving, always move*able*. Europe has imagined content and imagined contours: literature plays a role in shaping and filling these, and in keeping them on the move, in rendering alternative cartographies imaginable.

It isn't just Europe's borders that are kept on the move; it is also the axes determining its internal arrangements. As she reminds us,

> neither Switzerland nor Czechoslovakia, not even Austria lie at the centre of Europe, which, after all, extends to the Urals. If one wants to be precise, the centre is more likely at Minsk or Witebsk, and the continent's highest mountain is in no way Montblanc, but the weathered Elbrus in the Caucasus, 800 meters higher.[5]

In so doing, she intimates how much more is at stake in allocating centrality than the merely geographical. By decentring western Europe, she encourages us to recalibrate our co-ordinates of and for the European continent. What might be the ramifications of taking seriously the injunction to shift the centre of gravity eastwards; to question the assumed westernness of Europe?

While thus asserting her right, in a creative, artistic capacity, to re-imagine the land and the continent of her birth, Moníková also registers that the mutability of these borders has worked in more violent ways. She describes her native Czechoslovakia during the divisions of the Cold War: "I experienced instead a country, a Bohemia no longer by the sea—the armies came and shifted it to where it belonged, to the edge of the steppes."[6] Shakespeare might have moved Bohemia to the sea, but soldiers shifted her home country metaphorically eastward.

Europe has difficult histories, including those that drew a dividing curtain across it, and state-sanctioned memorial culture is often too static to do justice. Resources for renegotiating relationships to the past can be found in literature, and so can more flexible ways of memorialising and remembering: "we could celebrate Josef K. Day."[7] Celebrating "Josef K. Day" would serve to honour those who are "unexpectedly invited to visit a courtroom or the police"[8]—whose numbers, in that Bohemia no longer by the sea, might have been rather high. This is a different means of remembering—and of remembering a different constellation of human beings—than official memorialisation might allow. Fiction here serves to articulate alternative relationships to Europe's pasts, and to geographies steeped in those pasts.

In the rollicking journey described in Moníková's novel *The Façade*, Europe's continental borders wither into irrelevance as they leak into Eurasia.[9] Eurasia brings with it a smorgasbord of tricks and possibilities. One character, Dobrodin, opines,

> Europe, what is that? Speaking on a macro-geological scale, we are part of a tectonic plate. The political squabbles on its surface are laughable when compared to what is happening in the earth's mantle. I was part of a deep-bore project on the Kola Peninsula last year; it was enough to make you call all men your brothers on the spot. And it is pure luck that our plates have fused so tightly, forty miles thick… We Eurasians belong together.[10]

Dobrodin points in the direction of things shared not on a national, or even merely *trans*national, scale but to some extent on a *planetary* one. Another character's "migration in the opposite direction, to tribal origins",[11] across the Bering Strait from Alaska to the USSR, has a similar inflection. The Bering Strait, which is cut and divided by Mercator projections of the world, is the contact zone between the United States and Russia, and between North America and (Eur)Asia. Projections of the strait often entail a visually counter-intuitive depiction in which Russia is positioned on the left. As the passage along which early humans are purported to have migrated from Asia to the Americas, these "tribal origins" are possibly also origins to which humankind is heir: a *planetary* inheritance, perhaps.

The move into Eurasia, as delineated here, segues Europe into Eurasia and Eurasia into the planet. This move, too, has temporal dimensions. There is a Soviet-bureaucratic temporality in which one's aims are forever deferred by an incomprehensible, Kafkaesque administrative apparatus. Such, for instance, is Dobrodin's (deliberate) obfuscation of a flight schedule:

> "You can't leave just like that, my little doves, not only because it would make us very sad, but also because there is no flight to Chabarovsk today."

"Didn't you tell us yesterday that there would be one today?"

"I did. It's all my fault," Dobrodin says with a smile. "And it left right on schedule. At seven this morning. The one at six this evening goes to Tura. The flight schedule for winter started today. Those two flights alternate from here on out. You can fly to Chabarovsk tomorrow and to Tura the day after. On even days in the morning, on odd days in the evening."[12]

The arrangement and apportioning of time here work according to rules that seem impossible to grasp. Its absurdity is only rendered more apparent when one of the travellers, Podol, tries to understand it. Once they have landed—unexpectedly—in Tura, Siberia, he questions a local geologist they meet on a bus:

"Is today an even- or odd-numbered day?" Podol suddenly thinks to ask.

The man apparently doesn't understand. "Oh, the date? It's the end of November." He mulls it over, "The twenty-ninth or the thirtieth. Around here we say that a purga can get your days and nights mixed up. One day more or less doesn't matter."

He laughs.[13]

The taiga of Eurasia and its arctic snowstorms produce yet other temporalities. Not structured according to a calendar or watches (as arbitrary, bizarre and capricious as these are shown to be), but by seasons, by the weather, and sometimes by whim; a temporality that certainly has no interest in time zones dictated by the Greenwich Meridian. Regardless of the date— to all appearances, an unsolvable mystery anyway—, as the geologist tells them: "You're going to have to wait out the *purga*. That may be ten days. Or longer."[14]

Moving from Europe into Eurasia counters a closed European continent, reminding us of planetary inheritances and migrations. The shift from a western European

Image from Alex La Guma, *A Soviet Journey*, originally published by Progress Publishers, 1978

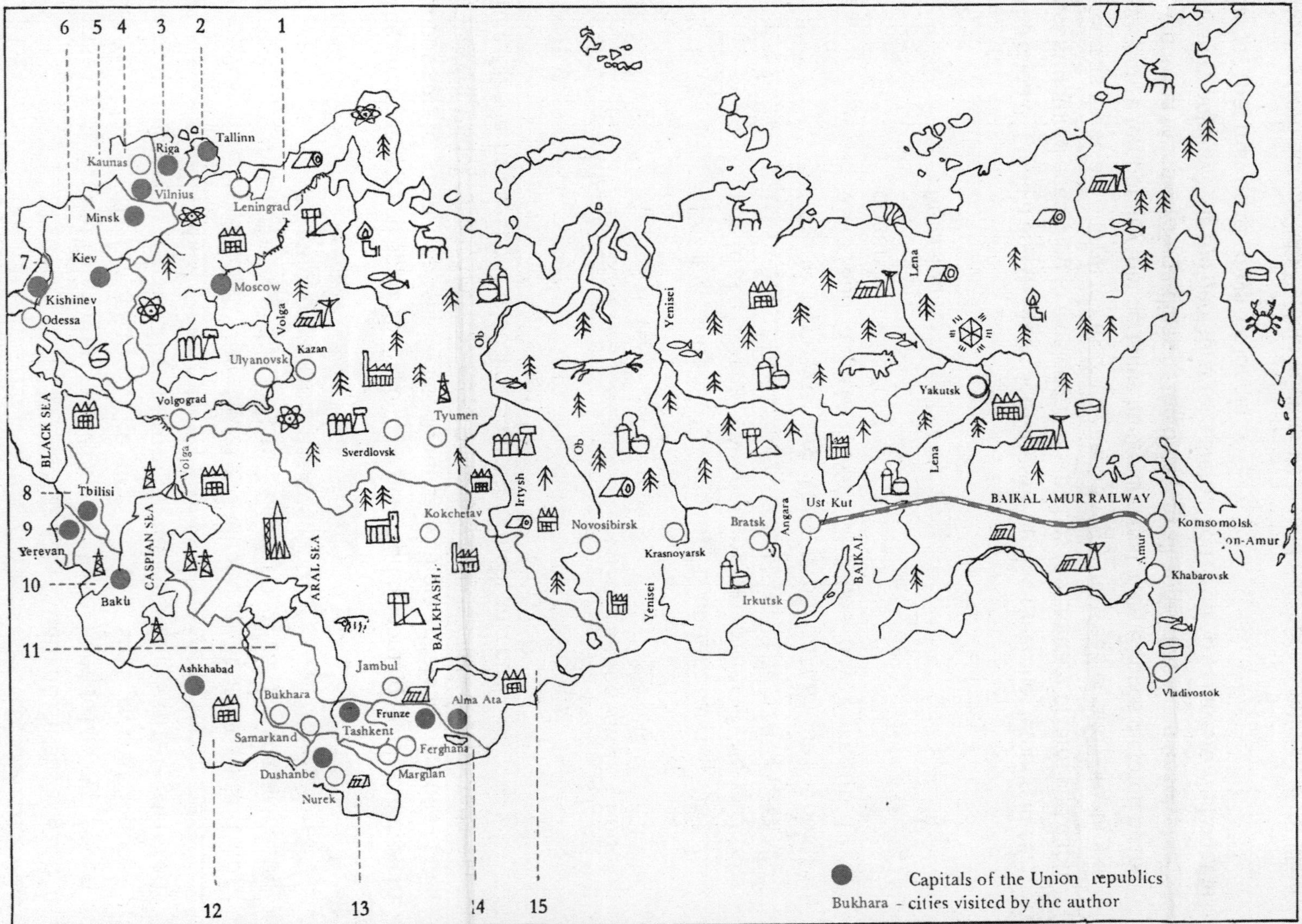

Figures stand for Union republics:

1 Russian
2 Estonian
3 Latvian
4 Lithuanian
5 Byelorussian
6 Ukrainian
7 Moldavian
8 Georgian
9 Armenian
10 Azerbaijan
11 Uzbek
12 Turkmen
13 Tajik
14 Kirgh
15 Kaza

centre to Eurasian centres, as enabled by such imagined journeys, works not only spatially, but also temporally: literature serves as a resource for unmaking the tyranny of imperial time and cartographic control.

Further Europes swim into focus when imagined from wider afield too: a last trip, via South Africa. Alex La Guma, novelist and communist, marks the next itinerary point on these Other European journeys. La Guma was invited to the Soviet Union in 1975 and wrote a travelogue of his experiences there. His journeys encompass expanses from Irkutsk to Kaunas, and as he is moved to note, the Soviet Union is a unit that makes a hard border between Asia and Europe inherently tricky. He observes, "we were crossing into Lithuania, but the landscape took no notice of borders and did not change – after all it is all the USSR."[15]

La Guma's Soviet Eurasia works in direct contravention of the spatial and temporal mappings promulgated by western imperialism. Colonial narratives posited Europe as a self-creating centre of the world, its self-constitution exclusively its internal prerogative. Traditional Orientalist stories sought to imaginatively create and impose a world in which the global South should be relegated to perennial peripherality. These colonial peripheries should be taught to look to the European metropolitan centre as aspirational: the home and origin of a civilisation and culture that imperialism's civilising mission presented as eminently desirable.

Pauline Podbrey, another South African communist, captures the dubious valence of this purported civilizational point of origin in the use of the phrase the "Old Country" by white South Africans:

> The "Old Country" that Uncle Bill assumed was ours—and it therefore followed that we must long for it—was, of course, England, a land that none of us had ever seen. It was a conceit common among English-speaking South Africans… to refer to England as "home."[16]

Many English-speaking white South Africans imagined a past belonging to them to be housed in western Europe—where one kind of past was located, and also where a never-to-be-fully-achieved future was projected. The so-called civilising mission implicitly entailed an assumption that, if it was lucky and tried hard enough, colonised Africa might one day become what western Europe was already.

While violently prescribing a future for the colonies, these imperial narratives also denied them a past, fleshed out through narratives of the global South's "discovery" at the moment of colonial encounter.

This isn't the story La Guma's travelogue allows to be told. In his imaginary, inflected by his coming from South Africa, there emerges a Europe that also belongs to Eurasia; a Europe that, in fact, imaginatively becomes a subcontinent of the larger landmass. His cartographic configuration decentres Europe and performs, rather, western Europe's peripherality—or possibly, its irrelevance. His centre of gravity lies with international socialism and its decolonial affinities; his sextant takes its coordinates from (South) African celestial bodies and a Eurasian horizon; his triangulations are calculated according to the aligned interests of the global South and the Soviet Union.

His journeys through Eurasia are also guided by alternatively modulated temporalities: pointing to histories of interconnectedness that don't operate in relation to a European centre, and that never did. La Guma observes that "what was known as 'the great silk road' of old times—linking Byzantium with China—crossed the south of Kazakhstan, as well as the caravan trails to South-Western Siberia. These gave rise to settlements and cities."[17] His journey into the central Asian Soviet Union calls on him to take a long view of history from this angle of sight, which speaks to a Eurasian network of connectivity in existence before any presumed or invented inevitable centrality of Europe. His elided histories of interconnectedness stage a closely networked world that also includes his native continent of Africa:

> One saw one's own ancestry among the exhibits under Timokhin's care. Didn't that Siberian mask look like a Dogon monkey mask from Dahomey (now Benin)? Was that not a Khoi-Khoin bow? A statue from some ancient Egyptian period. All men had started with similar social organisation.[18]

His imagined pasts draw a space already invented as Eurasian closer to his home continent, intimating the possibility of crossed ancestral paths. His Eurasian spaces further offer up contestations of the backwardness otherwise so often attributed to central Asia—in renditions of a, first tsarist and later Soviet Russian, civilising mission in these regions. He sees the local pride in the "history of Tajik astronomy—they had a long association with the subject, dating back to before the Persians."[19] Encounters with this space do not seem to allow the making of Eurocentric histories; such narrativising simply doesn't work in and for these imagined worlds.

Significant to this world's imagining of pasts and origin stories is the lack of a will to exclusivity. While Europe's imperial civilising mission required the quashing of other stories to those of western European reason and religion, La Guma's meetings with the peoples of Eurasia suggest varied stories that are happy to live alongside each other. In Kazakhstan, his guide, Amangeldeh, relates how the local mountains came to be:

> There is a legend which says that when the world was born, God looked down on Kazakhstan and saw the flat empty steppes. He felt sorry for those living in such desolate emptiness, so he took a handful of rocks and tossed it down as a sort of compensation and so we got the Blue Mountains.[20]

In response, La Guma offers a different narrative of the origin of mountains:

> There is an African folk-tale, from Tanzania, I think, which gives another explanation for how mountains came to be. It says that long ago the earth was smooth and flat and even all over, but one day she arose to talk to the sky. When the two of them had finished their chat the earth took leave of the sky and started to return. But she did not reach home all over. Some parts of her became tired on the way and stopped where they were.[21]

So mountains came to be: some parts of the earth not making it all the way back from their visit to the sky. La Guma's "another explanation" claims no universality and no supremacy for itself. On another occasion, he relates the story of how

> "Stars were first made in South Africa, you know." I told him that South African tale of

> the young African girl who sat warming herself by a wood fire one night and played with the ashes, taking them in her hands and flinging them up to see how pretty they were when they floated in the air. As they floated away she put more wood on the fire and stirred it with a stick and the bright sparks flew everywhere and wafted high into the night. They hung in the air and made a bright road across the sky, a road of silver and diamonds.
> "It's still there," I said. "They call it the Stars Road or the Milky Way."[22]

La Guma ends his anecdote: "if we invented the stars, it must have been your people who invented the sun."[23] The account of his journey imagines and produces a world that is shared and inclusive, in which different (hi)stories can accommodate each other and need not strive to win out over each other.

La Guma's travelogue also reveals the capacity to envision alternative futures and demarcate different aspirations. While the imperial civilising mission constructed colonial western Europe as the world's most advanced civilisation, La Guma contests this version of civilisation and its much-propagated desirability: the "capitalist system, disguised under … 'Western civilisation,'"[24] has brought with it racism and colonial oppression, and consequently is presented as the source of problems to which the Soviet Union proffers solutions. As such, his narrative locates civilizational futures elsewhere. In one alternative temporality, then, the global South is condemned to backwardness, not because it is less civilised than the "west," but because it is struggling with problems caused by the colonisation perpetrated *by* the "west," which has married racism to capitalism, and deferred the more desirable endgame of perfect socialism. When La Guma relates the financial hardships of South African workers expected to survive on a very meagre wage, a "withered farmer" replies: "It was like that in the time of the tsar."[25] South Africa's present is placed in line with the Soviet Union's tsarist past.

Advancedness is attributed not only in terms of proximity to socialism, but also in terms of approximating a society free of racism. La Guma recounts the reaction he experiences from Soviet citizens vis-à-vis the racism of apartheid: "Most Soviets I have met find racial discrimination difficult to comprehend and it usually takes a lot of explanation."[26] Apartheid and its racism are construed as inconceivable to the Soviets.

Elsewhere, La Guma explains the situation in his home country to some interested workers: “they listened, looking extremely puzzled, almost uncomprehending. They had never experienced such a state of affairs.”[27] The Soviets’ ability to live ostensibly without racial discrimination shows them as clearly superior to and *ahead* of both apartheid South Africa and the supposed fountainhead of civilisation presented by colonial western Europe. Not only has the Soviet Union created a racially egalitarian society, for La Guma, it has also produced one which regards women as the equals of men. This makes of it the most progressive space of the travelogue’s imagined world.

This is a doggedly utopian rendition, not least signalled by the ardent communist’s wilful blindness to the gulag system. Injustice and discrimination certainly *did* exist in the Soviet Union, and the propagated narrative that they didn’t make it difficult today to confront pasts whose existence is denied. La Guma’s imagined world is helpful in combatting one dangerous narrative, while perpetuating another. But for him, struggling against apartheid at home, it seems the more urgent fight was to be fought against the colonising-capitalist west.

La Guma’s alternatively envisioned future not only makes a more socially just world imaginable for a readership with his priorities, but extends further into the cosmos, into planetary futures, as the Soviet Union represents the “opening of a new era in world history,” which inaugurates a vision of the future: “the Soviet socialist culture … is … seen as the prototype of a future world communist culture.”[28] He describes how “somewhere in the general area … was the Baikonur space centre where they were then preparing to launch the Soyuz-Apollo project … in the general vicinity a great cosmic event was being prepared … they had come to mount the stars, those who had lived under feudalism only a century ago.”[29] He relates how “above the greenery, silvery domes poked like futuristic craft, glittering in the sun. One thought of HG Wells’ *The War of the Worlds*—the Martians had landed.”[30] Stories of the past can be folded into each other in the world imagined by his travelogue, and the future lies, not in any erstwhile colonial centre, but in a Soviet Union whose enormous potential stretches out into the universe. The itinerary ends here.

La Guma’s Eurasia is a far cry from Stoker’s “wildest and least known portions of Europe,”[31] and it implicitly undercuts figurations of Fortress Europe by intimating how easily Europe as a closed category is imaginatively dissolved—which isn’t to say that its borders are so easily disarticulated for those who try to cross them today. But seeking out resources for rethinking what Europe is, can, and should be, is perhaps a worthwhile task. Moníková’s multiply shifted Bohemia by the Sea hints at how arbitrary and imaginatively malleable borders might be. The worlds offered up by these writings portray journeys—take their readers on journeys—that bypass western Europe altogether, and meaningfully question its assigned status as any kind of origin of culture and civilisation, as the birth place of human rights, as a template for dealing with difficult histories, as enviable or aspire-able, and as representing what the rest of the world should want its future to look like.

It seems apparent that the question of which literature we choose to read and make more visible is also integral here. The traditional British canon Stoker belongs to will make a different world to the non-canonical Europeanness of Moníková's imaginary; as, in turn, the non-European La Guma will have other priorities and see things differently again. A cumulative contestation of (west) Eurocentric (hi)story-telling and envisioning of futures emerges from literature's ability to cultivate a capacity for re-imagining worlds. This ability also works to formulate alternative *aspirations*, to craft and accumulate political imaginations not derived from western Europe. In this way, literature can resist assignations of marginality and teach of (western) Europe's own implicit global peripherality, of its borders' mutability and malleability, and of ways to keep imagined centres on the move. Literary journeys might travel beyond Mercator maps and Greenwich Meridians, to re-navigate the axes for determining how to *move with the times*.

1 Bram Stoker, *Dracula* (New York: Norton, 1986), 9.

2 Stoker, *Dracula*, 11.

3 Stoker, *Dracula*, 10.

4 "Bei meinem täglichen Blick auf die Karte verschiebe ich die Grenzen von Böhmen des öfteren, mal nach der historischen Vorlage von Großmähren, mal nach Shakespeare, der wußte: Böhmen liegt am Meer. Es wäre allemal sinnvol, die Vorschläge der Dichter zu bedenken, statt die Teilung der Welt Politikern zu überlassen, die nicht lesen" (Libuše Moníková, *Prager Fenster* (Munich: Carl Hanser Verlag, 1994), 9). Translations of Moníková's *Prager Fenster* are my own.

5 "Weder die Schweiz noch die Tschechoslowakei, nicht einmal Österreich liegen im Zentrum Europas, das schließlich bis zum Ural reicht. Wenn man es genauer haben will, liegt die Mitte eher bei Minsk oder Witebsk, und der höchste Berg des Kontinents ist mitnichten der Montblanc, sondern der verwitterte Elbrus im Kaukasus, achthundert Meter höher" (Moníková, *Prager Fenster*, 23).

6 "Dafür erlebte ich ein Land, ein Böhmen, das nicht mehr am Meer lag – die Armeen kamen und rückten es dorthin, wo es gehören sollte, an den Rand der Steppe" (Moníková, *Prager Fenster*, 57).

7 Libuše Moníková, *The Façade*, trans. John E. Woods (London: Chatto & Windus, 1992), 169.

8 Moníková, *The Façade*, 169.

9 I build here, to some extent, on ideas developed elsewhere (Lucy Gasser, "Towards Eurasia: Remapping Europe as 'Upstart Peripheral to an Ongoing Operation'" *Postcolonial Studies* 22, no. 2, 2019).

10 Moníková, *The Façade*, 216.

11 Moníková, *The Façade*, 227.

12 Moníková, *The Façade*, 233.

13 Moníková, *The Façade*, 281.

14 Moníková, *The Façade*, 281.

15 Alex La Guma, *A Soviet Journey: Impressions of the USSR* (Moscow: Progress Publishers, 1978), 215.

16 Pauline Podbrey, *White Girl in Search of the Party* (Pietermaritzburg: Hadeda Books, 1993), 15.

17 La Guma, *A Soviet Journey*, 82.

18 La Guma, *A Soviet Journey*, 193.

19 La Guma, *A Soviet Journey*, 68.

20 La Guma, *A Soviet Journey*, 114-5.

21 La Guma, *A Soviet Journey*, 115.

22 La Guma, *A Soviet Journey*, 131-2.

23 La Guma, *A Soviet Journey*, 132.

24 La Guma, *A Soviet Journey*, 230.

25 La Guma, *A Soviet Journey*, 148.

26 La Guma, *A Soviet Journey*, 175.

27 La Guma, *A Soviet Journey*, 67.

28 La Guma, *A Soviet Journey*, 98.

29 La Guma, *A Soviet Journey*, 93.

30 La Guma, *A Soviet Journey*, 68.

31 Stoker, *Dracula*, 10.

On Other Poleis

SIKHO SIYOTULA

Bokoni, 2018
Inkjet Print on Cotton Paper, 60 x 100 cm

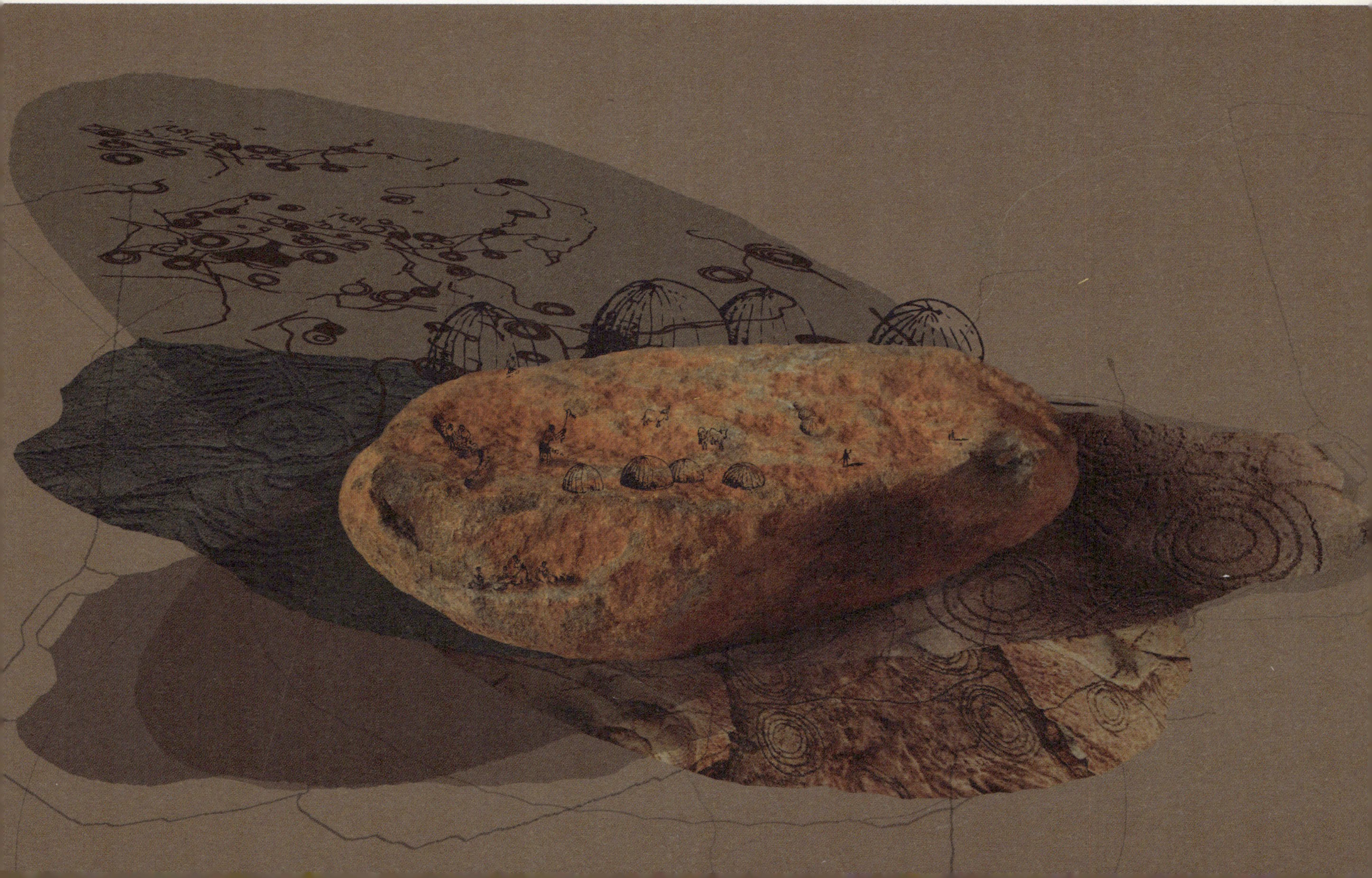

SIKHO SIYOTULA

Cosmic Dust, 2018
Inkjet Print on Cotton Paper, 60 x 100 cm

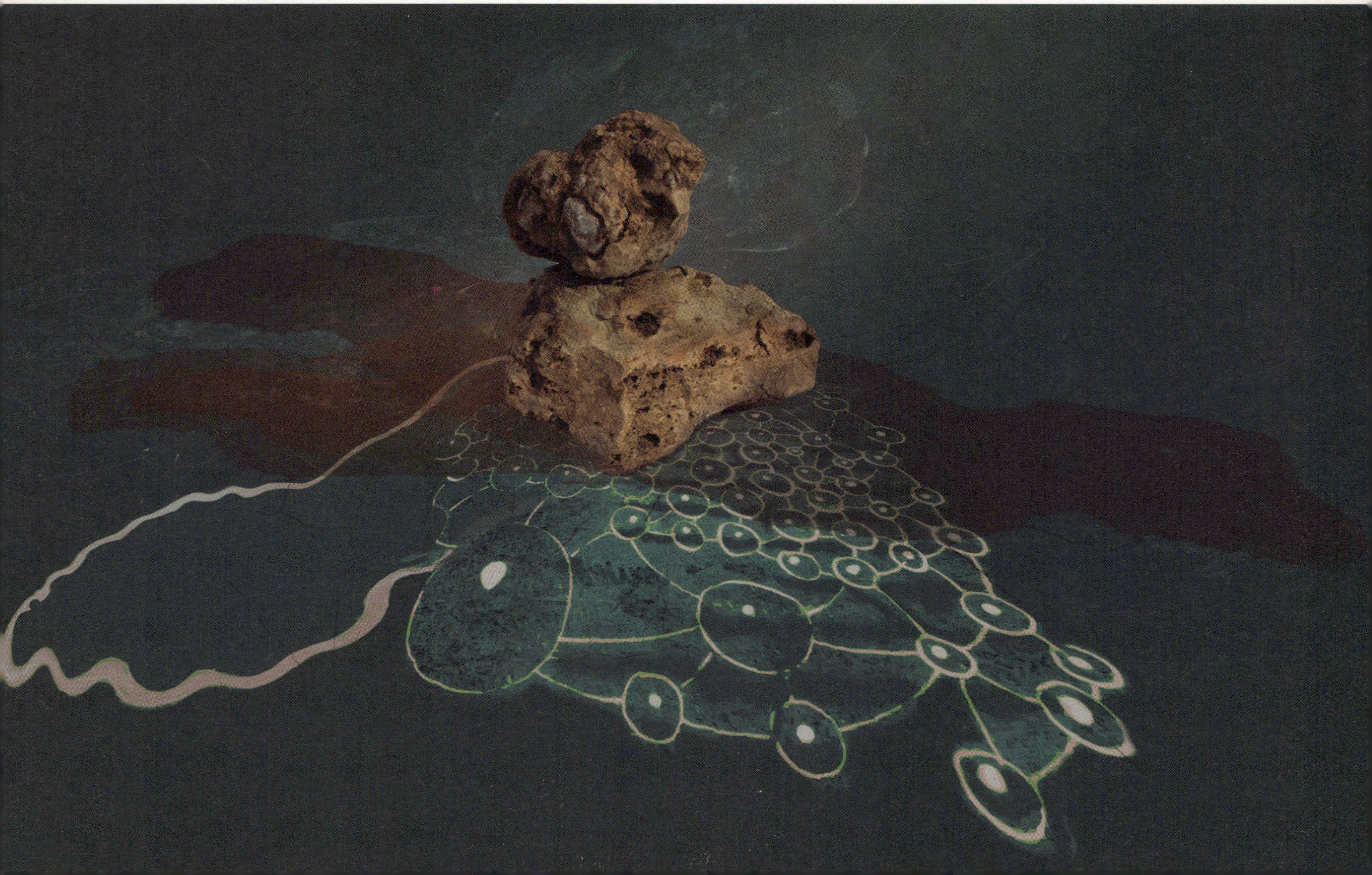

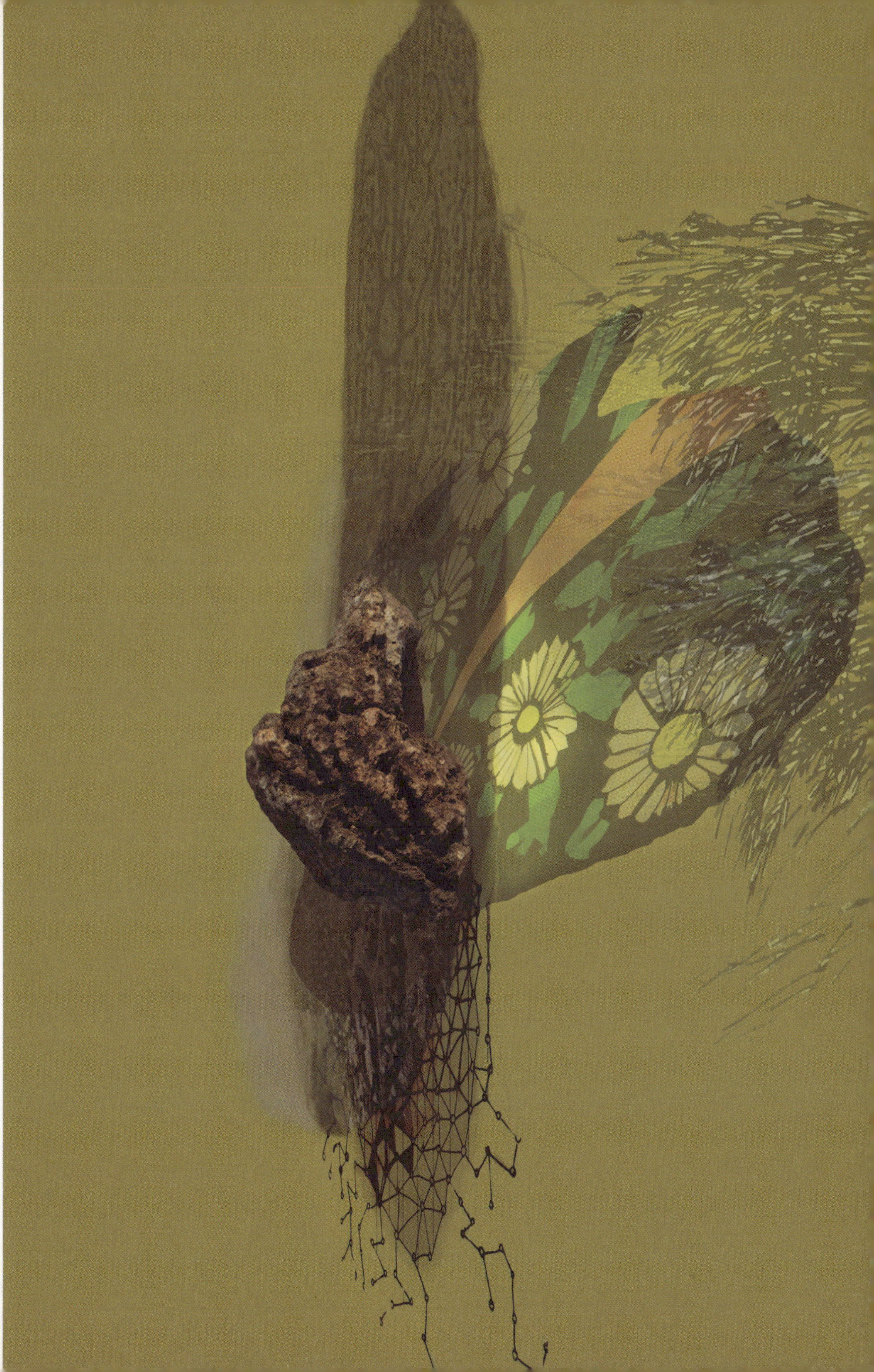

SIKHO SIYOTULA

Maru's House, 2018
Inkjet Print on Cotton Paper, 60 x 100 cm

SIKHO SIYOTULA

Pretoria, 2018
Inkjet Print on Cotton Paper, 60 x 100 cm

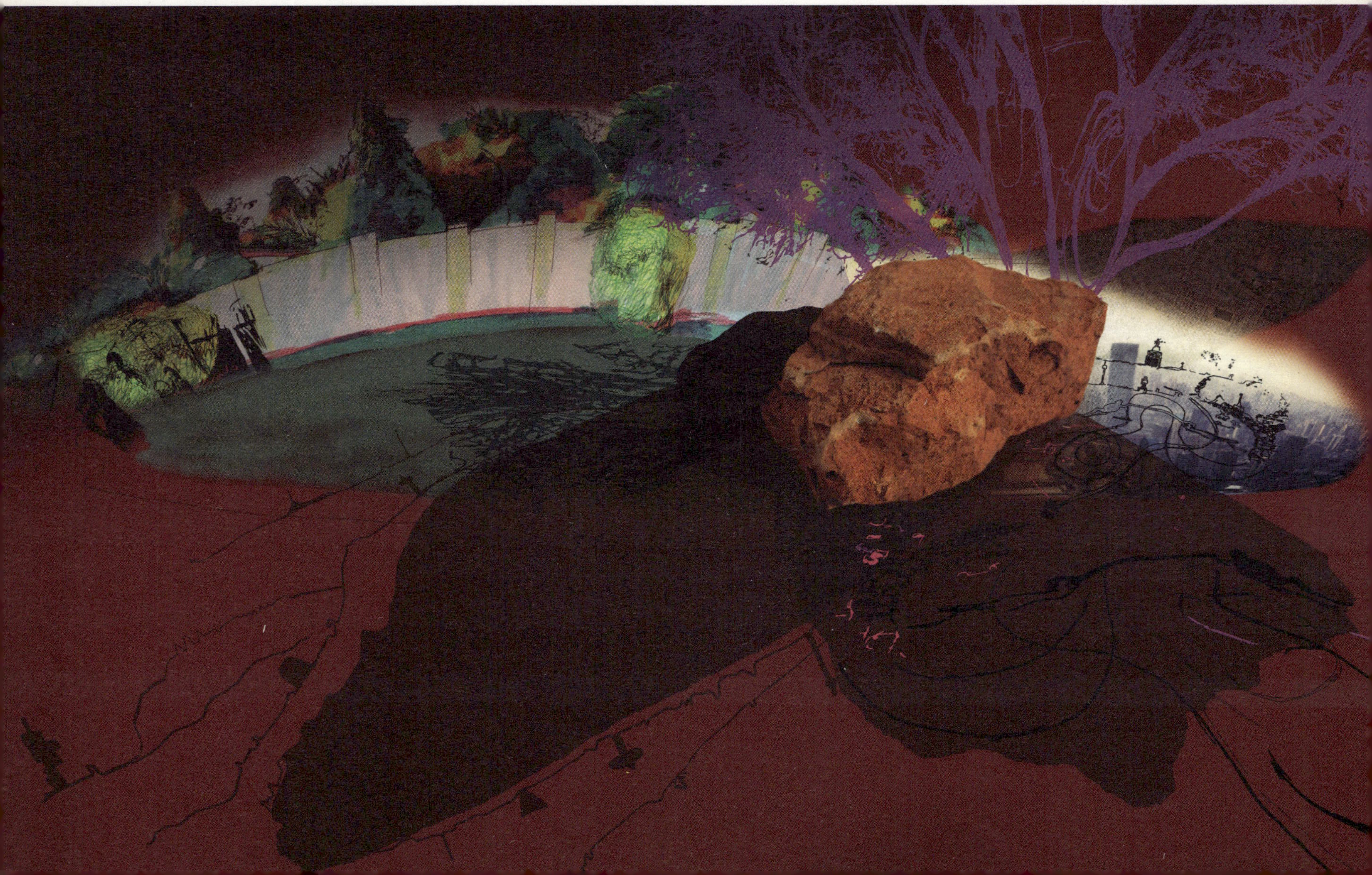

On Other Poleis

On Other Poleis is part of a larger body of work investigating the visualisation of Late Iron Settlements in archaeological publications of the late nineteenth, twentieth, and twenty-first centuries.

In an attempt to visualise "usable" African history, remainders of Southern African Late Iron Age settlements (second millennium AD, 900-1800) are animated through illustration, across the late nineteenth, twentieth, and early twenty-first centuries, by researchers, as well as in African nativist and nationalist rhetoric. Embedded in this animation are Eurocentric, formative interpretations of the settlements stemming from colonially inscribed ethnographies.

The visualisation of Southern African Late Iron Age settlements has multiple meanings and uses in contemporary Southern Africa. By visualisation, I mean the consideration of both the object—the "physical" visual interpretation of ruins—and its imaginary—the interrogation of the function and meaning thereof. Southern African Late Iron Age settlements here refer to Late Iron Age settlements "discovered" in Southern Africa from the late nineteenth century. Located on the borders of modern-day Botswana, Zimbabwe, South Africa, and stretching to Late Iron Age trading posts in Mozambique, this northern region has buried in its landscape the ruins of the earliest known settlements in southern Africa. Stonewall architecture is a distinct characteristic of such settlements. Stonewalled settlements like Mapungubwe, Khami, Great Zimbabwe, and Bokoni are believed to have belonged to complex societies involved in the cultivation of crops, working of ivory, mining of gold, and long-distance trade.

In the change from an apartheid state to a democratic one, the visualisation of Mapungubwe in South Africa has become essential to nationalist rhetoric in search of pasts alternative to dominant Eurocentric colonial history and visual culture. The pyramids and sphinxes of Egypt, the ruins of Great Zimbabwe, San rock paintings, Benin bronzes, and African masks are often similarly used. As ancient capitals, Mapungubwe and Great Zimbabwe, in particular, symbolise past political power and pre-colonial African presence in Southern Africa. As such, they speak to contested questions of land and ownership in Southern African democracies. The artefacts discovered here attest to pre-colonial achievement and demonstrate human, regional, and global interregional connectivity. Finally, such visualisations present a pre-colonial hub of cosmopolitanisms on a scale never imagined in colonial histories of "indigenous" communities, thought of as the ultimate "other" of global modernity. As a tool in nationalist rhetoric, such visuals are used to destabilise colonial power, and that of the apartheid state, particularly its hold on the writing and framing of Southern African history.

Archaeologists, anthropologists and historians—through their visualisation of Late Iron Age Settlements—have been central actors in the production of images of this past with authority. Their visual outputs direct what about the past is seen and how it is seen. This is so even when they consider the images they create as secondary to the primary research presented. While the visualisation of Southern African Late Iron Age landscapes is an interdisciplinary subject, the involvement of image-centred disciplines using visual cultural methodologies remains minimal. Visual cultural methodologies, as with images in Southern African Late Iron Age settlement research, often act as supplements to other primary concerns, and are seldom engaged with critically. Working outside frameworks critical of images, representation, and what images do, the problems in formative interpretations are easily replicated and perpetuated through uncritical circulation. Lively discourse is taking place amongst scholars of Southern African Late Iron Age settlements with regards to an over-reliance on formative interpretations of such ruins. Current research encourages a move away from the authority of such interpretations and a return to critical studies of material culture. As with the authority of Eurocentric formative interpretations of Southern African Late Iron Age research currently being reconsidered, the visuals accompanying Southern African Late Iron Age research also need to be critically revisited, using appropriate visual cultural methodologies informed by postcolonial and decolonial frameworks.

Eurocentric and western-colonial history books have made much of Europe's modern centres of power, cultivated in the ages leading up to and during the European Age of Discovery. *On Other Poleis,* as the title suggests, is an exploration of other poleis. Poleis outside of these assumed European centres of power; Southern African Late Iron Age poleis, to be exact. The body of work is a component of a two-fold research project involving, in the first fold, textual analysis and, in the second, an image-making process. The first fold surveys the cultural production, circulation, reproduction, and theorisation of images accompanying archaeological, anthropological, and historical Southern African Late Iron Age Research. A curated archive of images is the byproduct of this survey. Played out as a sequence, this archive animates the changing history of Southern Africa across time. Reflecting the late nineteenth, twentieth, and early twenty-first centuries, the archive in motion is a stop-frame animation of the history of imperialism, specifically the visualising of the history of others as a tool for domination. Carefully examined, it also archives a history of counter-visuality.

Designed to intercept and disrupt the repetition and reproduction of a problematic archive, the body of work *On Other Poleis* was conceived as an intervention beyond critique. Its images combine computer-aided drawings, photo-documentation and the photo-manipulation of the documentary, archival and artistic impressions of selected archeological landscapes. The image-making process involved a synthesising of my phenomenological experience of these landscapes during field research with images from the archive. Images are scanned, placed, cropped in Adobe's graphic editors photoshop and illustrator. The programs help layer, warp, erase, transform, and then eventually flatten images. As original images move through the programmes, their architecture directs how images gain and lose qualities. I half-jokingly think of this process as Adobe translating the Iron Age.

The images draw attention to the cultural politics of representation in order to interrogate: what and who is being made visible in the visualisation of settlements accompanying Southern African Late Iron Age research; what forms of materiality and spatiality are pictured and performed; and finally, how this is materialised and what effect such visualisations have on the people who experience them.

On Other Poleis was on display at the Haus der Kulturen der Welt, Berlin, during the *minor cosmopolitan weekend*, from the 6th to the 8th of December, 2018.

[

the *minor cosmopolitan weekend* remembered

illustrations by Nik Neves
photography by Camila Gonzatto

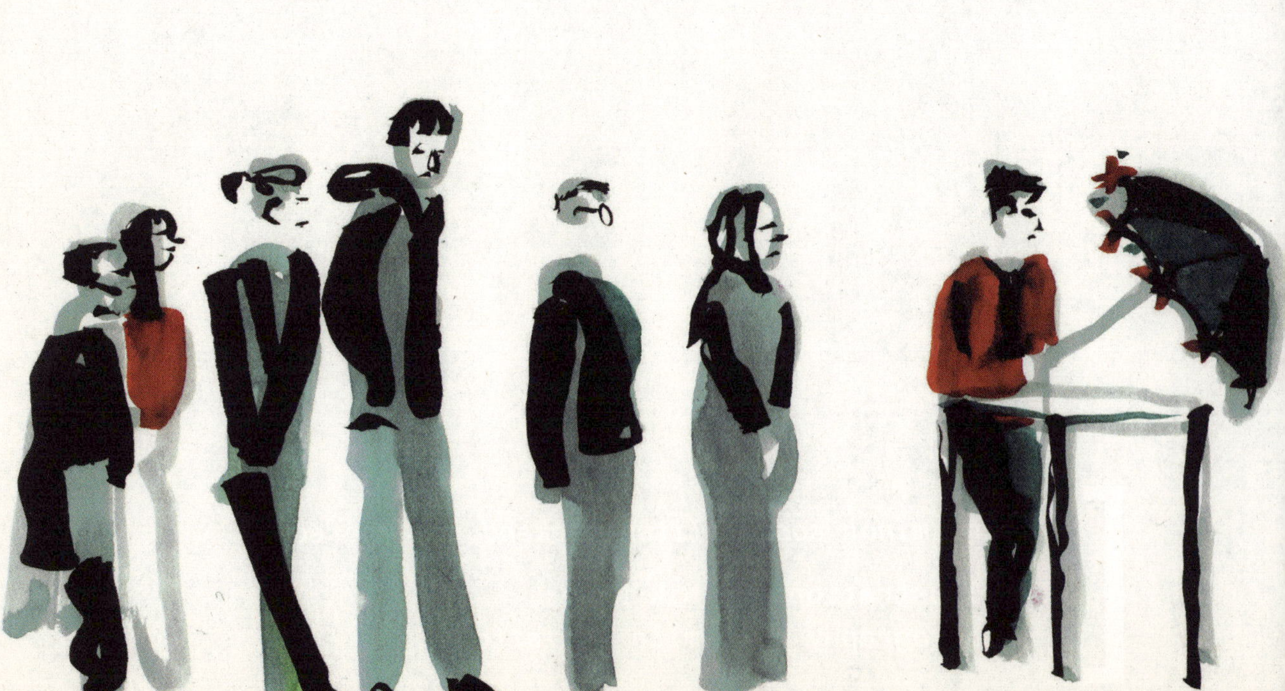

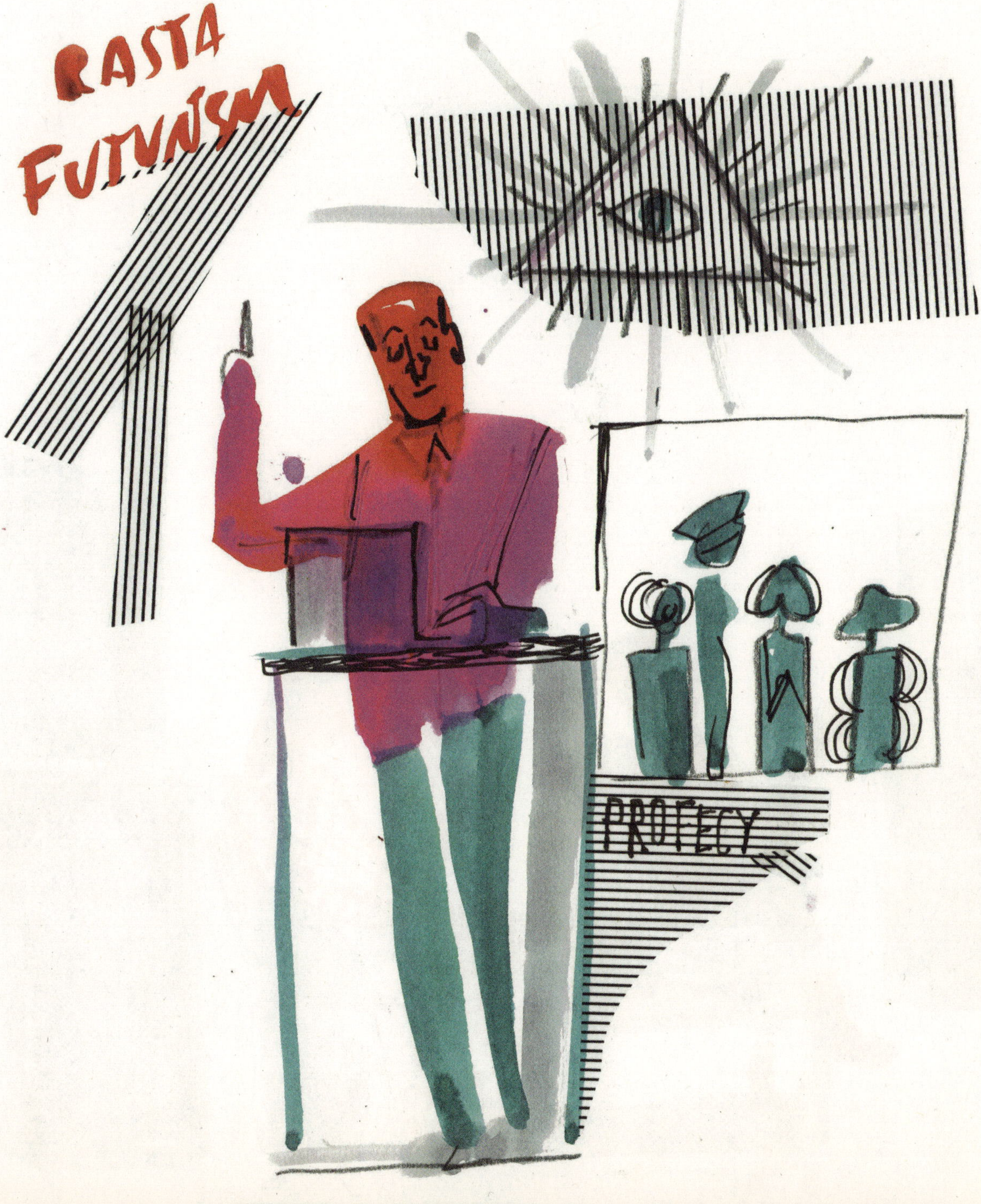
RASTA
FUTURISM
PROFECY

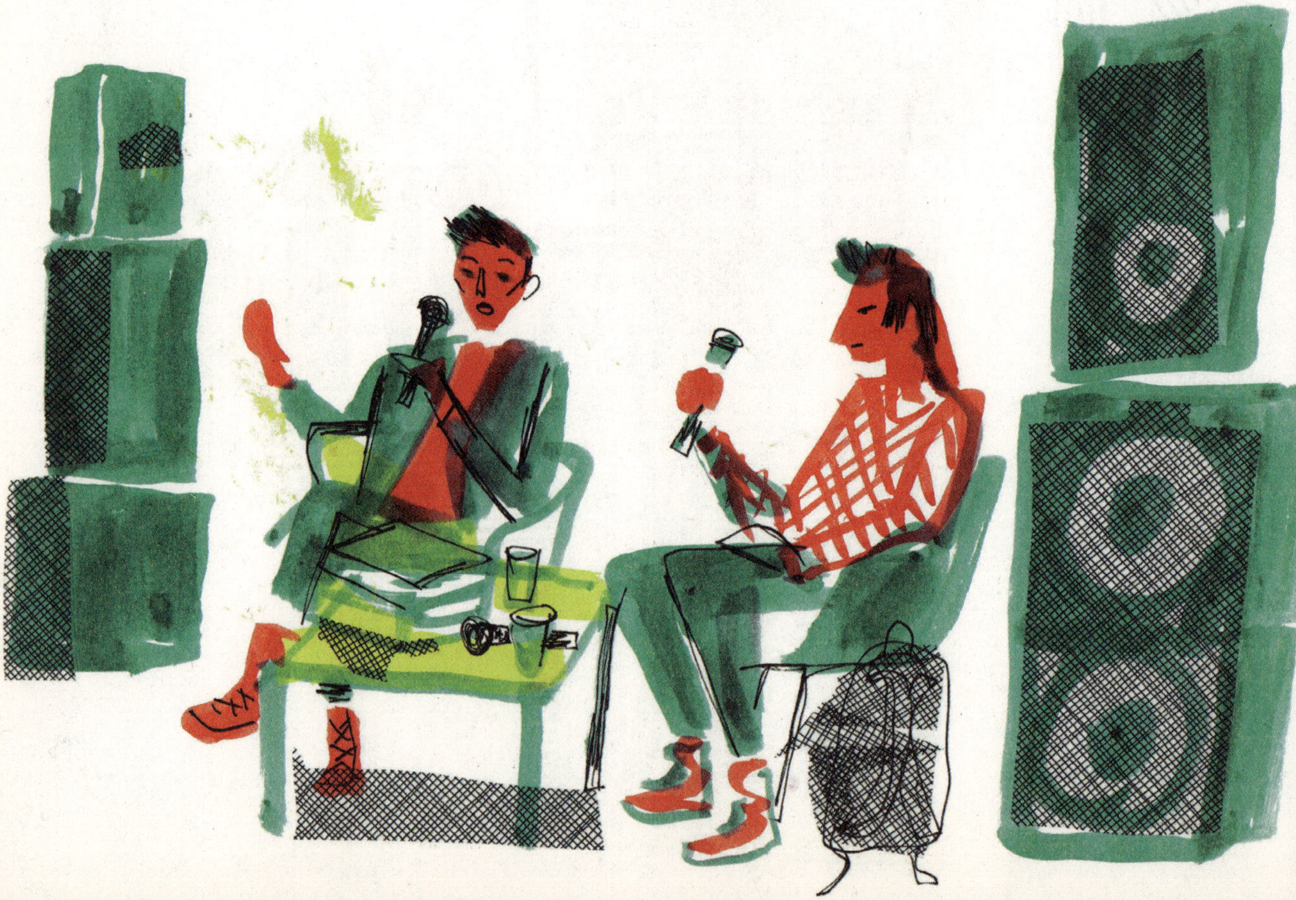

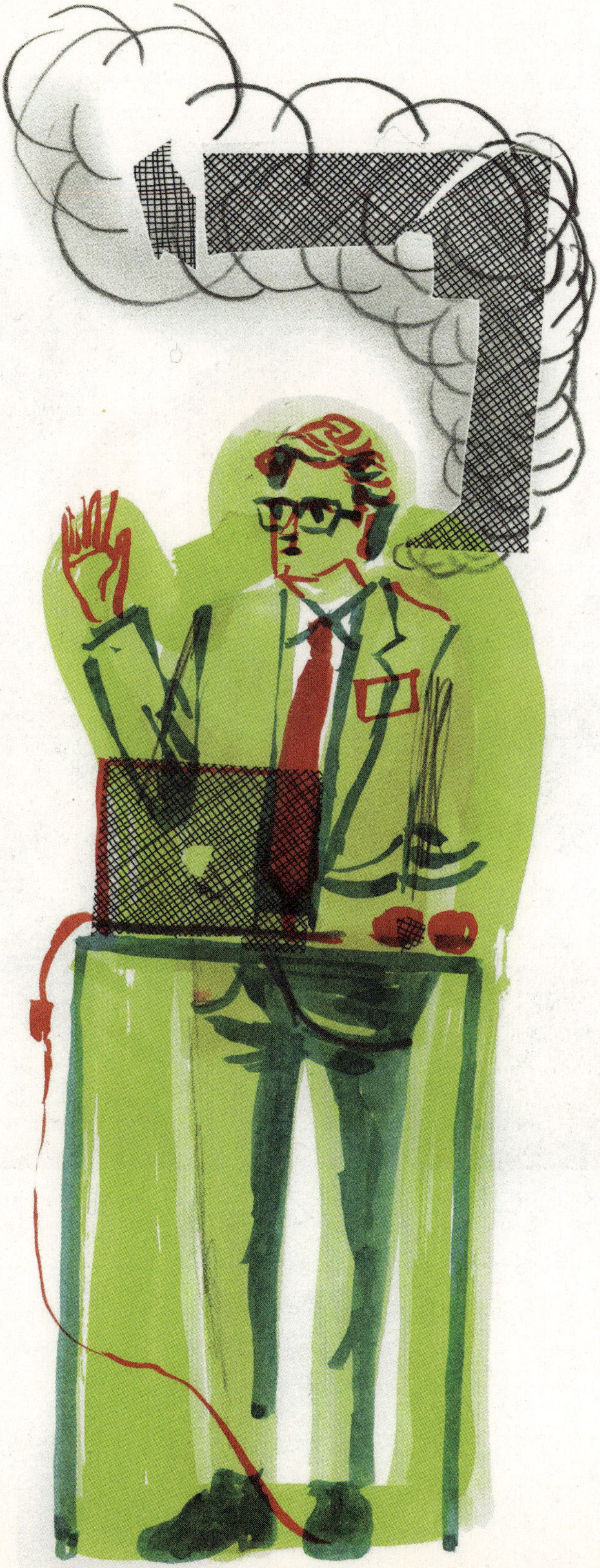

the same
Empty space
from our bodies
is the same
empty spaces
in the ENVIRONMENT.

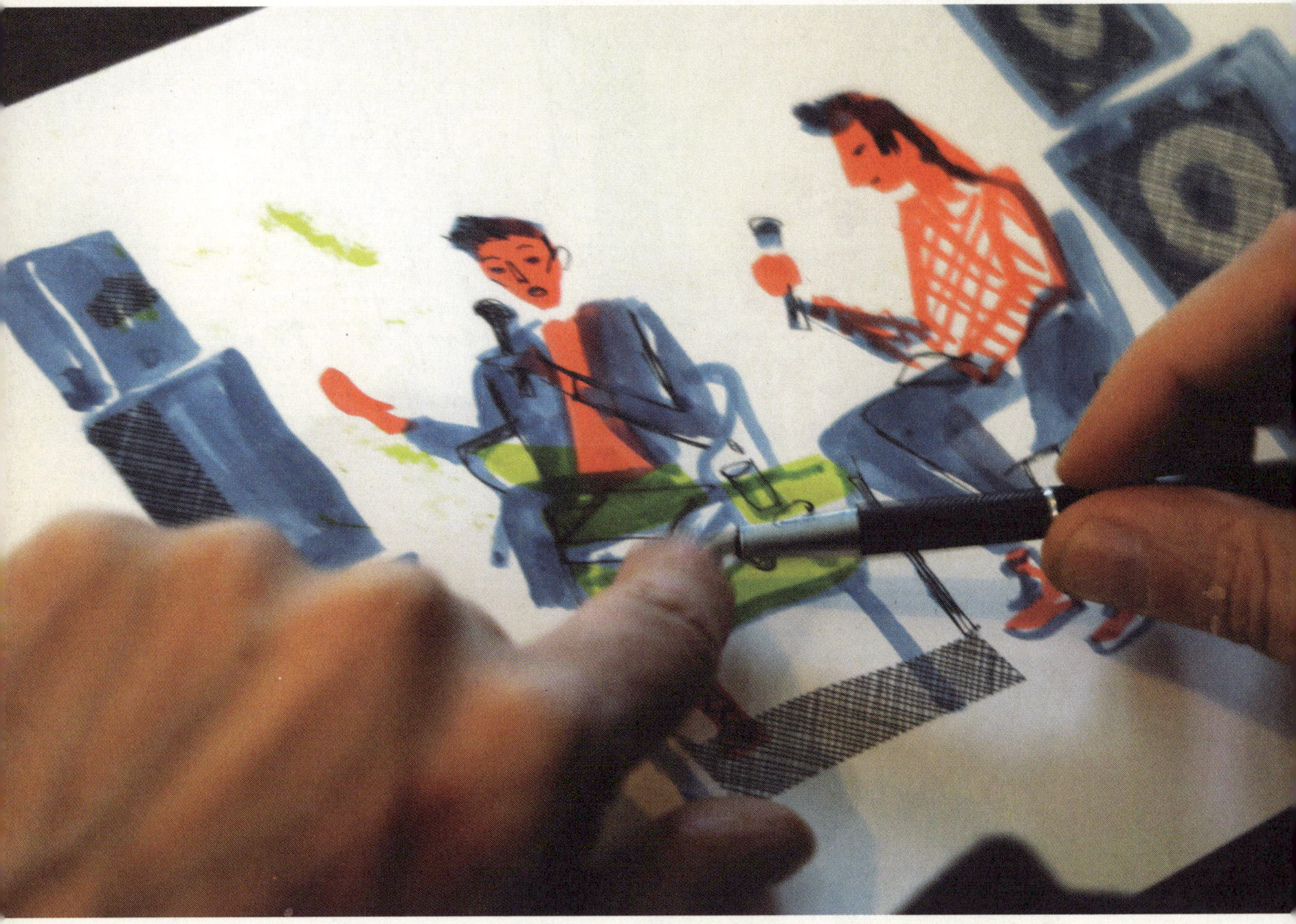

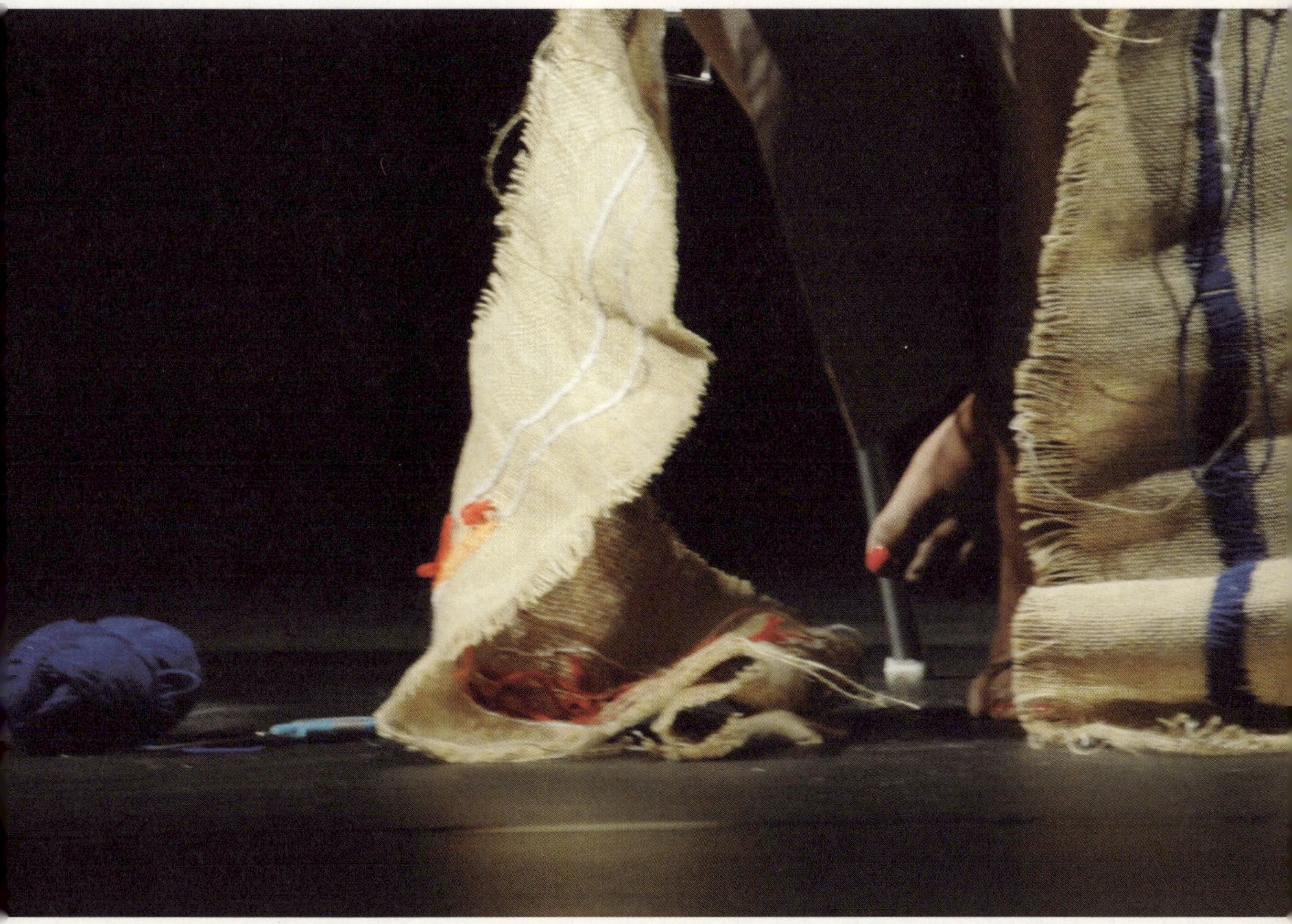

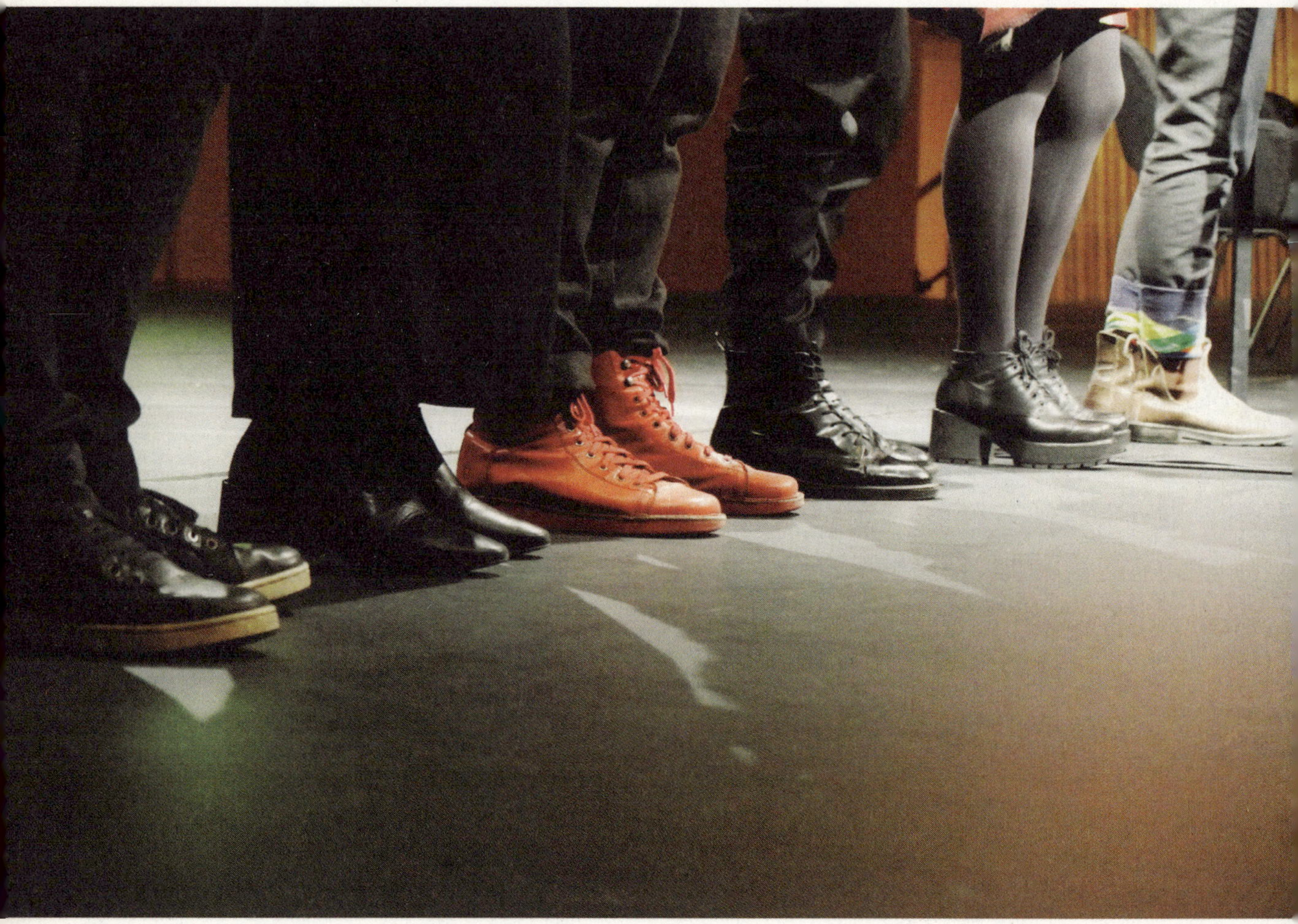

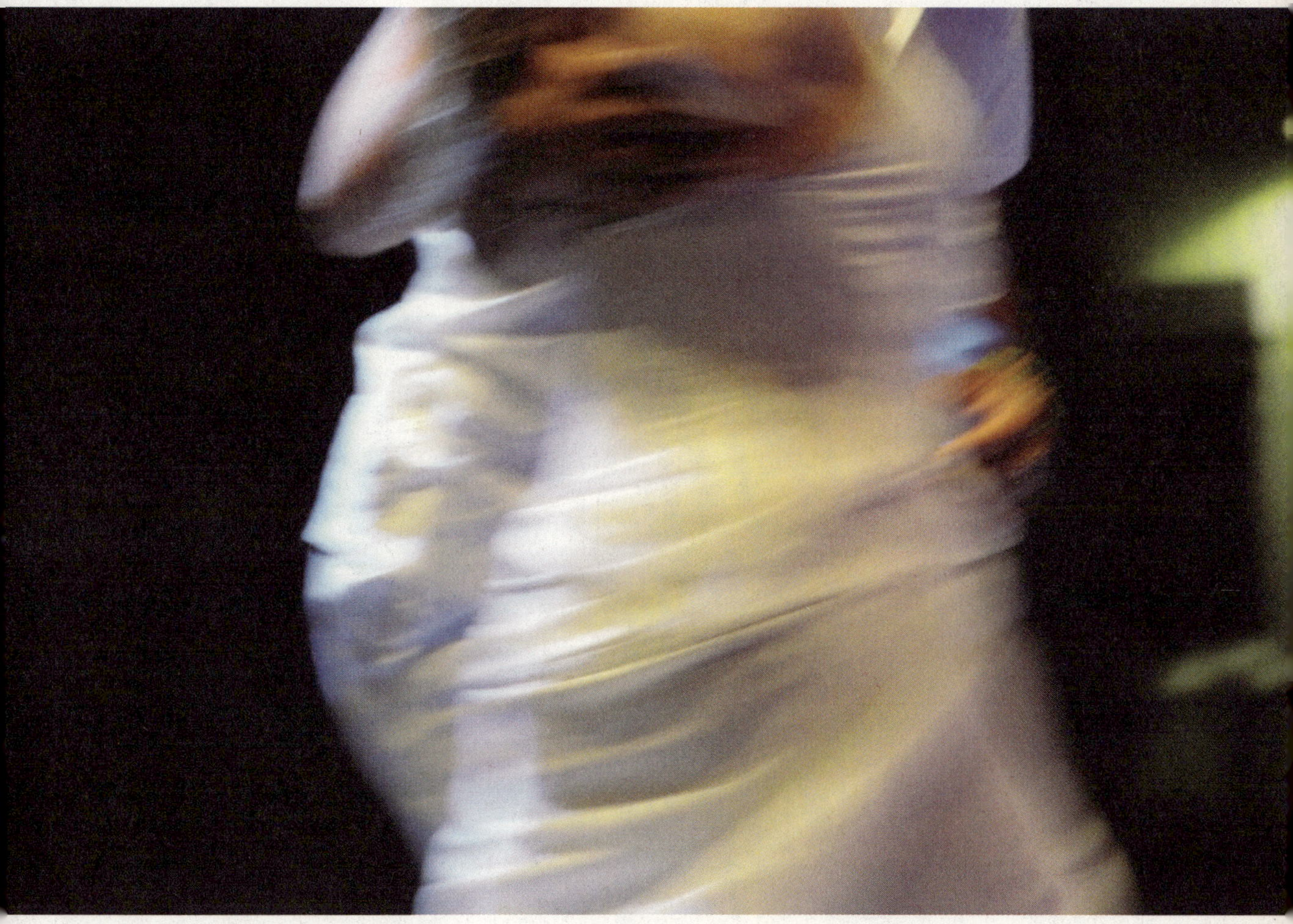

WHO SUSTAINS THE FLOURISHING OF THE WORLD?

03

FLOURISHING OF THE WORLD? WHO SUSTAINS THE FLOURI
HO SUSTAINS THE FLOURISHING OF THE WORLD? WHO SUST
HE WORLD? WHO SUSTAINS THE FLOURISHING OF THE WOR
FLOURISHING OF THE WORLD? WHO SUSTAINS THE FLOURI
SUSTAINS THE FLOURISHING OF THE WORLD? WHO SUSTAI
HE WORLD? WHO SUSTAINS THE FLOURISHING OF THE WOR
FLOURISHING OF THE WORLD? WHO SUSTAINS THE FLOURI
HO SUSTAINS THE FLOURISHING OF THE WORLD? WHO SUST
HE WORLD? WHO SUSTAINS THE FLOURISHING OF THE WOR
FLOURISHING OF THE WORLD? WHO SUSTAINS THE FLOURI
SUSTAINS THE FLOURISHING OF THE WORLD? WHO SUSTAI
HE WORLD? WHO SUSTAINS THE FLOURISHING OF THE WOR
FLOURISHING OF THE WORLD? WHO SUSTAINS THE FLOURI
HO SUSTAINS THE FLOURISHING OF THE WORLD? WHO SUST
HE WORLD? WHO SUSTAINS THE FLOURISHING OF THE WOR
FLOURISHING OF THE WORLD? WHO SUSTAINS TH FLOURIS
SUSTAINS THE FLOURISHING OF THE WORLD? WHO SUSTA

Rosa Barotsi, Saima Akhtar, and Clio Nicastro
(In Front of the Factory Collective)

Introduction: Film, Women's Work & Labour Organizing

> Impressed by the rise of factories in the nineteenth century, Marx showed us forms of capitalism that required the rationalization of wage labor and raw materials. Most analysts have followed this precedent, imagining a factory-driven system with a coherent governance structure, built in cooperation with nation-states. Yet today—as then—much of the economy takes place in radically different scenes. Supply chains snake back and forth not only across continents but also across standards …[1]

In recent years, as we celebrate the rise of several global and local women-led labour movements, we also bear witness to a mainstreaming of precarious labour practices historically associated with women's work.[2] Piecework, zero-hour contracts, home-based freelance work, micro-financing, and outsourcing have characterised this tendency globally. For a while now, feminist scholars have been demonstrating how work performed by women has remained invisible because it happens within the private space of the home, or it is not directly or regularly remunerated,[3] often remaining outside official GDP calculations and resulting in the classification of working women as "dependents."[4] These scholars have long asked themselves what "development" statistics would have looked like if women's work and other subsistence labour that does not participate in the market economy had been taken into account in the calculation of the GDP.[5] Because this type of work has been historically flexible, straddling artificial lines between productive and reproductive and public and private spaces, women's work has functioned as one of the blueprints for this new phase of neoliberal labour exploitation, which some are calling the feminisation of labour.[6]

What's new today is not precarious labour itself. In fact, for the last century precarity has been the dominant form of access to income for a majority of the population in many parts of the world—including those subjected to colonialism, immigrants, or women workers in the Fordist era.[7] What appears to be changing, however, are discursive and institutional approaches towards precarity. The types of flexible labour that belonged to the informal sector, and which excluded workers from welfare and similar means of protection, are now being partially incorporated into the formal sector through deregulation and privatisation. Discourses of personal responsibility and entrepreneurship have also served to justify and promote a lack of worker protections.[8] Today, these unsafe and unwaged labour conditions are reinforcing the burdens already placed on marginalised groups. But as multinationals aggressively infringe upon workers' rights to unionization and collective bargaining, women's and labour rights movements will also continue to struggle.

This section, "Who Sustains the Flourishing of the World?," shines a light on visual narratives that arise from and about women's work and labour activism. Here, we offer a set of propositions for activists and image-makers to reflect on. It is our hope that collective thinking on past and present forms of labour organising, and their visual representations, will contribute to and engage with a broader array of minor cosmopolitan images of struggle.

Our contributors, filmmaker and geographer Mary Jirmanus Saba, and professor, activist, and filmmaker Vivian Price, present a series of open-ended questions about work, gender, labour organising, and environmental justice. They examine how film can act as both a tool for change and a way to upset "major" cosmopolitan narratives. Jirmanus and Price arrive at their visual and scholarly work with backgrounds in activism and union work. In their own ways, they provoke us to think about how the production and circulation of images is central to representations of labour and the movements associated with them. In our view, their films also suggest that if we are to understand current shifts towards precarity, we must take a closer look at collective representations of labour and its gendering.

Domestic Labour, Space, and Film

As an introduction to Jirmanus' and Price's essays, we suggest that visual representations of women's labour can provide invaluable insights into our new world of work, as well as the future of domestic and home-based labour in a globalized market. Recent anxiety about employment has centred on issues historically connected with women's work. Visual culture has been seminal in registering shifts in labour practices, as well as our gendered perceptions of labour and the separation between spaces of work and life. The Lumière brothers' *Workers Leaving the Factory* (1895), arguably the first film screened publicly, presented an almost entirely female workforce rushing past the figurative and literal barrier between work and non-work: the factory gate. Since then, audio-visual representations of women's work have continued to have a powerful effect on our understanding and performance of labour.

In our own research, we have come to realise that the "home"—as a built environment, affective sphere, and ideological tool—has often acted as a laboratory for broader strategies of labour exploitation (and resistance). Across changing social and political contexts, labour in the domestic sphere has traditionally hovered between what is considered productive, unproductive and reproductive. As David E. Staples points out, due to "its apparently contingent but actually continuous and expansive nature," home-based labour "offers a kind of illusory freedom to women (and to men somewhat differently), often in exchange for the dubious status of 'independent' or 'self-employed' worker." [9] Our contemporary labour landscape is reminiscent of the ways in which domestic and home-based work has historically been broken down and rendered insignificant, while at the same time being central to the reproduction of capitalist labour relations.[10]

As scholars working on these issues, we noticed that there has been a surge of interest in labour and visual media scholarship that specifically examines representations of working women in recent years.[11] Yet, the role of image-making and visual culture (including films, photographs, advertisements, popular media, and design) in the gendering of domestic labour in relation to the larger world of work has hardly been addressed.

Our initial interest in visual culture and domestic labour therefore focused on moving images, including fiction films, documentaries and archival film, highlighting a crucial link between domestic and non-domestic labour spaces.[12] At the end of World War II, this link seemed to be based on competing views of efficiency and time-management. Mid-twentieth century industrial films depicted Taylorist-inspired time management strategies as a way to expedite labour in the "home" as well as on the factory floors of booming US automotive industries. For example, in *The Easier Way*, a 1946 informational film about time-motion study commissioned by General Motors, the inefficiency of a middle-class wife's unpaid housework is used to advance an argument about the benefits of factory-based scientific management.[13] The husband, Bob, a motion study expert in a GM factory, tries to convince his dinner guest, a factory assembly-line foreman, of the benefits of motion study for his workers. He takes his wife, Marge, and her housework as an example: "Now take this simple job of setting the table. Women do it the hard way." "Now Bob," says Marge, "you can't run a house like a factory." Bob responds: "Why not? Think of the effort you'd save. Maybe you wouldn't be so tired at the end of the day." In this case, housework is taken to be a valid (if less serious) arena for experimentation with time-management strategies primarily meant to be enacted in the factory.

By contrast, in *Umberto D* (Vittorio De Sica, 1952), an Italian neorealist film from the same period, the housework routine of a paid domestic worker is presented as dead time: a symbol of halting narrative progression and productivity at a time of economic crisis and post-war disillusionment.[14] Caught in long sequence shots without dialogue, the young maid's kitchen chores dilute time rather than organise it. By some accounts, this scene of small, mundane gestures set the stage for a revolution in cinema's narrative economy.[15] That such a huge task was placed upon housework was no accident. As film scholar Domietta Torlasco put it: "Well before other forms of labour in the new global economy erased the line between work and life, housework (from cleaning and cooking to child-rearing) was always that with which we are never done."[16]

In just these few examples, we can already see that cinematic depictions of housework are presented as productive or unproductive based on the medium, the geopolitical context, and the audience to which they cater. These films aren't alone. Similar themes continue through a wide range of forms of visual culture today: in the evolution of the *Signora Candy* Italian washing machine adverts,[17] the subversions of gendered labour in the soap-opera-homage US television series *Jane the Virgin* (2014-2019), and US documentaries such as *Europlex* (2003), which show how race and class shape perceptions of domesticity. What is also interesting (and under-researched) are the many films that show the domestic sphere as spaces of workplace horror, including *The Shining* (USA, 1980), *The Maid* (Singapore, 2005), *A Maid for Each* (Lebanon, 2016), *Creepy* (Japan, 2016), and, most recently, *Parasite* (South Korea, 2019).

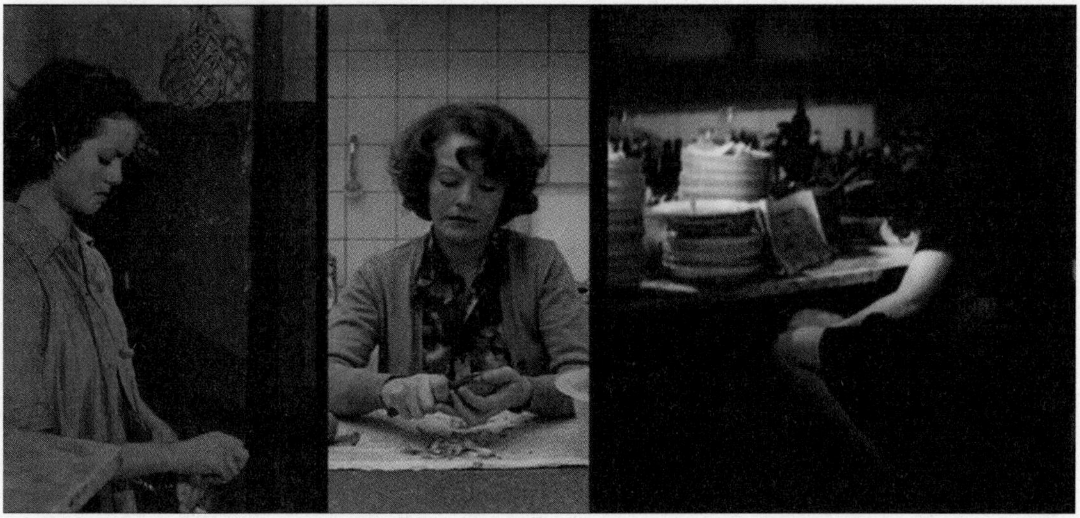

Philosophy in the Kitchen (Domietta Torlasco, 2014)

Also integral to this visual analysis is the way that urban and architectural spaces contribute to the visual culture of domesticity and housework. Examples can be traced back to Frank Lloyd Wright's use of the column-free, open-floor house plan to promote housework as pleasurable, the sentiment of which has now been translated into the free and flexible workspaces of Silicon Valley, including Google, Facebook, and Microsoft. The recent Netflix series *Follow This* (2018), based on short-form documentaries that follow Buzzfeed journalists as they produce their investigative stories, is a relevant example where the corporate workspace is framed positively as flexible, laid back, and cozy. Seen in this way, it also has subtle undertones that mirror 1970s ad campaigns for the modern kitchen.

The complexities of the "home" construct in relation to employment and labour organising resonates in the work of both Price and Jirmanus. Their films are part of an exciting body of cinematic work that closely examines collective representations of labour. They shed light on undervalued work and workers, and offer ways to shift the conversation towards organising against this devaluation—which often takes place at the margins of visual culture.

Feminist Filmmaking, Collective Memory, and Labour

Together, Vivian Price's *Transnational Tradeswomen* (2006, henceforth *TT*) and Mary Jirmanus Saba's *A Feeling Greater Than Love* (2017, henceforth *Feeling*) are striking testaments to the infinite possibilities of feminist filmmaking. Together, they open up questions about the relationship between form and content. They present two stylistically different films that are part of the same struggle—which is to centre women's historic and contemporary contributions to the fight for worker's rights.

From the start, both films are irrevocably anchored to their narrators, but in modalities that are fantastically different from one another. In *TT*, the narrator is expositional. In voiceover, Price lays out the motivations that drove her to make the film and defines her position as a filmmaker. She tells the viewers about her background as a labour activist, her training as an electrician, and the motivations behind making a film about women construction workers around the world. In the first few minutes, viewers have a sense of the filmmaker and her point of view. In contrast, the narration of *Feeling* moves between landscapes and people and text like a ghost. In the opening sequence, the voice of a union organiser informs the viewer where they are, and what they are doing there: the film begins in Nabatiyeh and the surrounding villages in the south of Lebanon, during a protest at the Regie tobacco factory building. But then, in the form of an intertitle, Jirmanus cuts into the film to ask: Where to begin? Images of present-day Lebanon are replaced by archival interludes that make an attempt at historical reconstruction. After the first short sequence, therefore, the film alerts the viewer to the film construct. Jirmanus takes the viewer along in the process of historical reconstruction, of archive-making, and her own doubts about these processes. In this sense, the two films differ in their narrative style: *TT* has an audible narrator who walks us through the film's storyline, while *Feeling* has an illusory narrator who plays with the storyline, mixing past and present.

In *TT*, Price journeys around the world in search of tradeswomen and their struggles to gain recognition for hard-earned skills and labour rights. Price and her collaborators travel from the US to China, India, Pakistan, Thailand, Singapore, Taiwan, and Japan and document women in a variety of occupations. Price primarily focuses on women who work in construction, but interviews a variety of workers within this sector, including brick-makers, drivers, electricians, plumbers, and masons. The problems women face in the construction sector are multiple and context-specific, but the continuities are striking as well. For example, women in this industry struggle to have their labour recognised as skilled work, and the workers' associations representing them work tirelessly towards this goal. What becomes clear by the end of the film is that the terms "skilled" and "unskilled" are ambiguously defined as women search for suitable jobs. What many contracting firms consider as skilled work, for example, is gendered as masculine and fiercely guarded by sexist and traditionalist tropes regarding women's abilities and place. This, as Price shows, is as much true in the so-called Global North as in the South.

Feeling takes us on a journey, too, but between the past and the present. In it, Jirmanus traces the Lebanese labour movement from the 1970s onwards. The film moves very little geographically—from Beirut to South Lebanon and back—and yet, it travels through Lebanese labour history via links between past and present struggles and protests. The film focuses on two strikes from the early 1970s, shortly before the outbreak of the Civil War: one at the Regie tobacco factory in the South of Lebanon, in Nabatiyeh, and another at Beirut's Gandour chocolate factory. Rather than attempting to reconstruct a straightforward history, Jirmanus uses a range of different materials: archival footage, interviews, documentaries, fiction films and re-enactments. These materials are used to fail purposefully at arriving at some form of truth. The film shows the discordant effects that collective memory can have, depending on who recorded it, who remembers it, and who forgot it.

Despite the decade gap between the films' production, they are undeniably tied by their efforts to illustrate how women's work has been consistently undermined and made invisible in labour discourse and history. While *TT* shows how women's physical labour is rendered invisible because it remains "unskilled," *Feeling* demonstrates that women's work in the labour movement is erased from history through historical reconstruction. *TT* makes clear that one of the main hurdles women in the construction sector face globally is the gendered division of skilled work. In South Asian countries, where some construction sectors employ as many women as men, a lack of opportunities for skilled training and the burdens of family responsibilities are compounded by intransigent discursive clichés about women's innate inability to work in the trades, therefore excluding them from skilled work, higher pay, and job security.

In *Feeling*, labour organising emerges as a variation of skilled work, as explained by the women who participated in the strikes. Yet, by the end of *Feeling*, and in spite of all the leadership efforts put in by women during protests and strikes, a union organiser named Nadine reveals that her male communist comrades still see her and other women as the "sandwich-makers" of labour organising. In other words, the women are viewed and treated as care workers whose sole occupation is to provide support to men. This question of skill as a foil for the exclusion of women is also reflected in the distribution of the film itself. As Jirmanus herself recounts in her piece, the distribution of *Feeling* in Lebanon was obstructed by the old (and male) left guard's active hostility to the film on the basis of her own presumed lack of ability and knowledge.

In *Knocking on Labor's Door*, labour historian Lane Wyndham flips the script of the supposed downturn in union membership in the USA by tracing the history of workers who tried to form unions and were met with employer resistance. Wyndham asks, regarding the 1970s as the decade of marked decline in private-sector organising in the US: what if I tell that story a different way? Rather than solely looking at dwindling union density within workspaces, she notes that the number of workers who turned up to vote at National Labor Relations Board (NLRB) elections each year were more indicative of "tremendous organising efforts," solidarity, and resilience.[18]

There is no doubt that canonical narratives are hard to change. In *TT*, there are scenes in which it seems like skilled women construction workers have to constantly prove that they exist, even as they stand in front of the people who deny their existence, like contractors looking to hire. An example is when a male contractor, discussing a woman labourer named Ranganayki and her qualifications as a mason, refuses to believe in the notion of a skilled woman worker. He engages in near-absurd rhetoric when faced with her union representative who lists her skills—including her strength, experience, training certificates, and work ethic—but to no avail.

Similarly, in the first half of *Feeling*, Jirmanus asks her viewers: if I tell the story again, will the outcome change—if I tell it differently? In the south of Lebanon, Habib describes how he and his co-workers occupied the Regie building in 1973. He recalls how he gave his car keys to a comrade who drove through Nabatiyeh

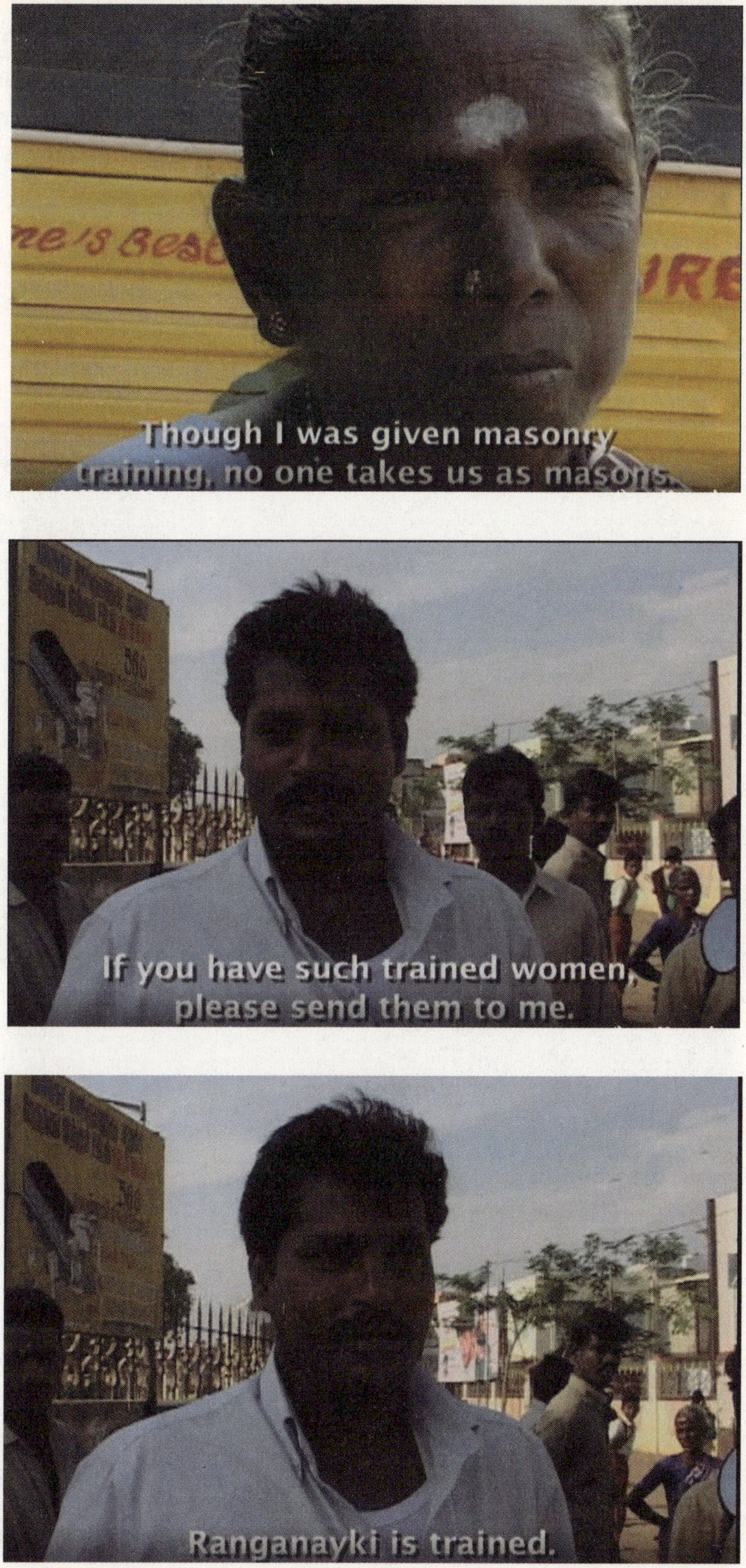

Transnational Tradeswomen (Vivian Price, 2006)

and the surrounding villages and urged people to join workers occupying the Regie tobacco factory building. The film goes back to its opening sequence. This time there is an added detail that makes the reconstruction explicit: the very shot that opened the film is shown again, and Najib, the driver, adds: "These events happened on 23 January, 1973." The feeling is one of being unmoored.

In *Feeling*, Jirmanus' failed search for representational images of the Lebanese labour movement ends with lament: "We can't access images of our labour movement's past. Would anything change if we could?" The film then tells the

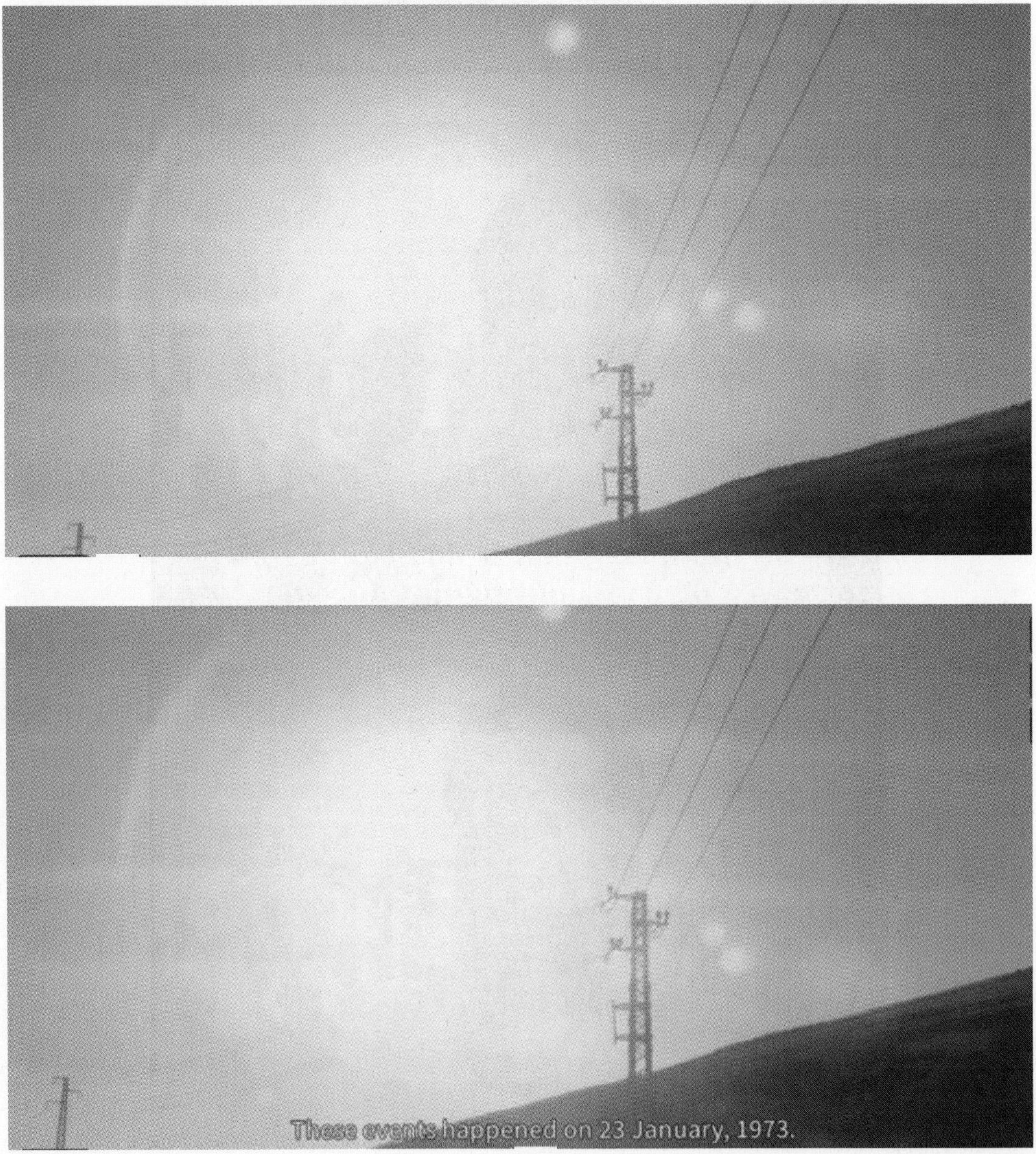

A Feeling Greater than Love (Mary Jirmanus Saba, 2017). Opening shot (top); Minute 48 (bottom)

story of Hajje Khadra in Kfar Roumman, who tore the rifle from a soldier's hands as he tried to beat her with it. But the documentary images of Hajje Khadra in the Communist party film from that period, The *Leaves of the Poor are Gold* (1974), betray this oral history. A young Hajje is shown only talking about food prices and getting beaten at the protest: "Not about fighting back." Jirmanus films present-day Hajje, watching herself on the TV screen. She is adamant: that is not me.

Yet, this is the point. Despite missing archival images, or conflicting oral histories and memories, the exercise that these two films engage in, of the reconstruction

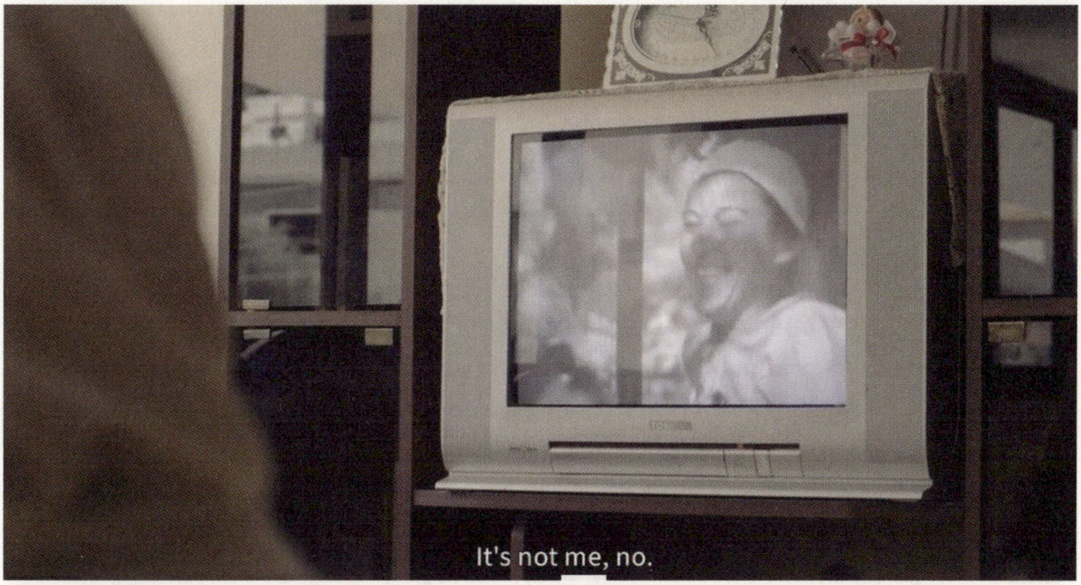

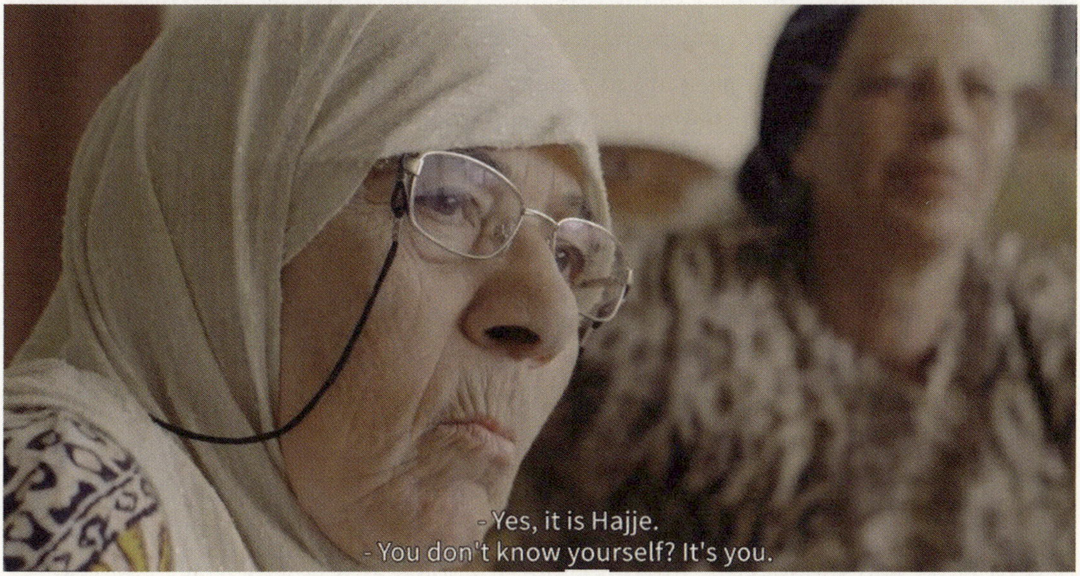

A Feeling Greater than Love (Mary Jirmanus Saba, 2017). Two Hajjes.

of women's experience of labour, in labour, and being left out of labour, are precisely what we need for the historical record. The act of filmmaking, which Price and Jirmanus do so provocatively, illuminates women's participation in organising and working.

The films destroy the so-called "sandwich-maker" stereotype and powerfully render women's presence in the labour market, both visibly and audibly. But the question of domestic work persists. As the two films show, domestic work can also be seen as both a question of space and of time. In some sense, domestic work takes place in a specific environment—the manifold iterations of "home." But in another, domestic work is about taking care of communal life and sustaining others, which is also a question of time.[19] The permutations of this responsibility are much more fluid than the false division between proverbial "homes" and "factories." In *TT*, Price visits a building site in Thailand, where five families (made up of around twenty people) have set up makeshift spaces that function as home for the duration of the construction work. Women workers, who are also family carers, are surrounded by both their laundry lines, pots, and pans, as well as their trowels and cement mixers.

Housework, as we mentioned previously, can be viewed as productive or unproductive based on the parameters of its visuality. In *Feeling*, there is a scene in which this dialectic plays out as well. The film shows the home of a former Gandour chocolate factory worker discussing her and her friends' tasks on the assembly line. They chat about unpaid overtime and the sense of precariousness cultivated by foremen on the job, as the camera pans to their hands, which are cleaning and sorting dishes and cutlery. The two women use objects on the dining table—a pack of cigarettes and grapes—to mime the efficiency of their gestures on the assembly line. This scene is where some of the most potent imagery of factory work and women's work in cinema converge: the restaging of the assembly line on a dining table can serve as a reminder of the infamous discourse of the indifference or inability of cinema to cross the factory gates.[20] The close-up of women's hands doing both housework and (restaged) assembly-line work echoes and challenges discourses of nimble-handed women and their natural ability for precise and repetitive tasks.

In the end, Price and Jirmanus make clear that precarity is not a new condition of the labour market. Today, as the security of "standard employment" is attacked from all sides, it's even more urgent for us to pay attention to the way gendered and racialized workers have resisted and organised for themselves at pericapitalist margins. These films are powerful reminders that both global capital and labour movements rely on such workers for their sustenance.[21] In the pieces that follow, Price and Jirmanus give us hope, and suggest that images of internationalist solidarity may in fact be able to "connect the tissues" and act as "feminist comrades."

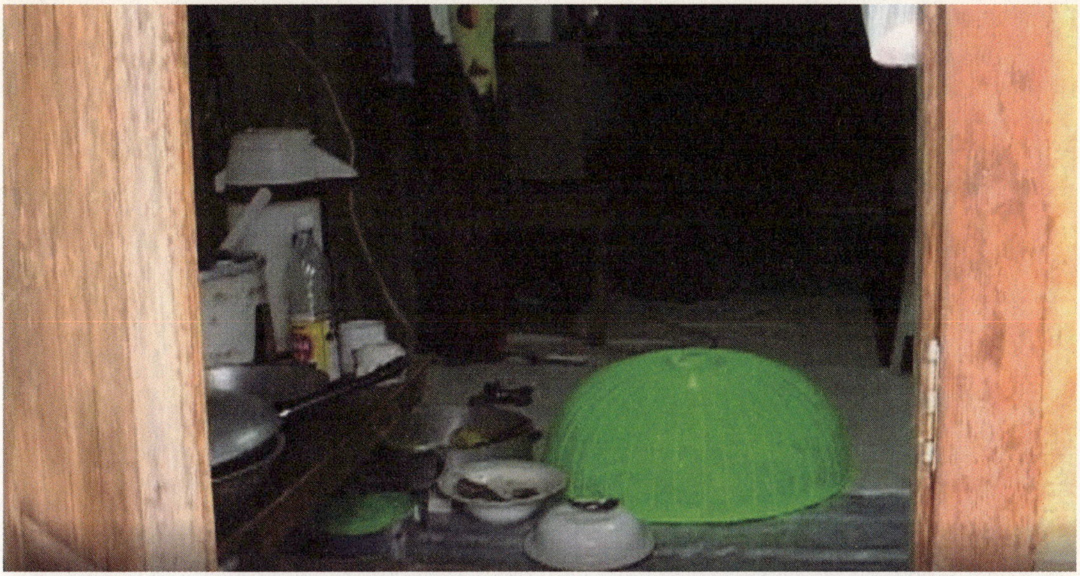

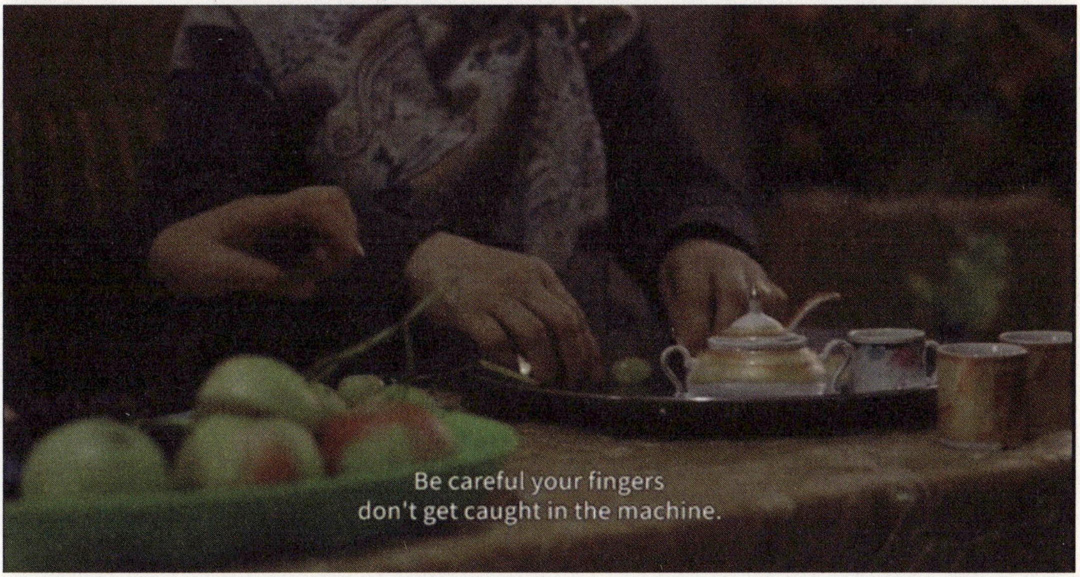

Domestic/Work. Transnational Tradeswomen (top); A Feeling Greater than Love (bottom)

This text was written by Rosa Barotsi and Saima Akhtar, with input from Clio Nicastro. Our collaboration is inspired by a series of workshops and symposiums titled *In Front of the Factory* and held at ICI Berlin Institute for Cultural Inquiry from 2016-2018. This section is based on a panel we organised for the *minor cosmopolitan weekend* at Haus der Kulturen der Welt on December 6-8, 2018, and supported by the RTG minor cosmopolitanisms.

1 Anna Lowenhaupt Tsing, *The Mushroom at the End of the World: On the Possibility of Life in Capitalist Ruins* (Princeton: Princeton University Press, 2015), 61.

2 Related movements in the last decade range from #metoo, the Paro Internacional de Mujeres (International Women's Strike), the fight for Universal Basic Income, or the Sin Tierra movement in Brasil; to the Greek Finance Ministry cleaners' protest, Donne per Taranto, the New York Domestic Workers United, and many more.

3 Christine Delphy, *Close to Home: A Materialist Analysis of Women's Oppression* (New York: Verso, 2016), 228.

4 Raffaella Sarti, Anna Bellavitis, and Manuela Martini, "Introduction," in *Gender at the Crossroads of Home, Family, and Business from the Early Modern Era to the Present*, eds. Raffaella Sarti, Anna Bellavitis, and Manuela Martini (Oxford: Berghahn, 2018), 22.

5 Angela Miles, "Women's Work, Nature and Colonial Exploitation: Feminist Struggle for Alternatives to Corporate Globalization," *Canadian Journal of Development Studies/Revue canadienne d'études du développement* 22, no. 4 (2001): 858.

6 Sarti, Bellavitis and Martini, "Introduction," 42.

7 Carla Arconte, *Impiegate alla Società Terni: Lavoro e scritture di donne in un'acciaieria* (Narni: CRACE, 2010), 47.

8 Kim van Eyck, *Flexibilizing Employment*, Working Paper No. 41 of the InFocus Programme on Boosting Employment through Small Enterprise Development Job Creation and Enterprise Department, International Labour Organization, 2003, p. 13.

9 David E. Staples, *No Place Like Home: Organizing Home-Based Labor in the Era of Structural Adjustment* (New York: Routledge, 2007), 3.

10 Lisa Adkins, "Contingent Labour and the Rewriting of the Sexual Contract," in *The Post-Fordist Sexual Contract: Working and Living in Contingency*, eds. Lisa Adkins and Maryanne Dever, (London: Palgrave Macmillan, 2016), 2.

11 Jennifer L. Borda, *Women Labor Activists in the Movies: Nine Depictions of Workplace Organizers, 1954–2005* (Jefferson: McFarland, 2010); Elena Gorfinkel, "The Body's Failed Labor: Performance Work in Sexploitation Cinema," *Framework: The Journal of Cinema and Media* 53, no. 1 (2012): 79-98; Barbara Mennel, *Women at Work in Twenty-first-century European Cinema* (Champaign: University of Illinois Press, 2019).

12 Our series has included the following events: *IN FRONT OF THE FACTORY: A Lecture by Silvia Federici; The Globalisation of Women's Work and New Forms of Violence Against Women*, ICI Berlin, 9 July 2018, https://www.ici-berlin.org/events/silvia-federici/; *IN FRONT OF THE FACTORY: As workers leave the factory, What's left behind?* Workshop, ICI Berlin, 9 July 2018, https://www.ici-berlin.org/events/as-workers-leave-the-factory-whats-left-behind/; *IN FRONT OF THE FACTORY: Out of Work: A Screening and Conversation with Domietta Torlasco*, ICI Berlin 19 June 2017, https://www.ici-berlin.org/events/out-of-work/; International conference and film programme *IN FRONT OF THE FACTORY: Cinematic Spaces of Labour*, ICI Berlin, Berlin, May 2016, https://www.ici-berlin.org/event/744/. We would like to thank ICI Berlin for its invaluable support.

13 The film can be accessed freely on the Huntley Film Archives YouTube page, https://www.youtube.com/watch?v=pEkqxgP_Ibk.

14 Cesare Casarino, "Images for Housework: On The Time of Domestic Labor in Gilles Deleuze's Philosophy of the Cinema," *differences* 28, no. 3 (2017): 67-92.

15 Gilles Deleuze, *Cinema II: The Time-Image* (London: Bloomsbury Publishing, 2013 [1985]).

16 Domietta Torlasco, "Philosophy in the Kitchen," *World Picture* 11 (Summer 2016), http://worldpicturejournal.com/WP_11/Torlasco_11.html.

17 Enrica Asquer, "La 'Signora Candy' e la sua lavatrice. Storia di un'intesa perfetta nell'Italia degli anni Sessanta," *Genesis: Rivista della Società Italiana delle Storiche* V, no. 1 (2006): 97-118.

18 Lane Windham, *Knocking on Labor's Door: Union Organizing in the 1970s and the Roots of a New Economic Divide* (Chapel Hill: University of North Carolina Press, 2017), 3.

19 Miles, "Women's Work," 874.

20 Harun Farocki, *Workers Leaving the Factory* (Berlin: Goethe-Institut, 1995).

21 Staples, *No Place Like Home*, 12.

Mary Jirmanus Saba

Feminist Internationalism: From Solidarity to Sandwiches

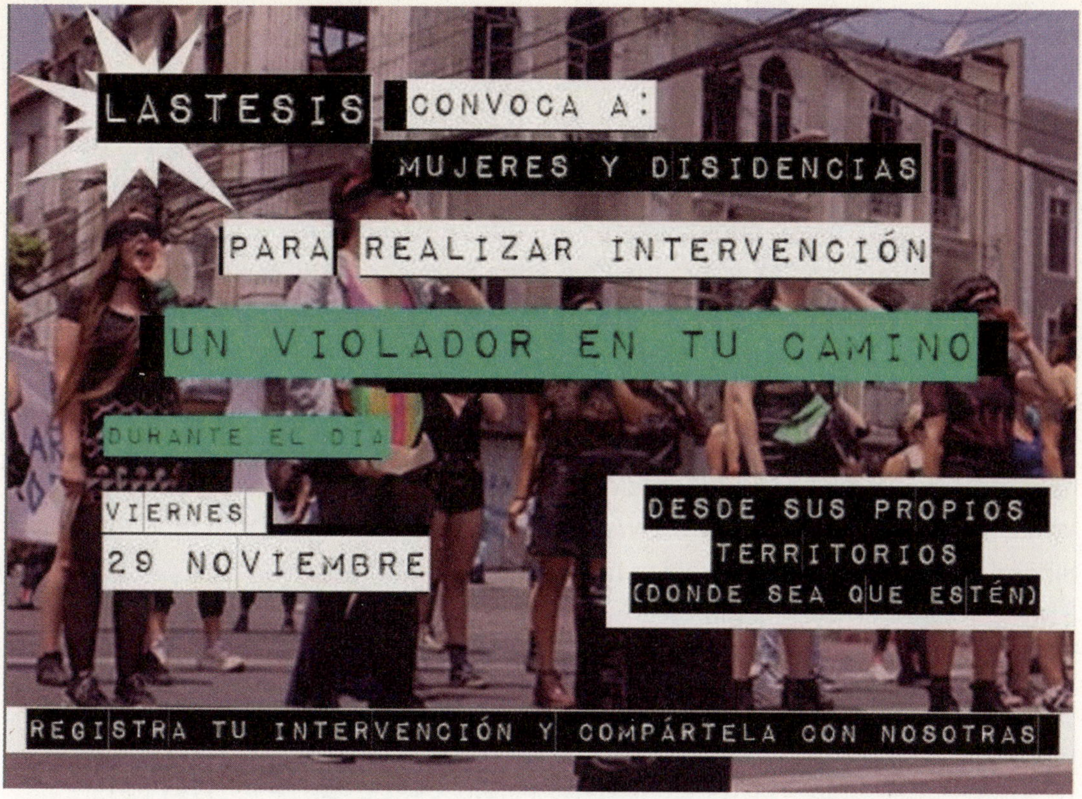

Intervención UN VIOLADOR EN TU CAMINO de colectivo LASTESIS

El estado violador es un macho opresor

(The rapist state is a patriarchal oppressor)

So goes the biting internationally resonant line of the feminist dance performance "El violador eres tu," initiated by Chilean artist collective Las Tesis in massive demonstrations, ongoing in Chile since early October 2019.

Amidst these massive protests, directly sparked by a proposed metro fare rise, but building up to encompass cost of living, inequality, and a renewed drive for a constitutional assembly, Las Tesis arranged an intervention they called "El violador eres tu." They responded to a call for action: fuego acciones en cemento, to take performance outside the theatre, into the streets. On November 20, 2019, a group of women cut traffic in central Valparaiso, and initiated a dance performance with simple moves, arranged to a techno-y rhythm with lyrics chanted in unison.

The action connects individual violence against women with a state apparatus of control and patriarchal governance of all aspects of life.

I have never been to Chile, but if Chilean protests spaces are anything like Beirut, or anywhere else I've protested en masse, these are prime for feminist intervention. At their best, these public spaces are dominated by the performance of muscular nationalism; at worst, they are sites for systematic sexual harassment. Perhaps that accounts in part for the enormous local success of Las Tesis' first intervention on November 22, leading them to put out a call over social media to repeat the intervention on November 25, International day for the Elimination of Violence Against Women. This time, masses of women turned out for the protest held in Santiago de Chile, Valparaiso, and also Mexico City, Berlin, Paris, New York. Youtube, Twitter, Instagram were filled with videos of women repeating the didactic dance moves and precise lyrics.

Jane Gaines once called this visual mimesis, the aspiration that what we see on screen will repeat in our bodies. I don't think she anticipated it quite like this.

Across the internet, women chant and dance in unison: "It was not my fault, not what I was wearing, not where I was standing. You are the rapist," placing the fault for sexual violence on the oppressor—not the woman—as well as on the pervasive and omni-powerful patriarchal system more broadly.

Such feminist internationalism is rarely so visible. It is also rarely so practically effective.

I participated in a group dance once—it was during one of the many Israeli bombings of Gaza (so many since Hamas won municipal elections in 2006, that I've lost track of which). I don't remember the lyrics. I remember feeling vaguely embarrassed and vanguardist. Not because I was embarrassed by the message, but because there was something about exposing myself as an Arab in a Zionist milieu, because the simplified dance moves performed in unison felt so rigid, so white. My body, before my brain, rejected the moves which unified me with the American Anti-Zionist Jews who had planned the protest. The key differences in our personal stakes, flattened by the movements not of my making.

This one seems different. No Violador protests are organized where I live at the moment (Boston), and so I participate vicariously via Instagram and Twitter. I watch if this will make it to Beirut, where there are also unprecedented mass protests (it eventually does), and I feel ambivalent when a few male bloggers retweet their Arabic translations of the Chilean lyrics. At home, later, I find myself chanting the lyrics silently while vacuuming: "the rapist state is a patriarchal oppressor,"

I repeat my favorite line over and over. An anthem for girl power, far more operative to smashing the patriarchy than anything by Lady Gaga.

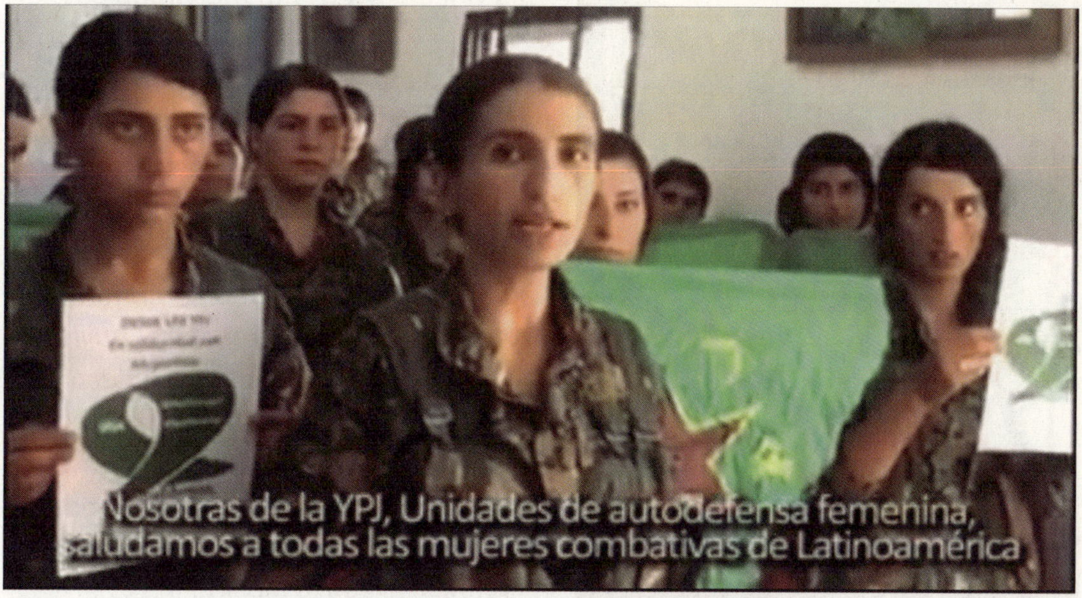

Mensaje de las YPJ a las mujeres argentinas

When I began to think about Feminist Internationalism several months back, it was in a political moment marked more by isolation than urgent aesthetics and internationalist creativity. Feminism is perhaps even more necessary in such times. I came across a video made by YPG fighters in Syria expressing solidarity with the abortion legalization initiative in Argentina. In the video, a line of women dressed in fatigues stand behind a spokeswoman in what appears to be a converted schoolroom. Framed photographs of women's faces, ostensibly party martyrs, hang behind them. The low-resolution camera pans across the fighters as the spokeswoman reads a statement of solidarity: "In the women's self-defense units, we not only fight militarily against ISIS but our main goal is to build a new society with free women. And so we declare our solidarity with women in Argentina in their fight for universal access to free, safe abortions."

For months, a massive campaign to legalize abortion galvanized feminists across Argentina, producing declarations of solidarity from across the world. The bill promised to legalize abortion before 14 weeks, making abortion free and accessible in all public and private hospitals. Building on the momentum of the anti-feminicide campaign "Ni Una Menos" (Not one less), it passed Argentina's lower congressional chamber, and was narrowly defeated in the Senate. Had it passed, the proposed bill would have been a major victory for legalized abortion in Latin America. Many argued it would also be a victory for feminism internationally.

Articulating the linked nature of struggles, the YPJ video ends with the women chanting, in Kurdish, "Ni Una Menos: Not one less, by illegal abortion."

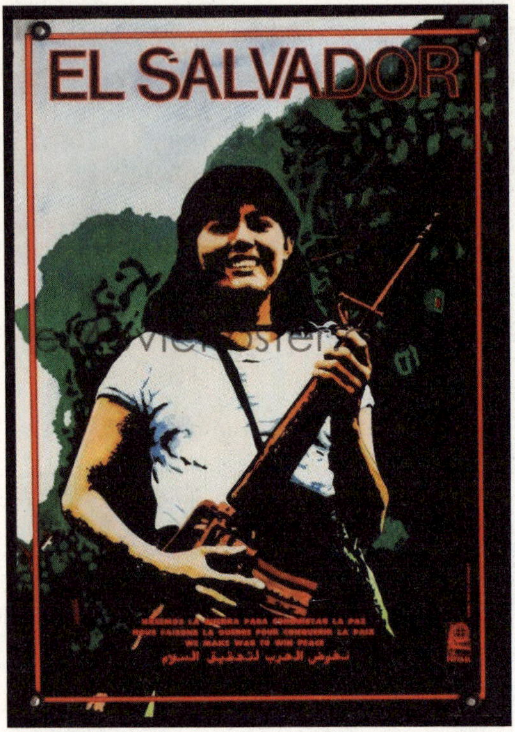

This video stayed with me—troubled me even—for weeks. I contemplated its DIY aesthetic and affinities to the newsreel declarations of tricontinentalism. Complete with military fatigues, low-fi art direction, and direct camera address, it could have been one of the scenes Jean-Luc Godard and Anne-Marie Miéville ostensibly discarded from *Ici et Auillers* (1976) for being too didactic. Indeed the iconography of Kurdish women fighters is almost identical to OSPAAAL posters about El Salvador in the eighties, and the textual structure of the declaration resembles closely Leila Khaled's party-approved declaration in *Red Army/ PFLP A Declaration of War* (1971). What to make of these aesthetic links?

Assuredly, the artistic collaborations that accompanied or resulted from that period of third world coordination mainly mirrored the movement's broader blindness to questions of patriarchal dominance and the gender division of labor. Or at least they did not overtly critique it. The widely circulated image of a Salvadoran fighter with a Kalashnikov in hand echoes within these images of Kurds in Syria, even as it repeats the Sandinista Slogan "HACEMOS LA GUERRA PARA CONQUISTAR LA PAZ," We Make War To Win Peace. It does not ask who made what decisions in that war, and how, let alone who, did the dishes, raised the children. With the distance of thirty years, it's hard to see these images without simultaneously acknowledging that the movements of tricontinentalism were largely defeated/failed. As Saldaña Portillo has brilliantly argued, those failures have as much to do with their aspirations to out-of-touch ideals of the new man and development ideologies, as they do with imperial intervention. And while the YPG aesthetics apparently resonate with internationalists today, is this militant aesthetic trapped within the form and vision of its internationalist forefathers?

My hesitancy is compounded by another afterimage. I find myself associating this self-authored image of YPG fighters with those glamorously portrayed on the cover of US-based, media conglomerate Condé Nast-owned women's magazine, *Marie Claire*. That widely circulated issue focused on their opposition to Islamic Fundamentalism and their advocacy for universal abortion in a tenuous geopolitical alliance with Western Feminism. And indeed, the issue's publication appropriately coincided with the US declaration of an armed alliance between Kurdish forces in Syria and the US military. The women became sentimentalized willing martyrs, risking everything for women's rights and western (i.e. anti-Islamic) values. This is underscored in the Marie Claire article by the women's insistence that they are all volunteer fighters. Initially remarkable, the statement becomes complicated if seen through a critique of uncompensated care work's contribution to capitalist value production. Through this lens, fighting ISIS (and facing additional gender-based violence and possible death in the process) becomes one more unpaid task asked of Kurdish women living in Syria. Conveniently bracketed off from the YPG's socialist aspirations and gender-based class critique, a geopolitically agreeable version of Kurdish militant feminism was presented to the public.

While the Argentinian-solidarity video certainly received a far more limited circulation than Marie Claire, it too does little to challenge that narrative. My reservations about this video stem less from that uncomfortable alliance, than from a desire for something more. At its most basic, the YPG video is a message of support across borders: we too—they say—struggle for putting gender difference at the center of our local struggle. And yet, it is a certain version of gender difference—one that, perhaps unintentionally, extrapolates from class and women's unpaid labor—that multiplies across our screens. A certain *kind of feminism* becomes syndicated. What is left is a sentiment, a feeling of not being alone. This sensation is indeed key to feminist alliance. And yet, much like the feminist hashtags of the past few years, it elides other images of feminist labor.

Whose labor is left out? Arguably those much less glamorous, and far more prevalent feminist forms and actions.

I would like to think through some of these questions—of labor—feminism—and internationalism—and their limits, in relation to my own experience circulating a feminist film, and to likewise think through some of the questions of potentiality of image-making and circulation.

I needed to work my way out of a practical problem, and feminism intimated to offer solutions.

I had made and distributed a film on the labor movement in Lebanon—a domain over which men typically have a monopoly. A *Feeling Greater Than Love* (2017) revisits two famous strikes in the 1970s, one by workers, one by farmers, which are symbolically central in the Lebanese left's collective memory as the starting point of a revolutionary process formed by a powerful secular coalition of workers, farmers, students, and intellectuals that was cut short by the Lebanese Civil War (1975-1990). In addition to shedding some doubt on the ideological unity of this coalition, the film features women—working- and middle-class and intellectuals—as central to the movement[1]. Even before the film made its way back to Lebanon, it began sparking virulent reactions from the exclusively male old-guard leadership, who dismissed the film, and me, as out of touch, and suggested—both quite publicly, and through interpersonal channels—that it misrepresented the movement, and therefore shouldn't be seen.

I hadn't set out to make a feminist film. In a time of seeming political impossibility (the late 'oughts, and twenty years after the "end of history"), I set out to make a film that recuperates lessons from the successes and failures of the working class movements of the 1970s. I had watched the handful of contemporary films that revisit this period (among them *Alfaro Vive Carajo* (2007), *The Weather Underground* (2002), *My Perestroika* (2011)), finding that many of them viewed this past through a neoliberal cast, towing the line of "we didn't change the system, but we changed"). The more hopeful, albeit melancholy ones, like *Chile Memoria Obstinada* (1999), took a critical-memory view of the past, reflecting on what memory of this past might be able to invoke. And while these past moments of possibility were produced by working class movements, unsurprisingly, perhaps, given the class character of their directors, most of these films privileged intellectual organizational labor and viewpoints over perspectives of working-class people and their intellectual and collective political work. That is, these films depoliticized the questions of class and actual bodies on the ground, to focus instead on intellectual labor done primarily by middle- and upper-class party leadership.

I aimed to avoid this trap, and to make a film that was not narrated by the movement leadership. Rather, it would recenter labor and the pivotal political work of working-class and non-leadership actors. In a sense, my commitment to class—aspiring to have the story told as much as possible by workers—was what led me to the women.

In Gandour factory, like in many confectionary factories across the world, young women were the primary labor force. Internationally, scholars have pointed out that this was simultaneously about political economy and power relations—women could be paid less, did not expect job permanency (because it was thought they should leave when they married), and were seen as suitable for the more "delicate" work of moving and boxing candies. In Lebanon, they were sub-

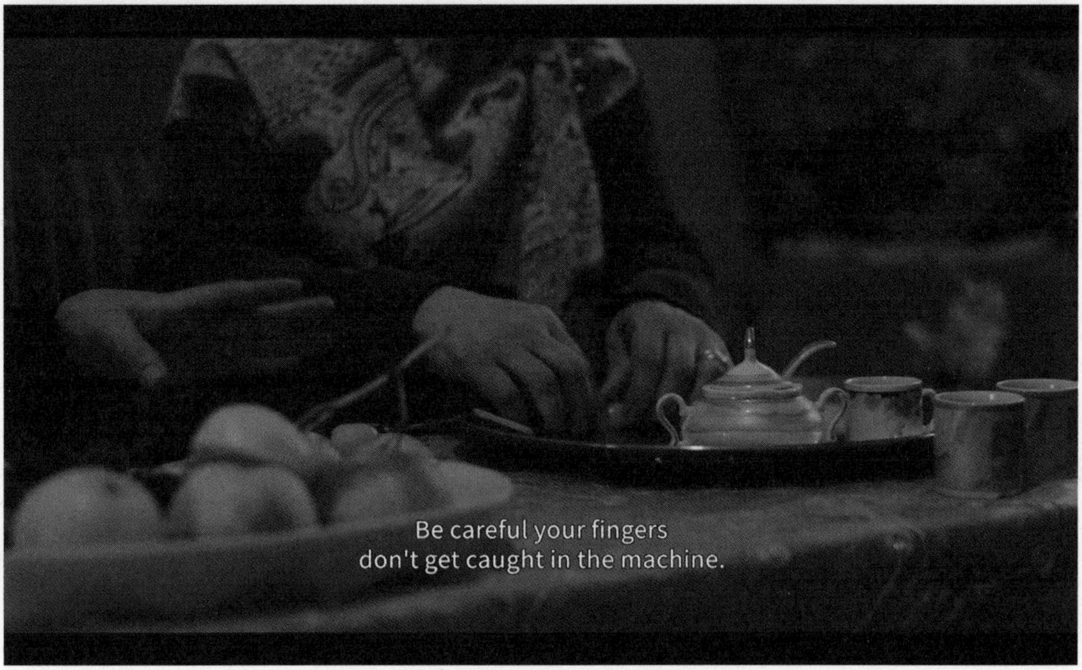

View: vimeo.com/417749880/213f3d5168

ject to the same kinds of draconian working conditions, lower pay than their male colleagues, almost no possibility of job mobility, and what several called "humiliating" daily body searches to make sure they hadn't "stolen" anything, inevitably underscored by the threat of sexual harassment from supervisors.

I surmised, if the strike at the majority women-staffed factory had full participation, then surely these women, who had even more reason to demand improved working conditions, must have been a major force in it. For reasons particular to Lebanon, and more general ones, I had a hard time finding the women. Of these, even fewer agreed to be filmed and do so under family duress, on the condition that their identity not be obvious to their family.

The women I speak with, without fail, all match their descriptions of factory work with a repetitive motion of the hands, as if the movement itself invokes the memory, and not the other way around. Work changes us, our bodies and our minds. In the first such scene, three women ex-workers use objects like coffee cups—implements of domesticity—as stand-ins for biscuits they once packaged for a living. They reminisce about contradictory emotions—the pride they felt for being self-taught machinists, able to repair the machine they worked on when it broke without calling the mechanic—the camaraderie of being brought together with others from work—along with exploitation: low wages, forced overtime, unequal pay compared to their male colleagues, and arbitrary treatment from their bosses, which led them to go on strike.

Maybe it's in this sense that feminism is sensational, as Sara Ahmed writes; it "relates both to the faculty of sensation and to the arousal of strong curiosity, interest, or excitement." I would add, it is simultaneously embodied.

Without fail, in revisiting their working days, the women express mixed emotions—a sense of loss for the relative independence and camaraderie of factory work, along with the denouncement of exploitative working conditions.

This ambivalence resonates with a Portuguese art writer, to whom I show the film while it is still in montage. She recalls similar hand gestures in a Portuguese film about women workers, of which she cannot recall the title. Images lead to an unplanned solidarity between Portugal and Lebanon in 2016. It is where my mind goes when faced with relentless criticism of my own work methodology. Although the stakes are considerably lower than in a factory strike, and quite different, it is images that I turn to for the solidarity and direction I crave.

Do images communicate across space and time?

When those images engage marginal spaces and forms of labor—like women tobacco workers linked across a monopoly industry with colonial contours—can images be feminist comrades in struggle?

In my research, I discover women are also the backbone of the tobacco farming industry. An otherwise unsuccessful search for audiovisual media on these strikes leads me to a newsreel film, The *Leaves of the Poor are Gold* (1974). It recounts the 1974 tobacco farmer uprising. Interviews with both participants and union leadership structure the film. Meanwhile in the fields—tobacco workers plough, plant, harvest, pack and prepare their crop. Underscoring its cyclic nature, the process repeats. I filmed the same, surprisingly similar, labor process decades later. The movements of tobacco processing have changed little. The director interviews women. But women are also the majority of those in the fields, or sitting on the floor stringing thousands of leaves.

A basic surface observation principle: these images from Puerto Rico are practically interchangeable with my own images, taken decades later and thousands of miles away. The labor process in this monopoly production industry is virtually the same. The crop, how it is planted, harvested, processed, sold. That is the organization of the labor process. Capital flattens difference and distance in the interest of continued accumulation. And indeed, the economic structuring of both Puerto Rico and South Lebanon are products of centuries of colonialism of various forms. Tobacco is one of the world's most concentrated industries: with

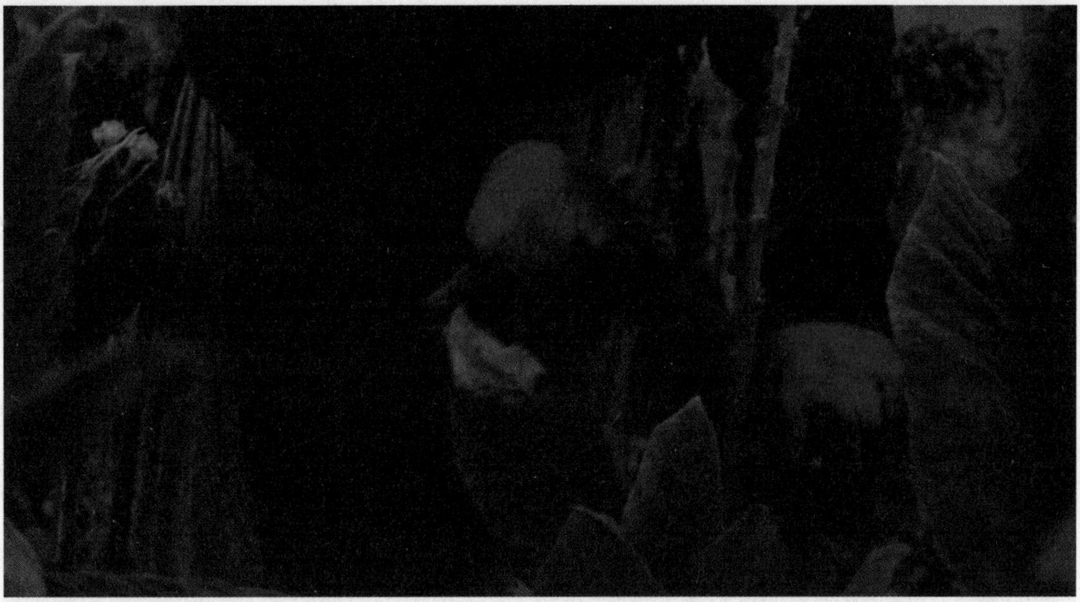

View: vimeo.com/417759724

only five companies controlling 26 percent of production and sale. The political implications of this vast global concentration of wealth are significant—for the workers on whom this industry runs.

Women tobacco workers are central to—if largely written out of—Lebanese social history. The 1946 Lebanese labor law was passed largely thanks to mass pressure galvanized around a workers strike in which militant women tobacco workers played a leading role. The same is true in Puerto Rico. So many of these workers are women, doing the household picking and sorting, in addition to the work to maintain the labor force.

What if they stopped working? My favorite and most romantic part of Marxism: the labor theory of value. Poetic in its simplicity: without workers, there is no accumulation.

This is also the presumption of the Global Women's Strike. To imagine the consequences if women refused to work. But how to organize this global women's work stoppage if women are isolated and atomized and disconnected as domestic workers in their own households? If their industrial and service labor is regularly made invisible? These images across space and time are feminist comrades in struggle—telling each other, and observers, that women perform the labor upon which this industry, in fact global capitalism, rests. And yet—history hasn't worked this way. That is, these images have not been allowed to function as such. Fragmented, isolated, partial, much like the work of domestic labor.

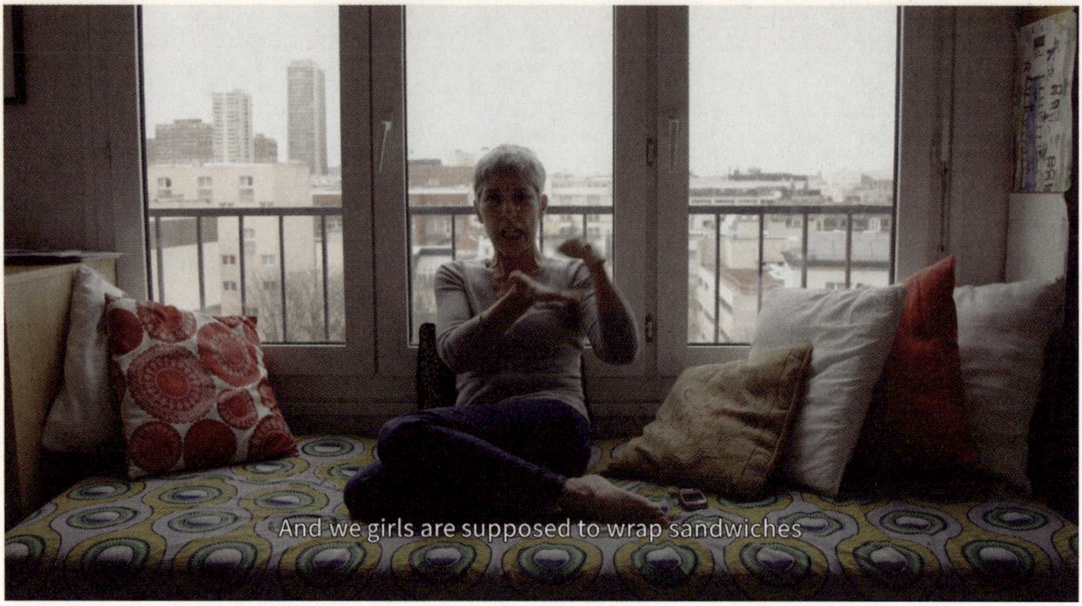

View: vimeo.com/293588315

Simultaneously, and as *A Feeling Greater than Love* began to circulate internationally, it started eliciting an opposite reaction—one more hushed, occasional, and fragmented—from women who felt the protagonists' stories resonated with their own experience of social movements.

I showed the film in Poland, and a young journalist approached me who had done work on Solidarity. She has written a book, in which she recounts how the women instrumental to the Polish protest movement were asked to make sandwiches once the dust had settled. In Japan, a Korean student articulates the same story from the present day.

The sandwiches story is repeated back to *Warde*, one of the main figures in my film, and also appears in a seminal film made forty years before: *With Babies and Banners* (1979), a collaborative project excavating women's role in the 1936 UAW strike in Flint, Michigan.

Over and over, this story of the sandwiches. Women who had once had political purchase as comrades—or so they thought—are told to make sandwiches, after the revolution ends. I start to think about this. Not stews. Not elaborate rice dishes. Sandwiches, a quick food so that the revolutionary men can get back to work. No time to waste, I guess, on things like dismantling organizational hierarchy or the patriarchy.

I like to play a game called "where were the women." It's very simple, and goes like this: in this summarized declaration from the 1st Encuentro de Cineastas del Tercer Mundo, held in Algeria, in 1972, where were the women? There is only JOSEPHINE (Guinea Bissau). Her name in all caps, with no identifying characteristics. I ask around informally, contact the researchers who unearthed this document. Who is Josephine? Where were the women?[2]

The principle of internationalist images—of images that communicated our commonality in anti-capitalist struggle across context and place—underlay the Encuentro de Cineastes del Tercer Mundo and the affiliate Third World Cinema Committee, which it sparked. In their two meetings, Algiers, December 1973, and Buenos Aires, May 1974, they resolved to combat the functional role that cinema plays in solidifying individualistic and racist ideologies by supporting the production of cinema that, in form and content, undercut imperialism and served the interests of popular struggle. Part of their commitment—which seems to have continued, only more informally, after the 1974 meeting—was to translate and screen each other's films, and to commit to third world co-productions (now to be called "South South"), based on the principle that imperial film funding would only serve imperial ends.

The various Third World Film Festivals inaugurated after the Tricontinentalism Conference in 1966 Havana enabled a physical dialogue between form, politics, and content that linked aesthetic approaches between third world countries and artists. In their documentation, the Encuentros and Festivals don't appear to have considered gender of concern to anticolonial struggle, nor a relevant question in their aesthetics and practice. I ask a prominent Arab director about her experience of these meetings. She states simply that she had no experience, since "we were not invited."

Viewing these documents from a distance of almost fifty years, the diagnosis and proposed solutions are still relevant. While non-western filmmakers now have broad access to non-commercial cinema originating in other parts of the Global South, these films largely encounter one another and receive their sanction at major European festivals. Proliferation of the festival-affiliated film market and related development workshops and funds mean that national origin (or race / gender) stand in for *difference* within a form that offers more of the same. Global cinema translates experience to a neoliberal framework—the logical political economic continuity of the framework critiqued by the Encounter. And funding for the most seen and circulated continues to originate from Europe and to a lesser extent, North America. This critique is not new—although it may be under-argued. Those that have breached the subject have often pointed to the internet as a place for unfettered exchange—corporate control and algorithms aside.

More often, the images from internationalism have found a re-purposing in the world of contemporary art, often divorced from their initial militant function. For the artists who present them, they become a commodity for trade in artistic value production in an international art market. The proposition that these works could have served to practically coordinate struggle, to suggest solutions, to reorient thinking against colonialism and transnational capital becomes an afterthought, much less an intention to revisit these functions.

But what if we could? To re-frame the question posed by the Third World Cineastes, what kinds of practices of exchange could enable us to frame differences and commonalities, and in fact practically coordinate across borders and experiences?

A different essay might have ended with Las Tesis' beautiful, and still ongoing, adaptable performance, lauding it as an ideal type for Feminist Internationalism. And indeed, the embodied critique of this performance in the streets has more far-reaching potential than any on-screen film. And yet I have a sense that we could do much more. That images could politicize repetitive, isolating reproductive labor, carework that unites the overwhelming majority of unrecognized and uncompensated work globally. That the internationalist feminist images that would truly shake the intersecting structures of oppression to its core exist, but have not yet found each other.

I write this essay with a deliberately—difficultly—utopian bent. Because what we do not imagine can never be possible, but—as another patriarch of the left once said: be practical, demand the impossible. It must be that all such political ruptures are unfathomable until they happen.

1 It suggests, both subtly and more directly, that not incorporating them as serious political actors was a central factor in the movement's failure. The film is particularly critical of the move from mass union politics—a form with room for different kinds of political leaderships—to militarization, the atypical hierarchal organization.

2 Where was Sara Maldoror? Heiny Srour? Jocelyne Saab? Many others …

Vivian Price

Times are Changing, Minds are also Changing: Patriarchy, Neoliberalism and the Construction Industry

In the Spring of 2006, I completed *Transnational Tradeswomen*, a film that looks at the gendering of work and the impact of globalization on women construction workers in six Asian Countries: Thailand, Taiwan, India, Singapore, Pakistan, and Japan. The inspiration for the film came from my interest as a former union electrician and tradeswomen's advocate to know more about where women work in the construction industry historically and how the gendering of work differs in various cultures and political economies. My focus is on the sexual division of labor, but the racialization of labor, whether by ethnicity or tribe or region or caste is present as a subtext. My interest in making the film heightened after I attended a workshop on women construction workers at the Beijing Conference on Women in 1995, where I met women construction workers and organizers from many countries. Ruth Manorama, a renowned activist from India, attended that conference, and urged women from the global north to travel to India and other places in the global south and learn more about women construction workers to stimulate international support for workers facing difficult conditions.

I felt that a documentary connecting the issues among women in various countries might contribute to understandings that would further labor solidarity. Following the idea outlined in the *minor cosmopolitan weekend* blurb, I examine *Transnational Tradeswomen* to trace the "productive tensions between the local and the global, the individual and the collective, and the specific and the universal."[1] The film questions a homogenizing narrative about the gendering of work, looking deeply into the experiences of women working in labor-intensive societies who are pushing against gender restrictions and in some cases for collective workers' rights.

A strong theme of the film underscores how transitions in political economy and technology affect workers, particularly women workers. The film interviews workers and advocates to reveal the difficulties of life within the harsh conditions of heavy manual labor for all workers involved, how patriarchal barriers make it difficult for women to gain skills and skilled employment in changing times, when foreign companies with mechanized technology are changing the economy and the labor market. Writing about the stories of women related in the film, Bipasha Baruah states, "Their stories disturb commonly held notions of progress and show how globalization, modernization, education, and technology do not always result in gender equality and poverty alleviation."[2]

Transnational Tradeswomen makes the case that women have worked in labor-intensive construction for hundreds of years. Family-based work arrangements are common, with women and children and men working together, not unlike the English mines before the Mines Act of 1842. Countries with a large informal sector tend to employ many women, while in the formal sector, under greater state regulation, the workforce tends to be male, with more technology and fewer employees.[3] In India, the informal sector constitutes over 90 percent of the workforce. Construction work is also stratified by caste, with longstanding traditions delegating certain kinds of work to the various castes and subcastes.

India's construction workforce numbers about 30 million, with women accounting for about half, distinguishing it from other countries depicted in the film, and providing the starkest example of the issues of globalization, mechanization and the struggles against patriarchy by women workers. India also offers examples of union organizing, mass protests, and several models of skill-training programs.

One of my main hosts was Geetha Ramakrishnan, a key organizer of informal sector workers, slumdwellers and fisherfolk in Tamil Nadu, and the joint secretary of the nationwide union Nirman Mazdoor Panchayat Sangam (NMPS); my translator on my first trip was Devi Kumar from Kerala, who showed me construction sites in Delhi and her home state. Before looking more in-depth at these phenomena in India, it's informative to look at a broader continuum of women working in construction as represented in other countries in the film.

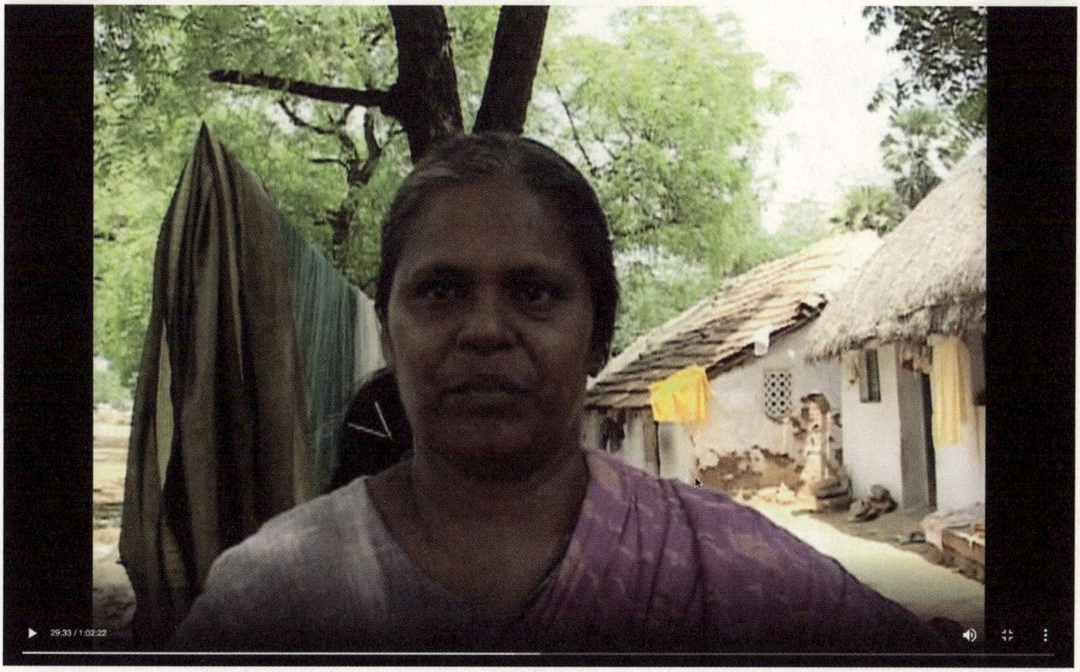

Geetha Ramakrishnan, joint secretary of the nationwide union Nirman Mazdoor Panchayat Sangam (NMPS), 2002. Screenshot courtesy of the author.

The long tradition of women construction laborers in Asia

In Pakistan, women from the Rajput Odh traditionally work alongside men. Sobia Aslam, a Pakistani woman journalist living in Lahore, agreed to shoot this segment. She went to the outskirts of the city, engaging the help of her parents to interview many of the women and men who work in construction about their lives, with the backdrop of the village streets and houses, the chickens and the goats. The Aslams went to a nearby construction site, capturing footage of women in their twenties carrying piles of bricks and cement and helping the men move other construction materials. Answering the questions of Sobia's parents, the women told fragments of their stories, acknowledging that their fathers and husbands were the ones who actually received their pay.

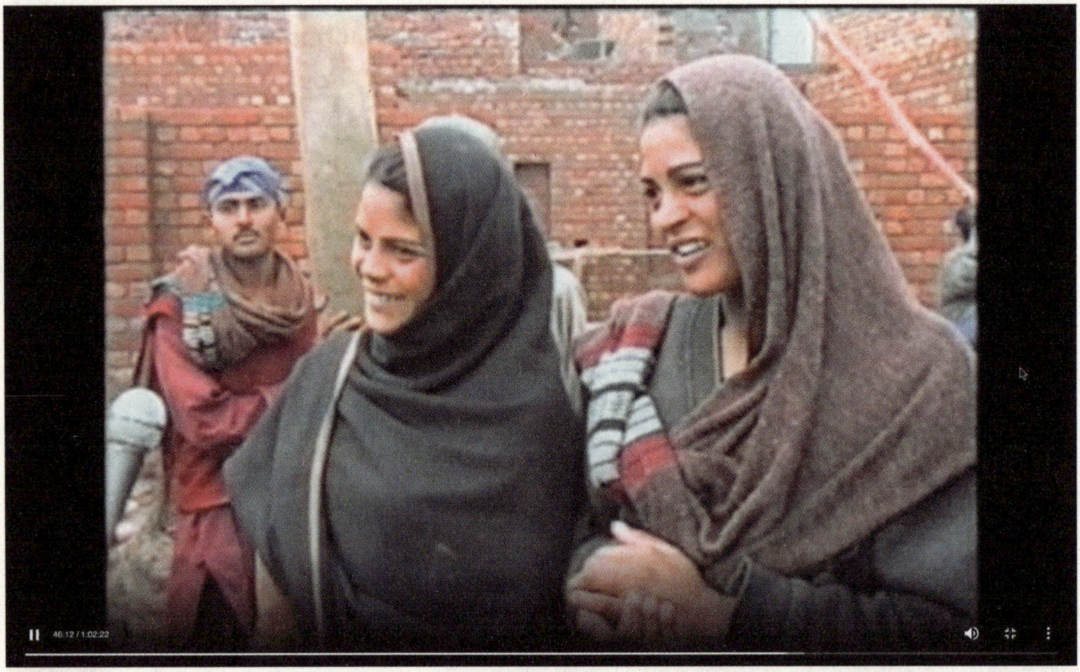

Two sisters, Kausar and Fatima, at a construction site in the outskirts of Lahore, Pakistan, 2005. Screenshot courtesy of Sobia Aslam.

In the 1920s and 30s, the British colonizers of Malaya, soon to be Singapore, began employing Chinese immigrant women known as Samsui to work in the construction of the city-state when the entry of male Chinese workers was restricted. The Samsui did not work as part of family units. They came as teenagers and were relegated to digging, mixing cement, carrying loads, and working inside buildings cleaning up cement pours with hammer and chisel. They worked into the 1960s, most not marrying, living in tiny apartments, sending money home to China.[4] A Taiwanese scholar connected me to a young journalist in Singapore,

Sim Chi Yin. She brought me to the apartment of a Samsui woman in her nineties, who spoke about how the machines on the construction site replaced her and her colleagues decades earlier.

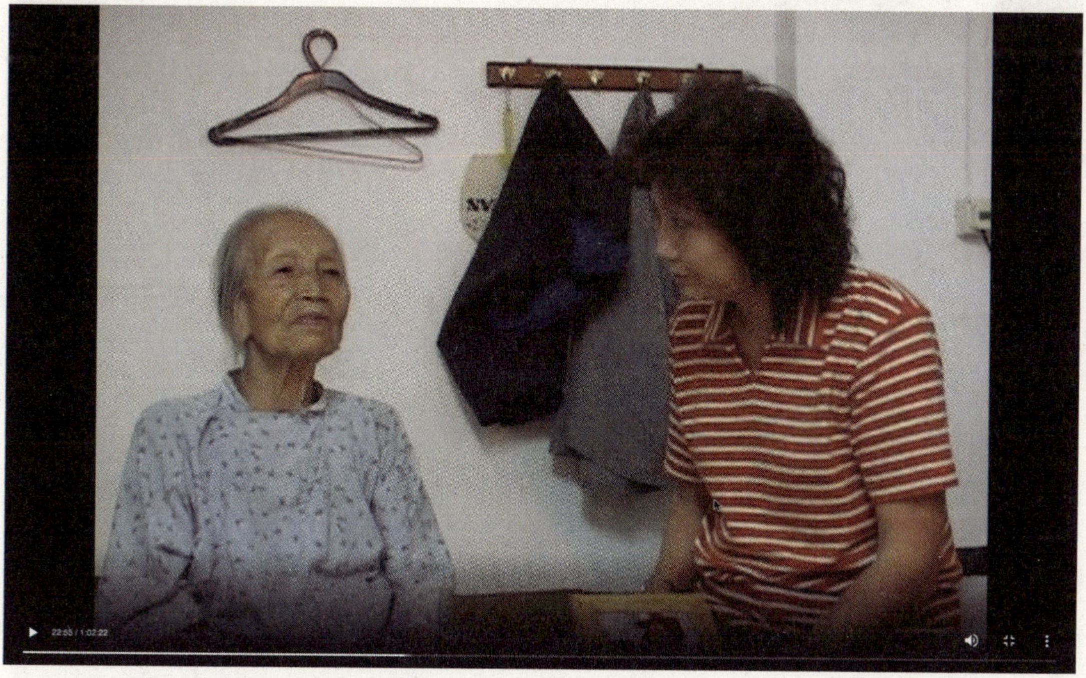

Visiting a former Samsui laborer, Madame Loh, in her home in Singapore, 2004.
Photo courtesy of the author.

Attending a conference on gender and globalization, I met scholars and graduate students Boonsom Namboonsom, Tippaya Rasameechan and Sani Navinit, who took me to various construction sites in Bangkok, explaining the conditions and interviewing workers. Thailand has a large informal sector, a seasonal workforce that divides its time between agriculture and construction. Farmers in the north-east region of Isan suffer from both displacement and farms being divided up among family and becoming too small to support everyone. Many workers from that region come with the whole family to where construction is taking place near Bangkok, the capital, and live on the site till the job gets done. We visited one of the small camps. In Thailand, women hand-mix and apply the concrete and climb scaffolding and nail wooden framing, but generally are not accepted or trained to do what is considered skilled work. Yet there are some families who accept that women can work as skilled masons, and we also filmed a woman named Jin, who expertly applied cement to the walls of an apartment being remodeled, as part of her family's crew.

I was in Kaoshiung in Southern Taiwan for a film festival and asked my host, Mr. Huong, from the state public sector union, to take me to see women construction

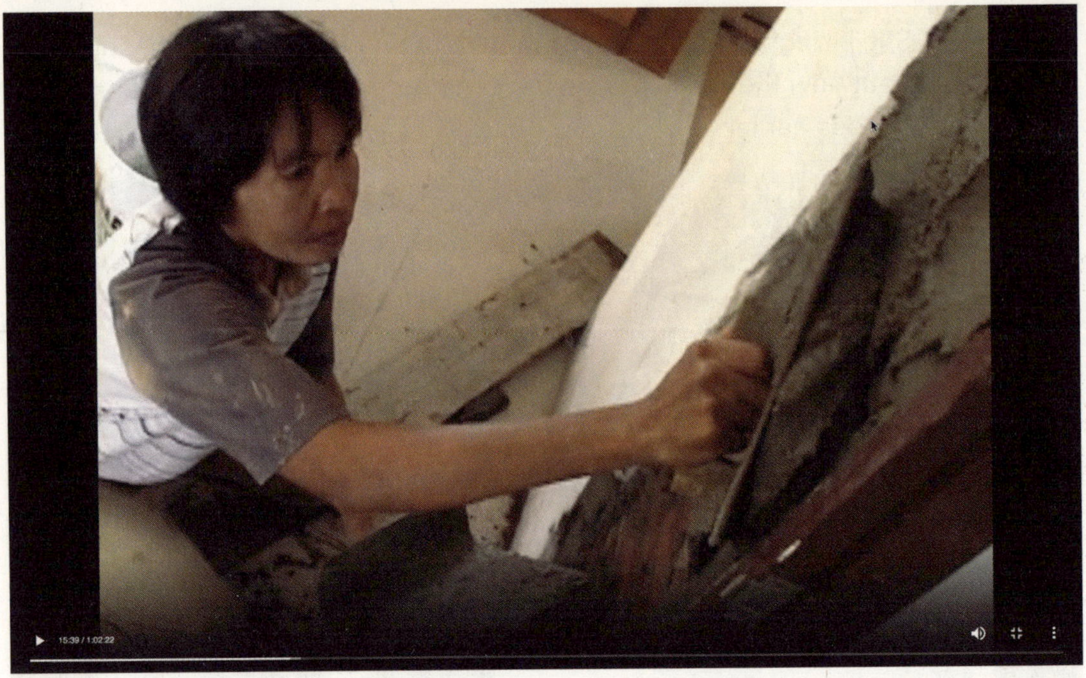

Jin, a mason, works with her family on construction in Bangkok, Thailand, 2004. Screenshot courtesy of the author.

workers and interview them. Taiwan still has traces of the family-based agriculture and construction economy. As the country has become more developed, employers recruit male workers from other countries to work in factories and in construction, and fewer women are employed in the construction sector. Mr. Huong took me to speak with his friends, a Taiwanese husband and wife working together remodeling a shop in a strip mall. The wife shoveled the ingredients for concrete into a wheelbarrow, mixed it and wheeled it where it was necessary, while her husband and other male workers did the masonry work applying it to the wall. On the way, we passed a woman working in a group of roadworkers filling potholes with asphalt, and then stopped to meet another woman working as a temp doing heavy labor at a store badly damaged by an earthquake.

Emiko Aono, a Japanese labor activist, shot the segment of the film in that country. Women used to work in construction as part of traditional family units in Japan and some of the elders still do. Industrialized Japan has a shortage of workers and runs a program to bring over Bangladeshis and Brazilians, among others, on work visas to do blue-collar labor. A construction boom in the 1980s that created a shortage of skilled workers, together with the development of Western-style liberal democracy in that country, produced The Equal Employment Opportunity Law of 1986.[5] This brought some women into skilled construction jobs in the big cities. The film depicts an older woman, Yoshiko Hiraide, who was trained to be an architect, climbing scaffolds and nailing boards along with her

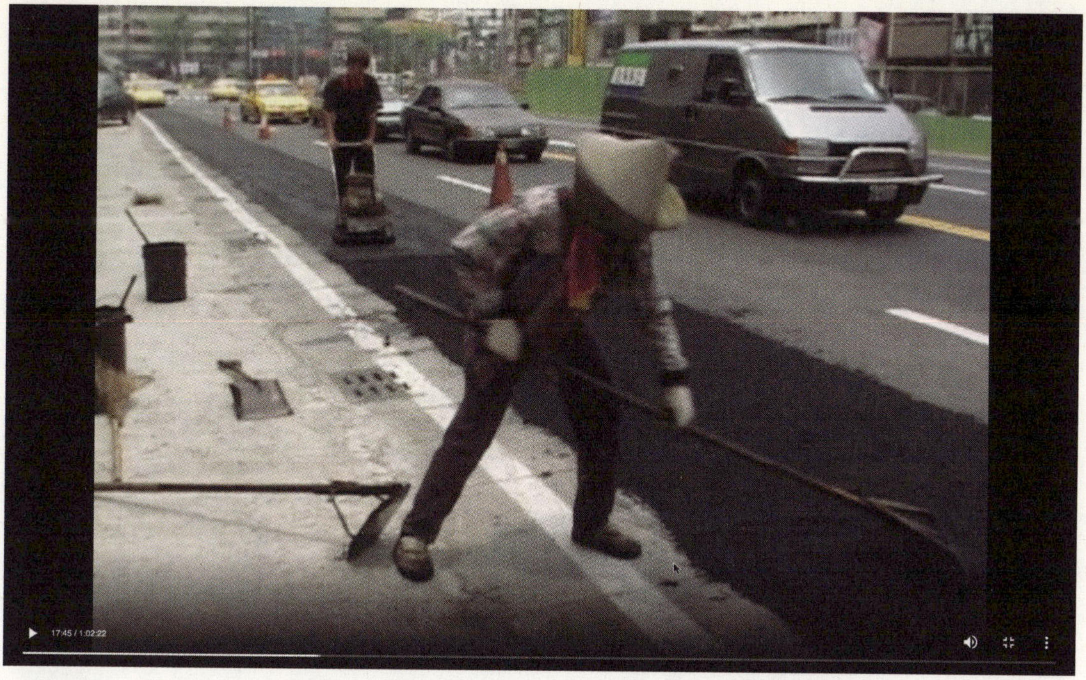

A woman on a road repair crew in Kaoshiung, Taiwan, 2004. Screenshot courtesy of the author.

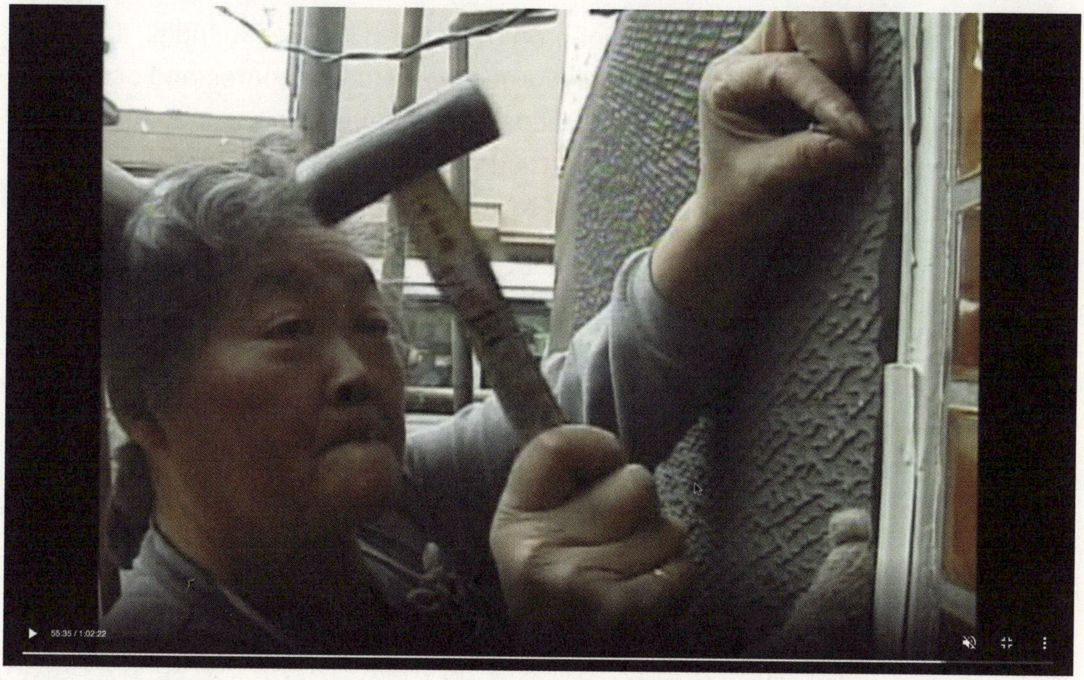

Yoshiko doing carpentry work in Tokyo, Japan, 2004. Screenshot courtesy of Emiko Aono.

aged husband who has a disability; two women cement truck drivers working for a company, who spoke about the problems of "eve-teasing" (sexual harassment); and Keiko Watanabe, a woman who became a plumber and is having a hard time being accepted by her peers. These women were all doing work considered "male." Yoshiko represented the older pattern of a family team, although she was doing the same work as her husband. Watching Masami Tashio drive the cement truck, hop out and steer the heavy chute into place and guide the cement into place, shows that she is clearly in control of her job. The same is true watching Keiko standing on a ladder handling a large drill motor to puncture a wall for a large pipe. She's managed to get the training she needs. But Keiko expresses that she is not getting the big jobs she wants to work on nor is she taken seriously as a plumber and it is making her want to quit.

In each national setting, patriarchal barriers make it difficult for women to gain skills and skilled employment in changing times. Looking at the six countries portrayed in the film, it becomes clear that technology on its own does not equalize the workplace for women. Even when women gain skills, a supportive environment is important for them to get employment and more training and to want to stay in their field.

Indian women construction workers: training and protests

As construction is such a large area of employment for women in India, it is all the more important to understand how women workers, advocates and contractors view the situation. Transnational Tradeswomen goes into some depth to show the work women do on large construction sites. As Annette Barnabas, D. Joseph Anbarasu, and Paul S. Clifford write, there are myths, "lies" about what women can and can't do: "The men construction workers and the contractors are of the opinion that the important barrier for women to become masons in construction sector is that the job involves working for long exhaustive hours and women are not fit physically."[6] They continue:

> The common belief is women are scared of heights … The prejudices like women are scared of heights and physically not fit have to be challenged and changed. At present, women climb up the scaffolding carrying loads of bricks and sand on the head, work in multi-floor buildings with ease as chithals, and they perform all the tasks done by men like digging, breaking stones and some of the tasks of the masons. So women have the same potential and the courage like men to do masonry work.[7]

Footage shot in Chennai, the capital of Tamil Nadu, Southern India, and near and in Delhi, portray these descriptions vividly. One woman after another is crowned by other workers with a large container of cement or pile of bricks on her head, then walks great lengths or up numerous flights of stairs to deliver her load. Women are called "chithal," little helper, even if they do some of the heaviest work on the site.

Mathew Cherian, a Board Member of the Mobile Creche, an NGO that provides daycare to children on construction sites, explains in the film that there are three types of construction. The A class, in the city center, is highly mechanized and mainly male. The B class can be found throughout the cities and uses some machines, and there, as well as in the C class, where little machinery is used, both men and women are employed. Much of the training for the B and C class construction is informal on-the-job training, but for men only, making it difficult for women to do anything other than the hard labor:

> In India, the men construction workers join construction sector as unskilled workers. After a few months, they are asked to do the semi-skilled work of periyal or manvettial and paid more wages. While they work as periyal or manvettial, they start assisting the masons in certain tasks and receive spot practical training for masonry work. But this type of informal training is not extended to women construction workers in construction sector because of the worldview of people, gender discrimination …[8]

Training is one thing but getting hired is another. In a number of places in the global south, NGOs have been setting up training programs to prepare women to get better-paying skilled work, especially as the demand for unskilled work is diminishing. Neoliberal policies open up opportunities for foreign companies to win construction contracts in India and other countries in South and Southeast Asia, bringing in large machinery that pushes out intensive construction practices and reduces employment.

The Self-Employed Women's Association (SEWA) saw the need to create training programs as women were displaced from textile mills in the 1990s in Gujarat.

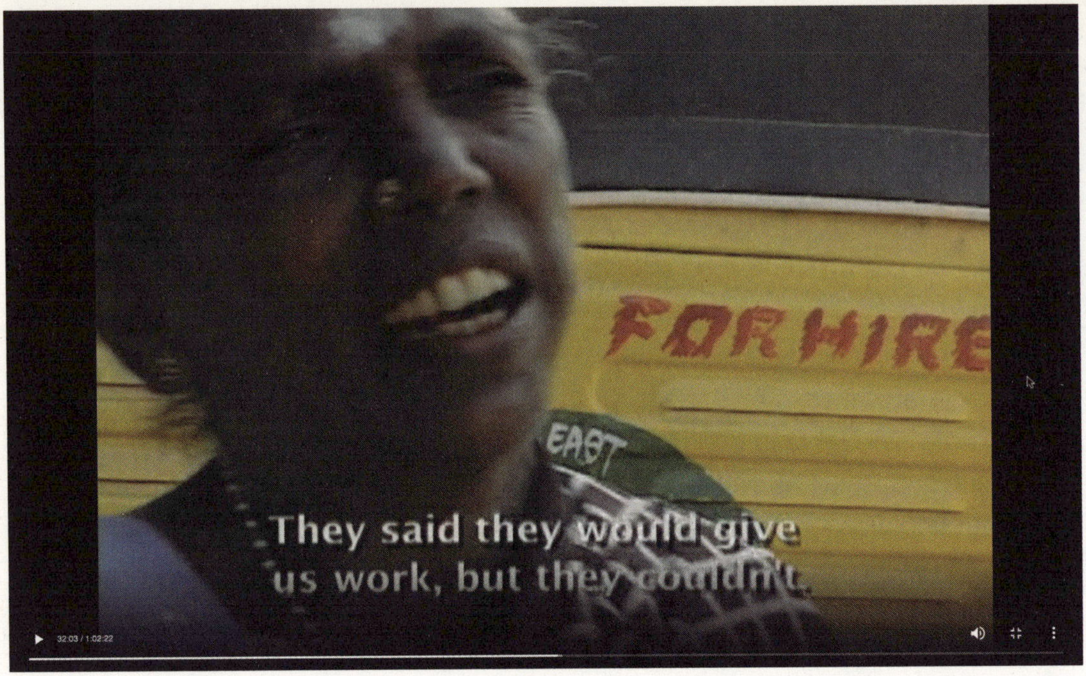

Ranganayki speaking to Padma about her concerns, Chennai, India, 2004.
Screenshot courtesy of the author.

The more recent Mahila Housing Trust's Karnika School for Construction Workers went even further, building relationships with contractors to provide a career path for women who get training, yet women graduates report having to work for free to prove themselves and making half of what male masons do when they are hired.[9] Baruah adds, "much evidence suggests that it is easier for women to acquire the skills than to subsequently find employment as skilled workers. In country after country, the experiences are similar: women face tremendous social and cultural barriers in entering the traditionally 'macho' construction industry."[10] There are similar difficulties faced by women in the global north, because even when there is formal apprenticeship, this has to be translated into actual job conditions, where mentoring is critical for mastering skills.

In 2002, I went to Ahmedabad to attend a conference on women construction workers and went to the outskirts of town where SEWA was holding training at that time. *Transnational Tradeswomen* contains a clip from that training, in which women are putting up a brick wall. Another clip shows a program for survivors of domestic abuse to fabricate doors and windows, sponsored by an architect in Kerala.

But it was in Chennai where much of the Indian segment is shot. I was welcomed to many events at Geetha's house, which was a hub for meetings, meals, staging protests and hearings. Geetha arranged for me to interview a group of women workers, with Padma, an advocate and organizer, as a translator. They told us stories about their youth and how many of them had to choose between construction work and domestic work to make ends meet. One of the women, who was in her fifties, was the mother of Selvi, a young organizer in the NMPS. Ranganayki was still being hired to carry headloads but was trying to become a mason. She had twice taken a 45-day training program through the union. Her interview turned out to be a pivotal one in the film and provided a way to represent the tensions that I saw women experiencing around work in many parts of India.

Padma talked with Ranganayki on a doorstep near the corner labor market on a hot and dusty October day. Ranganayki spoke about her pessimism about finding skilled work, despite the training she got from the union. After the conversation we moved over to the corner, where a contractor was looking for male workers to hire. Padma launched into a spirited confrontation with him over hiring women only as unskilled transporters of material. During that exchange, Ranganayki left, was hired by another contractor to do headload work, not missing out on a day's pay, but her daughter, Selvi, stood by and listened. Padma, with a captivated audience of workers who joined in at points, interrogated the contractor. I held the microphone and camera to catch as much as I could of what was a dramatic scene. I inferred its meaning by catching phrases of Tamil, by gestures and expressions of emotion, and by understanding that this was a street-corner hiring hall. The contractor started quite amiably answering Padma's questions, as I learned later, regarding paying women less because "they could not do men's

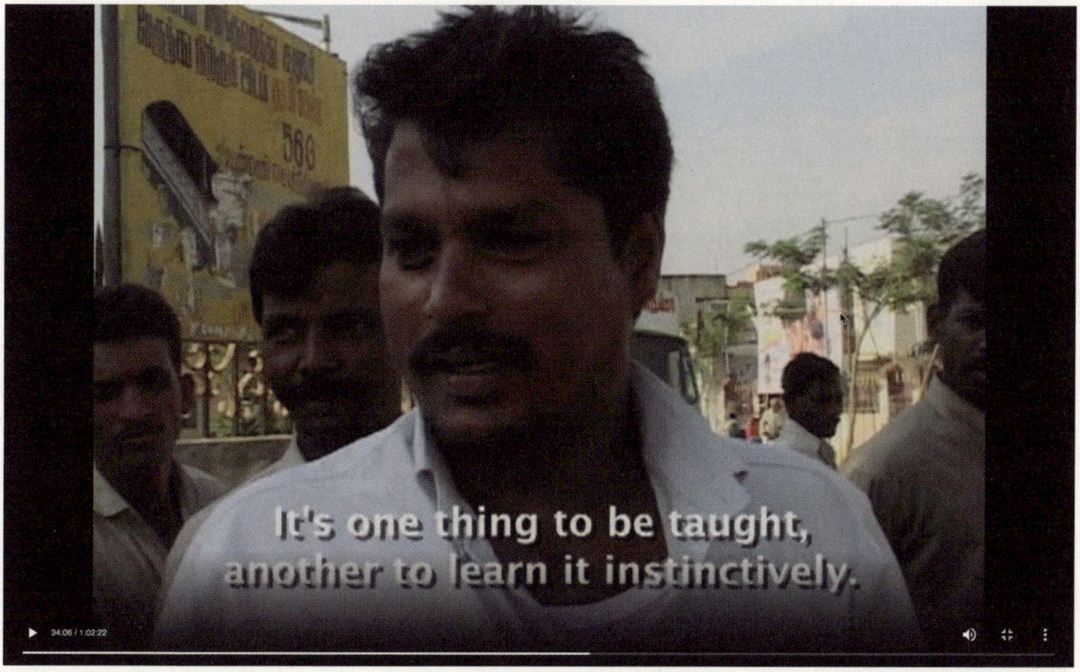

Interview with contractor in Chennai, 2004. Screenshot courtesy of the author.

work." But he grew increasingly agitated and arrogant as the questioning continued. He presented a clear point of view from a contractor's position, namely that he doubted if women could do the work men do even if they were trained to, because men learn their work "instinctually." Moreover, he knew women could not afford to work a day for free to prove themselves, as he would demand they would. Padma challenged him, and the women started laughing, including Selvi, who jumped into the discussion at the end. The scene underscores that it is not enough to train women for them to be able to get skilled construction work.

Hiring women as skilled workers requires a profound shift and flies in the face of patriarchal values, as well as having a financial cost:

> Recognition of the women laborers' ability means parity in wages. So, it is a collective denial of their ability to perform the masonry tasks. Women laborers agree with the view that cultural habits die hard, but those cannot be cited as the reason for denying women their place in the work spot. The men are also well entrenched in their expectation of passivity, obedience, and respect from women laborers. Conceding women the roles of masons or supervisors will challenge the hierarchy and even the notion of men's work.[11]

Longstanding customs and an interest of reserving better-paying jobs for men are entrenched in religious ideas as well. The primary goals of Geetha's organizing were to improve workers' lives and conditions, but also to raise political demands and build solidarity across gender and caste. Within this context, Geetha was interested in challenging ideas and practices of women's subordination. She invited me to attend and to film the ceremony of Ayudha Puja as it was celebrated in her house, and at another venue. Ayudha Puja is a day in which workers honor their tools. It is one of the last days of Navaratri, a nine-day Hindu holiday celebrating the incarnations of the major goddesses, Devi, Lakshmi and Saraswati.

I watched the workers build an altar in Geetha's courtyard, an elaborate activity which involved many hours of festooning the altar with flowers and fruits, and the rubbing of hallways and doors with special fragrances and oils. Her office was blessed, and bricks, the metal baskets for carrying them, and trowels were on display around the altar. I stood off to the side and filmed the late-afternoon crowd surrounding the altar, the insertion of rupee notes into the bricks held in a basket by the women as they carried off ceremonial headloads. As daylight dimmed, the men began a ritual of taking their trowels and smartly cracking a brick in half, then setting a burning piece of incense on the trowel, circling the tool and wafting its smoke around the altar. As I held my shot, while one after another man performed this ceremony, I saw one of the construction foremen gesturing to Ranganayki to come towards the altar and to take the trowel and perform the same ritual.

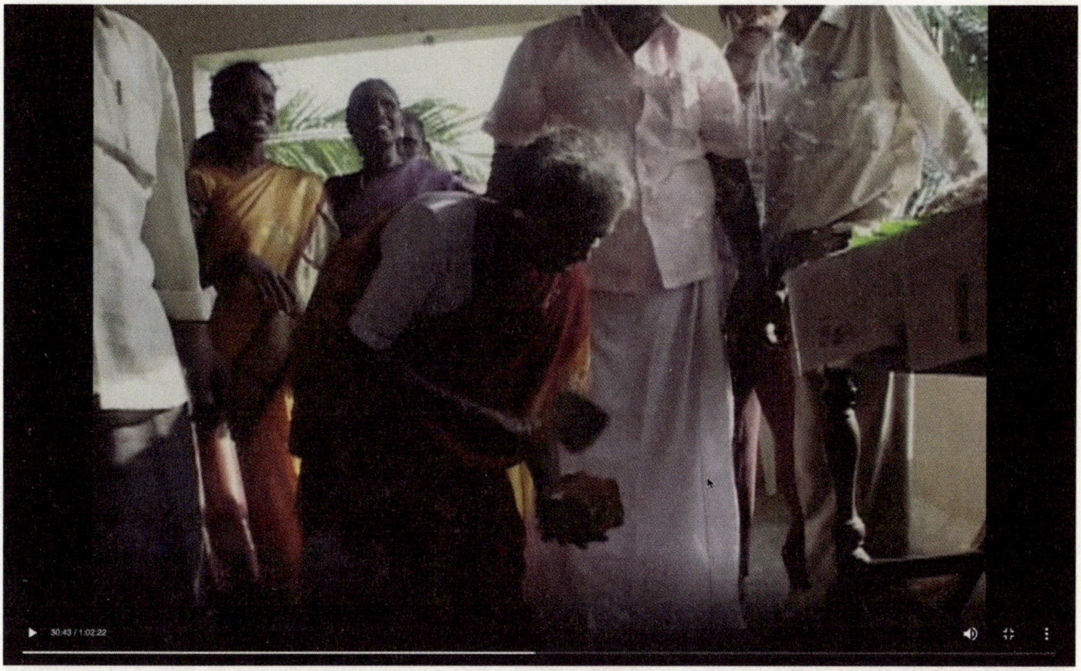

Puja on the porch of Geetha's home, Chennai, 2004. Screenshot courtesy of the author.

Early in the film, Ruth Manorama explains that there is still a belief in many parts of India that, because they menstruate, women are not supposed to use construction tools. The taboo against women going to certain places or doing certain kinds of work because they are unclean is a belief held by a number of orthodox religious groups, including in Hinduism and Judaism, and is in the Old Testament, Leviticus 15:19. I asked Geetha about the foreman inviting Ranganayki to take the trowel, making a gesture as if to say that the fact that she was welcome to join the men in this custom was unusual. She explains in the film that "times are changing and minds are also changing."

Creating solidarity and promoting venues for cultural inclusion are noteworthy activities for fostering acceptance of change. Baruah argues that raising consciousness is critical for women to move toward equity:

> It is also important to bear in mind that legal interventions and policy reforms do little or nothing to challenge the underlying social norms and customs that inhibit women's participation in the construction industry. Education and consciousness-raising initiatives that raise awareness among women as well as men about women's equal entitlements to quality employment are just as crucial as policy reforms and state actions that protect women's interests and facilitate their agency.[12]

I witnessed several intense strategy meetings on Geetha's porch, where people celebrated Ayudha Puja, and saw many people come by to consult with her. She invited me to attend rallies in Chennai and I briefly joined a three-month pilgrimage across villages near Madurai. It was organized as a political protest by the union against privatization and to enforce legislation for construction workers' rights. India is known for its democratic constitution and wide-reaching legislation for

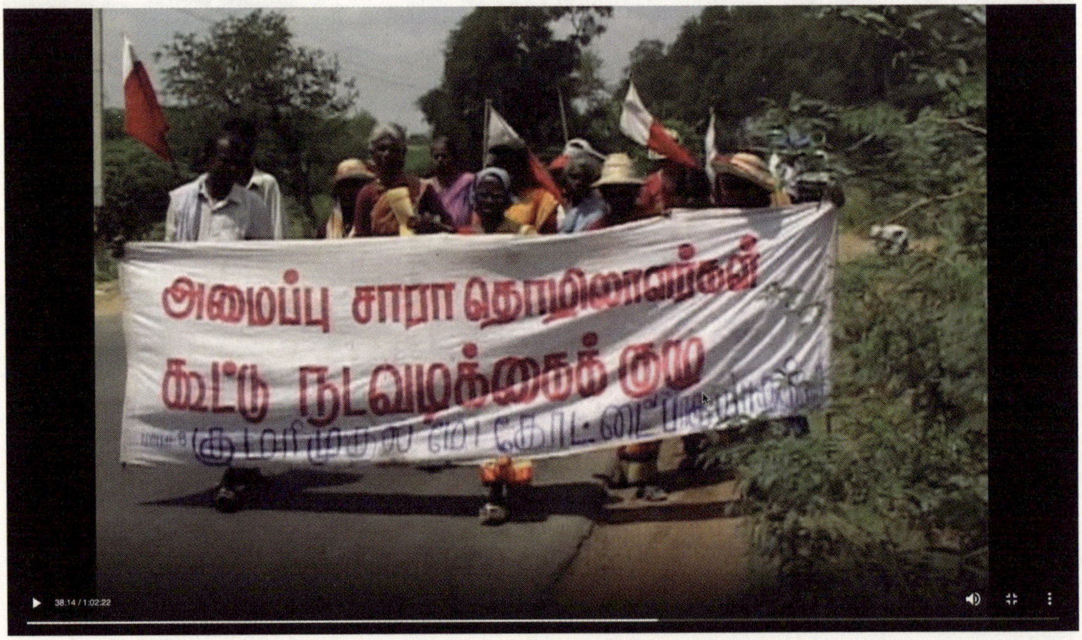

Construction Workers Pilgrimage outside of Madurai, 2002. Screenshot courtesy of the author.

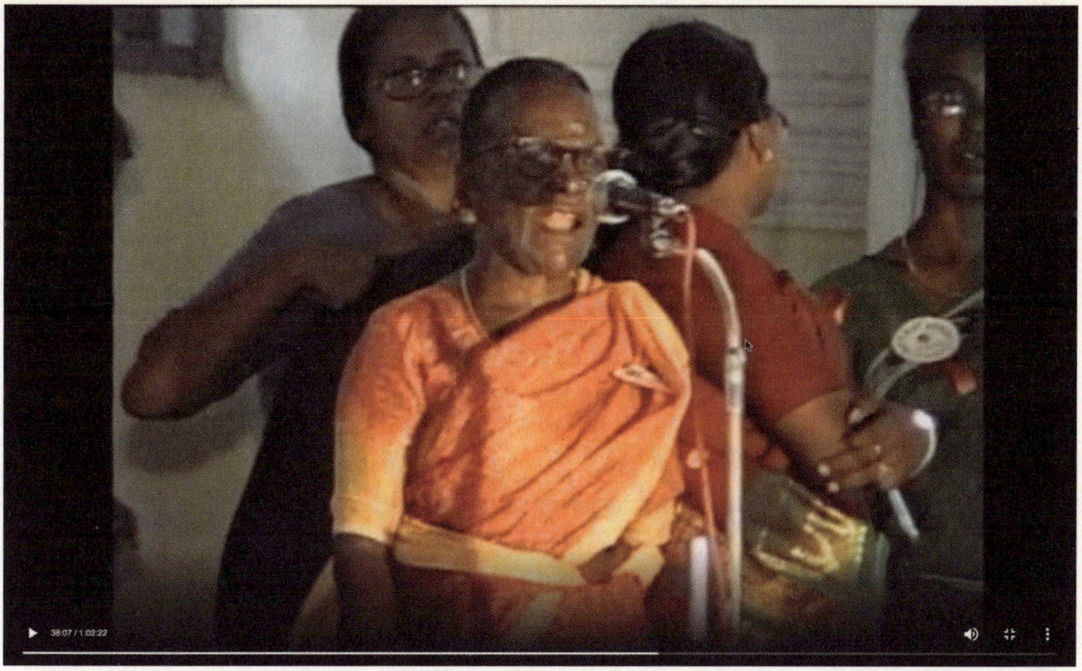

Rhadama speaking at the hearing, Chennai 2002. Screenshot courtesy of the Geetha Ramakrishnan.

the protection of workers, but these mainly protect people in the formal sector.[13] Geetha and the NMPS were involved in getting the Building and Other Construction Workers Act passed, together with a tax (cess in Hindi) to support the welfare boards created to monitor and protect construction workers throughout the country. The pilgrimage was a local grassroots movement, with people in the villages putting up the workers as they marched from place to place. They were joined by supporters from the environmental movement that was concerned about the cutting down of the forests and rampant dam building that was jeopardizing rural peoples' way of life, as well as the ecosystem.

NMPS questions the way mechanization was being rapidly introduced into South India in particular, eroding the work of the manual workers, many of them women. They engaged in protests against globalization, which displaced workers in construction, agriculture, manufacturing, without providing a safety net for those who were unemployed. *Transnational Tradeswomen* shows scenes of women attending the National Commission for Women's public hearing on the impact of globalization on women, held in Chennai in September of 2002. Rhadama, one of the workers I met on the pilgrimage and interviewed at Geetha's, testified at the hearing.

Devita Singh, co-founder of Mobile Creche, talked about the economic policies that have brought foreign companies to bid on projects all over India. They bring more advanced technology while avoiding labor-intensive practices: "Instead of creating jobs for people," she says, "they put people out of work."

Turning away from the Technological Fix

Transnational Tradeswomen explores the gendering of work that keeps women relegated to manual labor, but also challenges the idea that the introduction of technology and access to training results in gender equality. The Women in Development approach to gender equity, popular in the 1980s, asserted that modernization would raise the standard of living of countries in the "third world."[14] The notion was that human capital development would empower women and that, as skilled workers, they could increase their pay and better their conditions. That has not proven to be the case, as the examples discussed above, as well as in the film, demonstrate.

The idea that technology and training will solve social problems still resonates today. It has many proponents in the debate over how to address climate change, including corporations and some unions. For example, engineering breakthroughs (such as carbon capture) are expected to find a way to maintain employment in fossil fuel industries, and skill-training will guarantee a plethora of jobs in an expansive sustainable industry. Relying on the "technological fix" to address these problems simplifies the social issues involved. Nora Räthzel and David Uzell call the use of this concept in climate change solutions "ecological modernization," a perspective which overlooks the role of policy and structural conditions.[15] Similarly, skill-training in preparation for an energy transition without clear social policy about the meaning of growth, who gets the work or what work is actually needed, opens up many controversies, ranging from manual workers adapting to more technical employment to how to avoid reproducing already existing inequities of race and gender.

The construction industry is embedded in the growth paradigm, so much so that the questions of technology and employment are linked to environmental futures. Stefania Barca and Emanuele Leonardi argue that there is a deep connection between patriarchy and the persistence of the fossil fuel economy: "In its modern-industrial form, this gender order has given men the role of breadwinners, making them bargain for wages that heavily discount their health and safety, or accept job blackmail that compromises the health and safety of entire communities and their territories."[16] Rather than confining the fight to racial and gender equity in a capitalist or colonial regime, the climate emergency inspires a rethinking of how to fundamentally reimagine our way of living.

1 From the event description of the *minor cosmolitan weekend*.

2 Bipasha Baruah, "Gender and Globalization: Opportunities and Constraints Faced by Women in the Construction Industry in India," *Labor Studies Journal* 35, no. 2 (2008): 200.

3 Annette Barnabas, D. Joseph Anbarasu, and Paul S. Clifford, "A Study on the Empowerment of Women Construction Workers as Masons in Tamil Nadu, India," *Journal of International Women's Studies* 11, no. 2 (2009): 121-141.

4 Mariano Sana, review of *Remembering the Samsui Women: Migration and Social Memory in Singapore and China*, by Kevin E. Y. Low, *Contemporary Sociology* 43, no. 3 (2016): 324-6.

5 Barbara Molony, "Japan's 1986 Equal Employment Opportunity Law and the Changing Discourse on Gender," *Signs: Journal of Women in Culture and Society*, 20, no. 2 (1995): 268-302.

6 Barnabas et al., "Empowerment of women construction workers," 121.

7 Barnabas et al., "Empowerment", 126.

8 Barnabas et al., "Empowerment," 129.

9 Baruah, "Gender and Globalization," 216.

10 Baruah, "Gender," 215.

11 Barnabas et al, "Empowerment," 126.

12 Baruah, "Gender," 219.

13 G. Gopalakrishnan, G. Brindha, "A Study on Employee Welfare in Construction Industry," *Technology* 8, no. 10 (2017): 7-12.

14 Gina Koczberski, "Women in Development: A Critical Analysis," *Third World Quarterly* 19, no. 3 (1998): 395-410.

15 Nora Räthzel and David Uzzell, "Trade Unions and Climate Change: The Jobs versus Environment Dilemma," *Global Environmental Change* 21, no. 4 (2011): 1215-1223.

16 Stefania Barca, Emanuele Leonardi, 'Working-class Ecology and Union Politics: A Conceptual Topology," *Globalizations*, 15, no. 4 (2018): 487-503.

AMBIGUOUS UTOPIAS

04

I M I U T I M I U T I M I U T I M
A B G S O A B G S O A B G S O A B
S I U   P S I U   P S I U   P S I
  G O U I   G O U I   G O U I   G
  U U T A   U U T A   U U T A   U
A O S O S A O S O S A O S O S A O
M U   P   M U   P   M U   P   M U
B S U I   B S U I   B S U I   B S
I   T A A I   T A A I   T A A I
G U O S M G U O S M G U O S M G U
U T P   B U T P   B U T P   B U T
O O I   I O O I   I O O I   I O O
U P A A G U P A A G U P A A G U P
S I S M U S I S M U S I S M U S I
  A   B O   A   B O   A   B O   A
U S   I U U S   I U U S   I U U S
T   A G S T   A G S T   A G S T
O   M U   O   M U   O   M U   O
P A B O U P A B O U P A B O U P A
I M I U T I M I U T I M I U T I M
A B G S O A B G S O A B G S O A B
S I U   P S I U   P S I U   P S I
  G O U I   G O U I   G O U I   G
  U U T A   U U T A   U U T A   U
A O S O S A O S O S A O S O S A O
M U   P   M U   P   M U   P   M U
B S U I   B S U I   B S U I   B S
I   T A A I   T A A I   T A A I
G U O S M G U O S M G U O S M G U
U T P   B U T P   B U T P   B U T
O O I   I O O I   I O O I   I O O
U P A A G U P A A G U P A A G U P
S I S M U S I S M U S I S M U S I
  A   B O   A   B O   A   B O   A
U S   I U U S   I U U S   I U U S
T   A G S T   A G S T   A G S T
O   M U   O   M U   O   M U   O
P A B O U P A B O U P A B O U P A
I M I U T I M I U T I M I U T I M
A B G S O A B G S O A B G S O A B
S I U   P S I U   P S I U   P S I
  G O U I   G O U I   G O U I   G
  U U T A   U U T A   U U T A   U
A O S O S A O S O S A O S O S A O
M U   P   M U   P   M U   P   M U
B S U I   B S U I   B S U I   B S
I   T A A I   T A A I   T A A I
G U O S M G U O S M G U O S M G U
U T P   B U T P   B U T P   B U T
O O I   I O O I   I O O I   I O O

Tom Holert

Surrealism's Peripheries

> The German observer is not standing at the source of the stream. This is his opportunity. He is in the valley. He can gauge the energies of the movement. As a German he has long been acquainted with the crisis of the intelligentsia, or, more precisely, with that of the humanistic concept of freedom; and he knows how frantically determined the movement has become to go beyond the stage of eternal discussion and, at any price, to reach a decision; he has had direct experience of its highly exposed position between an anarchistic Fronde and a revolutionary discipline, and so has no excuse for taking the movement for the "artistic," "poetic" one it superficially appears.[1]

Thus, at the outset of his 1929 essay on Surrealism, subtitled "The Last Snapshot of the European Intelligentsia" and published in the journal *Die Literarische Welt*, the *world* of literature, Walter Benjamin situated himself as a "German" dwelling at the geographical and cultural edge of the French Surrealist movement and therefore at the receiving end of the creative energies it produces. Drawing on the topographical metaphors of stream, source, and valley, Benjamin conjures an image of the avant-garde movement's temporality, or rather speed, the perception of which is determined by the beholder's excentric position. For Benjamin, the German experience of the years after the end of World War I, the disillusionment with the intellectual and political developments since 1918, provides the necessary distance from which Surrealism's urgency and decisionism could be appreciated.

Benjamin's topology of Surrealism may have also been motivated by the fact that this literary and artistic movement has been committed to a reconsideration of the political and cultural geography of its times. Based on an aesthetics, epistemology, and methodology that were organized around figures such as *defiguring*, *defacing*, and *debasement*, the critical modality of *de-centering* likewise featured in Surrealism's portfolio of strategies. Amid its spectrum of criticalities, deconstructions, aggressions and auto-aggressions, the questioning of any geopolitical consensus was of key importance to Surrealist discourses around ways of world-making and world-undoing, and particularly for the ways in which colonialist-capitalist center-periphery relations were to be unsettled, revolutionized, undone.

One of the icons of Surrealism's de-centering impulse is *The World in the Times of the Surrealists*, a map that was originally published in a June 1929 special issue of the Brussels-based illustrated journal *Variétés*, guest-edited by André Breton and Louis Aragon.

The theme of the issue was *Le Surréalisme en 1929* and the map was obviously inserted to represent the world as conceived by the Surrealists at that very moment in history. Probably drawn by the painter Yves Tanguy, but as likely based on an idea developed collectively, the fold-out world map nonchalantly does away with geographic objectivity, showing several missing countries and a wandering equator. The United States, Japan and all European countries west of Germany and Austria have vanished, while many Pacific territories have been enlarged considerably. As Jacqueline Chénieux-Gendron and Andrew Eastman point out, "What this map shows—one could even pencil them in—are the multiple circulatory movements between countries and continents that Surrealism promoted and supported, making emigration a magnetic attraction, a voyage of initiation, or the reverse."[2] What's more, this map could be considered "a snapshot of the Surrealist movement's anti-imperialist and anti-fascist ideals in 1929."[3]

According to David R. Roediger, the Surrealists' world map could be read as a collective, affirmative response to poet Paul Valéry's question, in his "The Crisis of the European Mind" (1919), whether Europe "will become what it is in reality?—that is to say, a little tip of the continent of Asia."[4] The imagined map visually shrinks Western Europe and the United States down to what the Surrealists saw as a more appropriate size, taken from the perspective of countries that have not yet been spoiled by western imperialism. Through the removal of all overly industrialized, capitalistic, and mechanized countries, a sort of "human scale" is regained.[5]

Roediger thus interprets the 1929 Surrealist map as an early attempt to identify Eurocentrism as a problem and, conversely, to project a nonwhite counter-mapping. The Surrealists' cartography encouraged and even cultivated idiosyncrasy and inconsistency, galvanizing "the active imagination of new worlds."[6] The issue of the journal *Variétés* in which the Surrealist world map was published (with the originator's name replaced by "XXX" in the table of contents) supported such active imagination of new worlds through hinting at a "nouvelle géographie élémentaire," as in Paul Nougé's article of the same title, or through invocations of a non-European "art sauvage," as in an article by Paul Éluard in the same issue.

Paul Nougé was a Belgian Surrealist and frequent collaborator of René Magritte. The text "Nouvelle Géographie Élémentaire," however, is not by Nougé himself. Instead, Nougé here presents a manuscript found in the personal archive of Clarisse Juranville, a nineteenth-century educator and author of numerous books on the moral upbringing of young girls, as well as of introductions into botany and literature. Nougé and Magritte were instrumental in promoting Juranville to become one of the most worshipped writers and artists in the Surrealist pantheon. Nougé introduces the presentation of the short text by calling it, in the preface, a "Traité de géographie" for children and grown-ups, which Juranville did not finish in her lifetime.[7] However, judging from the text that Nougé may have revised to his liking, Juranville was interested in a geography of the small scale, the immediate environment, the phenomenological experience of the world as simple yet fluid, encouraging her readers to admit the ephemeral and malleable nature of geography: "Vous êtes partout sans être nulle part," you are everywhere but nowhere.[8]

Combining a radical revision of imperialist cartography with such attention to the existential geography of the wandering mind and embodied experiences in the *Variétés* issue can be considered as programmatic for the Surrealist project of de-centering contemporary geopolitics mentioned before. However, this enterprise of de-centering, taken in a more general sense, was of course not free of certain biases of patriarchy, sexism, primitivism, etc. The Surrealists regularly failed to act as the radical intellectuals they flattered themselves to be, and they more than once failed to meet their self-image as radical destroyers of bourgeois-capitalist binarisms and hierarchies. This failure became particularly palpable in moments of performances of humility and blindness, as demonstrated by an infamous 1929 collage showing sixteen male Surrealists in photographs made in a mechanical photo-booth, surrounding the image of a female nude: Breton, a part-time collagist, assembled the leading Surrealist men on the border of a reproduction of a painting by René Magritte, quite literally on this image's *parergon*/periphery, to watch, with their eyes closed, over the mystery of femininity and language.

Jacques Lacan's later, much disputed theory of "woman as lack" is preemptively staged here in one of the more infamous self-portraits of the group, whose members pose at the margins, as "marginal," while celebrating the image of the woman as word, as that which cannot and, arguably, need not be seen.

It took a while, 56 years, until feminist art historian Whitney Chadwick reversed the logic of Breton's 1929 photomontage on the back cover of her 1985 *Women Artists and the Surrealist Movement*.

Here, leading surrealist women artists such as Frida Kahlo, Leonor Fini, Valentine Hugo, Leonora Carrington, Eileen Agar, Alice Rahon-Paalen, Remedios Varo, Susch Eluard, Rita Kernn-Larsen, Kay Sage, Jacqueline Breton, and Lee Miller are grouped around a black field filled with endorsements of the book by women art historians (such as Lucy Lippard, Linda Nochlin and Ann Sutherland Harris). It is a feminist counter-pantheon of Surrealism, introducing a reversed and revising gaze on the movement's history and its canonizing logic and effects.

Chadwick's selection of women Surrealist artists and poets, certainly incomplete, also pointed—if indirectly—to other kinds of marginality, as well as to the intersectionality of gender, race and geopolitical location. For instance, the geographical peripheralism of Surrealism may be seen as represented by numerous artists not originally from France, and of whom at least three, the Mexican artists Frida Kalho and Remedios Varo, and the Argentinian/Italian painter Leonor Fini, were working from non- (or rather para-)European backgrounds.

For some time now, the "surréalisme péripherique" has become the subject of art historiographical revisions. Surrealism, the most influential avant-garde movement in the visual arts and literature in the 1930s, was highly successful in opening branches and outposts, in forming alliances with avant-garde artists, writers and groups outside of Paris, outside of France, outside of Europe. Postcolonial takes on this story of global success, however, have stressed the necessity "to treat Surrealism as an international discursive field that was shaped as much by artists from the [global south] as by artists from Europe."[9] Such a view, it is argued, "disallows the erroneous assumption that Surrealism was 'essentially' a 'European' language somehow 'imposed' on easily manipulated Third World artists."[10]

It is not possible to go into any detail here of how surrealist poetics and aesthetics were being appropriated and transformed in contexts of literary and visual production outside of Paris and outside Europe. However, the remaining part of this essay will attend to the repercussions of Surrealism in Taiwan and Japan during the 1930s. Taipei-based director Huang Ya-Li's 2015 essay film *Le Moulin* extensively, extravagantly and effectively charts the characteristic mix of tensions, attractions, fascinations and partial repulsions with regard to Paris Surrealism in the Windmills Poetry Society's circle in Taiwan.

The self-confidence of those on the assumed receiving end of the avant-gardist streaming of ideas and images cannot be underestimated. Already in 1924, the year of the publication of Breton's *First Surrealist Manifesto*, 22-year-old Japanese poet Kitasono Katsue introduced the poetry of Breton, Aragon, and Éluard to Japanese audiences in the magazine *Bungei tanbi* (Literary Aesthetics). Three years later, Kitasono, Ueda Toshio, and Ueda Tamotsu wrote *A Note—December 1927*, acknowledging their indebtedness to Surrealism's practice of a deranging of the senses.[11]

Originally, Kitasono Katsue wanted to become a painter. However, after a literary friendship and time spent in Tokyo, broiling with new ideas and a cosmopolitan lifestyle, inspired by Hirato Renkichi's 1921 Japanese Futurist manifesto, Kitasono decided to become a poet. As Eric Selland recounts, by 1924, Kitasono had become involved with a group of fellow poets who published Japan's first Dadaist magazine, *Ge.Gjmgjgam.Prrr.Gjmgem* which marked the beginning of a long-term involvement with experimental, iconoclastic creation; of particular importance was the magazine's introduction of the usage of katakana words in poetry, combined with the deployment of foreign words and images that appeared both in katakana script and the alphabet.[12] Kitasono's Surrealist poems were collected in his 1929 anthology *Shiro no Arubamu (White Album)*. After the publication of his poems,he became instrumental in running the experimental VOU club, a poet's collective through which he channeled his theory of "ideoplasty," which later became supported by Ezra Pound who eagerly promoted Kitasono and VOU in Europe and the United States, connecting "ideoplasty" with his own theory of the ideogram in his 1938 *Guide to Kulchur*.

In the 1929 *White Album*, Kitasono also inserted diagrammatic poems such as *Legend of the Airship* and *Plastic Surgery Operation*.[13] They are reminiscent of the ideograms of Guillaume Apollinaire and other early concrete poets as well as of the diagrams of Marcel Duchamp and Francis Picabia, but they also seem to have a distinct quality of their own. "Semiotic Theory," likewise included in *White Album* (and translated into English by John Salt), is an extended, dandyish meditation on whiteness as *decoloring*, and arguably a reflection on the pressures inflicted upon Japanese culture by Western modernism's rule of whiteness. In another reading, the poem might as well celebrate an art deco lifestyle as the epitome of late 1920s contemporaneousness, with the "I," the "self," and the "decolorized boy" somewhat hovering in a hyperreal void.

[…]
*
silver cubist doll
silver cubist doll
flower and mirror
statics

*
white architecture
far suburban sky
far

*

sky
sea
rooftop garden
cigarette smoking boy, decolorized boy
alone
space

*
magic-making noblelady's magic-making silver boy
magic-making noblelady's magic-making silver boy
reflected in red mirror
reflected in red mirror
white hands and eyebrows and flowers
I
space

[…]

decolorized boy
distant sky
hyacinth
window
white landscape

*
it is happy lifestyle and me
it is happy ideas and me
it is transparent pleasures and me
it is transparent manners and me
it is fresh appetite and me
it is fresh love and me
memories of blue past
all dumped in ink bottle

*
mechanics is dark
plants are heavy

*

white tableware
bouquet and book of poems
white
white
yellow

*
white residence
white
pink noblelady
white distant view
blue sky

*
trumpet aristocrats all wear red bandannas

*
evening formalwear
evening formalwear
evening formalwear
evening formalwear
evening formalwear
boring

Interestingly, by considering the subjects of fashion, textures and colors featuring so prominently in "Semiotic Theory," Kitasano, like other Japanese surrealists, was to be criticized by fellow poets. He was accused of wearing Surrealism like a dress, surrendering to a reactionary lightness and weakness, while merely covering or camouflaging a dependency on the oldest traditions of Japanese poetry.[14] Miyoshi Jūrō, a poet publishing in the *Waseda* literary magazine, as well as a writer of proletarian plays and film scripts, was very direct in his repudiation of Kitasano's artificialist poetry:

How is Surrealism being translated against itself in Japan? How it is being mistranslated? And furthermore, how will those reactionary poets, those

> highbrow poets, skillfully redesign the camouflage clothing of this mistranslated Surrealism, this Surrealism translated against itself, remaking it in the Japanese style, then hiding themselves stylishly behind it? … What kind of meaning does this have for society? … I will merely say here how disgusting and how intolerable it is to see you Japanese Surrealists wear this stylish camouflage of Surrealism that hides the truth.[15]

Criticism of Surrealism and Surrealist attitudes and stylistics as being too entrenched in bourgeois aesthetics, and too invested in the interests of the consumerist capitalist self, to be able to become the revolutionary force it aspires to be, is a common feature of left-wing dismissals of the movement. But such criticism may have different, specific functions, meanings, and undertones in non-European contexts. Miryam Sas, in her history of Japanese Surrealist poetry, emphasizes the Japanese reading of Western Surrealism as a specific misreading, a substitution, a "misprision."[16] Majella Munro, in a recent account of Japanese interwar Surrealist visual art, clarifies, partly based on reports in secret police files, that Surrealism was probably less dismissed as decadent than as a subversive artistic element of communism.[17] It therefore remains important to attend to the relations being established to Western art and ideas on both sides of the pro- and anti-Surrealist divide in places like Japan in the late 1920s and early 1930s.

As art historian Chinghsin Wu emphasizes, by the time surrealism arrived in Japan in the 1920s, Japanese artists had already established a solid knowledge of the European avant-garde, on the basis of which some were interested in producing art in the Surrealist vein, in a double movement of assimilation and distinction from Western Surrealism:

> An important aspect of the commensurability of Japanese, and later Chinese, surrealism was the pervasive conviction that not only could Asian artists produce surrealism that measured up to the highest standards of Western theorists, but that Asians could produce a surrealism that was superior to or surpassed that of Westerners.

Interestingly however, the distinctions drawn by Asian surrealist artists and theorists, and in some cases their claims of superiority, for the most part were not predicated on racial or cultural distinctions or ideas of national uniqueness. Rather, even the distinctions that Japanese and Chinese artists claimed for themselves were characterized within a fully commensurate lexicon of modernist scientism and rationality.[18]

Painters such as Abe Kongō, Tōgō Seiji, and Koga Harue self-confidently displayed such distinctiveness, staying firmly within the modernist paradigm. They seem to have looked for a standpoint of their own whilst refusing to turn to an idea of tradition drawing on national or ethnic heritage. At the same time, Surrealism as a style and a method met resistance from critics such as Miyoshi, the sociologist Ueda Toshio or the painter Kambara Tai, the latter a card-carrying member of international Futurism in the 1920s who, like many other young Japanese artists, later associated himself with the proletarian movement and abandoned his previous avant-garde practice. Surrealism, considered to be stressing the inner life of dreams and fantasy rather than looking for the reality of economic and social struggle, was accused of escapism, hence everyone tried to get some distance from it.[19]

Moreover, the particular European avant-gardism and anti-bourgeois affect of Surrealism may have been lost on Japanese artists and poets, for reasons linked to the constant and frantic ruptures in Japanese society since the Meji Restoration in the nineteenth century, "with its deep impact on society and the arts." As Thomas Hackner argues: "In Japan, the historical avantgardes were not perceived as a fundamental rupture with a longstanding tradition or a fundamental paradigm shift, but as just another new trend. The 'rupture' if there was one, had been the Meji Restoration …"[20]

Returning to *Le Moulin*'s rendering of Taiwanese Surrealist poets such as Yang Chih-chang, Li Zhang-rui, Lin Xiu-er and Zhang Liang-dian—who searched for a way to foster an aesthetics of pure art while also struggling to establish a new tradition of Taiwanese literature and poetry in the face of Japan's political and cultural colonialism—, it would be interesting to ask to what extent Surrealist aesthetics were suitable for the support of an anti-colonial agenda and minor cosmopolitan counter-realities.

If considered as less of a rupture than a trend in the Japanese context of the 1920s and 1930s, how might references to and affiliations with European Surrealism have worked differently in Taiwan in that period? Could the colonized Taiwanese poet make different use of the Western avant-garde than a member of the Japanese literary world? To what extent did Surrealism's twisted centre/periphery topology (as embodied in the 1929 surrealist world map) become even more twisted in the complex geopolitical centre-peripheries that unfolded between Japan and Taiwan?

The author of these lines neither disposes of the knowledge nor the linguistic means to contribute any substantial answer to these questions. Writing at the periphery of the East Asian histories of modernist literature and art as well as outside of the disciplines that attend to these histories within Western academia, I am all but entitled to claim any particular insight into the "misprision" (Myriam Sas) or "synthetic indigenization" (Majella Munro) of Western Surrealism in the respective contexts of Japanese and Taiwanese art worlds of the 1920s and 1930s. The reason for nevertheless feeling impelled to attend to these highly situated histories of exchange, translation, emulation, assimilation, and appropriation at all, is entirely owed to the experience of watching Huang Ya-Li's *Le Moulin* a few months after the closing of an exhibition that I had co-curated (*Neolithic Childhood. Art in a False Present*, c. 1930, at HKW, Berlin). The latter project was marked, due to the way it was conceptualized, by a significant lack of references to the resonances and repercussions of European interwar avant-garde art and theory in East Asia. The desire to close the gap of knowledge and first-hand experiences of Taiwanese and Japanese Surrealist poetry and painting was spurred by Zairong Xiang's contribution on "transdualism" to the exhibition's conference and publication and his subsequent invitation to participate in the 2018 *minor cosmopolitan weekend*. Rather than relegating them to this text's periphery, the endnotes, I am including these remarks here, as I intend to underscore the always already fragile position of someone standing in the "valley" (to recall the peripheral vantage point that Walter Benjamin deliberately inhabited in the late 1920s, as the appropriate place from which to engage with the creative energies originating in Paris Surrealism). Huang Ya-Li's speculative meditation on the historical possibilities and impossibilities of developing an independent avant-garde voice in colonial Taiwan in the 1920s and 1930s, by the members of the Tainan-based group that called itself "Le Moulin," provided me with the kind of incentive to dwell on the periphery of a provincialized Europe—if for the sole purpose of humbly working towards establishing a personal, episodic relationship to the histories of artistic and anti-colonial struggles and apathies unfolded in *Le Moulin*.

1 Walter Benjamin, "Surrealism. The Last Snapshot of the European Intelligentsia," in *Selected Writings. Volume 2, Part 1 1927–1930*, trans. Rodney Livingstone et al., eds., Michael W. Jennings, Howard Eiland, and Gary Smith (Cambridge, MA: The Belknap Press of the Harvard University Press, 1999), 207.

2 Jacqueline Chénieux-Gendron and Andrew Eastman, "Surrealists in Exile: Another Kind of Resistance," *Poetics Today* 17, no. 3 [Creativity and Exile: European/American Perspectives I] (Autumn 1996): 437-451, here 438. Specifically, Chénieux-Gendron and Eastman mention Paul Éluard's and Jacques Viot's trip around the world in the 1920s, the 1927 voyage from Yugoslavia to Paris by Marko Ristic, Jacques Herold who, in 1930, travelled from Romania to Paris, Enrico Donati's trip to New York in the late 1930s, similar to Marcel Duchamp's travelling back and forth between New York and Paris since 1915, Michel Leiris' participation in the ethnological Paris-Dakar expedition in 1933, or the trips artists such as Kurt Seligmann and Wolfgang Paalen made after 1939 to the regions inhabited by First Nation peoples, as well as the various wanderings of Leonora Carrington, which led from Great Britain to Mexico, passing through France, Spain, the United States.

3 Kae Yamane, *The Map as Muse. Exploring the World of Artists' Maps* (Department of Geography, School of Arts and Sciences, Rutgers University 2013).

4 See David R. Roediger, "Plotting against Eurocentrism: The 1929 Surrealist Map of the World," in *Colored White: Transcending the Racial Past* (Berkeley: University of California Press, 2002), 171.

5 Roediger, "Plotting," 173.

6 Roediger, "Plotting," 173.

7 See Paul Nougé [and Clarisse Juranville], "Nouvelle Géographie Élémentaire," *Variétés. Revue mensuel illustré de l'esprit contemporain,* numéro hors série et hors abonnement [Le Surréalisme en 1929] (1929): 16-17.

8 Nougé [and Juranville], "Nouvelle Géographie," 16.

9 Susanne Baackmann and David Craven, "Surrealism and Post-Colonial Latin America. Introduction," *Journal of Surrealism and the Americas* 3, no. 1–2 (2009): i-xvii.

10 Baackmann and Craven, "Surrealism."

11 See Chinghsin Wu, "Reality Within and Without: Surrealism in Japan and China in the Early 1930s," *Review of Japanese Culture and Society* 26 (December 2014): 190.

12 Eric Selland, "Book Review: Shredding the Tapestry of Meaning—The Poetry and Poetics of Kitasono Katue (1901-1978), by John Solt," *The New Modernism. Japanese Modernist & Avant-Garde Poetry, Translations, Explorations*, https://ericselland.wordpress.com/2010/04/02/book-review-shredding-the-tapestry-of-meaning-the-poetry-and-poetics-of-kitasono-katue-1901-1978-by-john-solt/.

13 See samples of the diagrammatic poems here, https://www.thing.net/~grist/ld/japan/DIAGRAMS.HTM

14 See Miryam Sas, *Fault Lines. Cultural Memory and Japanese Surrealism* (Palo Alto: Stanford University Press, 1999), 64-65.

15 Miyoshi Jūrō, "Chōgenjitsushugi nado [Surrealism, etc.]," c. 1935, cit. Sas, *Fault Lines*, 64.

16 See Sas, *Fault Lines*, 38-41.

17 Majella Munro, *Communicating Vessels: The Surrealist Movement in Japan, 1923–70* (Cambridge: The Enzo Press, 2012); see also Michael Richardson, "Charting an Amorphous Past: Surrealism in Japan," *Art History* 37, no. 5 (November 2014): 998-1001.

18 Wu, "Reality Within and Without,"189-190.

19 See Wu, "Reality," 190.

20 Thomas Hackner, "Worlds Apart? The Japan-Europe Avant-Garde Relationship," *Decentring the Avant-Garde*, eds. Per Bäckström and Benedikt Hjartarson (Amsterdam: Rodopi, 2014), 211.

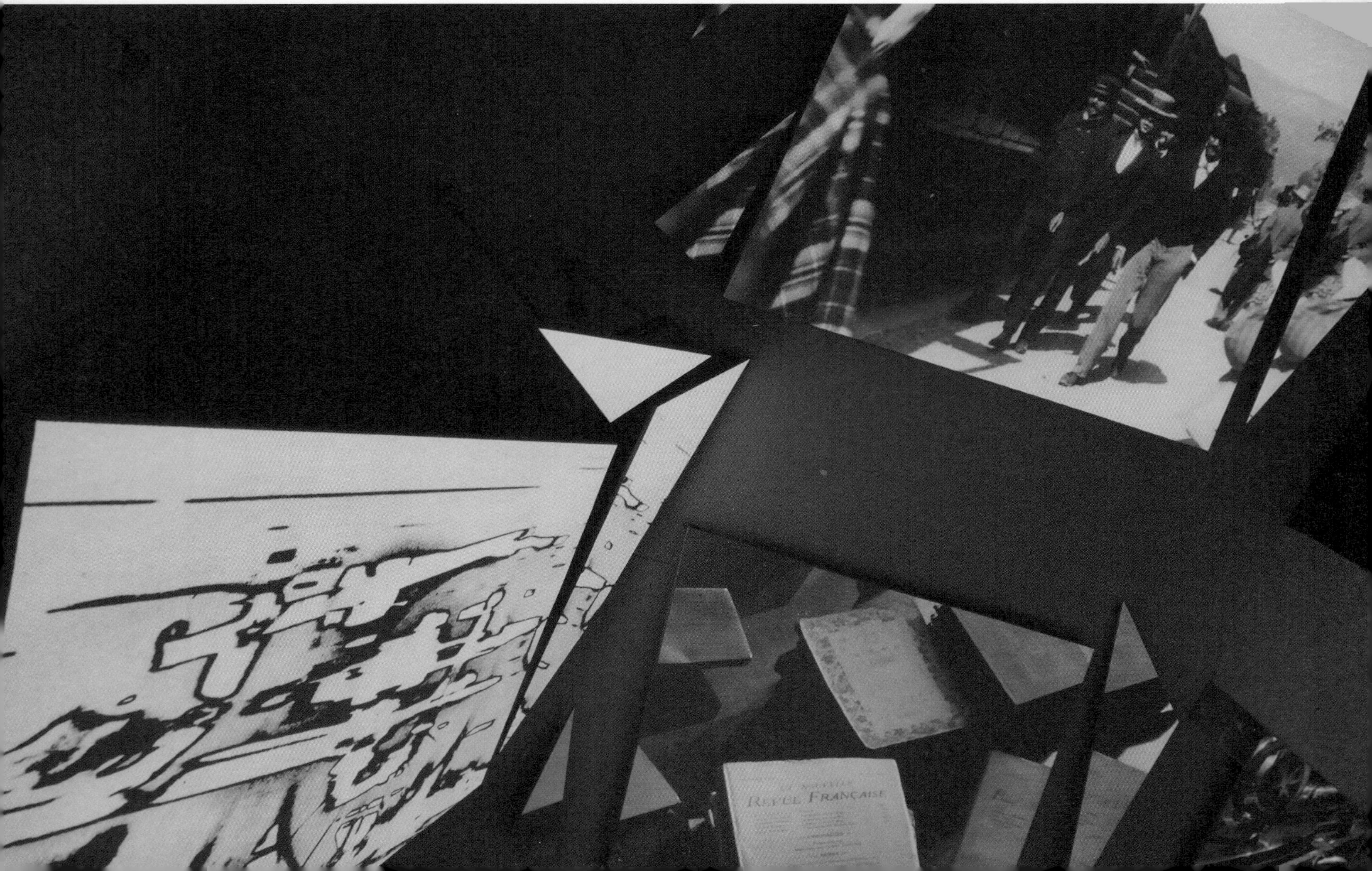

Projection of the film *Le Moulin* (Huang Ya-Li, 2016) and related film fragments in the section “Speed Drives the Future” at the exhibition *Synchronic Constellation*. Courtesy of Huang Ya-Li and Roots Films

For more information about the film and the exhibition, https://constellation.ntmofa.gov.tw/home/en-us

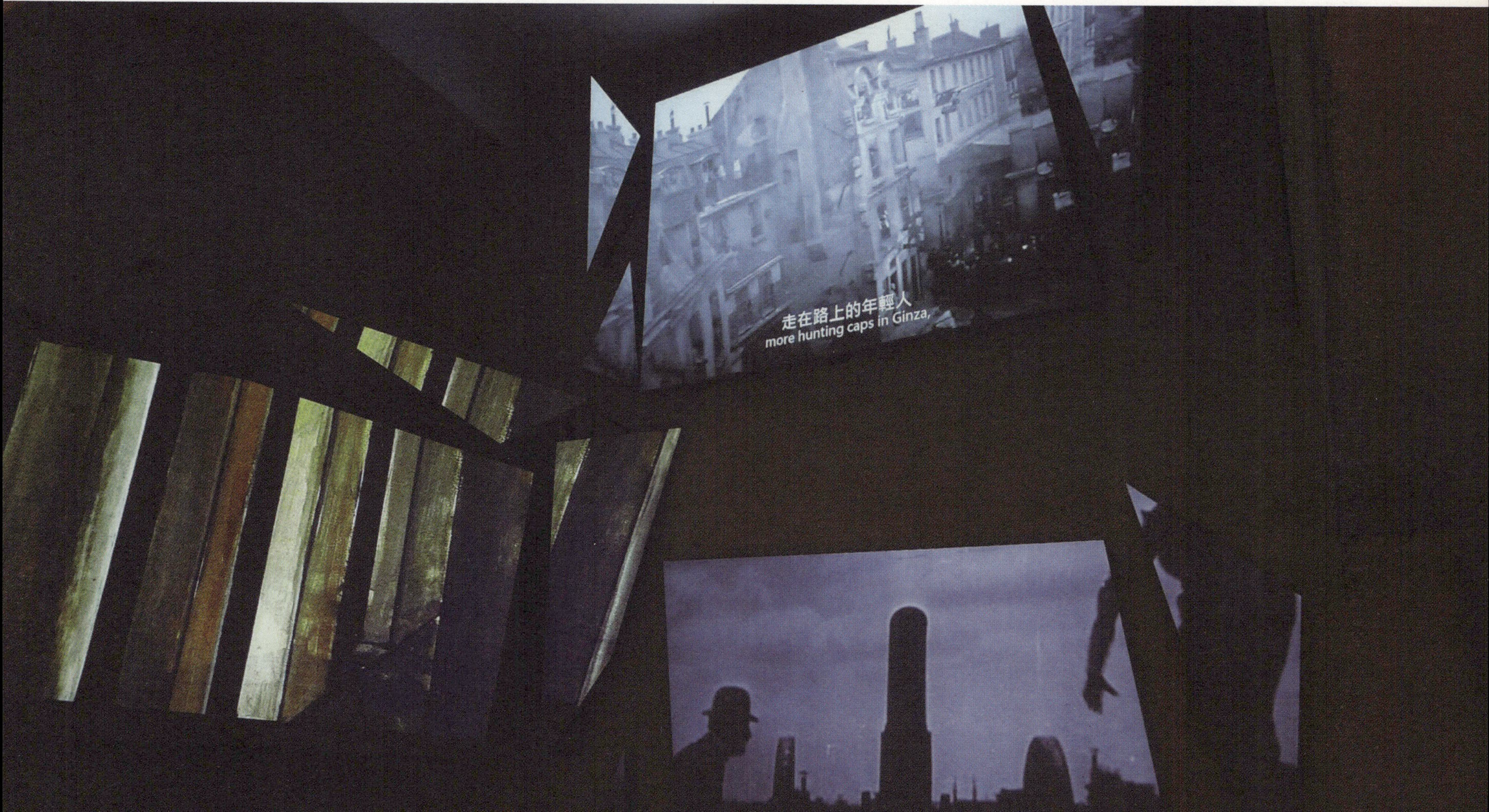

From the section "Emergence of Modern Art and Culture" of the exhibition. For more information about the objects pictured, visit https://constellation.ntmofa.gov.tw/home/en-us/Exhibition%20theme/13440.

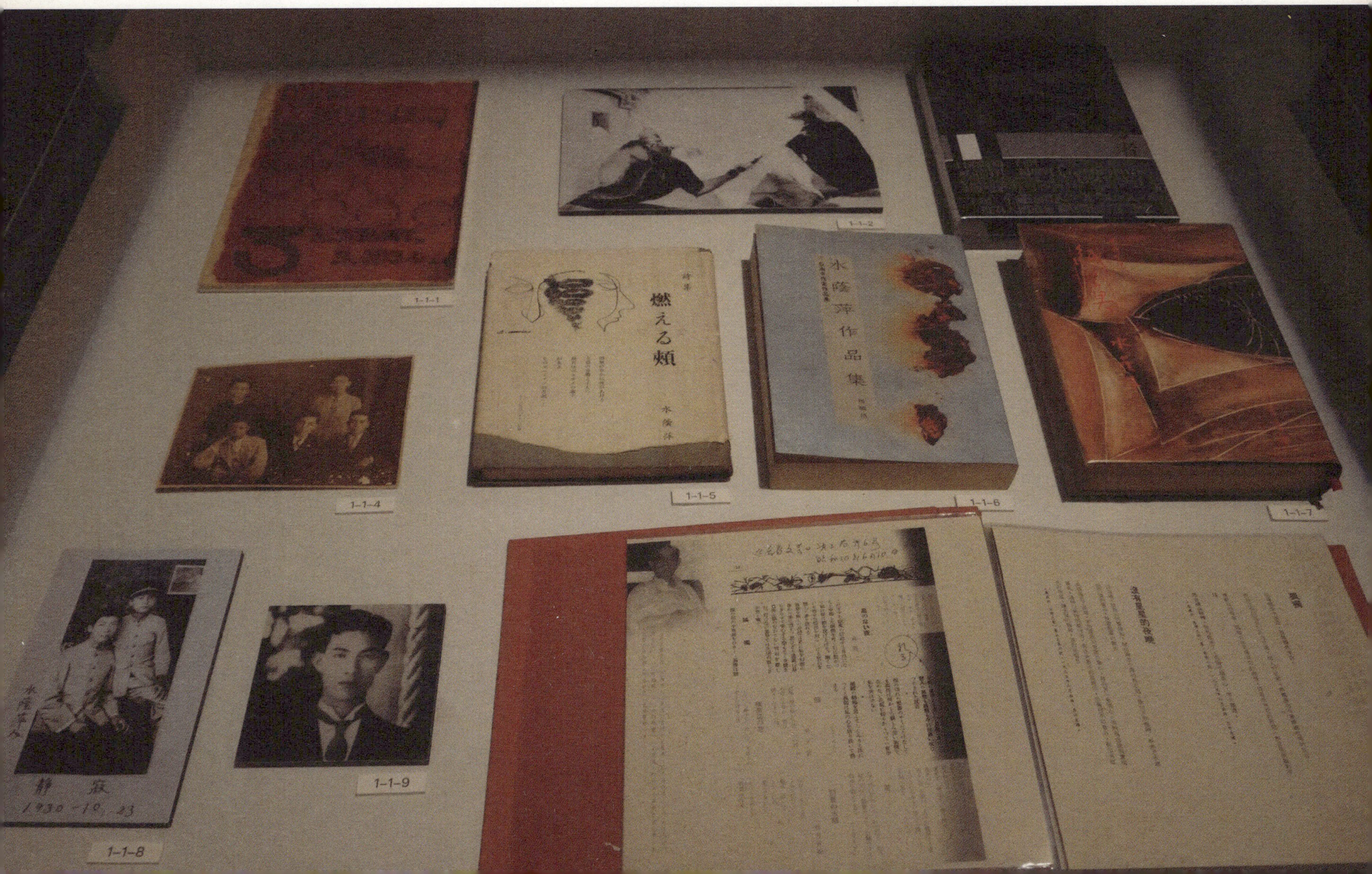

From the section "Emergence of Modern Art and Culture" of the exhibition. For more information about the objects pictured, visit https://constellation.ntmofa.gov.tw/home/en-us/Exhibition%20theme/13440.

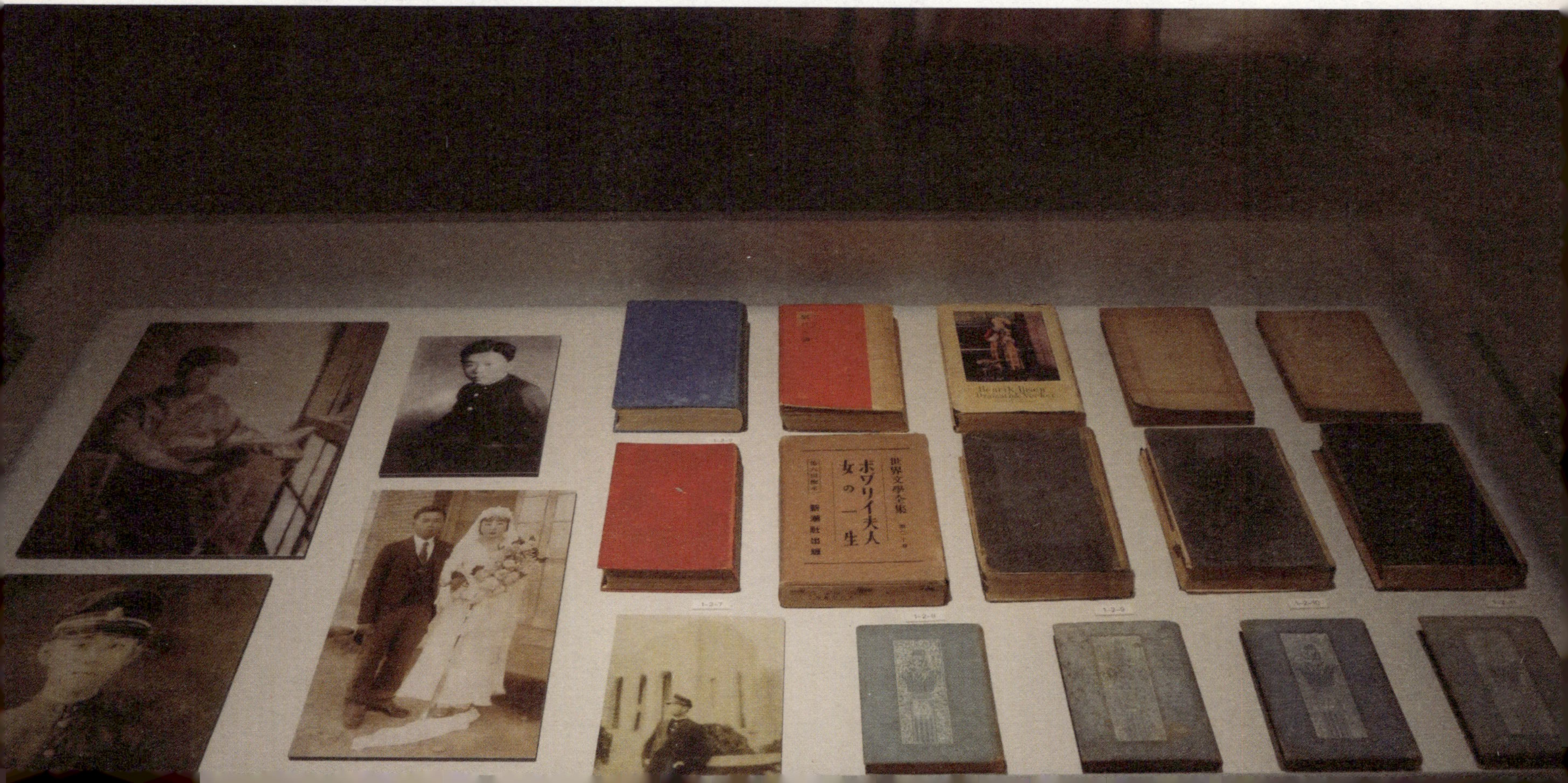

Curatorial Statement
Synchronic Constellation – Le Moulin Society and its Time: A Cross-Boundary Exhibition
29 June – 15 September 2019 at the National Taiwan Museum of Fine Arts

Curatorial Team: Huang Ya-Li, Sing Song-Yong, Iwaya Kunio

In the southern lands of Taiwan ninety years ago, a rare flower bloomed. Its name was "Le Moulin Poetry Society." Established in 1933, this poetry society was jointly founded by Japanese and Taiwanese poets, including Yang Chih-chang, Lin Hsui-erh, Li Chang-jui, Chang Liang-tien, Kisi Reiko, and Toda Fusako. In keeping with the new spirit, intellectualism, and lyricism of the time, modernist poetry was the focus of creativity, publication, and literary ideology. In the annals of Taiwanese literary history, the fate of this literary association born during the Japanese colonial era was meteoric, disappearing as quickly as it rose to prominence. At the end of the 1970s, Le Moulin Poetry Society reemerged on the horizons of Taiwanese literary history, igniting heated discussions regarding pre-war Taiwanese modernist literature. Le Moulin Poetry Society was the subject of the 2015 film, *Le Moulin*, which, on the one hand, posited it within the literary context of the Japanese colonial era and opened up connections to the global modernist trends and movements; and on the other hand, retraced precious fragments from the life experiences, cultural inspirations, and historical incidents encountered by the group of Taiwanese and Japanese poets.

Based on the background described above, the "Synchronic Constellation - Le Moulin Poetry Society and its Time: A Cross-Boundary Exhibition" hopes to further deepen and extend the wave roused by modernist literature and art culture in the Western world and in East Asian countries from the beginning of the 20th century to the 1940s with Le Moulin Poetry Society as a core; and from this, rethinks ways in which Taiwan's cultural workers in the colony formed relationships with Japan, China, Korea, Europe and America. At the same time, it contemplates key historical events and their effect on the lives and destinies of Taiwan's cultural and literary workers.

Le Moulin Poetry Society was at a spatio-temporal intersection, located in a star cluster of history, radiating shimmering light. With this as a center, it broke through linear space and time and moved outward to traverse the historical pulse of prewar and wartime literature, art, theater, photography, music, film, and other artistic paradigms, to detect and receive the electrical current emanating from the world.

"Emergence of Modern Art and Culture" originates in the cities of a new century and a modernist sensibility. "Meditations on Modernity: Translation and Creation" explores the dream chasing artists exploring the Eastern embrace of Western trends. "Speed Drives the Future" forges the truths of a mechanical Utopia. "Collective Response to Surrealism" is a down-to-earth avant-garde dialectic. "Civilization of Machines and Illusions in Art and Culture" constructs the cross-regional artistic practice of the new spiritual artist. "Literature – Anti-Colonial Voices" bears witness to the cultural resistance of the arts society movement. "The Dialectic of Art and Reality" contemplates the distance between aesthetics and politics. "Local Color and Exotic Imagination" is an exposition on the parallax between the local and the foreign realm. "War, politics, decision" describes painterly mirages of war. "A Long White Night" mourns the poet and the aphasia of historical remnants.

This interdisciplinary art exhibition does not only belong to history, but it belongs moreover to the contemporary. Le Moulin Poetry Society transcended the boundaries of art, moving from literature and film into the art museum. Here it encounters and dialogues with a cornucopia of exhibition objects from various artistic paradigms including original works, reproductions, audio-visual files, documents and texts, bringing the imagination to life in formats that combine new media technologies including sound effects, multimedia installations, and graphic design.

Above the stars, the windmill that symbolizes the poetry society seems like a flower, and dazzles like starlight when it spins. Shimmering, fascinating, and touching, it is an eye of history that ignites literary thought and ideological movements.

ONCHI KOSHIRO

Diving, 1933

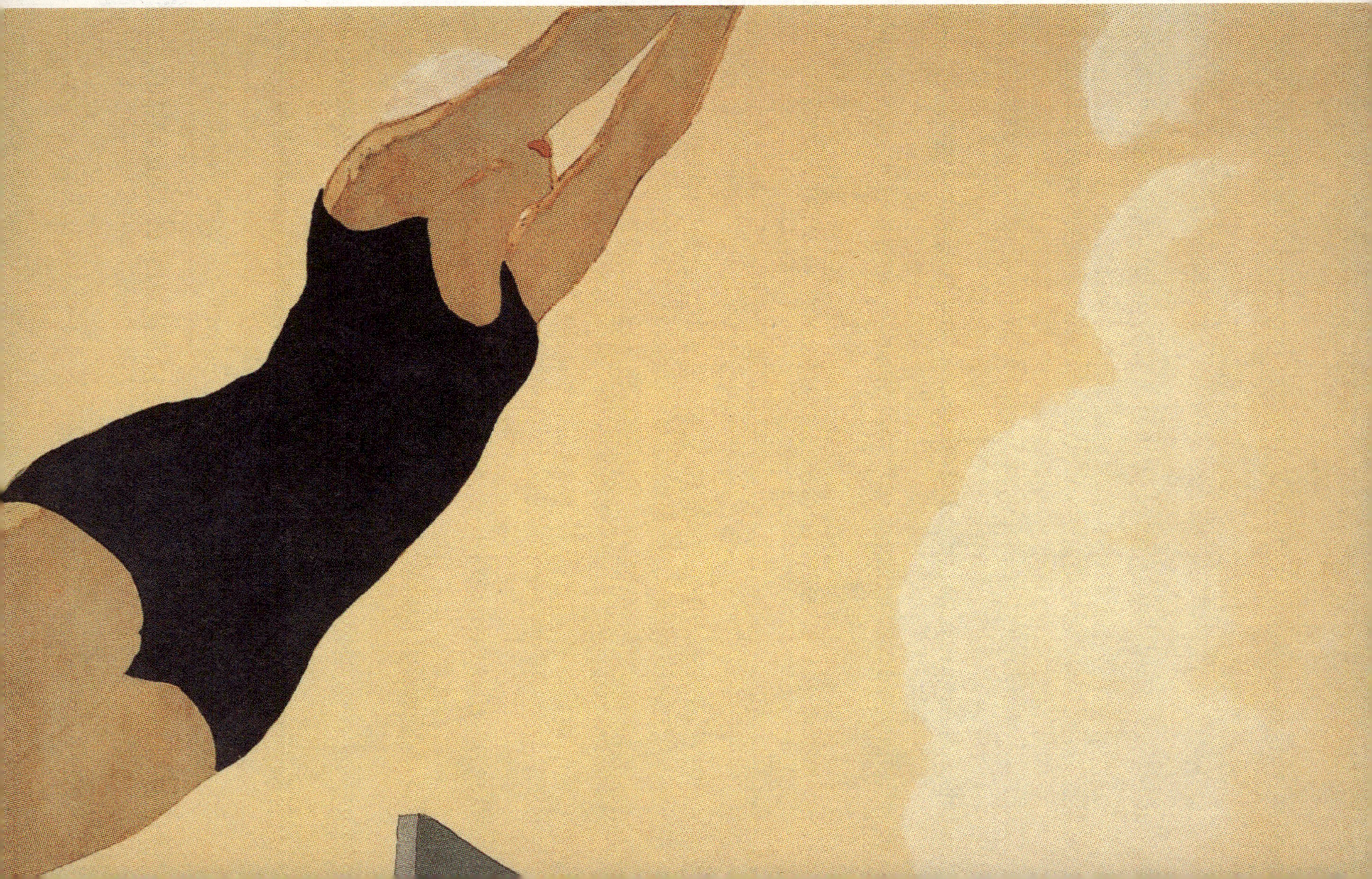

From the section "Meditations on Modernity: Translation and Creation" of the exhibition. For more information about the objects pictured, visit https://constellation.ntmofa.gov.tw/home/en-us/Exhibition%20theme/13439.

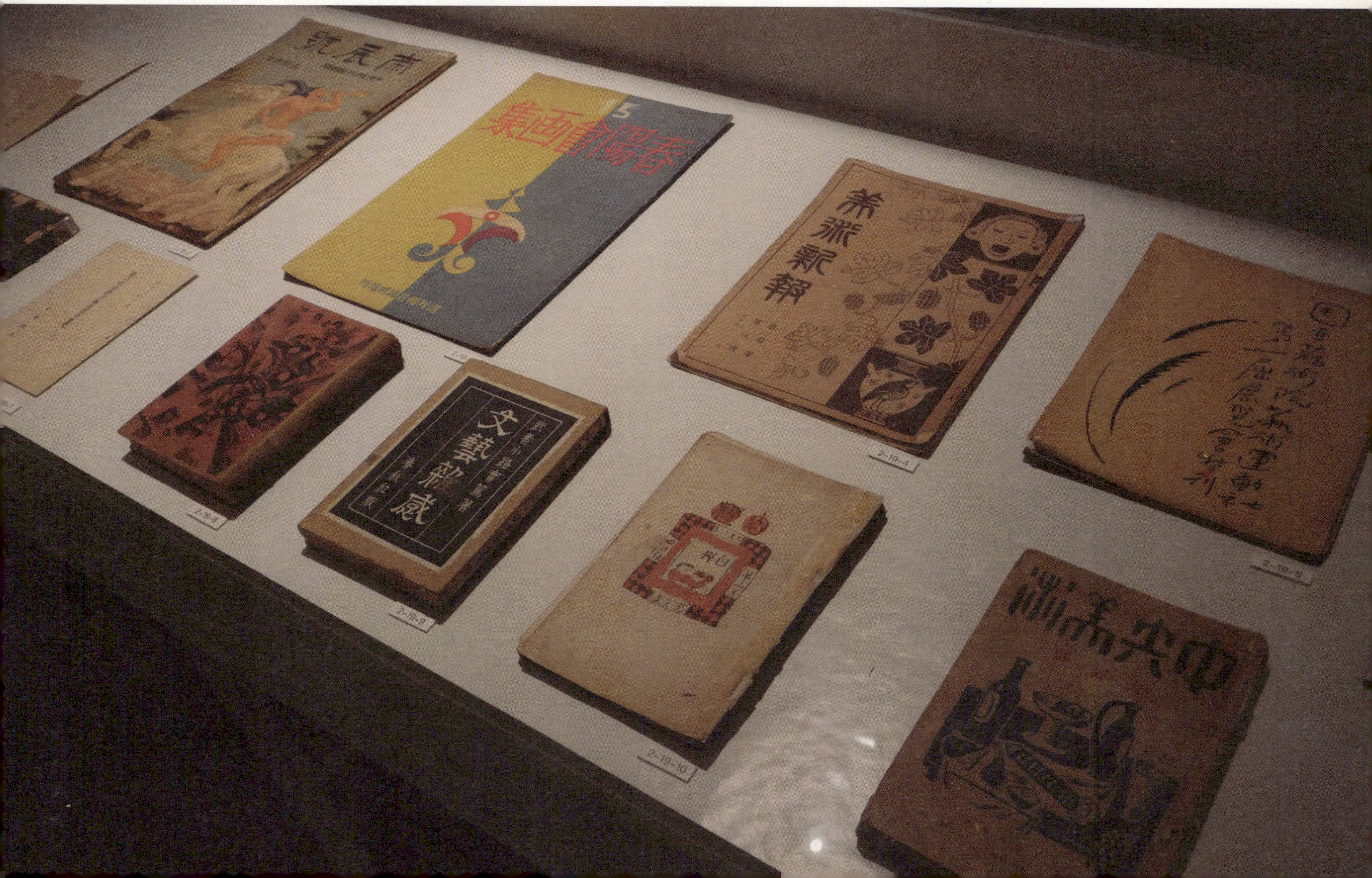

From the section "Meditations on Modernity: Translation and Creation" of the exhibition. For more information about the objects pictured, visit https://constellation.ntmofa.gov.tw/home/en-us/Exhibition%20theme/13439.

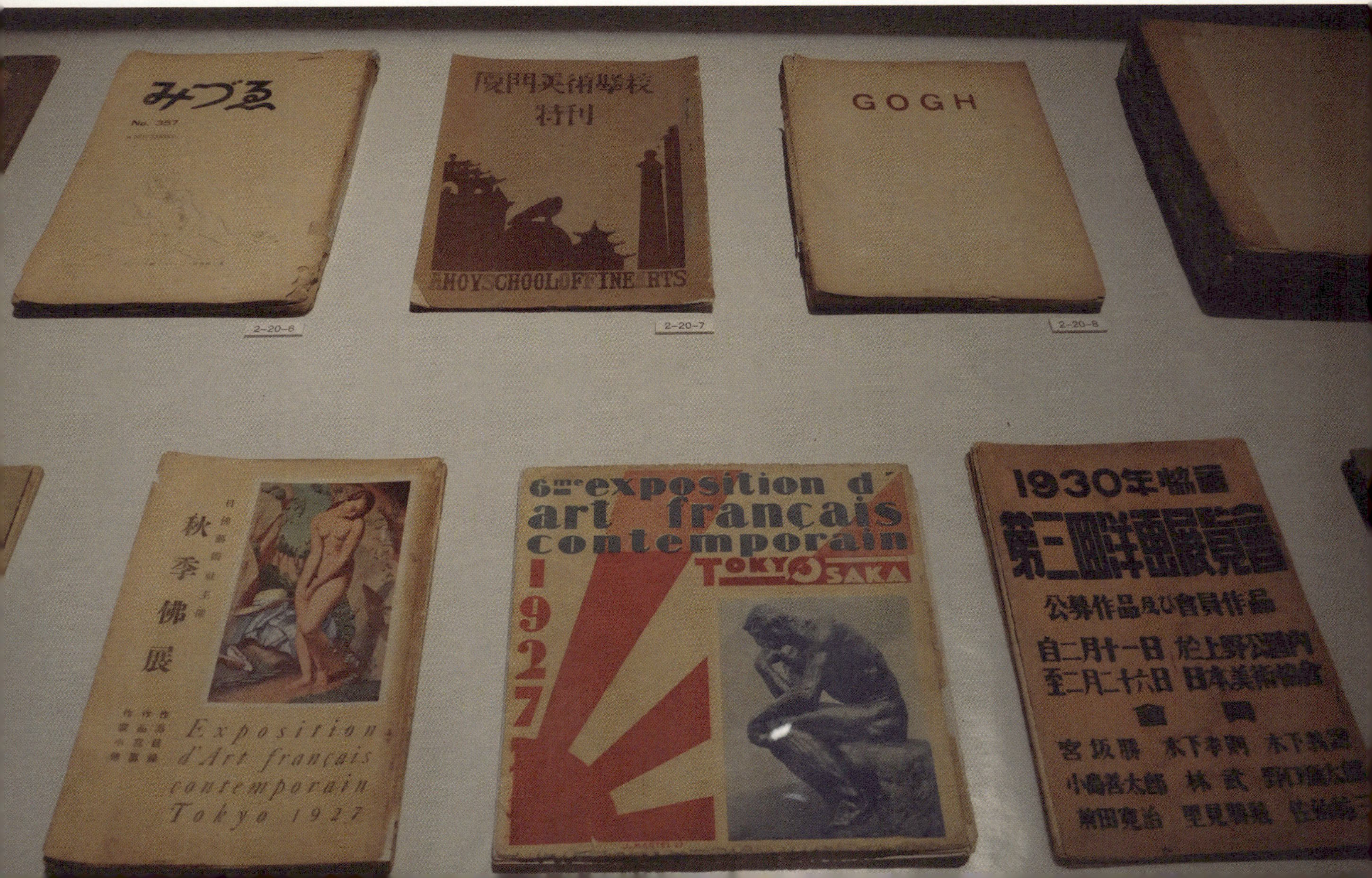

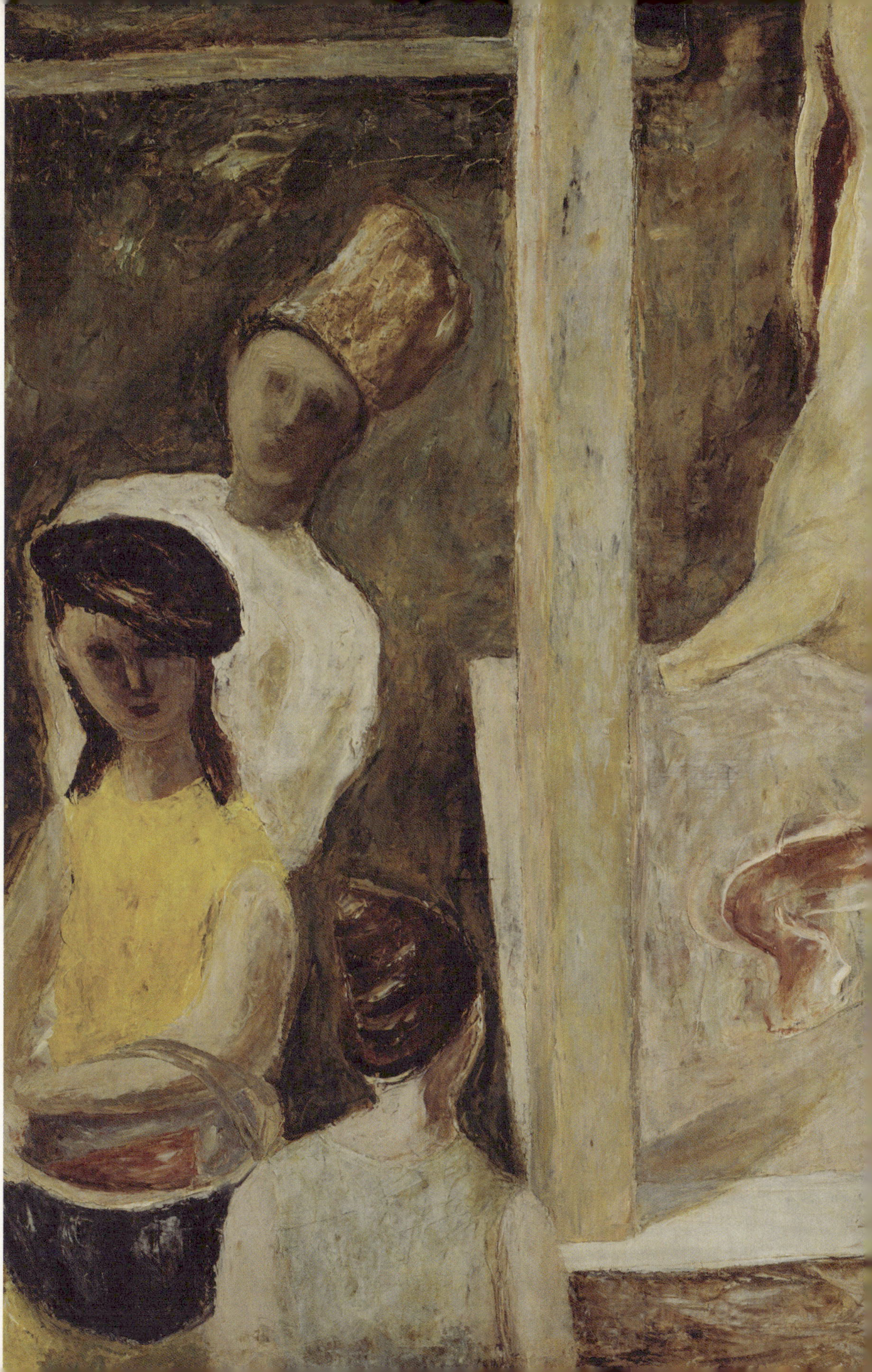

LIU CHI-HSIANG
Butcher Shop, 1938

NAKAYAMA IWATA

Butterfly, 1941

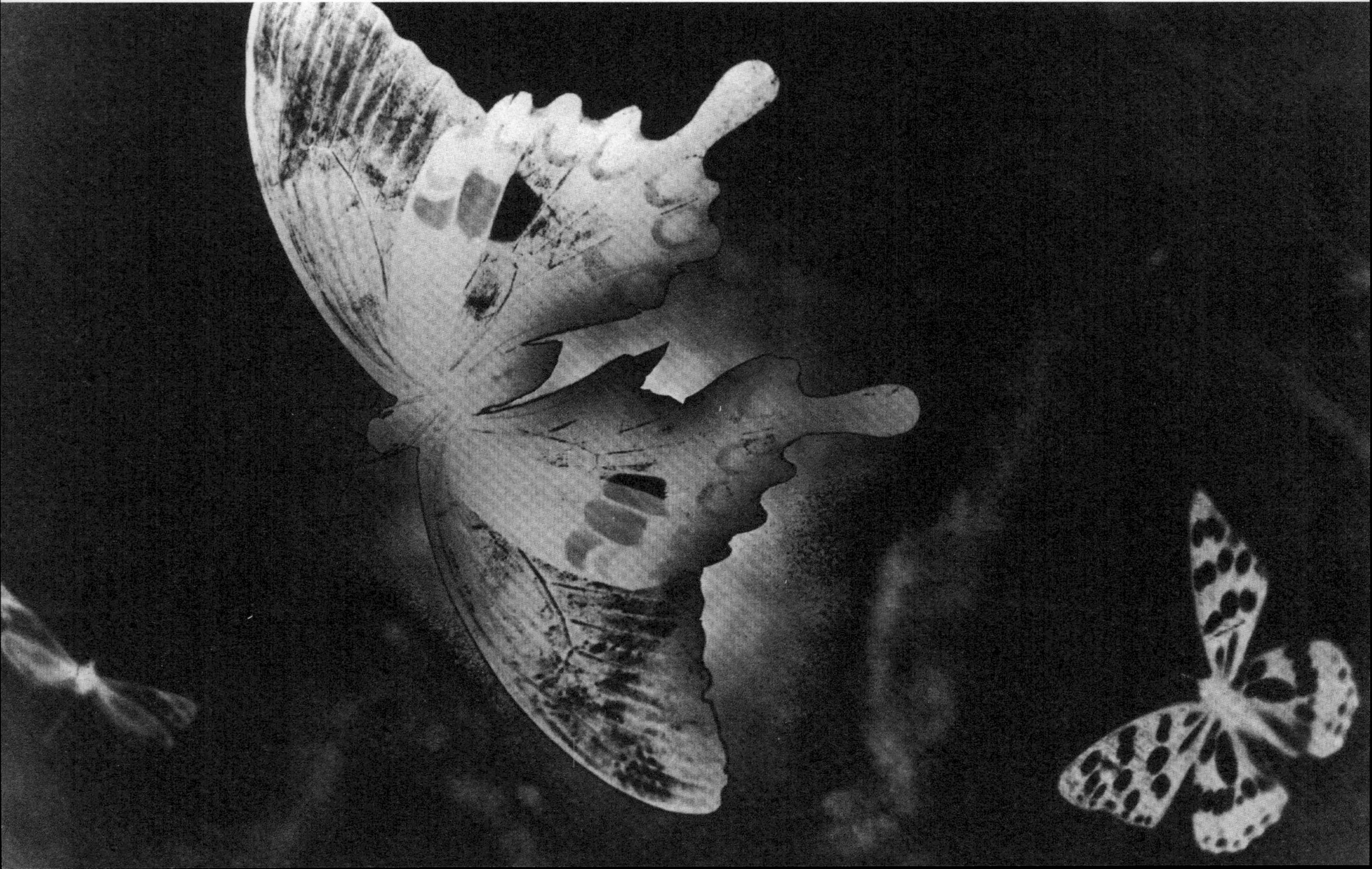

James Burton

Ambiguous Utopias: Science Fiction and Minor Cosmopolitanism

Part One: Ambiguous Utopias

The fact that numerous critics and cultural theorists have recognised the critical potential of science fiction (SF)[1] for exposing, challenging, and thinking beyond dominant hierarchies and structures of power would seem to recommend it to those interested in pursuing ideas and possibilities of minor cosmopolitanism(s).

For the purposes of this chapter, I take minor cosmopolitanism(s) to indicate projects, practices, and lines of thought that are critical of unethical exercises and unequal structures of power, particularly as these structures and activities are embedded within what could be conceived as "major"—e.g. normative, mainstream, institutionalised, governmental—conceptions of and approaches to cosmopolitanism. In this sense, minor cosmopolitanism(s) are likely to share with various other cosmopolitan perspectives some form of principled commitment to values such as openness, inclusivity, equality; yet the minor perspective will be attentive to ways in which these ideals or principles have been undermined in certain large-scale social, political, and cultural cosmopolitan projects and perspectives. Indeed, in many cases this will entail exposing the ways some such projects, in the name of cosmopolitanism and/or some of its associated values, have become indistinguishable from those larger power structures that these principles ought to challenge, such as coloniality, patriarchy, or various forms of cultural normativity. I will also, in Part Two of the chapter, develop a more specific notion of minor cosmopolitanism emphasising the local/small-scale, in relation to works of SF engaging with these concerns.

Where "cosmopolitanism" in the phrase "minor cosmopolitanism" implies a continuity with more familiar conceptions of cosmopolitanism, "minor" implies an opposition. Such a dynamic is likely to lead to a complex relationship to cosmopolitanism generally, in which various aspects of its established imaginaries, ideas, principles, and other resources may, at some points, prove useful to minor cosmopolitanism(s) and, at others, require subjecting to radical critique—whether simply to expose their destructive effects, or to retool/reimagine them for a minor cosmopolitics. This is seen, for example, in various postcolonial engagements with the term "cosmopolitanism" by thinkers such as Homi Bhabha, Paul Gilroy and Kwame Anthony Appiah.[2]

This condition is arguably similar to that of much critically-oriented SF. It depends and draws upon certain established elements of science fiction as a genre and body of past works, along with its defining tropes, while at the same time recognising and in some cases working through the imbrication of these tropes, images and ideas with various cultural-political structures of dominance and oppression.

Another way of describing/conceiving this shared ground between minor cosmopolitanism(s) and critical SF would be that each has a complex or ambiguous relationship to understandings and modes of utopianism that are part of its heritage, embedded within its contemporary form, yet which it must simultaneously treat with suspicion and subject to critique.

The recurrent, if not core, utopian element within various expressions of cosmopolitanism, can be identified in the fact that most aim at a "better" world, and on a scale (global if not cosmic) that transcends historically existing realities. Even where cosmopolitanism is taken as a more everyday outlook rather than a worked-out project or social model, it tends to be aspirational, looking towards a not-yet-existent reality in which all or most sentient beings would live according to a similar outlook.

Those sceptical of utopianism often find particular cause for concern in the grandness of its ambition and scale—and it is precisely these aspects that are most in need of critique and challenge in major historical cosmopolitan projects—, from the universalisation of a bourgeois Western European idea of human rights, to the instantiation of global institutions such as the United Nations, to countless projects of global economic "development." And yet, any minor cosmopolitanism that would identify such projects with a dangerous degree of grandeur, arrogance, and/or blindness to the detailed structures of social injustice, can be expected, more often than not, to remain in accord with a basic utopian principle of hope that a better world may be possible. In other words, it is not the idea of a world in which all people would be accorded the same rights, freedoms, opportunities, and conditions that is to be challenged, but the idea that a given self-proclaimed cosmopolitan or utopian project is actually interested in or capable of producing it.

If this ambiguous approach to utopianism is somewhat implicit in discourses and projects that take a critical interest in cosmopolitanism, it has tended to be explicit in discussions of the critical power of SF. This was certainly the case with the first wave of academic commentators on science fiction starting in the 1970s. At a time when utopia and utopianism were increasingly viewed with suspicion for their perceived neglect of the practicalities and messiness of socio-political and material reality, a number of Marxist thinkers found in certain writers of SF new utopian possibilities attuned, rather than oblivious, to such obstacles. Raymond Williams, for example, identified in certain (then) recent works of SF, especially those of Ursula K. Le Guin, "a general renewal of a form of utopian thinking."[3] Fredric Jameson identified SF's political importance in its capacity to expose the impoverishment of the utopian imagination in the late capitalist (post)modern era, while also giving rise to its renewal (even if largely by virtue of this exposition), in works by authors such as Le Guin, Samuel Delany and Philip K. Dick. He saw in SF "a structurally unique 'method' for apprehending the present as history," by which it was able to "body forth … the atrophy in our time of what Marcuse has called the utopian imagination, the imagination of otherness and radical difference."[4] Darko Suvin, meanwhile, situated certain types and works of SF within a long utopian tradition, but with a modern critical-theoretical force. Suvin influentially developed Ernst Bloch's concept of the "novum" as a critical term to indicate the key element in an SF narrative that causes a divergence from the reader's (and author's) implicit "norm of reality," seeing this as key not only to a work's aesthetic effects upon the reader, "but also to its ethico-liberating qualities, its communal relevance."[5]

The trait that these critical theorists were finding so valuable in (some) SF could be described as a treatment of utopia as necessarily ambiguous (but nevertheless necessary). Such a notion is invoked directly in the subtitle of Le Guin's 1974 novel *The Dispossessed: An Ambiguous Utopia*.[6] This descriptor, and the narrative as a whole, imply that while a utopian principle of hope for a better world remains vital, any attempt to construct this better world, whether in narrative imagination or practice (if indeed the two can be separated), will result in something necessarily imperfect and incomplete. This notion is consciously dramatized in Le Guin's short piece from around the same time, titled "The Ones Who Walk Away from Omelas" (1973), which can be read as a direct reflection in the form of a fiction-thought-experiment on the necessary imperfection of any given utopia, in its depiction of a seemingly emancipated, joyous society whose existence is possible only by its continued acceptance of the horrific torture of an innocent child. Her earlier novella, *The Lathe of Heaven* (1971), by placing in the hands of its central characters the power to change the world literally overnight, dramatizes the dangers of a certain kind of utopian attitude held by one who believes with zealous certainty that they know what is best for others, if this is accompanied by power.

These and other notable works from the era, such as Joanna Russ's *The Female Man* (1975), Samuel Delany's *Triton* (1976) and Marge Piercy's *Woman on the Edge of Time* (1976), either develop utopian scenarios with constitutive flaws that require working through, or juxtapose utopian visions against non-utopian and dystopian depictions that bear directly on the conditions of possibility of their utopian elements. Appiah's suggestion that cosmopolitanism may be considered "the name not of the solution but of the challenge"[7] could equally be applied to "utopia" as dealt with in such works.

Yet the critical or ambiguous utopianism of such works arises not just as a retooling of utopianism, but in tension and dialogue with established elements within science fiction as a genre and body of works that would seem, if anything, to reinforce values antithetical to any kind of critical politics. A widespread popular perception of science fiction as a genre, especially in the late 20th century, associated it, not without reason, with uncritically patriarchal, imperialist, heteronormative, and rational-modernist perspectives.[8] Certainly, Le Guin, Delany and others were doing new and different things with science fiction, but they were working *with* and *within* it as genre and mode, rather than doing something different altogether. That is, while their work may be taken to belong to a wider category of speculative fiction, unlike other examples of the latter, such as the works of Jorge Luis Borges, or Adolfo Bioy Casares' *The Invention of Morel* (1940), they also situate themselves squarely within the narrower generic sphere of science fiction, drawing on key tropes such as space travel, fantastic journeys, alien encounters, time travel and so on in recognisably "science-fictional" terms.

In other words, these authors were consciously working with and within traditions and generic tropes, themes, and imaginaries that they knew well and appreciated, rather than wholly deconstructing or fundamentally reinventing the genre. For this reason, I would suggest that they did not introduce a critical imaginative potential into SF, but, rather, discovered, cultivated, and made more radical use of a potential that was already discernible in the early history of modern science fiction, even where its apparently normative values seem most prominent. Rather than seeking to divide SF into two broad types, one patriarchal, imperialist, capitalist, normative, the other radical and critically attuned, it seems more apt to suggest that there is an ambiguity within SF that frequently sees elements of these two putative types mixed together, such that the dominance of one may always be, and often is, at least partially countered or destabilised by elements of the other. SF certainly does operate at times, and especially in the first half of its career to date (from, say, the late nineteenth century to around the time of the Second World War), to support and project certain ideas and values of capitalist imperialism; but at the same time, there is a critical-utopian potential that is either always-already present, or which repeatedly begins to emerge. Whether this is due to the interests and psychology of particular authors, or to do with the nature of certain key traits that attract both writers and readers to the genre, would be hard to say; yet it's at least plausible that the kinds of thinking and imagining that SF tends to undertake and inspire lend themselves to modes of "thinking otherwise" that will always hold the potential for upsetting whatever other mainstream or normative values are at work. The idea, for example, of radically other worlds, cultures, ways of life, being; the possibility of moving between cosmic and local scales; the openness and freedom of imagination to conceive of things as other than they appear to be—all of these key traits and capacities of SF writing seem particularly suited to the critically political, utopian imagination, even though (as with utopian thinking in general) these possibilities might equally lead down politically very different paths.

Moreover, this is not a subdued or immanent potential that is only manifest in SF from the late 1960s onwards. Rather, it is always manifest in some places, arguably from the beginnings of science fiction as a modern genre. As John Rieder compellingly argues, we may take this in part to arise from—rather than despite—the colonial context in which it first develops. His study of the emergence of modern science fiction in the late nineteenth and early twentieth centuries explores the many ways such writing expresses colonialist desires and fantasies, embodying and thus disseminating ideological tenets of imperialist modernity, such as belief in the power of "progress," primitivism, and the hierarchisation of racial difference.[9] But at the same time, he recognises that any work taking up elements that have become generic staples, including those that have become associated with the values of colonial modernity, necessarily addresses them in its own individual way, and that this leads to a variety of engagements and positions that are seldom simply repetitions of a single, straightforward (in this case colonial) outlook. Nor does this result in a simple division or categorisation of texts as either "colonial" or "anti-colonial," "naïve" or "critical." This not only applies to obviously satirical or critical approaches to an existing generic form, such as the "lost tribe" scenario as taken up in H. G. Wells' "The Country of the Blind" (1904) and Charlotte Perkins Gilman's *Herland* (1915). It can also be identified in other, more apparently straightforward and commercially successful examples of adventure writing from the period, such as H. Rider Haggard's *King Solomon's Mines* (1885) or Arthur Conan Doyle's *The Lost World* (1912): these are not, for Rieder, simplistic endorsements of colonialist attitudes, but able to "register the emotional ambivalence and historical complexity of colonial situations just as richly as the more explicitly satirical-utopian works do."[10]

Similarly, David Higgins, in an article dealing explicitly with cosmopolitanism in SF, recognises early science fiction as "a key site where the ideological dream-work of imperialism unfolds," such that it is able to function not only as an enabler but also "as a powerful critical literature of empire."[11] Though Higgins perhaps seeks to make starker distinctions between critical and non-critical approaches than Rieder, he likewise sees SF as possessing a richness and range of political/ideological possibilities by virtue of its capacity to address "the philosophical and institutional operations of imperialism more fully than any other genre of cultural production."[12] These conditions, he suggests, are crucial to the richness of Le Guin's explorations of the difficulties in cosmopolitan projects' attempts to move beyond the imperialist values and tendencies that often accompany ideas and instantiations of cosmopolitan structures.

Higgins sees a key aspect of the value of Le Guin's work in in the ways it experiments with different forms and possibilities for cosmopolitan frameworks, perspectives and ways of organising and relating different forms of life. The novels sometimes referred to as "the Hainish cycle" (the Hain being a common ancestor of the diverse species that feature in them), usually involve the activities and efforts of a large interstellar body that seeks to integrate different species and their cultures within a shared network of interests, for the sharing of knowledge, trade, and other mutual benefits.

Novels set in an earlier era, such as *Rocannon's World* (1966), feature the League of All Worlds, which takes a heavy-handed approach to integration that resembles Cold War U.S. neo-imperialism: "its aim is universal inclusion, but the terms of this inclusion are different for different peoples, and it is ultimately an inclusion that prioritizes one economic way of life at the expense of others."[13] Higgins identifies the League as a manifestation of a "weak cosmopolitanism," one that claims to uphold certain values of equality and fairness, but in so doing justifies imposing them, by force or coercion if necessary, on others. Novels set in a later era following the collapse of the League and the long, slow rebuilding process—notably *The Left Hand of Darkness* (1969)—see a new cosmopolitan organisation called the Ekumen having taken its place. The Ekumen and its representatives, such as the protagonist of *Left Hand*, Genly Ai, are governed by a "strong cosmopolitanism," an ethical outlook that places a much more fundamental value on responsibility towards and respect for the other's difference. There is a clear proximity between this strong cosmopolitanism and the minor cosmopolitanism(s) that are the preoccupation of this volume (though I will argue below for making a distinction between certain applications of the terminology of weak/strong and minor/major in relation to cosmopolitanism in SF).

However, the experimentation underway with respect to cosmopolitanism in the Hainish stories does not simply amount to critiquing bad models and trying to imagine and present better ones. Rather, it is a matter of the ongoing intertwining of critique and invention: the earlier novellas do not just offer a critique of neo-imperialist cosmopolitanism, but explore the difficulties which beset it at various scales, from the intimate to the global to the interstellar. From these explorations emerge various elements of a strong cosmopolitan ethics, along with an appreciation of the kinds of conditions that give rise to them and the kinds of obstacles that would be faced in embedding them into practice on a massive scale. In this way, the difficulties of the path from one to the other, the transgenerational efforts (and thus patience) that are required, can be taken into account as part of Le Guin's "developing philosophy and practice of cosmopolitanism,"[14] rather than the earlier novels being understood as less successful or valuable than a novel like *Left Hand*, in which a strong cosmopolitical structure has been instantiated.

In the second half of this paper, I will address precisely this question of the instantiation of a viable larger cosmopolitical structure, with reference to some specific works of SF, starting with Le Guin. I will argue that the problematic faced here is not simply that of "scaling up" from a local or interpersonal ethical relation to a macro-level socio-political organising structure; but rather, of the necessity of maintaining the texture of this local strong cosmopolitan relation continuously throughout. For this reason, I will suggest that it is useful, in some contexts, such as those I will discuss, to employ the terminology of minor cosmopolitanism in preference to (or at least as a supplement to) the weak/strong terminology Higgins applies to Le Guin.

Part Two: Minor Cosmopolitanism in SF writing

In the previous section, despite a few references to particular works, I have largely been considering SF's minor cosmopolitan potential in general or generic terms. In this section, I would like to address a particular mode found in some works of SF by which I think major and minor forms of cosmopolitanism are set in productive tension. This brings out various of their mutual imbrications and complex interdependences, opening up resources for the imaginative exploration and development of key minor cosmopolitan questions, principles, ideas, and problems. This mode or trope involves setting the cosmic scale of struggles for intergalactic peace against the local, personal scale of interactions between (initial) strangers, as they develop bonds of understanding, companionship, and friendship. I will briefly consider three examples of this trope, beginning with its place in Le Guin's Hainish novels, in a manner that I have already begun via Higgins' account of strong cosmopolitanism above. The other two examples are Clifford Simak's *Way Station* (1963) and Octavia Butler's Earthseed novels.

First Example: *Rocannon's World* (Le Guin)

Personal relationships, developed against the background of larger-scale attempts to construct an ethically viable cosmopolitical framework of governance (the League of All Worlds, the Ekumen), repeatedly occupy central positions in Le Guin's novels. I do not think it is incidental that these relationships develop between characters who are culturally and biologically—or, for emphasis, we might say xenologically[15]—distant from one another.

This can be said even of the single encounter, lasting only a few minutes, between representatives of different worlds that marks the culmination of the Prologue to *Rocannon's World*.[16] Semley, inhabitant of a remote planet on the periphery of the League of All Worlds, makes what is from her perspective a magical journey to an archaeological museum at the centre of the empire. Her encounter there with a scientist, the titular Rocannon, triggers a series of events that will lead to his adventure on the world from which she has travelled. Higgins notes that the radically different perspectives of these two protagonists (enhanced metafictively by Le Guin's employment of conventional elements of elf-and-dwarf-style fantasy writing when presenting Semley's perspective, and more conventionally technocentric science-fictional tropes when presenting Rocannon's), "jarringly juxtaposes the epistemologies of imperial center and periphery," in the process disrupting the colonial gaze by dramatizing the imperialists' extreme failure to comprehend Semley's world and her subjecthood.[17] However, we ought also to note that, despite this mutual incomprehensibility and absence of shared cultural reference-points, the brief exchange between them displays, in a moment, intimations of the kind of openness and mutual respect that one might associate with a strong cosmopolitanism.

I would, however, like to make a distinction here between the strong and the minor with regard to cosmopolitanism. To the extent that they both represent an ethical position of radical openness to the other, I understand them as effectively the same. However, where Higgins sees strong cosmopolitanism as scalable from the interpersonal to the governmental level, I would suggest a conception of minor cosmopolitanism as retaining the interpersonal manifestation of this ethical relation as an irreducible core. Any adequate realisation of minor cosmopolitanism on a larger scale would in this sense need to be conceived as a continuation or extension of these interpersonal relations: there could be no macropolitical structure that would correspond, at the larger scale, to a strong cosmopolitanism without retaining this minor—in the sense of locally, interpersonally embodied—structure.

Semley seeks a necklace viewed as having great power and significance among her people, which has been acquired by the museum as a xenoarchaeological artefact. On hearing her claim the necklace and request its return, Rocannon hands it over without resistance: the centre cedes its power to the periphery in the face of the Other. Of course, returning an appropriated artefact is not a radically anti-imperial gesture, nor one deserving of much praise. Nevertheless, where historical steps and gestures towards countering imperialism (such as the official abolition of slavery, or an imperial power's granting of independence to one of its former colonies) tend to result from a range of political and pragmatic pressures, this one is undertaken with no sense of pressure or recognisable threat other than Rocannon's own conscience, and his face-to-face encounter with its claimant.

For Higgins, the scene (and its consequences) both present and implicitly critique the weak cosmopolitanism in which difference is tolerated and managed only as part of a strategy for maintaining the larger empire. His argument is that the novel's later "recovery of Semley's voice on its own terms, and Rocannon's ultimate efforts to reform the League once he realizes the damage it has done" represent "the beginnings of a strong cosmopolitan ethics."[18] However, I think we can already identify such ethics, if in a non-formalised embodied form, in this exchange at the opening of the novella. In Higgins' account, the incipient strong cosmopolitan ethics emerging from the critique of weak cosmopolitanism in *Rocannon's World* anticipates its institutionalisation into a "normative politics"[19] in novels featuring the Ekumen. But might we not also consider these instances of a stronger cosmopolitan ethics, exhibited in the local relationships among small groups of individuals, to have a constitutive, rather than preparatory role in any successful version of a more extended, strong cosmopolitanism?

Indeed, might we not in fact question the very compossibility of strong cosmopolitanism and normative politics? It seems to me that if we take minor cosmopolitanism to encompass both a strong cosmopolitan ethics and the small-scale manifestation of such an ethics—found in the relationships between small numbers of individuals, in single acts of hospitality and kindness—we may find it easier to retain a sensitivity to the risks any form of normativity poses for such an ethics. That is, where a strong cosmopolitanism lends itself to a conception of ethics as a set of principles that may be expressed at various scales, the notion of a minor cosmopolitanism that includes these strong cosmopolitan principles also maintains a sense of their inseparability from the face-to-face, interpersonal, embodied register: it can never be purely institutional, or legal, or governmental, but can only take on a normative, governmental form as an emergent property of (or at best as a subsequently added complement to) these minor relations taken en masse, rather than their condition.

The significance of the early encounter between Semley and Rocannon is that a moment of respect and trust, of hospitality, of acceding *without condition* to a request, takes place between them, despite the sense of their radical mutual alterity that has been established by the juxtaposition of their respective fantastical-metaphysical and imperial-scientific worlds, and by the obscurity that characterises the world of each for the other. Later, Rocannon's own journey on Semley's planet will repeatedly be shaped by the formation of bonds, companionships and friendships with local inhabitants in which, again, the acceptance of a degree of obscurity, of impenetrable mutual strangeness or alienness, becomes a condition rather than an obstacle.

The Left Hand of Darkness is set millennia after Rocannon's World, when the League has collapsed, and, after a long and slow process, been replaced by the Ekumen, the looser, more genuinely anti-imperialist institution that Higgins' associates with a fuller realisation of a strong cosmopolitanism. Yet, notably, the means by which the Ekumen extends itself, making contact and forming relations with other worlds, species and cultures, takes place through minor, interpersonal forms. The protagonist's role as "First Mobile" is to make first contact with the people on a planet named Winter, as an envoy of the Ekumen. There is no question of using the vastly superior technological and military power of the Ekumen's other worlds to persuade a new world to join it:

> The first news from the Ekumen on any world is spoken by one voice, one man present in the flesh, present and alone. He may be killed, as Pellelge was on Four-Taurus, or locked up with madmen, as were the first three Mobiles on Gao, one after the other; yet the practice is kept, because it works. One voice speaking truth is a greater force than fleets and armies, given time; plenty of time; but time is the thing that the Ekumen has plenty of …[20]

The Ekumen has plenty of time, not because it is more important than any individual, but because it operates in accordance with an ethic of selflessness, in which the absolute refusal to employ force in reaching out to integrate with another culture is inseparable from the willingness of individual envoys to take on the role of First Mobile and the risks it entails. If killed, the envoy is not sacrificing themselves for a greater good; they are simply governed by the same minor cosmopolitanism that prevents the institution from sending anything other than a single, well-informed but absolutely vulnerable individual. Rather than going into a detailed reading of the whole novel, we may note that one-to-one relationships, and the difficulties of overcoming one's own prejudices regarding what constitutes personhood (including how one relates to another person, especially, in this case, in terms of gender, sexuality and intimacy), remain crucial throughout to the protagonist's capacity (or not) to successfully introduce the nations of Winter into the Ekumen.

Second Example: *Way Station* (Simak)

In Appiah's account of cosmopolitanism, he develops a notion of conversation as one of its necessary, constitutive elements: not just in the sense of everyday communicative interaction, but in terms of more general "habits of coexistence: conversation in its older meaning, of living together, association."[21] This might function fairly well as a descriptor of the kinds of scenarios I'm describing, in which trust, companionship, camaraderie, and kindness are manifest, regardless of whether they form part of a lasting friendship. Conversation in this combined sense is central to Clifford Simak's *Way Station*, which, again, foregrounds minor cosmopolitanism in simultaneously the "small, local" (conversational) and "strong" senses; and sets it in tension with efforts at cosmopolitanism that are to a large extent "major" in corresponding ways.

Way Station opens with a two-page evocation of the horror, destruction, waste and senselessness of war—specifically, the American Civil War, from which the novel's protagonist, Enoch Wallace, emerges as an unlikely survivor. His experiences have left him with a deep antipathy to war, but also, almost paradoxically, a certain habituation to certain aspects of it: he carries his rifle with him whenever he ventures out of his house, seemingly with no intention of using it, and hunts strange animals for sport in a (probably) virtual environment. Perhaps the seeming contradiction finds its resolution in the fact that he is ultimately prepared to kill another if they are unswervingly bent on (and about to enact) the all-out mass destruction of war—amounting, arguably, to a kind of cosmopolitan self-defence. It is perhaps for this reason that he is chosen to man the interstellar "way station" of the novel's title.

Enoch has been granted superhuman longevity in exchange for maintaining and operating a way station—a node on a cosmic transport network that allows galactic travellers passage via Earth to (relatively) distant stations and locations. The station is built on the site of his family house, which retains its outward façade, but has internally become an enclave of alien technology—both in the mechanisms that enable it to function as a means of interstellar travel and which prevent him from ageing, —and in the various artefacts, gifts, and discarded objects that travellers passing through have left behind. Enoch is intensely concerned about the prospect, following the Second World War, of a third that would be terminal for humans. Using an alien form of logic developed by "the mathematicians of Mizar" to study a wide range of factors (including technological developments, birth rate economics, popular tastes and various other data) he is convinced that humanity's self-destruction is approaching: "the Earth was headed straight for another major war, for a holocaust of nuclear destruction."[22]

It later transpires that peace is similarly fragile at the intergalactic level, a topic that preoccupies the alien who effectively becomes Enoch's "handler," whom he dubs "Ulysses" (among themselves, Ulysses' people do not use proper names). The novel's plot eventually sees the two of them, with support from unlikely others, collaborating to avert conflicts on a series of levels, from the local to the cosmic. In this sense, the question of cosmopolitanism looms over the narrative, as the counterpart of the images of all-out destruction that form its frame. However, the larger-scale cosmopolitan structures (the diplomatic global and cosmic networks maintaining peace) are only saved by a kind of *deus ex machina*, a mysterious artefact that, through the characters' combined efforts, eventually finds its way into the right hands. The more effective model of cosmopolitanism here, arguably, again comes instead from the more "minor" relationships among the individuals and small groups that enable this outcome.

As very often in Le Guin, the crucial elements of the minor cosmopolitan relations manifest in Simak's novel can be identified in the combination of forms of companionship, friendship, solidarity, and trust *on the basis of* (rather than by overcoming) mutual incommunicability, unknowability, alienness. Where a weak or major cosmopolitanism is likely to function on the basis of a degree of transparency—of a confirmation that we are all neighbours, citizens, and in these senses "the same"—this minor version entails the acceptance of the other's radical unknowability, the impossibility of full communication between two alien entities (all entities being to some degree alien to one another—even if, as noted above, the xenological difference between conventionally SF aliens and earthly humanoids can help emphasise this).

This is seen repeatedly in Enoch's few relationships with others, starting with Ulysses. In their very first encounter, Ulysses masquerades as a thirsty human wanderer who has found his way on to Enoch's homestead by accident. Their first interaction consists of hospitality being shown to a stranger, Enoch drawing up water for him with a pump, and Ulysses returning the gesture. As if to underscore that it is the gesture itself that is important, the first sign that Ulysses is not all that he seems comes when Enoch notices that his guest is not sweating, despite it being a very hot day and his supposed thirst. The strength of the friendship that can be observed between them across the rest of the novel can arguably all be traced back to this first encounter. Having opened up, without question, to a stranger, Enoch's openness is unshaken by the revelation that this stranger is not from another country, but another star system, and the unique request that follows.

Another instance of a relationship built on, rather than through, the overcoming of incommunicability and obscurity, is Enoch's relationship with Lucy Fisher, a local deaf girl whom he ends up protecting from her abusive father (triggering one of the more local conflicts that need to be resolved towards the novel's end). Lucy is largely isolated from ordinary human communication and sociality—yet Enoch has formed a largely wordless friendship with her. Certainly, there is a degree of idealisation in her description and Enoch's perception of her (as there was, in fact, in Rocannon's somewhat exoticising initial reaction to Semley): "He stopped and watched her and thought how full she was of grace and beauty, the natural grace and beauty of a primitive and lonely creature."[23] And yet—perhaps because of the regularity with which, in other contexts, exoticisation turns out to be a prelude to something more menacing—the actual innocence of their relationship, marked by simplicity, genuine warmth and the absence of self-interest, is all the more apparent.

In order to communicate with the vast, diverse range of lifeforms that pass through his way station, Enoch has developed a certain facility with a kind of galactic sign language called "pasimology," which is "adaptable to many different means and methods of expression"[24]—and thus able to account for the fact that not all beings will communicate through words, sounds, visible symbols (and that they will have radically different anatomical structures, technological prosthesis, thought patterns, etc). He does lament that pasimology isn't available to Lucy—yet there is clearly no shortage of trust and communication between them. Again, perhaps to underscore the significance of a certain kind of hospitality towards strangers, the first time we encounter Lucy she offers Enoch a drink of water from a spring, using a cup made of folded birch bark. Subsequently, she brushes his forehead with her fingertips, and in response he "put[s] out a hand and [lays] his broad palm against her cheek, holding it there for a reassuring moment as a gesture of affection."[25] Then they leave with mutual gestures of farewell. Again, there is a sense that their strong relationship is based on their lack of knowledge of one another, their non-exchange of detailed communication, rather than hindered by it.

What I am treating here as a kind of minor cosmopolitan relationship (trust/companionship/potential friendship built on an accepted lack of knowledge of one another) is perhaps most clearly—if least subtly—manifest in Enoch's relationship with his postman. By the time the novel is set, Enoch has established a rapport and trust with Winslowe Grant without feeling that he has to explain the obvious strangeness of his circumstances. Like other locals, Grant cannot have failed to notice that Enoch does not seem to age; and yet he has sought neither to exploit this knowledge, nor to press for an explanation. After giving Enoch a gift—a carving made from one of many pieces of alien wood Enoch has provided Winslowe over the years—the postman affirms: "I like you. I don't know what you are and I ain't about to ask, but anyhow I like you."[26] This simple relationship later leads to Winslowe playing his part in helping resolve some of the local conflicts that end up besetting Enoch, as he simultaneously struggles to deal with those taking place on a global/cosmic scale.

Again and again in *Way Station* (as elsewhere in Simak's fiction), characters demonstrate their mutual respect and affinity by *not* prying, *not* knowing and registering that they *do not need to know* everything about one another's lives: the relationships between them seem to exhibit an uncodified, automatic, and interpersonal respect for "opacity" in Édouard Glissant's sense.[27] Even Claude Lewis, the CIA agent investigating Enoch, defies expectations by attempting as far as possible to observe and understand without interfering in his affairs. About halfway through the narrative, he takes something from Enoch's land that he shouldn't have—in the process unwittingly desecrating an alien grave and fomenting a scandal that threatens the collapse of galactic peace. Yet on being confronted by Enoch, he agrees to have the remains returned as quickly as possible, taking Enoch's statement of its importance at face value—and follows through on his promise. (There is a marked absence of the scene—now an expected cliché in mainstream film and television narratives dealing with incredible otherworldly events—in which a protagonist presents a sceptical authority-figure with shocking evidence to win them round). As in the case of Semley's necklace, the return of what has been taken does not excuse the theft, but demonstrates an uncommon openness to trusting and responding to another being —without demanding explanation or justification—, where the expected norm in such contexts would be the intensification of existing unequal power relations and the re-entrenchment of mistrust.

War—the experience, memory, fear, threat and possible imminence of war—looms over all these relationships and over the whole narrative. As the direct effect of the breakdown of socio-political relations on epic scales, war among many parties is effectively the counter to cosmopolitanism, the sign and result of its absence or failure. Since the actions of Enoch and various other characters are, knowingly or unknowingly, geared towards averting this failure, it may seem that it is these contributions that render them significant and give them meaning. However, I would suggest that their significance is in the minor cosmopolitanism they embody, set up as a model against those larger ("major") global and galactic cosmopolitan forms and structures that are in the process of failing. Although this juxtaposition is at times unsubtle, its re-articulation in straightforward terms across the novel simultaneously manages to underscore both the difficulty, and the ultimate simplicity of what is required in order to reach a genuinely peaceful form of coexistence. As Winslowe the postman puts it: "it don't much matter what any of us are, just so we get along with one another. If some of the nations would only take a lesson from some small neighbourhood like ours—a lesson in how to get along—the world would be a whole lot better."[28] In reading this as a general position presented by the novel as a whole, it would seem advisable to read the phrase "small neighbourhood" here as referring to the set of relations among Enoch and his various allies and companions, rather than the literal rural neighbourhood in the area in which the novel is set (which is the site of plenty of mistrust, conflict and inequality).

What these examples point towards is a notion of knowledge of the other that is based purely on how they appear to behave, react, how they relate to others—and does not require any particular penetration into their "inner" personality, their "true essence" etc. Such an approach is arguably already implicit in what Higgins terms the strong cosmopolitan ethics associated with Emmanuel Levinas, Jacques Derrida or Judith Butler. But among many other things, what we may derive from these smaller scale instantiations of such an ethics within immediate, lived relationships—which I am choosing to see as a particular kind of minor cosmopolitanism—is that any larger scale institutionalisation must be built up of such relationships as its very texture. It may be possible to state an institutionalised, codified version of strong cosmopolitanism in, for example, a legal constitution or a declaration of rights; and it may be possible to develop detailed legislative and (to some extent) policing authorities to help reinforce them. But ultimately, minor cosmopolitanism has to be lived and reiterated locally across a sociocultural structure: the minor does not scale up.

Third Example: *Parable of the Sower* (Butler)

In referring to these particular examples of SF, I am not seeking to make the same point repeatedly or show that each exhibits precisely the same model. Rather, while each of these instances points towards the notion of the minor (local, interpersonal, small-scale) dimension as essential to the possibility of a larger-scale extension of strong cosmopolitanism, each of them also imagines and explores such an extension in its own particular way, in the process bringing into focus different potential obstacles and ways of approaching them. We could apply Rieder's point—that specific works within a genre are always something more than instances of that genre—to a putative sub-genre of minor cosmopolitan SF: each example, as also singular, necessarily does more than simply exemplify the characteristics of the genre, and sometimes develops in active tension with them.

Whereas the previous two examples, I think, point towards the necessity of extending or "growing" a minor cosmopolitanism, rather than seeking to translate or scale or abstract it into a larger, normative, institutional form, my final example arguably offers an imaginative exploration of *how* this growth might take place—though this amounts to an outline of what is, of course, only one among many, many possible pathways.

Octavia Butler's *Parable* novels depict the collapse of US society in the 2020s under the increasingly destructive effects of climate change and ever-growing social inequality.[29] As a child, the protagonist, Lauren Olamina, is far more attuned than most to what is happening, and foresees the inevitable collapse of the old social structure. She uses the short interim time to prepare, trying to work out and gather what will be useful in the world-to-come: equipment, knowledge, and, importantly, ethical principles—which she begins to enshrine and develop within an almost-secular religion she comes to call "Earthseed."

There is no space here to touch on all the ways these novels might be valuable for all manner of critical-utopian and minor cosmopolitan projects.[30] However, it is possible to point to a few key elements that are salient for considering a minor cosmopolitanism as I have characterised it here, starting with the use of religion. It would be apt—if the notion is not considered self-contradictory—to describe Earthseed as a religion of immanence. Its only stable principle with regard to the transcendental is that "God is change": like Baruch Spinoza's "God = nature" ("*deus sive natura*"), its uptake as a principle effectively renders irrelevant the question of whether there is some kind of transcendental entity that could be called "God," or "God" is simply a convenient name for a general principle of existence. Either way, it is the principle, and the further principles Lauren attaches to it, that are important.

An upshot of the principle that "God is change" is the acceptance of continual change—and therefore continual adaptation—as a necessity of life. Appropriately, though she works out her religion in advance of the full social collapse, Lauren does not initially publish the principles of Earthseed and circulate them in the hope of drawing followers. Rather, having prepared it as an outlook, vision, way of life, she gradually shares parts of it with others as she comes to trust them and be trusted by them, as part of the growth of their relationships. In this way, Lauren is able to have a plan for her minor cosmopolitan network, a direction of growth that points towards a cosmic scale—for the "destiny" of Earthseed is "to take root among the stars"[31]—and yet to allow the growth towards this scale to continue to take place in a minor register, one relationship at a time.

In this regard, it is not incidental that, when Lauren first sets out on her journey to survive (and ultimately build something new) in the remnants of the former world, whose inherent violence and insanity have now been unleashed from any semblance of "civilised" restraint, she is accompanied not by her family, a partner, or neighbours, but with relative strangers. Though *Parable of the Sower* begins with Lauren's life within a large family at the heart of a fairly close-knit community, few of her family or friends survive its being overrun by violence. She gradually accumulates new companions, friends, associates (eventually, perhaps, followers) through diverse accidents and experiences of mutual dependence, feeding in intimations of her vision for their future in small doses. This group become the community to which she gives the name "Acorn."

That most of her companions, and those they add to their group, begin as strangers is thus not a weakness but a strength. Reflecting on what she is attempting, Lauren notes that she does not want a tribal community or a gang: "I don't want gang types with their need to dominate, rob and terrorize."[32] Despite the risks and vulnerability this initially entails, building a community through encounters with strangers has benefits in the long run, for a minor cosmopolitan project. A brief conversation between Lauren and one of her earliest companions, Zahra, makes clear how different their lives and experiences have been until now. While Lauren comes from a relatively well-off, middle-class community, Zahra has grown up among the "street poor." As they begin to establish a bond, we see that this is not simply the result of a purely ethical (e.g. strong cosmopolitan) embrace of radical alterity, but also of a pragmatic appreciation of their mutual differences. Their different skills complement and benefit one another, as Lauren imparts knowledge she has gained from books and teaches Zahra to read, while Zahra shares the skills and techniques she has acquired through years of experiencing the kinds of harsh conditions that they must all now face.[33]

The kind of community Lauren hopes to build will reject certain principles associated with the problems of the old civilisation, those which led ultimately to its collapse (especially those associated with toxic masculinity, such as hierarchical social structures, striving for domination, the encouragement of competition, etc).

In its fundamental respect for difference as well as opacity—indeed, in its embracing of mutual difference, alienness, as crucial to survival—Earthseed offers a minor cosmopolitanism in a similar vein to those located above in Le Guin and Simak. However, Butler's perhaps goes the furthest in recognising the obstacles to its realisation—and, indeed, in exploring the necessity of compromise that besets any utopian vision (however ambiguous) and may well completely undermine even the most carefully constructed and well-intentioned. As Alex Zamalin puts it, "Butler took black utopia in a more dystopian direction than ever before," informed by "a lifelong pessimism about the human condition," and yet still maintained "a tragicomic faith that something better, more enlivening, could emerge from the ashes of disaster."[34]

One of the results of this is that the potential utopianism in the *Parable* novels never shies away from the possibility, indeed, likelihood of its own undoing. This starts with early recognitions that survival will be virtually impossible without, to begin with at least, engaging in the kinds of violence (whether in self-defence or not) that Lauren and the members of Acorn oppose. Even in her reflections on not wanting her group to become a gang mentioned above, Lauren recognises the fact that it will not be this simple: "And yet we might have to dominate. We might have to rob to survive, and even terrorize to scare off or kill our enemies. We'll have to be very careful how we allow our needs to shape us."[35] Such compromise could always lead to the corruption and undermining of even the most well-meaning vision for the future (we could compare this to countless historical examples; in science fiction, a classic instance would be Paul Atreides' foreseeing, in *Dune* (1965), of how the resistance movement he leads against imperial oppression will eventually turn into an apocalyptic *jihad*). The second book, *The Parable of the Talents*, dramatizes these dangers as well as the ways any quasi-religious movement, no matter how oppressed and ethically sound, can solidify into an oppressive form as its doctrine and organisational structures are established and its leaders venerated.

The vision Butler presents—both in the utopian boldness of Earthseed, and the dystopian dramatisation of a collapsing world which frames it—simultaneously highlights the extent to which human survival may depend upon the realisation of something like Lauren's goals, and the extent to which existing human culture and behaviour threatens to block this realisation from almost every direction. This vision involves the implicit core principles that we've now identified in a few different SF examples of minor cosmopolitanism: first of all, the strong cosmopolitan ethics of respect and openness towards the radically other; second, the principle that these ethics—which are also a form of pragmatism once properly framed—must be manifest in actual interpersonal encounters and relationships; and finally, that any effort to expand such a minor cosmopolitanism to much larger scales cannot succeed purely through abstraction or reification into doctrine and hierarchical structures, but must simply grow. Yet Butler's framing of an optimistic vision within a pessimistic scepticism adds an exploration of the many ways in which, in practice, such elements of scaling will inevitably creep in—and thus, arguably, allows for further fabulative exploration and experimentation with ways one might counter their potentially derailing effects.

Conclusion

One of the reasons Jameson saw the renewal of a critical utopian spirit in some modern SF was that it revealed the incapacity of (post)modern capitalist society and culture to imagine itself otherwise. In revealing the limits of the utopian imagination, and confronting the reader with these limits, the ambiguous utopias of authors like Le Guin, Delany, and later Butler, almost paradoxically exhibit a utopian charge. Le Guin's *The Lathe of Heaven* epitomises this, Jameson suggests, in that it is particularly transparent about being concerned with "its own process of production"—that is, with the impossibility of realising utopia: "yet in the very process of exploring the contradictions of that production, the narrative gets written, and 'Utopia' is 'produced' in the very movement by which we are shown that an 'achieved' Utopia—a full representation—is a contradiction in terms."[36] It seems that the utopia produced here lies in the faint possibility that, by revealing these limits, their disruption or transcendence might just move a little closer to possibility. This seems to have been Mark Fisher's understanding in his updating of Jameson's postmodernity thesis, when he suggested that "even glimmers of alternative political and economic possibilities can have a disproportionately great effect. The tiniest event can tear a hole in the grey curtain of reaction which has marked the horizons of possibility under capitalist realism."[37]

Perhaps we may add to this, via another slight modification of Jameson, a particularly minor cosmopolitan articulation of this seemingly contradictory utopianism found within the apparent negation or impossibility of the utopian. Another way Jameson describes the latter is in terms of works of SF functioning as "unwitting and even unwilling vehicles for a meditation, which, setting forth for the unknown, finds itself irrevocably mired in the all-too-familiar, and thereby becomes unexpectedly transformed into a contemplation of our own absolute limits."[38] In plunging into the depths of the unknown, SF finds itself confronted with the familiar and the mundane. Yet within this familiarity, there lurks a deeper, more alien obscurity that leads into the unknown after all, as perhaps within the domestic space that Bowman discovers at the limits of outer space after being flung across the universe at the end of Stanley Kubrick's film *2001: A Space Odyssey* (1968). Thus, perhaps, we can make a further inversion of the logic of Jameson's statement: in addition to enabling a contemplation of the limits of the utopian imagination, minor cosmopolitan SF can be said to rediscover, within the "all-too-familiar," the very strangeness and unknowability of otherness upon whose embrace the possibility of a radically alternative future mode of existence might ultimately depend.

---

1 In the course of this paper, I alternate between the terms "science fiction" and "SF." The terms are more-or-less interchangeable to the extent that they refer to a vaguely defined but widely recognised phenomenon usually identified on the basis of some range of associated historical referents and generic traits—a "web of resemblances" (Paul Kincaid, "On the Origins of Genre," *Extrapolation* 44, no. 4 (2003): 409-19; John Rieder, *Colonialism and the Emergence of Science Fiction* (Middletown: Wesleyan University Press, 2008), 17), which remains recognisable despite the fact that some of these traits and associations are likely to be absent (and some more emphasised) in any given instance. I forgo any attempt at a definition of "science fiction," following Ursula Le Guin's view that there can be no such definitive definition that would be viable or useful ("Introduction," *The Unreal and the Real Volume 2: Outer Space, Inner Lands* (London: Gollancz, 2012), vii)—and trusting that the reader will recognise the web of resemblances implied. However, I sometimes prefer to use "SF" for what I take to be its connotations of a wider range of potential names, including "speculative fiction" and "speculative fabulation" which, partially following Donna Haraway, I take to lean towards those aspects of the genre or web that lend themselves to more critical, open and openly political modes (*Staying with the Trouble* (Durham: Duke University Press, 2016), 2-3).

2 Appiah, for example, is clear from the outset of *Cosmopolitanism: Ethics in a World of Strangers* (London: Penguin, 2007) that he approaches cosmopolitanism as a rubric "with some ambivalence," in the hope that it can be "rescued" (xi-xii). Meanwhile, as Sam Knowles notes, while Gilroy (rightly) identifies the imbrications of the terminology of "cosmopolitanism" with historical racism and colonial government, he nevertheless continues to use it with apparent approval at various points in his argument, effectively treating it as "a usefully ambivalent signifier" ("Macrocosm-Opolitanism? Gilroy, Appiah, and Bhabha: The Unsettling Generality of Cosmopolitan Ideas," *Postcolonial Text* 3, no. 4 (2008): 2-5).

3 Raymond Williams, "Utopia and Science Fiction," *Science Fiction Studies* 16, vol. 5, part 3 (November 1978): 203-214.

4 Fredric Jameson, "Progress Versus Utopia; or, Can We Imagine the Future?" *Science Fiction Studies* 27, vol. 9, part 2 (July 1982): 147-158.

5 Darko Suvin, *Defined by a Hollow: Essays on Utopia, Science Fiction and Political Epistemology* (New York: Peter Lang, 2010), 88.

6 Ursula Le Guin, *The Dispossessed* (London: Millennium, 1974). Delany subsequently presented his *Triton* (1976) as "an ambiguous heterotopia" in partial dialogue with Le Guin.

7 Appiah, *Cosmopolitanism*, xv.

8 See Joanna Russ, "Towards an Aesthetic of Science Fiction," *Science Fiction Studies 6*, vol. 2, part 2 (July 1975): 112-119; Istvan Csicsery-Ronay, Jr., "Science Fiction and Empire," *Science Fiction Studies* 90, vol. 30, part 2 (July 2003): 231-245; John Rieder, *Colonialism and the Emergence of Science Fiction* (Middletown: Wesleyan University Press, 2008); Louis Chude-Sokei, *The Sound of Culture: Diaspora and Black Technopoetics* (Middletown: Wesleyan University Press, 2016).

9 John Rieder, *Colonialism and the Emergence of Science Fiction* (Middletown: Wesleyan University Press, 2008).

10 Rieder, *Colonialism*, 24.

11 David Higgins, "Towards a Cosmopolitan Science Fiction," *American Literature* 83, no. 2 (2011): 331.

12 Higgins, 331.

13 Higgins, 338.

14 Higgins, 336.

15 The notion of a xenological distinction between two lifeforms, by implying that they originate from different planets (perhaps galaxies), potentially with fundamentally different environmental and climatic conditions, would seem (and is intended here) to indicate a difference even more radical than the difference between two diverse biological species existing within the same planetary ecosystem. It is, of course, perfectly conceivable for two entities from different solar systems to have much more in common than two lifeforms living within a few metres of one another, literally or figuratively under the same roof. Nevertheless, the notion of a xenological difference likely conjures, at least for beings who have yet to definitively encounter life from beyond their own planet, intimations of a far greater divide.

16 This Prologue is a reproduced version of a 1964 short story, "The Dowry of the Angyar" (later republished as "Semley's Necklace") which constitutes the first appearance of the Hainish universe in Le Guin's writing.

17 Higgins, 337-8.

18 Higgins, 338.

19 Higgins, 338.

20 Le Guin, *Left Hand*, 27.

21 Appiah, *Cosmopolitanism*, xix.

22 Clifford Simak, *Way Station* (New York: Open Road, 2015 [1963]), 75.

23 Simak, 41.

24 Simak, 43.

25 Simak, 45.

26 Simak, 50.

27 Édouard Glissant, *Poetics of Relation* (Michigan: Ann Arbor, 1997 [1990]).

28 Simak, 50.

29 There are two novels in the series, *Parable of the Sower* (1993) and *Parable of the Talents* (1998). Butler had planned to write a third.

30 For explorations of this value see, for example, Jerry Phillips, "The Intuition of the Future: Utopia and Catastrophe in Octavia Butler's *Parable of the Sower*," *Novel: A Forum on Fiction* 35, no. 2/3 (2002): 299-311; Peter G. Stillman, "Dystopian Critiques, Utopian Possibilities, and Human Purposes in Octavia Butler's Parables," *Utopian Studies* 14, no. 1 (2003): 15-35; Patricia Melzer, "'All That You Touch You Change': Utopian Desire and the Concept of Change in Octavia Butler's *Parable of the Sower* and *Parable of the Talents*," *Femspec* 3, no. 2 (2016): 31-52; and Alex Zamalin, *Black Utopia: The History of an Idea from Black Nationalism to Afrofuturism* (New York: Columbia University Press, 2019), 123-136.

31 Octavia Butler, *The Parable of the Sower* (New York: Grand Central Publishing, 2007 [1993]), 87.

32 Butler, *Sower*, 223.

33 This dependence on mutual difference can be read as an echo or restatement, in more earthly terms, of the biological dependence on radical difference at the genetic level that structured xenocultural relations between the Ooloi and humans in Butler's earlier *Xenogenesis* novels (1987-9), republished as *Lillith's Brood* (2000).

34 Zamalin, *Black Utopia*, 125-6.

35 Butler, *Sower*, 223-4.

36 Jameson, "Progress Versus Utopia."

37 Mark Fisher, *Capitalist Realism* (Winchester: Zero Books, 2009), 80-1.

38 Jameson, "Progress."

Rest Home

When I arrive in a new place, I ask: who are the locals here? Then I shut up and listen to them. Which mountains, rivers, villages, ancestors do they carry with them? Who are their living? Who are their dead? I question things and then I keep my opinions to myself. I don't expect to be listened to for a long time. I'm grateful if I am.

*

The word "Māori" means "unadulterated" or in German "unverfälscht."
For example, "wai Māori" is fresh water, and "wai tai" is salt water.

*

I climb your arms one verb at a time.
I polish your nails. Fix your hair.

You meet me anywhere and leave me changed.

The stingrays in the harbour so slick
and black and fleet.

Your very name means "to float."

We have all cried since the beginning.

The kingfisher is flying over the pūwharawhara.

The umbrellas drying in the stairway,
spiders on their backs.

*

Epeli Hau'ofa spoke of the ocean not as a separation, but as the ultimate connector. Grief can be like that, too: an ocean that connects all of our islands. Which other things which seem to separate us can eventually be understood, with a shift in perspective, as doing the exact opposite?

*

Indigenous Cosmopolitanisms vs. Indigenous Nationalisms ... this is a fascinating jumping-off point. Where do our loyalties lie? How can we navigate as global citizens with indigenous roots? How can I be a good Māori and live half a world away from my iwi, my bones, my whānau, my family?

I'm here not to answer questions. I'm here to pose more of them.

*

I arrived in this city as a writer on a scholarship, I stayed as a "Wahlberlinerin"—

although this "choosing to be a Berliner" is, of course, very much at the mercy of the Ausländer Behörde, the immigration department.

I live here by choice.

In other words, I am in the hugely privileged position of having "a home to go to."

*

If you can, while you read, I'd like you to listen to something. Listen to me reading this list of German vocabulary on this publication's website.

You can have it playing very quietly in the background while you read.
It might add to your experience, it might just be annoying.

Give it a go.

You can stop listening at any time.

*

In the early weeks and months after arriving in Berlin, I was overwhelmed by everything I didn't understand. I would switch on this vocab list, put my headphones in my ears and wade through the long grass growing on top of the Velodrom in Friedrichshain, walking a friend's hairy, crazy dog, throwing his ball, retrieving his ball, worrying about ticks. We don't have Lyme Disease in Aotearoa New Zealand.

Addiction to nostalgia. Addiction to novelty.

In Māori I would say:

tēnā tātou, tēnā tātou, tēnā tātou katoa.

Greetings to you all. I see you there, I see all those who stand behind you and beside you, living and dead.

Meine Damen und Herren; ich grüße euch, ich grüße euch, ich grüße alle

Ki a Papatūānuku, ki a Ranginui, tēnā kōrua, tēnā kōrua, tēnā kōrua.

I greet Papatūānuku our motherearth, and I greet Ranginui our fathersky.

*

How are you all doing, readers?

Did you realise people who attend conferences
and do post-doctoral study also speak like this?
Use words like motherearth and fathersky?
They're not even proper words are they?
How are you all doing?
Am I even for real?

*

Ich grüße die Erdmutter und den Himmelsvater. Ich grüße euch, ich grüße euch, ich grüße euch.

Ki ngā mate o tēnei whenua nei, ko ngā mate o ngā rau tau, o ngā tekau tau, o ngā rangi

kua pāhure ake nei. Haere ngā mate, haere atu ki te kāinga tūturu o te tangata, ki reira okioki ai.

I greet the dead of the centuries, the dead of the decades and of recent days. Farewell to you, our dead ones. Leave now, return to your origin-land and rest there.

Die Toten ihres Landes, die Toten der Jahrhunderte, der Jahrzehnte, der letzten Tage. Geht ihr Toten, geht zurück in euer Ursprungsland, und ruht dort.

*

On my mum's side my ancestors come from England and Bayern. Bavaria. The village of Oberammergau. A friend of mine in Aotearoa who would not describe herself as psychic says Of course you're going to Germany. Māori and German is not an easy combination to be, she says. Spiritually. It's time to heal that whakapapa, that genealogy, she says.

*

For around 800-900 years, Māori did not call ourselves "Māori" at all. If we identified with anything, it was with our tribes, our iwi (which also means "bone"); it was with our sub-tribes, our hapū (which also means "pregnant") and with our whānau, our family (which also means "to be born"). It was with our land, our whenua, which also means "placenta." Whenua. Whenua.

Unadulterated.

We can only presume that when settlers from Europe first arrived—my own ancestors among them—someone asked the question "Who are you people?" and the reply was probably "He Māori ahau—I'm just a human."

*

Shut up and listen. After a while, start asking a few questions.

In my travels, and there have been many by now, wherever I am I try to navigate by this tikanga, this protocol. Because I don't believe we need to choose between one or the other, either "Global Citizen" or living on the papakāinga. Tangata whenua, those of us who identify with our indigeneity, are usually very good at "both-and" rather than "either-or." Very important for people like me.

*

At this point, I indicate myself, wave my hand up and down my body, point at myself.

It's an entire Kosmopolitanismus up in here! I say, laughing.

*

I believe in whakapapa, in ancestry, in genealogy, as a way to learn and live and not as a way to exclude or oppress. I spent years in London, in Zimbabwe, lived for a time in Australia and Iowa. I spent years in Aotearoa learning Māori, waking up my tongue, because the violence of colonisation past and present beat the talk out of those kids that were my ancestors.

Now my Bavarian ancestors roll in their graves whenever they hear me mimic my Berlin friends: "Pass ma' auf Keuler!"

In New Zealandese I would say: "Listen up bro!"

*

If you can, while you read, I'd like to you listen to something else, now.
Listen to this song called "Rest Home," on this publication's website.

You can have it playing very quietly in the background while you read.
It might add to your experience, it might just be annoying.

Give it a go. You can stop listening at any time.

*

My father, his name is Valentine Rangiwaititi Baker. He was born in Ōtaki, which is a town in the rohe, the tribal area, of Ngāti Raukawa ki te Tonga. When he was seventeen, he joined the navy and when he emerged from that time, he had two new companions. Each has had a lifelong impact on him. One was tuberculosis, and the other was a love of scuba diving.

Because of the second one, he has lived for decades in an area which is not his tribal area, but which has sea temperatures a little warmer than the west coast, where he was born. He still lives there today, in a small town called Matata / Te Awa o Te Atua, between the east and the west of the bay known as Te Moana Nui a Toi.

My father and I and my sisters and I and my cousins and I and my Aunties and Uncles and I and my Grandmothers and Grandfathers and my Great Grandmothers and my Great Grandfathers and I, and all of them with each other … we all come from several marae on Te Ika a Māui and Te Waka a Māui, Aotearoa's North and South Islands.

One of these marae shares a peninsula with a colony of toroa, the Northern Royal Albatross. It is the only mainland nesting colony of these birds in the world. The toroa spends at least 85 percent of its life on the wing. Its wings stretch up to three metres.

Two months ago, in Berlin, I lay on a table while my friend Julie Paama-Pengelly, a tattoo artist and tohunga tā moko, worked hard and peacefully for two hours to reveal an ancestral print on my chin. The design pays homage to the albatross, because this kaitiaki, this guardian, connects me through sad and loving stories and history to all of the iwi to which I belong.

So now I live here in Germany and I wear a traditional tattoo, a moko kāuae, on my chin.

I have called this moko Te Ūkaipō: a deeply resonant Māori word for home. In its components, it translates as "the breast of the mother which feeds me, and on which I rest at night."

I gave this name to my moko kāuae because shortly after I had it done, a friend asked if I would look after something precious for him for a while—an instrument made of the wing bone of an albatross. This pūtōrino he had named Te Ūkaipō.

I have played her softly on stage to the people of Galicia, who understand the pain and joy of a mother language lost and recovered. I played her to the pohutukawa tree, an Aotearoa native which has nevertheless grown huge and old in the town of A Coruña there, shading the local police station. I played her loudly into the

Atlantic Ocean on the north coast of Spain as I travelled back towards Germany. I play her here at my Berlin home, where I sit while I'm writing this. Her voice wings out of my window to the huge chestnut tree in the courtyard of my building, as its last leaves fall and the day greys away into an early winter night.

*

Where is home for a toroa?
Is it Tangaroa and Hinemoana, the sea?
Is home to a toroa Tawhirimātea, the wind?
Or is a toroa most at home on its own wings?
How does it feel to fly and to rest at the same time?

*

"Point the canoe" is the title of a poem in my poetry collection "waha | mouth." It takes the form of a letter addressed to a writer friend I have never met in person, whose name is Kuukua Dzigbordi Yomekpe. We were paired up by a writing organisation called Kahini and wrote to each other from separate coasts of the world's largest ocean:

Kuukua it keeps us apart, or maybe
like Epeli says it joins us. We stand on either lip
of a moon-sized crater filled with Pacific, yet

we speak softly to each other and like fish
moving onto land the generations in our ears pick up
and move the message through, the next home is prepared,

and there's smoking earth-ovens warming our arrival.
You're there too Kuukua, perhaps you offer me a bowl of fufu
and we talk of Lake Michigan and that butterfly parent The Bay

Area from whom all other estuaries are most
freshly born onto your page. Point the canoe
and bring the island to it said Mau, the master

navigator from Satawal. I was twenty
and rudderless, no craft, no crew. I longed
to sit at his feet, have him teach me this –

not how to set sail but rather
how to set oneself still amid motion,

waiting only for the right home

to grow on the horizon.
Kuukua, my singular gift is for extrapolation.
I can't look at shellfish without thinking fritters

I talk of how much Atlantic I crossed
to walk beside the Hudson whose name
is Shatemuc, my plane a comic yellow shape

farting dotted lines across a brilliant screen,
the Seafather below an ice of impact. You and I know ice
and how to sing when you're made of it. We know it takes a
year to thaw. AAAAAA

I'm blinded in the right eye by the afternoon sun off the
Maton. AAAAAA
A dying ivy attempts the climb outside and Paraparaumu Beach
is salty enough for the breeze to carry it

the few kilometres to our green back yard.
In yours, the Ghost Ship stands offshore, television sets
and one entire roof after another will roll

in the white-tipped green waves. The woman from Japan,
a set of Mickey Mouse ears firm on her head as was the way
of her orchestra, stopped the music. She sat between

the banjo and the grand piano no bigger than a dinner plate
she gave thanks, love to shaken Christchurch, her voice
strong as her violin. A thousand of us breathed late summer air

off the mountain we share. In Titahi Bay I pictured
my great-great grandfather, his beard like Taranaki snow.
Christine and I scooped estuary mud through our fingers, threw

purple and lime-green seasmelling weed into the sparkle,
cars drove onto the hard sand and pulled up for picnics.
Through our fingers, blue sky and Central Park
in early blossom. AAAAAA

*

Philosopher, writer and scholar Epeli Hau'ofa spoke of the ocean not as a separation, but as the ultimate connector. I feel the sea, te moana, Tangaroa and Hinemoana, as a power and an ancestor and a responsibility that joins us all. Grief can be like that, too: an ocean that connects all of our islands.

*

I climb your arms one verb at a time.
I polish your nails. Fix your hair.
You meet me anywhere and leave me changed.
The stingrays in the harbour so slick and black and fleet.
Your very name means "to float."
We have all cried since the beginning.
The kingfisher is flying over the pūwharawhara.
The umbrellas drying in the stairway, spiders on their backs.

I climb your clothes. I polish your parachute.
Fix your keepsake.
You meet me in the body and leave me alone with it.
The screamtrains at the Bahnsteig, such a pulling
and such a machine. We have all dried.
The kingfisher is flying over the pūwharawhara.
The umbrellas drying in the stairway, spiders on their backs.

So far from the ocean I write with a paddle.
The house jolts with machinery here not quakes.
All the nouns are howling.Your very name means to float.
I sit in a pew and a monk sits behind me.
The sun is hitting a saint.
The rays are the rigging and our futures swing.

*

UK writer Simon Kuper observed in an article in the *Financial Times* that in the past—and still today, I would add, for many indigenous and smaller communities worldwide—older and younger generations mixed much more. Chronological age mattered so little that the "happy birthday" song—first published in 1912—was barely known until 1934. Now, segregated generations have segregated world views.

Perhaps we could desegregate our age nations, open our age borders, occupy and squat our rest homes and hospices and bingo nights and bridge clubs. We could once again begin to speak outside our chronology, learn and teach from and to each other.

In Māori it's the same word: ako—to teach, ako—to learn.

*

In Māori I would say:

Ka huri ahau ināianei ki te hunga ora, āra, ki a koutou kua mihi, kua pōwhiri mai nei ki ahau.
I turn now to the living, to those of you who have greeted me and welcomed me.
Nun wende ich mich den Lebenden zu Ihnen, die Sie mich eingeladen haben.
Koutou e nohonoho nei ki raro i o koutou maunga rangatira nei.
You who sit here in the shadows of your ancestral mountainchiefs.
Ihnen, die Sie am Fuße dieser majestätichen Ahnenberge liegen.

*

I te reo Māori ka kii atu au:

Ki a koutou me ō koutou maunga, ō koutou awa, ō koutou moana, ō koutou marae maha, tēnā koutou, tēnā koutou, tēnā koutou katoa.

Ich grüße euch und eure Berge, eure Flüsse, eure Ozeane und Seen, und eure vielen Dörfer. Meine Damen und Herren; ich grüße Sie, ich grüße Sie, ich grüße alle.

*

Ka kii atu:

Ko Tainui rāua ko Takitimu ngā waka.
Meine Ahnenkanus sind Tainui and Takitimu.
Ko Taranaki, ko Aoraki, ko Tararua ngā maunga.
Meine Berge sind Taranaki, Aoraki and Tararua.

Ko Ohau te awa, ko Tukorehe te tangata, ko Patumākuku te marae.
Der Fluss, dem ich angehöre, ist Ohau. Der geliebte Vorfahre, von dem ich abstamme, ist Tukorehe. Unser traditioneller marae, es heisst Patumākuku.

Anei ahau e tū nei, he uri, me kii he kākano i ruia mai i Hawaiiki nui, i Hawaiiki roa, i Hawaiiki pāmamao.
Hier bin ich, ein Nachkomme, ein Samen aus Hawaiiki nui, aus Hawaiiki roa, aus Hawaiiki pāmamao.

*

I love the English language.
I love it even more when it disappears.

*

Last of all I would say:
Ko Hinemoana Baker tōku ingoa.
My name is Hinemoana Baker.
Ich heiße Hinemoana Baker.

And:
Kia ora!
Be well!
Sei gesund!

Notes and acknowledgements:
Some aspects of this text seem very dated and naïve to me now, as I wrote and presented it in December 2018, long before the 2020 global Covid-19 outbreak. Although the pandemic has changed so much, I have chosen to leave my text unchanged. Many thanks to Silke Hilgers for her help with translating my traditional Māori greeting into German; to Marty Panapa for sharing Te Ūkaipō; to Victoria University Press for permission to re-print "Point the canoe"; to Teresia Teaiwa upon whose wings so many of us rest; and to all the whānau, friends and teachers who have helped me learn who I am, or at least, who I am for now. Tēnā koutou katoa.

VOICING THE minor COSMOPOLITAN

05

COSMOPOLITAN VOICING THE minor COSMOPOLITAN VOI
POLITAN VOICING THE minor COSMOPOLITAN VOICING T
ITAN VOICING THE minor COSMOPOLITAN VOICING THE
VOICING THE minor COSMOPOLITAN VOICING THE minor
NG THE minor COSMOPOLITAN VOICING THE minor COSMO
HE minor COSMOPOLITAN VOICING THE minor COSMOPOLI
COSMOPOLITAN VOICING THE minor COSMOPOLITAN VOI
POLITAN VOICING THE minor COSMOPOLITAN VOICING T
ITAN VOICING THE minor COSMOPOLITAN VOICING THE
VOICING THE minor COSMOPOLITAN VOICING THE minor
NG THE minor COSMOPOLITAN VOICING THE minor COSMO
HE minor COSMOPOLITAN VOICING THE minor COSMOPOLI
COSMOPOLITAN VOICING THE minor COSMOPOLITAN VOI
POLITAN VOICING THE minor COSMOPOLITAN VOICING T
ITAN VOICING THE minor COSMOPOLITAN VOICING THE
VOICING THE minor COSMOPOLITAN VOICING THE minor
NG THE minor COSMOPOLITAN VOICING THE minor COSMO

Irene Hilden in conversation with Anaïs Héraud-Louisadat

Of Voices, Noises & Colonial Traces

Archived for linguistic, musicological, and anthropological purposes, the historical sound recordings stored at what today is Humboldt University of Berlin bear witness to the objectifying and racializing scientific practices of their time. But they also elicit subaltern traces so far absent and silenced in historical narratives and dominant memories. As in most historical repositories, male presences dominate the Berlin sound archive (*Lautarchiv*). A rare exception is the sound file of a female singer named Venkatamma, born in the state of Tamil Nadu in Southern India. In 1926, the German linguist Friedrich Otto Schrader recorded her and other professional performers during a so-called India Show in Berlin. As one of many metropolitan sites, the Berlin Zoological Garden was an institution where People of Color performed in front of white audiences. Singing a traditional love song in Telugu, Venkatamma bursts into laughter after the second repetition of her piece. Inscribed and preserved on a shellac record, her laughing becomes a disruption of the rigid scientific procedure and archival order. In the following conversation, artist Anaïs Héraud-Louisadat and research fellow Irene Hilden talk about their respective approach to the sonic legacies of the Berlin sound archive. They share their thoughts on the broader historical context of a Eurocentric art and knowledge production in the first half of the twentieth century that fashioned practices of othering and exoticization.

Irene Hilden: In my writing on the Berlin sound archive, I often feel stretched to certain limits and fear not doing justice to the sonic material. This is the reason why I invited you to respond to my research and engage artistically with the sound archive's material. How would you describe your artistic and performative practice? How did you approach this archive and its historical sound recordings?

Anaïs Héraud-Louisadat: What has come to us today, almost one century later, through sound, text, and image, is an uncanny object. Neither the scientific nor the technical setting can be described as neutral. What I identify as content cannot be separated from its form. I hear Venkatamma's voice as part of a specific dispositive, which remains fragmented. There is her voice, there is the sound of the machine, there is the setting she was recorded in: the site of a human zoo. And finally, there is the historical time in which all of this was taking place. Still, she seems so close. If I try to picture Europe at the beginning of the twentieth century, I see the achievements of industrialization and technology and its implementation in everyday life and popular culture, no longer reserved for an elite. I see many intersections between entertainment industries, the field of scientific research, and war-related technologies and productions. The collections housed at the sound archive in Berlin are a compelling example: colonization allowed access to people from around the world. It offered the possibility to exploit their labor force, use them for anthropological research and displace them to Europe to be exhibited in the metropolis. Spaces such as colonial exhibitions or *Völkerschauen* attracted not only the interest of a huge number of visitors of the *white* urban middle classes, but also the interest of scientists. It is in this context that a young Woman of Color was recorded, leaving a trace that allows us to listen to her voice and sense her presence.

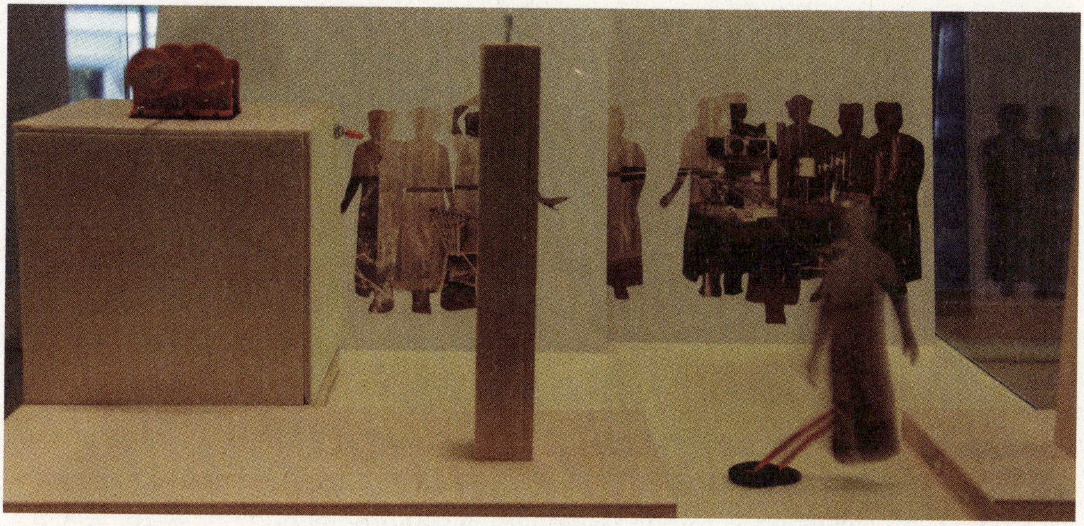

Anaïs Héraud-Louisadat: *REEL* (Installation: Sound, Text, Image). Photo: Paul Carlisle.

Irene: Your remarks remind me of Ann Laura Stoler's suggestions to consider both colonialism's archival content and form.[1] In my work, I am interested in seemingly minor details that nonetheless illuminate the colonial order of things through archival forms and practices. The approach of reading the archive both along and against the archival grain includes the investigation of structures of power and knowledge as much as modes of appropriation and subversion. Particularly against the background of sonic archives, I feel an urge to engage with the question of materiality and the specificity of sound, in contrast to visual and textual sources … Further, I am interested in practices and events that imply blurred dynamics of power and challenge a binary thinking of the subaltern and the dominant, periphery and metropolis. Engaging with Venkatamma's sound file, I began to see her as a colonial subject disrupting the scientific procedure through her laughter. I came to realize that the person recorded can neither be understood as an exploited and marginalized object nor as a subversive cosmopolitan from "below." Rather, I believe that the archival source tells us something about the ambiguity of intersubjective moments, alluding to the dialectics of systems of control and practices of appropriation. In my writing, I try to reconstruct the recording situations and draw on their entangled historical and epistemological contexts.

In doing so, I aim to complicate one-sided perspectives on colonial histories in and of the metropolis of Berlin.

All sounds of the world—the world of all sounds

Anaïs: For me, this advertising slogan, contrived by one of the then major gramophone companies in Berlin, stands as much for the commercial and scientific as for the artistic visions of the time: *All sounds of the world—the world of all sounds*. Unwinding and rewinding, this sentence alludes to a sonic loop or to the circular movements of the gramophone. The human voice printed on wax, possibly to be heard over and over again into the future. Yet, the recorded sound unveils a dissonance in the system: breaking out in laughter, the singer breaks the loop … Recording and archiving, collecting and classifying music, speech, and sound, all thanks to the technical possibilities of the gramophone, was not only a preoccupation of the scientific field but also of the artistic avant-garde. Artists were fascinated by the abundance of new and accessible technologies and influenced by the prevailing prejudices on *otherness* and primitivism. Against this backdrop, I found it particularly interesting to look at the work of the futurist movement, led by artists such as Filippo Tommaso Marinetti, a self-proclaimed Social-Darwinist. In his *Noise Manifesto* (1913), which is still an important compilation for contemporary composers and sound artists, Luigi Russolo tried to categorize the sounds of the city into different kinds of noises. Together with Attilio Pratella, Russolo started to investigate the field of sound and its classification, glorifying what they felt were the highest symbols of modernity: the metropolis, the machine, and especially the machine of war.

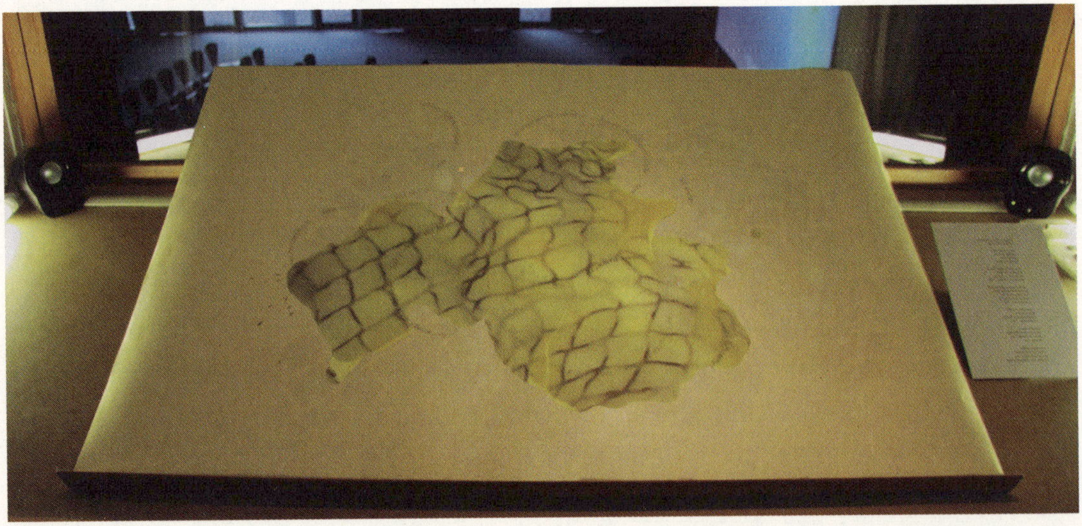

Anaïs Héraud-Louisadat: *REEL* (Installation: Sound, Text, Image). Photo: Paul Carlisle.

Absence & Presence

Irene: When examining sounds from the past, one has to be careful about the desire to read archival fragments as mere signs of historical subjectivity. Scholars like Anjali Arondekar[2] or Saidiya Hartman[3] warned us of attempts at archival recovery, stressing the impossibility of a consolidation between past and present. Hartman, for instance, demands to acknowledge the existing gaps and silences in the colonial archive. She urges us to respect the limits of what cannot be known … In my research, I aim at both mining and undermining the archival logics and blank spaces of the past—knowing that they cannot be separated from epistemic violence and coloniality. On another level, what animates me in my engagement with the acoustic heritage of the sound archive is feeling the need to come to terms with the colonial legacies of my own academic discipline of cultural anthropology, and to reflect on my own practices of knowledge production. I am aware that my postcolonial readings and mediations into archival absences and presences are as much a part of, and add to, the colonial archive, as the historical materials I am focusing on.

Anaïs: The absence of women and female voices in the sound archive's monumental project is still very striking to me. In your work, Irene, you have pointed out that scholars of the time did not seem to have considered the lack of female music and speech samples as a missing or incomplete part of their general research … This is, first and foremost, the reason for my engagement with this sound archive. The first connection I draw between me and the archival document is an empathetic relationship. I ask myself: what did she look like, what was her life like, what were her dreams? And then: am I at all allowed to identify with her, why do I feel the need to understand her laugh as an empowering gesture? This is another question that remains unanswered but that decidedly accompanied me in the realization of this work.

1 Ann Laura Stoler, *Along the Archival Grain: Epistemic Anxieties and Colonial Common Sense* (Princeton: Princeton University Press, 2009).

2 Anjali Arondekar, *For the Record: On Sexuality and the Colonial Archive in India* (Durham: Duke University Press, 2009).

3 Saidiya Hartman, "Venus in Two Acts," *Small Axe* 26 (2008): 1-14.

Liu Chuang

Bitcoin Mining and Field Recordings of Ethnic Minorities[12]

1

Towards the end of the nineteenth century, A French epidemiologist reported a new disease, An employee who had worked in the telegraph office for nine years discovered, He could no longer write certain letters that begin and end with a dot, Such as the letter I, U, and S, Whenever he tried to form these letters, His hands would become stiff and cramped, Then he switched to using only his thumb, But, within two years, His thumb became similarly afflicted, So he began using his index and middle fingers instead, But in only two months, They had become useless as well, Employing his wrist for this purpose, As a last resort, Worsened his disability substantially, For whenever he was forced to use his hands, His hands and arms would start shaking violently, Followed by the experience of over-excitement in the brain, This was an extremely common affliction among telegraph operators at the time.

In 2005, Apple quietly acquired FingerWorks, A gesture recognition company based in Silicon Valley, Mainly known for its Touch Stream multi-touch technology, Which is especially helpful for users with repetitive strain injuries, Three years later, The first iphone was released, A technology that would become a model for all mobile digital devices.

Today, Everyone is a user, And while electronic service providers claim to protect user privacy, They are cashing in on users' time, energy, intelligence and data, Provided by a host of different companies, Thus every user is a laborer, Eventually we will all become uberized, Generating profits for one app or another, Every second of the day, Workers building new infrastructure are at once online and offline.

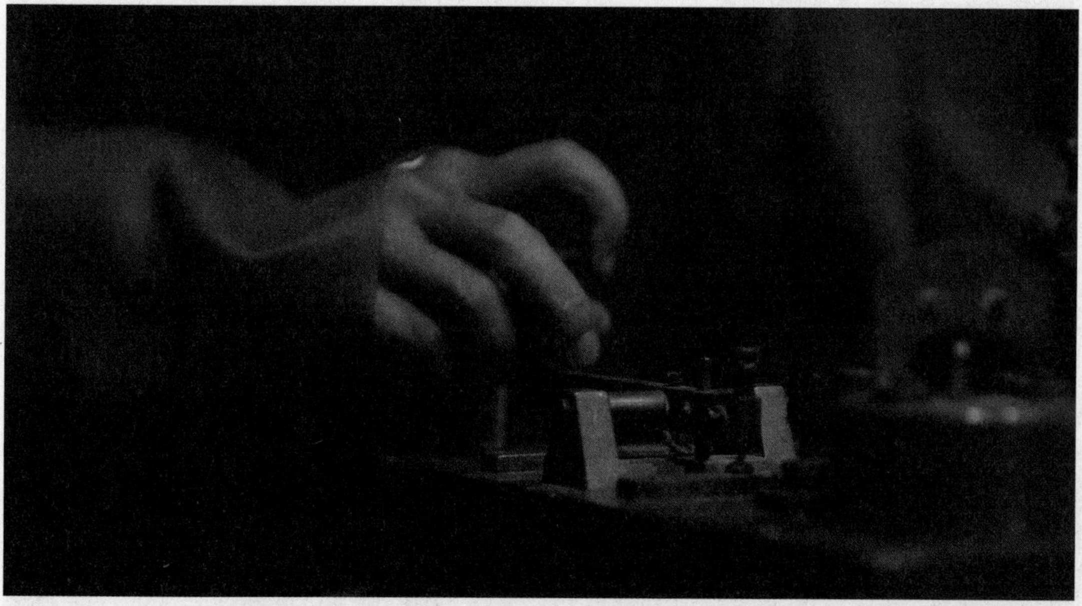

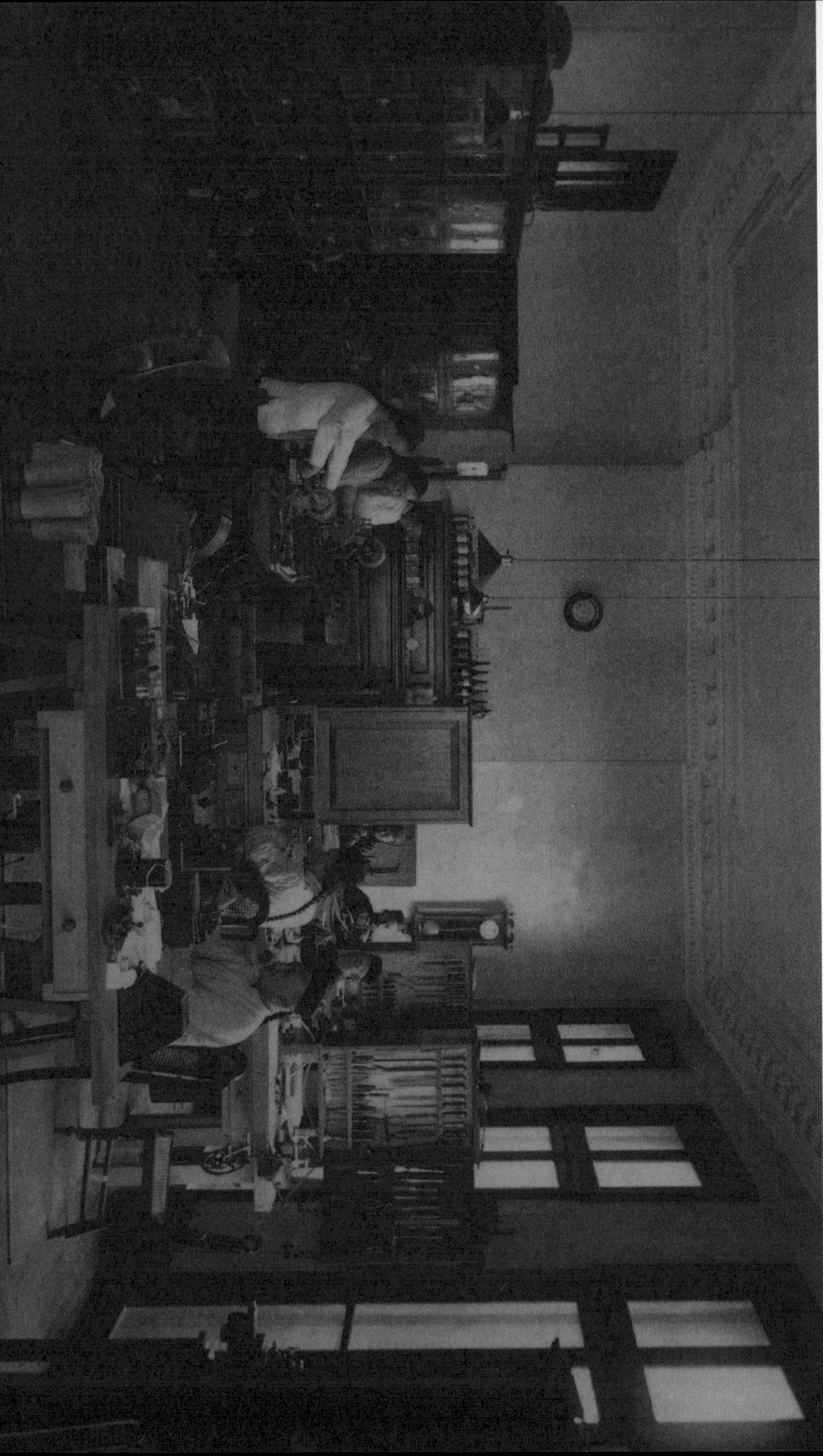

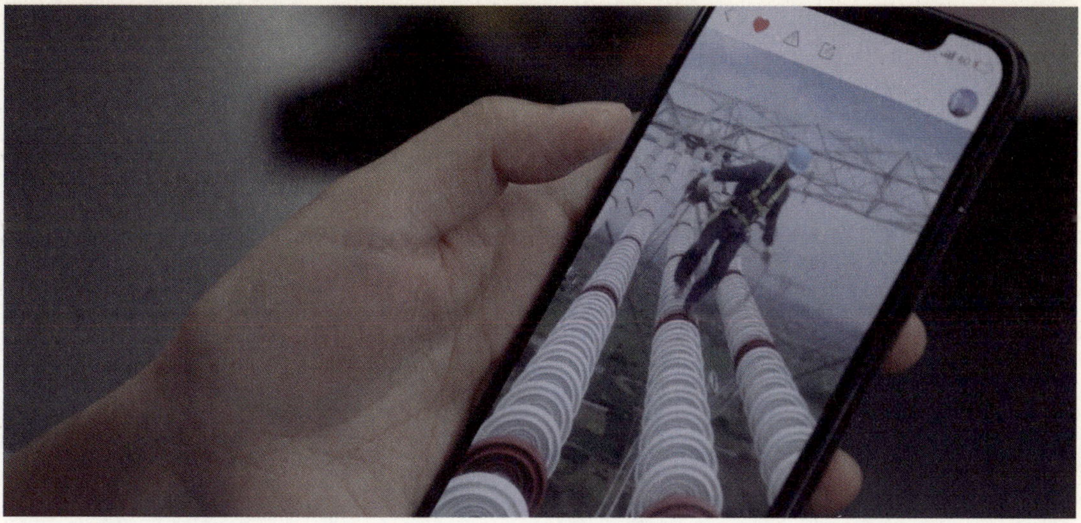

2

Maxim Gorky once described the hydroelectric power station, As able to tame a wild river. Pumped-storage hydroelectric power stations involve a type of energy storage used to supply high peak demands, They are made up of two reservoirs, One at a higher elevation, The other at a lower elevation, During peak hours, Water is sent from the upper reservoir to the lower one, To generate power, Then, between peak hours, It is pumped back to the upper reservoir using cheaper, Off-peak power.

Stalin once remarked that It is wasteful to let water flow into the ocean. The vast scale of dams, And their ability to provide extraordinary, yet safely-contained power for human purposes, Immerse us in a peculiar fantasy, From the elegant and awe-inspiring concrete crescent structure of the Hoover Dam to the incredible mass of the Three Gorges Dam, Today's dams are the hybrid product of the Cold War and nationalist dreams. Among the people who lost their land to hydroelectric power stations, Ethnic minorities comprise a disproportionate majority in the Philippines. All larger dams are located on minority-owned land, When Hòa Bình Dam was built,

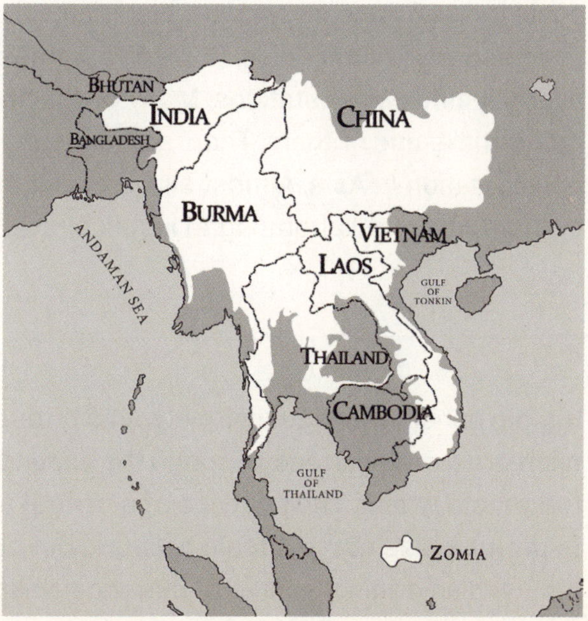

Zomia, according to James C. Scott.

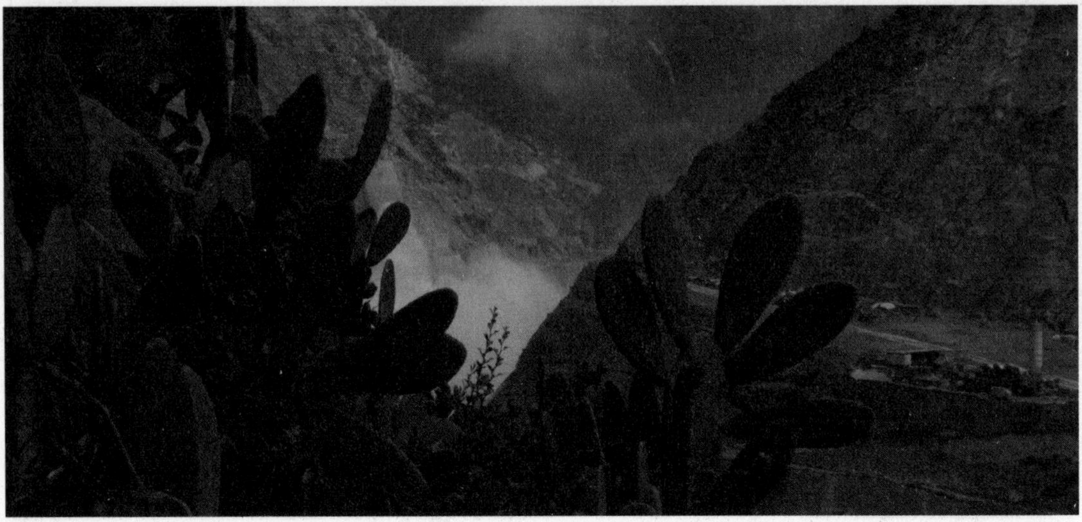

The largest of its kind in Vietnam. Most of the 58,000 people forced to migrate were members of ethnic minority groups. The Zomia that James C. Scott once mentioned in his book now has the world's highest concentration of bitcoin mining operations, Zomia refers to the area, 300 meters above sea level, That stretches from the highlands of central Vietnam to northeastern India, It spans five countries in Southeast Asia, As well as four provinces in southern China, It is home to an ethnic minority population of 100 million.

3

No need to be on site, Mobile control is enough, I'm in Shenzhen … I started bitcoin mining in 2011, Initially I was mining at home, But then the industry entered a crisis in 2012, An energy crisis, Electricity in cities became too expensive, Generating extremely loud noise, Someone suggested that, Since China has so many hydroelectric power stations, Many of which are abandoned, It would be a waste not to make use of them, Then, someone made a map With the address of every power station in Asia, Almost all were built in the last century, So we went to talk to them About collaborating to install bitcoin mines in there.

4

Bitcoin miners manage their networks through a Proof-of-Work (PoW) mechanism producing currency through the expenditure of CPU power and time, Satoshi Nakamoto writes, The absence of a central authority, Not only encourages miners to promote use of the Bitcoin network, But also provides Bitcoin's circulation system with an original source of currency, Nakamoto vividly compares this process to a kind of gold mining, Where all the gold obtained is immediately injected into economic activity, In order to maintain the pace of bitcoin production at approximately ten minutes per coin. The difficulty of mining new bitcoins is regularly increased, Forcing miners to chase after lower-priced sources of electricity, And build rooms filled with automated bitcoin mining equipment.

The roar of mining equipment is muffled by the sound of waterfalls at the hydroelectric power station, Until it is barely noticeable, Bitcoins, on the other hand, Are like the cloud above the power station, A quieter and more ethereal material embodiment of these infrastructures. Some believe The advent of Bitcoin is due to widespread resentment of sovereign nation-states' excessive money supply and interventionary currency policy, As well as a yearning for communal stigmergy in a gift economy.

After October, Sichuan would enter its drought season, We should deliver these bitcoin mining machines to Xinjiang, In winter, Xinjiang gets really windy, It has many wind power plants, And the electricity is cheap, So we leave our machines there, And in Spring, We ship them to inner Mongolia, Which is home to many coal-fired power stations, Before summer, Before the rainy season in Sichuan, We ship them back to Sichuan. Our miners are actually like beekeepers.

5

In *A Prehistory of the Cloud* (2015), Tung-Hui Hu discusses the militarized legacy of cloud-based computing, The digital cloud derives from older network technologies and politics, Where fiber-optic networks are broken into different layers or transplanted onto older networks, Through it, we can trace back to the earliest railway and telegraph networks, The digital cloud has also transferred control to these older structures of sovereignty, While Bitcoin ostensibly resists this centralized power structure, Its infrastructure is still built on it, Forming a symbiotic relationship with it, Just like the relationship between the ancient empire and its surrounding minority communities.

James C. Scott believes We might think of these mountain people as refugees, fugitives, Exiles. Those who successfully managed to exempt themselves From two thousand years of oppression in wet-rice cultivating countries, Enslavement, taxation, forced labor, plague, war, Bloodshed and everything about them, Their survival skills, social organization, ideology, Even their controversial culture based on oral heritage are carefully designed to elude state authority, They are scattered across rugged mountains, Their mobility, agricultural habitats, kinship structure,

Their highly adaptable national identity, As well as their patient wait for the millenarian leader promised by prophecy, Are all effective measures that both help them avoid rule by an external state, And prevent them from forming an internal state regime, What most of them want is to avoid assimilation by the Chinese empire already extant since ancient times.

In 544 BC, King Jing of Zhou wanted to cast a series of bianzhong or "chime bells" named wushe, The largest of the series is called Dalin, Never built before, Some natural phenomena produce heavy bass frequencies, Like earthquakes, volcanic eruptions, thunder and meteorite strikes. For King Zhou, the purpose of creating this instrument was to mimic these sounds, The instrument was expected to reverberate with powerful bass tones, In order to raise enough copper, King Jing launched the first currency reform in history, Reducing the weight of all recalled currency by half in order to make the instrument, While doubling the value of the reissued currency, Which led to inflation. According to historical records, The royal musician Lingzhoujiu tried to discourage the king, He said, after studying the customs of different places, The emperor is inspired, To write a song, And wishes to create a new instrument to play it, If the instrument were small without sounding too feeble, And big without sounding too bold, It would reach harmony, And that's called yuezheng, the ideal sound, The bell your majesty has just created, Emits an excessively cold sound, which is detrimental to your health, Its cost exceeds the budget, which is inappropriately indulgent, And it only serves to muffle the ideal sound, The sound produced by this instrument, Is unbearable to the human ear, It is not harmony, The King of Zhou did not follow his advice, Soon after the chime bell was made, The king passed away.

August 6, 1945, 8:15 a.m., An atomic bomb was dropped on Hiroshima, The overwhelming bass note of this explosion stunned the East Asian monarchs who were attempting to dominate the world, Thereafter, bass rumblings became less and less remarkable, The never-ending noise of the city, The roaring of airports, The hum of high-voltage current, Are like daily reverberations of World War thunder, But the number of explosives used to build infrastructure actually exceeds, The total sum of munitions expended in human warfare, The average loudness of a train station is 70 decibels, Bitcoin mine, 90 dB, The noise near an airport can reach 120 dB, People who regularly work in these places Frequently suffer permanent hearing damage. Active noise reduction is by now a highly developed technology, It uses a microphone to collect noise, Processes it with a series of circuits and algorithms calculated and developed by sound engineers, And generates a soundwave of equal amplitude but inverted phase to the noise, Which is then projected through a speaker, To interfere with and ultimately cancel out the noise, This is the mechanism of active noise reduction. Infrastructural hubs are primary environments for noise pollution, Under such a technological backdrop, Our environment becomes virtual, The infrastructure more and more difficult to detect, Which seems to lay the groundwork for a more extreme form of control.

Claude Bailblé once made a rather poetic remark, That the ear is not a homogenous organ, Merely given to serve the function of hearing, Tracing its origin, The ear amounts to just a piece of skin, Whose stereocilia function as sensors when disturbed by sound waves, Every bit of this skin is different, Gradually submerged in interior fluid, To capture sound from afar, The ear is cleverly hidden by the tibial cone, Operating delicately under its protection, It maintains the body's sense of balance, Sets the horizontal reference line for it, And helps with spatial coordination, It's what enables dancers to spin, run and jump during their performances.

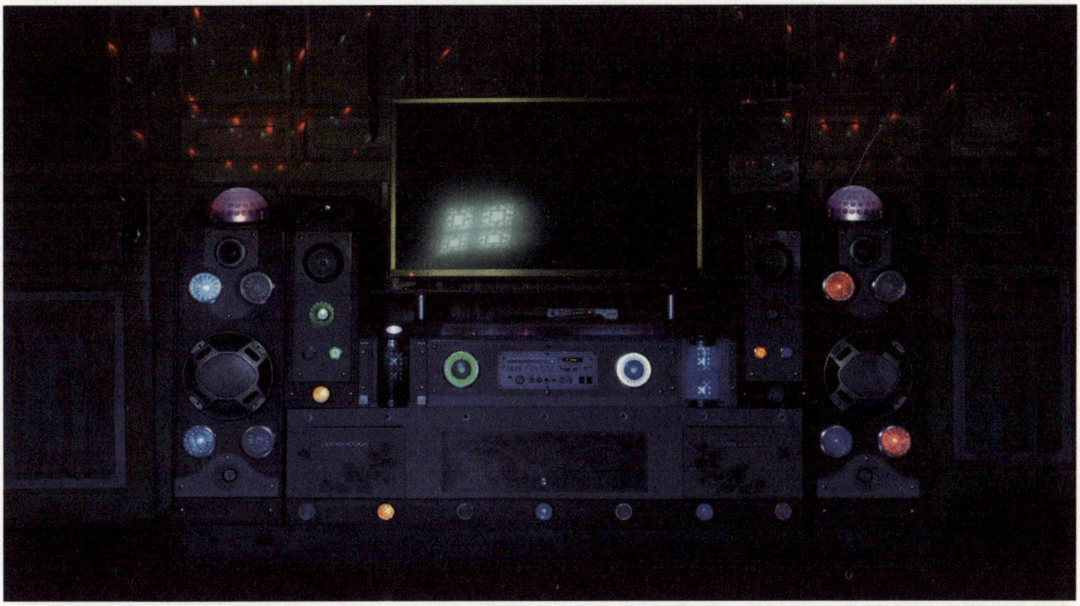

6

At the beginning of the twenty-first century, In order to acclimatize Zomia's minorities to television, Factories in the special economic zones utilized their excess capacity to invent the EVD, A classic Shanzhai product, A hodgepodge of all the electronic equipment of the day, Television, radio, recorder, DVD, Karaoke, Bluetooth, As well as Wi-Fi, But most importantly, a sound-to-light synchronization system, Initially conceived as a visual aid technology, To help the deaf and the hearing-impaired learn music, This technology was then used to digitize the nervous system of minority ethnic groups, And when the people finally adjusted to digital technology, The lights disappeared from the cabinets.

Hollywood East Star Trax, Was an electronic dance album, That was first released in Hong Kong in the 1980s, And when it took the Mainland by storm, Han youth became digitized, Some say, The modernization that took the Han a century, We achieved in just 30 years.

7

Where did these sounds come from?

Pete Seeger criticized those anthropologists making field recordings, For doing nothing more than moving music from one grave to another, From the site of cultural extinction to a museum, All in vain, However, perhaps it is precisely their archival recordings, That have allowed us to create fictions, In *Close Encounters of the Third Kind* (1977), Steven Spielberg imagines a musical dialogue between humans and aliens.

8

The astronauts arrived on a planet covered by oceans, Solaris.

Who was it?
She died 10 years ago
What you saw was the materialization of your conception of her
What was her name?
Hari
Everything began after we started experimenting with radiation.
We hit the ocean's surface with strong X-ray beams.
But it …
By the way, consider yourself lucky
After all, she's a part of your past
What if it had been something you had never seen before
but something you had thought or imagined?
I don't understand
As it turned out
the ocean responded to our heavy radiation with something else
It probed our minds and extracted something like islands of memory
Will she come back?
She will

And she won't
Hari the Second
There may be an endless number of them

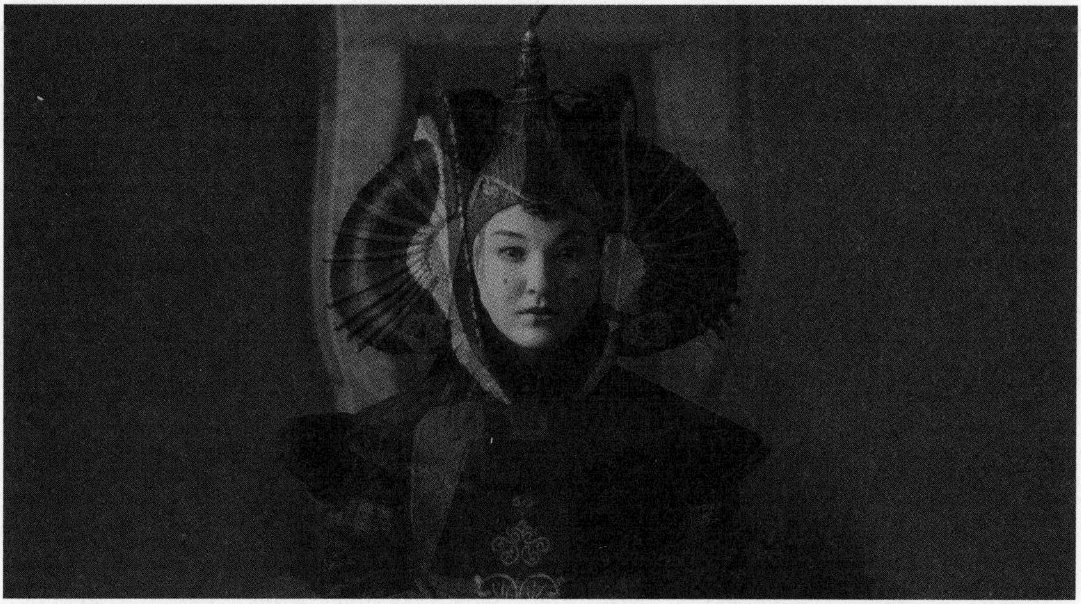

Races once extinct have now been resurrected on Earth, One is his wife on Earth who exists in his memory, While the other, in the spacecraft, Is a materialization of his memory, done by Solaris, Kris Kelvin experiences a mental breakdown, Originally colonizers of space, these astronauts in Stanisław Lem's works, Were ultimately colonized themselves by outer space, These Soviets, trapped in the universe and with their mind swallowed by Solaris, Subscribe to the norms of a modern, sovereign state, Industrialization, Cosmology, revolution, rationality and bureaucracy ... But they cannot make these things run on Solaris, They are what the Uruguayan writer Horacio Quiroga calls the "ex-men," A term that signifies the collapse of the relationship between empire, men, and subjectivity, A relationship that has hitherto been assumed to constitute the future world order.

---

1 *Bitcoin Mining and Field Recordings of Ethnic Minorities*, 2018 , 3 Channel Videos, 4k, 5.1 sound 40 minutes, Commissioned for Cosmopolis #1.5 : Enlarged Intelligence with the support of the Mao Jihong Arts Foundation, Courtesy of the artist and Antenna Space.

---

2 This text is the transcription of the English subtitles of the video artwork, which is narrated mainly in the language of the Mi-ñag people who live in the highlands of China's Southwestern region; and partly in Hakka.

Dong Bingfeng

Bio-Archiving: Shenyang Underground Music as History, Awareness, and Art in Action

> The aspiration of today's art [is] to become life itself, not merely to depict life or to offer it art products.[1]
>
> Boris Groys

1. A Short History

Chinese rock 'n' roll and its attendant artistic expressions have yet to be written into the history of contemporary Chinese art.

Several reasons may explain this. To begin with, even though contemporary art in China has evolved beyond traditional disciplinary confines, rock as an idea and form continues to be received as a genre in the music industry, despite its intimate interconnections with art practices. Secondly, the history of Chinese contemporary art remains tethered to systems and constructs of a Western, modernist art history that is centred on visuality. What lies beyond the realm of visual perception and aesthetic judgment, including the subject of this essay—underground music in Shenyang—has long been excluded from the discursive historiography of contemporary art in China.

Is rock 'n' roll an integral part of contemporary art in China? The following discussion of an exhibition I curated may constitute a partial response. In March and September 2016, the archival exhibition *Bio-archiving: Underground Music in Shenyang 1995–2002* was held, respectively, at Taikang Space in Beijing and the Lu Xun Academy of Fine Arts in Shenyang, the capital of Liaoning province. On view was a vast body of documents and records from the mid-1990s to the 2000s, grouped under the rubric of Shenyang underground music, and an even larger archive of art projects and audio-visual materials by performance artists, independent filmmakers, and experimental playwrights with longstanding collaborations with underground musicians. As I stated in the exhibition brochure, "the [strategy of] hybridity and juxtaposition recreates real historical conditions in order to shed light on the rock circle's strong sense of autonomy and resistance to being subsumed into the mainstream or coopted by capital, while pushing the boundaries of our own, often stagnant understanding of the ecosystems of contemporary Chinese art and culture."[2]

A panel discussion titled "Back to Locality: Rock Music, Art, and Cultural Politics in the 1990s" was held at the opening of the Taikang Space exhibition on March

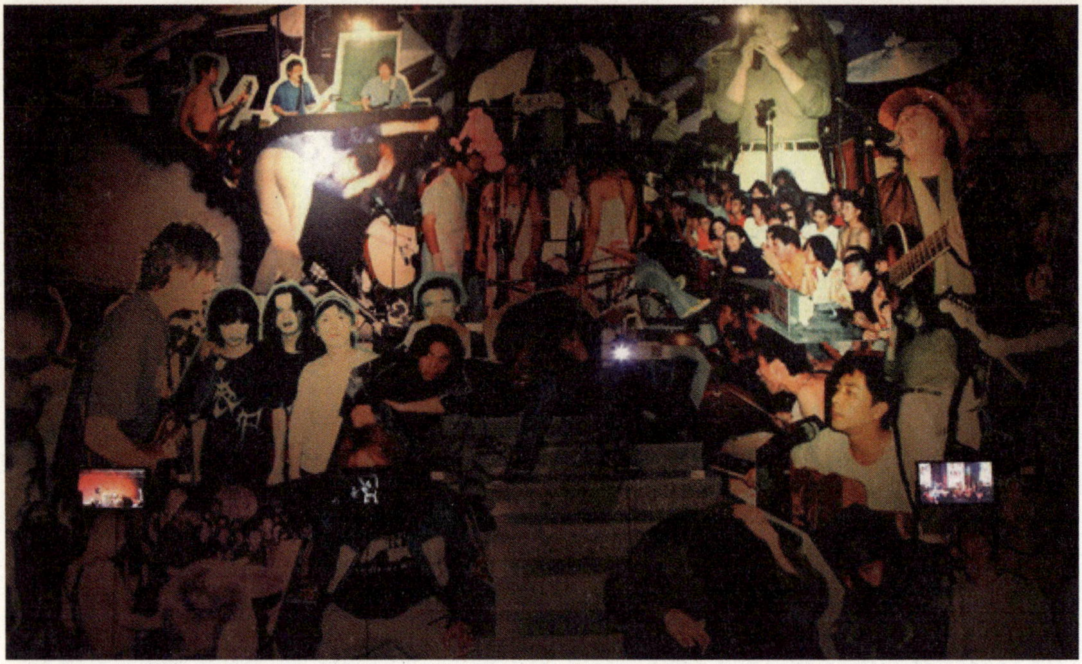

Exhibition Bio-archiving: Underground Music in Shenyang at Taikang Space, Beijing, 2016

17, 2017. Colin Chinnery, Jeph Lo, Li Juchuan, and Ma Zhongren were invited to speak as witnesses of nineties underground music and subculture in cities like Beijing, Taipei, Wuhan, and Shenyang respectively. Unsurprisingly, the exhibition received little feedback from the Chinese art world.

Bio-archiving was not an "artless" exhibition. Revisiting this history with the artists in question, we agreed to date the beginning of this period to the year 1995, which saw the rise of Cynical Realism in contemporary Chinese art on the global circuit, as well as with the momentous eruption of Shenyang underground music, with dozens of bands—such as Malignant Tumor in the End of Days (末日毒瘤), The Troublemakers (搅水男孩), and Dead Pills (死药丸)—emerging in a spontaneous, totalizing fashion that coincided with the surfacing of the city's subcultures.

Meanwhile, as the Beijing East Village art community was forced to disband in 1995, artist Ma Zhongren returned to his home city of Shenyang, where he organized a series of seminal music shows and facilitated interactions and collaborations between the music scene and other art practices. These preoccupation with not only art making but also questions of self-organization and self-institutionalization effectively instated the phenomenon of Shenyang contemporary art. The city's art schools, including the renowned Lu Xun Academy, were terribly parochial and occluded in their academicism and utterly unresponsive to ongoing social change. Viewed in this light, the year 1995 becomes an important turning point for both music and contemporary art in the city; any

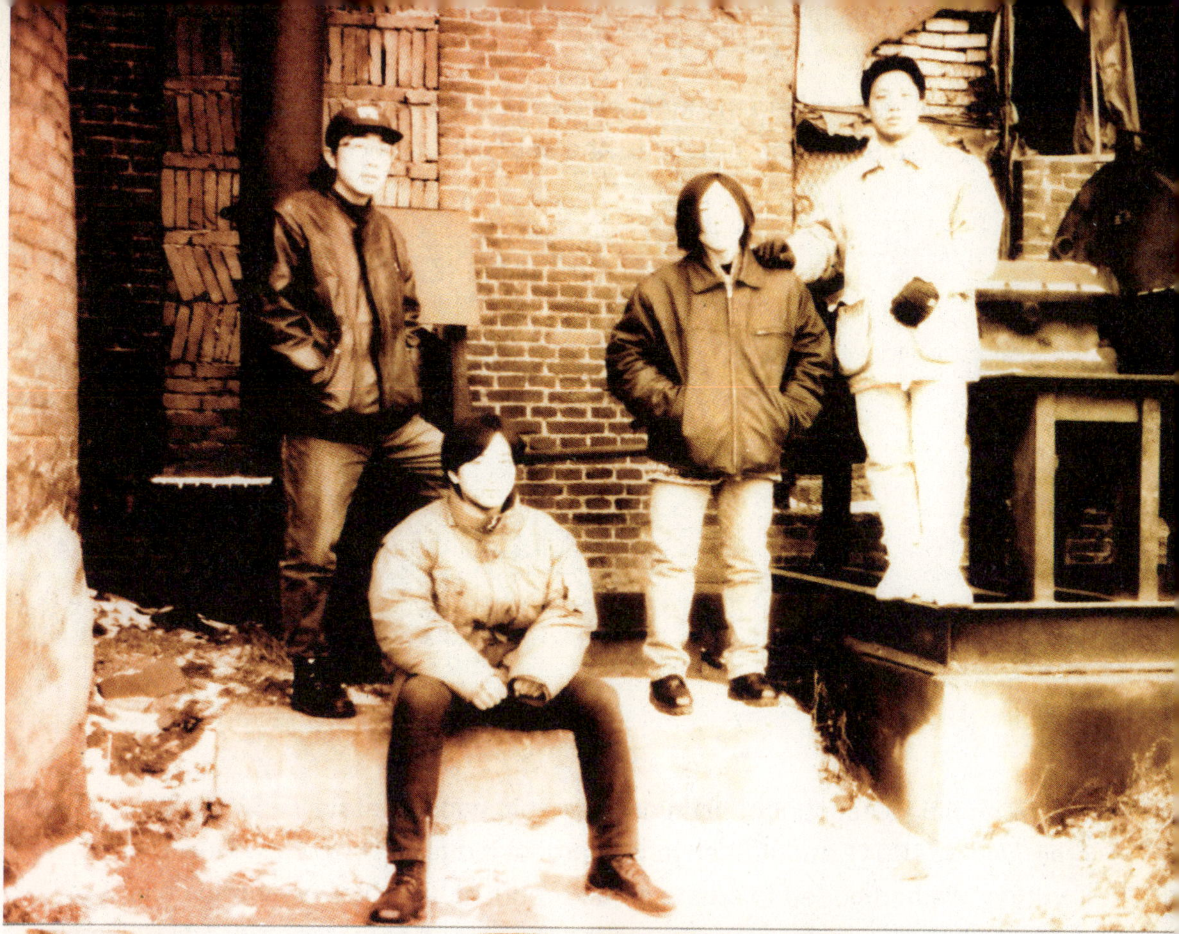

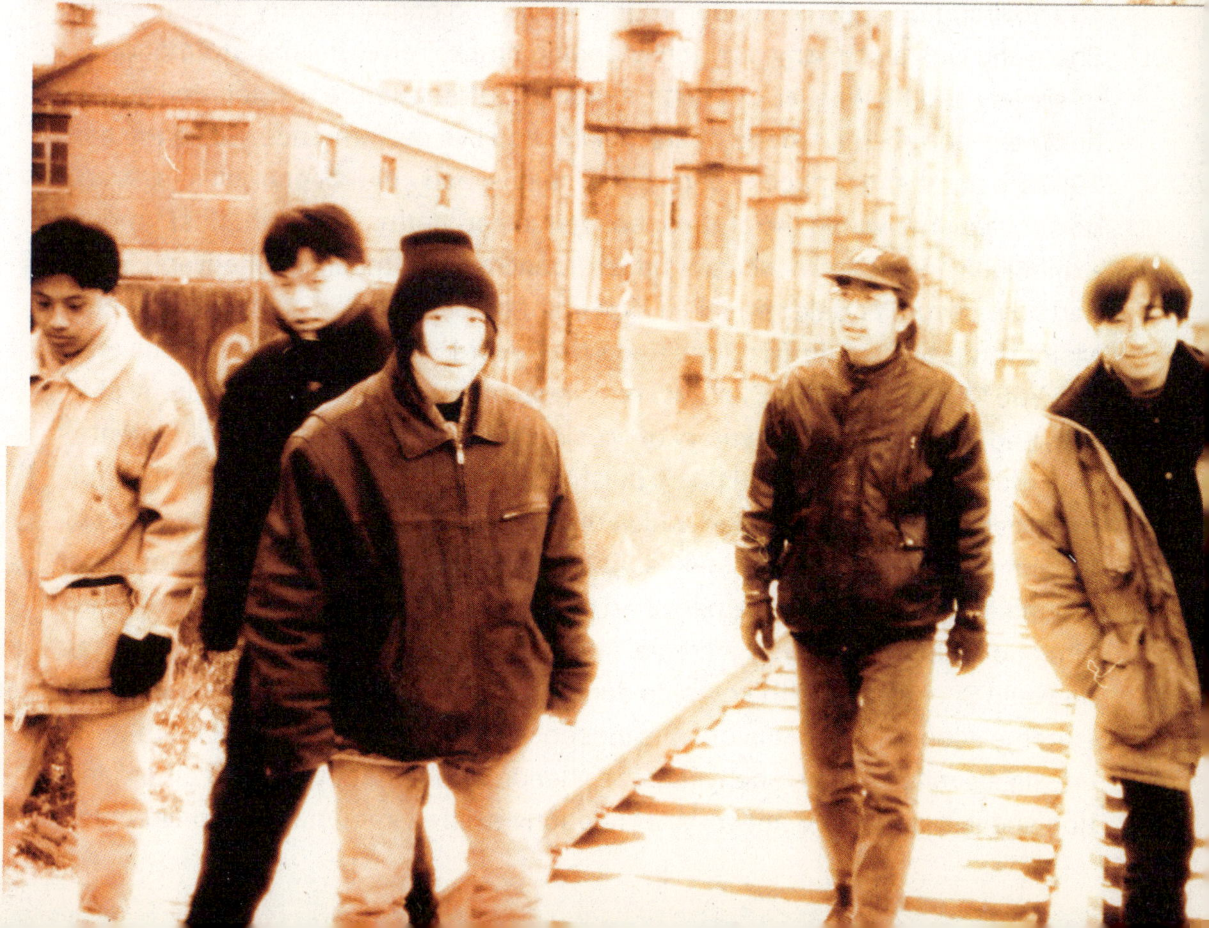

reflection on Shenyang in the nineties must necessarily synthesize and articulate these interdisciplinary art practices and subcultural phenomena.[3]

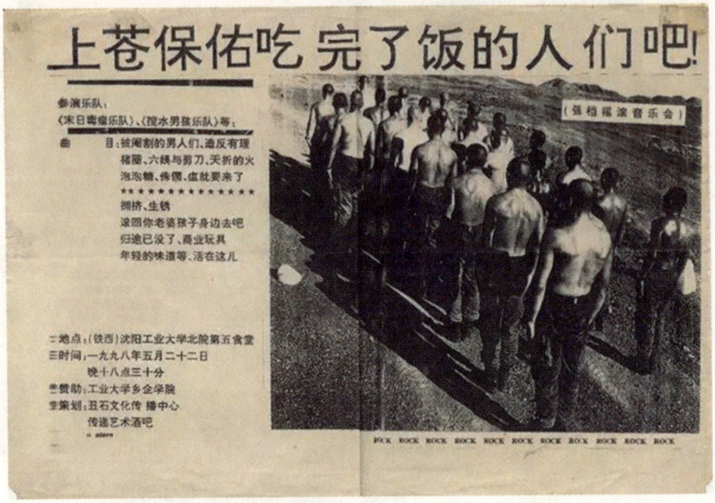

May God Bless Those Who Finish Their Dinner - announcement for a Rock 'n' Roll Concert in Shenyang 1998.

In Wang Bing's account of his nine-hour epic documentary *Tie Xi Qu: West of the Tracks* (2004), about Shenyang's largest industrial complex, Tiexi District, he writes: "We had hoped to create a new world; at last this very world collapsed."[4] The environment in which underground music and contemporary art evolved in Shenyang was also marked by the changing times. Torrential transformation of society and the dire lack of institutional art infrastructure precipitated an ad hoc, semi-commercial mode of art-making and live performance. Since the early 1990s, a number of spaces—bars, small salons, and cultural premises existing in power vacuums within the state or academic apparatus—began to host irregular exhibitions and performances of underground art and music in Shenyang, which had no museum or gallery-backed system of presenting and sponsoring culture. Major venues of the time include Red Wall Record Store near Liaoning University; Say You Say Me and Soft Clay, two bars located between Lu Xun Academy of Fine Arts and Shenyang Conservatory of Music; the short-lived bar Happy Elements; and, most importantly, the Hippies Bar, founded by Malignant Tumor in the End of Days lead vocalist Xiao Han, which played an indispensable role in the city's art and music scene in the nineties. At its peak, Hippies was the place for underground music shows, performance art, art exhibitions, as well as experimental film and theatre, serving as a crucial site for intellectual and cultural exchange between Shenyang and the outside during a period of drastic social change and extreme economic depression. It is indeed incredible to reflect back on that era—in a similar vein as Shenyang, the phenomenon of active artist self-organization and self-generated networks of relations existed in many second-tier cities

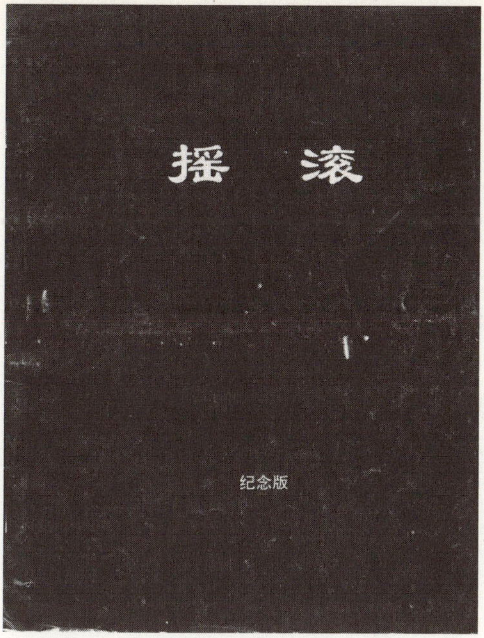

Rock 'n' Roll (magazine)

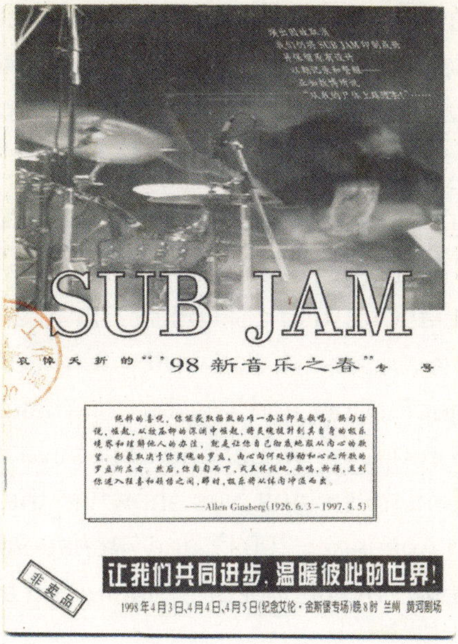

Brochure of the first underground music festival Sub Jam — in memoriam of the cancelled 98 New Year concert, Lanzhou, 1998. The Troublemakers had their first public appearance on this concert.

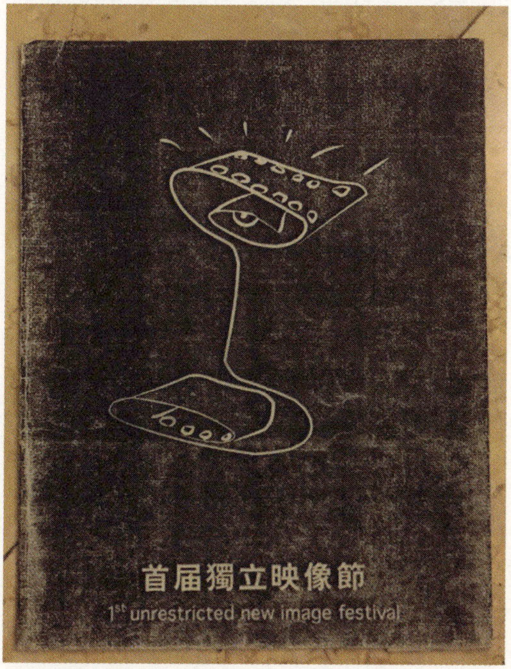

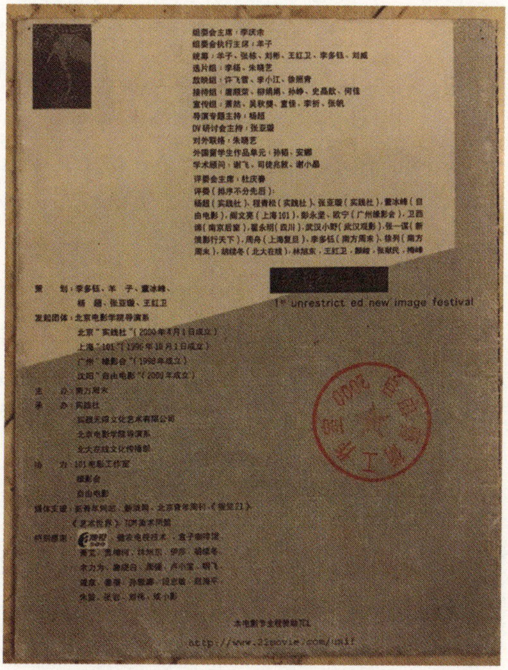

Program Brochure of the *1st Unrestricted New Image Festival* at Beijing Film Academy, 2001

around the country, such as Guangzhou, conveniently located in the Pearl River Delta and enjoying its proximity to Hong Kong; Wuhan with its punk scene; and Lanzhou, where the musician and critic Yan Jun was based.

As previously stated, this archival exhibition primarily consisted of materials from the underground music world, art shows organized by Ma Zhongren, and activities of the Cinema Libre group, initiated by myself and others in the late 1990s. Officially formed at Hippies Bar in 2000, Cinema Libre represented an intersection of the music, art, and writer communities in the city—Xiao Han, Dead Pills lead singer Fu Duo, and The Troublemakers lead A Bai were also key contributors to the group. Individual and collective work by Cinema Libre members and underground musicians was shown in the *1st Unrestricted New Image Festival* (Beijing Film Academy, 2001), and *Archaeology of the Future: The Second Triennial of Chinese Art* (Nanjing, 2005), including a sound art performance at its inauguration.

2. Life Itself and Representation

This history doesn't easily lend itself to a retrospective. Underground music in Shenyang could be considered underground inasmuch as it maintained conscious resistance to mainstream popularization and self-distancing from the Beijing-dominated rock scene. To reject commercialization is to make oneself impossible to commodify; sticking to the underground means staying close to reality as it takes place. Disadvantaged and nonconformist communities enthusiastically received realist lyrics and rowdy punk music that spoke directly to social issues. Their main Western influences included Sex Pistols, Nirvana, Pixies, and Red Hot Chili Peppers. As songwriter, vocalist, and worker A Bai put it, The Troublemakers' lyrics could be read as "evidence from below." Rage against the establishment was the common denominator between Chinese rock 'n' roll and the Shenyang underground. The price of growth finds expression in a manifesto such as: *Die before you get old*. The sudden eruption of underground music in the tumultuous nineties was the tour de force of contemporary art and culture in Shenyang, which reorganized and greatly facilitated the connection between art practices and real life actions.

Originating from the working class of Tiexi District, The Troublemakers' twofold toil on the factory floor and in underground bars attested to the nature of art/music as labour and exchange. Trained in medicine, Dead Pills lead, Fu Duo, often combined bloody, incendiary acts of body puncturing with savagely violent music in his live performances. Fu Duo's screenplay for the independent film *Droop* also tells of the roulette game of switching between grueling, benumbing everyday life and independent art/filmmaking, and of the accompanying sense of alienation. In the cracks of institutions and artistic actions, the artist finds a transient sense of autonomous life.

Boris Groys writes that "life can be documented but not shown,"[5] in reference to Italian philosopher Giorgio Agamben's idea of the *homo sacer*. Life beyond governance alone could be considered an exemplary life. The music and live performance of bands like Malignant Tumor in the End of Days, The Troublemakers, and Dead Pills suggest a relentless quest for proximity to the real—hence the realism—and possibilities of autonomous life on the outside or in the underground. Their fundamental pessimism toward life itself reflects a searing critique of existential conditions as well as of culture as a totality. In the epic song "Monument of Youth" alluding to the events of 1989, Xiao Han concludes Shenyang's decade of struggle with his lyrics:

> In the passing of time,
> you have lost your youth,
> inscribed in today's suffering the impulses and unrest.
>
> In those bleak memories,
> you once called for the light,
> your signs and slogans cracked the fissures of life.

The art historian Wu Hung remarks, "East Village artists favoured collective action, adopting performance as a platform for collaborative engagements, where photography, painting, installation, performance, and music were able to intersect and interact."[6] East Village artist Ma Zhongren transposed the ideas of collective, interdisciplinary practice to the music shows he organized, which helped catalyze the ecosystem of independent art and subcultural activities. In an interview, Ma Zhongren quotes Joseph Beuys: "art is a living organism, fluid and alive, flowing into all material governed by spirituality."[7] Like the musicians, Ma Zhongren's own performances in Shenyang attempted to address the relations between biopolitics and life as an artist in a palpable fashion. Both the "hour-long intervention in the life of others," titled *36 Volt Dial* (1995),[8] and the *Bathroom Show*, part of *Post-Infrastructure Art Show* (2001), reveal productive internal tensions in the necessary conflicts and frictions the artist must maintain with social institutions.

3. Art as Future-Oriented Action

The archive of the Shenyang underground on view at *Bio-archiving* evinces a perpetually liminal condition of life—transient practices of possible forms of life outside prescribed systems and ways of living. As connected as they were to a specific time, place, and community, these practices had the potential to reshape artistic life. At the exhibition, legible historical texts and invisible, deafening, mutually interfering music evoked and compelled the audience's own bodily presence.

In March 2001, independent filmmaker Yu Depeng, A Bai, and Zhao Guoxin initiated a performance project called *I Save Myself* at Soft Clay bar. Participants were asked to tie themselves up with ropes and then untangle the knots in five minutes in whichever way they liked, uttering the phrase "I save myself" before their final release. The three organizers, as well as Ma Zhongren, myself, and Yang Zhiming of The Troublemakers all took part in the action. In October of that same year, as a theatre group called Bad Temper Commune, Yu Depeng and A Bai put on a play titled *Happiness Supermarket*. The piece appropriated narratives of the Red Army's victory over Kuomintang troops to declare it an imperative for art to always be ready to combat the new ideological "reactionaries" of the day. The flyer reads:

A party for goodbyes
For the stupidity of inferiority
For the dissolution of purity
A life lived for death
A time for disintegration
A nation to be excavated
A technology to be upgraded
A flame to be put out
A burial, a burial.

Both events could be considered approximations of the theatre as Gesamtkunstwerk.

Importantly, beyond individual musician and band activities, the underground music world in Shenyang was interdisciplinary in orientation and practiced alternative institution-building as a form of self-organization. Hippies Bar founder Xiao Han started the indie magazine *Public Health* (which published one issue in 2000) fostering underground music and subculture in the three Northeast Chinese provinces. Active in the underground music scene and a founding member of the Cinema Libre group, I published *Culture of Street* magazine (a total of three issues, the first issue was published in 2000), which introduced experimental art and film while attempting to establish an international information and resource network.

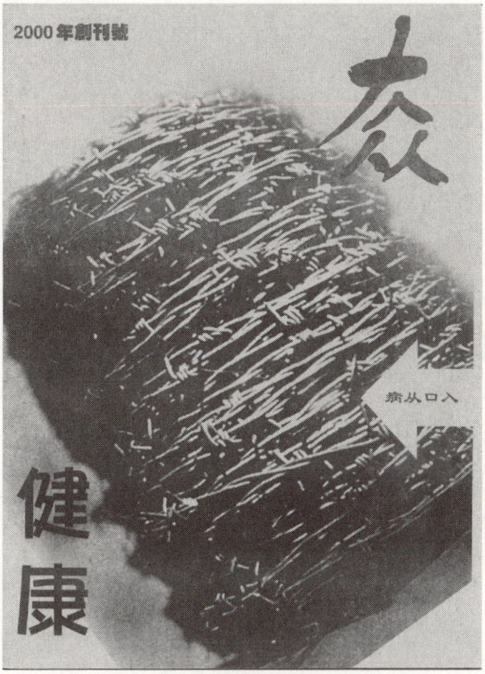

Public Health magazine, vol. 1, 2000.

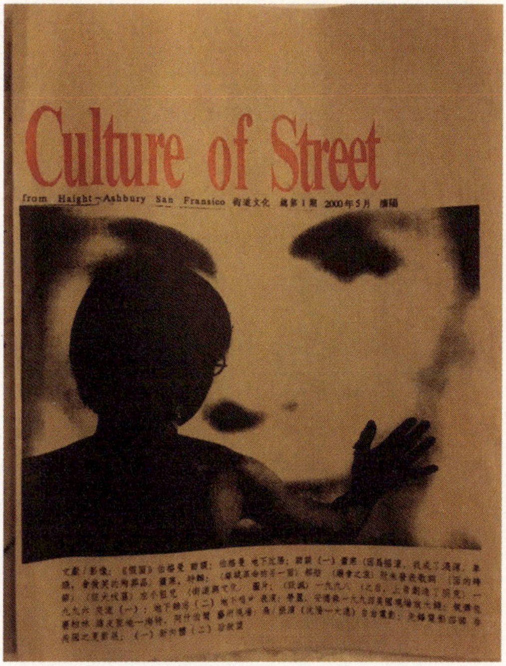

Culture of Street magazine, vol. 1, 2000.

Meanwhile, Xiao Han and Ma Zhongren played crucial parts in the Shenyang-based art collective K Space, organized by Ma Shang and advised by North Art Group member Ren Jian—all key figures engaged in and advocating for the artistic and community-building endeavours in Shenyang and the northeast region. Projects such as *Channel: The 1st Zhongxing Image Art Exhibition*, held in January 2002 in Shenyang, and *The 1st Northern Independent Image Exhibition*, at Beijing's Loft New Media Art Center in July 2002, best represented the collaborations between the underground music community and art groups like Cinema Libre and K Space. As Zhao Guoxin points out in his unpublished chronicle "My Participation in *The First Zhongxing Image Art Exhibition*," "the most important outcome of the event was that more people were involved." Curator Hou Hanru also wrote, in 2005: "[Self-organization] is not only a declaration of independence, but also a challenge to the establishment, a transcendence of 'multitude' itself."[9]

As is evident in the exhibition, *Bio-archiving* is an effort to integrate Shenyang underground music into the contemporary art landscape of the provincial capital and beyond. Its potential lies in identifying and transforming problematic patterns of conventional research on contemporary Chinese art. In other words, Bio-archiving is an incomplete discursive and historical reworking of certain ecologies and phenomenologies pertaining to the Shenyang underground that have yet remained undefined by contemporary art institutions. It is an alternative writing that departs radically from current conditions of biopolitical discipline, attempting to resist and transcend a "life-art" of some sort that leads to so-called artistic freedom. In his essay "Neue Slowenische Kunst—New Slovenian Art: Slovenia, Yugoslavia, Self-Management, and the 1980s," critic Aleš Erjavec observes that "[the band] Laibach ... found a discursive tool with which it was able to overcome symbolically the deadlock between a social reality that had drifted into populist totalitarianism and the discursive reality of an official ideology in which the official discourse promoted unlimited freedom."[10]

Only by upholding the practices of self-organization and radical anti-institutionalization could the Shenyang underground music and its associated art practices generate a response to contemporary art and social reality at a distance—an innate momentum and potential for continuous evolution, both historical and dynamically present.

---

1 Boris Groys, "Art in the Age of Biopolitics: From Artwork to Art Documentation," *documenta 11* (Ostfildern-Ruit: Hatje Cantz, 2002), 108-114.

---

2 Dong Bingfeng, "Preface to *Bio-Archiving: Shenyang Underground Music 1995–2002*," exhibition brochure, Taikang Space, Beijing, 2016.

---

3 Another case in point could be *From "Polar Region" to "Tie Xi Qu": Exhibition of Contemporary Art in Northeast China 1985–2006*, co-curated by Wang Huangsheng, Guo Xiaoyan, and Dong Bingfeng. The exhibition was held at the Guangdong Museum of Art, August 30–September 24, 2006.

---

4 Lü Xinyu, "Tie Xi Qu: History and Class Consciousness," http://page.renren.com/601539698/note/880149126/.

5 Groys, "Art in the Age of Biopolitics."

6 Wu Hung, Rong Rong's *East Village: A Moment in Chinese Experimental Art* (Beijing: Shiji Wenjing, 2014), 84.

7 Ma Zhongren, *East Village Performance Diary*, April 1995, unpublished.

8 Ma Zhongren, performance project plan for *36 Volt Dial*, October 1995. The performer sends nonstop information to the telephone station for one hour. The goal is to create a crisscross of behaviours through the performer's repetitive, continuous, and uninterrupted actions that interfere in and, at times, take over the flow of information. During the performance, other users' signals are consistently obstructed and prevented from reaching the station. The performance enacts an invisible intervention in the life of others, an effective way of bringing art into real life.

9 Hou Hanru, "BEYOND: An Extraordinary Space of Experimentation for Modernization," in *The Second Guangzhou Triennial*, Guangzhou Museum of Art (Guangzhou: Lingnan Art Publishing House, 2005), 31.

10 Aleš Erjavec, "Neue Slowenische Kunst—New Slovenian Art: Slovenia, Yugoslavia, Self-Management, and the 1980s," in *Postmodernism and the Postsocialist Condition: Politicized Art under Late Socialism* (Berkeley: University of California Press, 2012).

Julian Henriques and Zairong Xiang

Mumbo Jumbo, Jiggery-Pokery, Cosmopolitricks

Transcription of a conversation between Zairong Xiang and Julian Henriques on June 13, 2019 (transcript by Amina Balajo)

Zairong Xiang: I have prepared some questions that will lead us from cosmopolitics to tricksters and the trickster's relation to colonialism and queerness. For our *minor cosmopolitan weekend* event, you were given the task of thinking along what we have come to term “minor cosmopolitanism,” to tease out the tension between the so-called minor and the so-called cosmopolitan. Their alleged incongruence produces an open field of possibilities. At the event, you offered us a very intriguing concept that you draw from the Jamaican Rastafarian belief system and from sonic practice in reggae music, street technology and sound system. Just a very quick question regarding nomenclature to start with: could you tell us a little bit more about what the term *cosmopolitricks* refers to?

Julian Henriques: Yes. Well, I was inspired by your minor cosmopolitanisms and, as you just pointed out, the major/minor is a very interesting way of formulating the relationship—or, basically, a power relationship. But it's also a musical relationship, because you talk about minor keys and major keys and, traditionally, one is happy and one is sad. But minor, of course, also refers to minority in this context. It's a thing that we need to grapple with, because there's so much culture and tradition and … well, baggage which obscures the understanding of the Global North and Global South relationship.

As I was saying, the idea of minor cosmopolitanisms inspired me straight into the very rich cultural resource and vocabulary of Rastafarianism, which is a distinct and uniquely Jamaican phenomenon. It's a way of life, it's a musical tradition—but it's also got a tradition of what we call “reasoning,” which is sitting down in a group in what we call a “session” that can be musical or just spoken. So we've got a special theme we are doing, called “reasoning,” and we've got a place where we are doing it that is described as a *groundation* or a *ground nation*. And from that issues a whole set of interesting words and concepts; one of these is *politricks*. It's a word which is seeking to undermine, to destabilise, basically to overthrow what the traditional way of understanding things is. “Politics” becomes *politricks*, as a critique of the Jamaican government or, more generally, of authority. In this context, we also talk about overstanding as distinct from “understanding.” I think this, if you like, grass-root, bottom-up whole way of life and thinking can be useful in a much broader context than just Jamaican culture. So for my title, *politricks* is a way of using a resource from a particular Global South culture and putting it on a global, literally, a global stage. And so, thank you for your invitation!

Zairong: Thank you for joining us! The next question is very closely related to this. I think that *cosmopolitricks* is a very elegant way to avoid the overdetermination of something like "cosmopolitanisms"; even with the plural aspect of "-isms" and the "minor" that define it, cosmopolitanism still sounds quite totalising. It's a system of sorts that tries to encompass all existing people under one recognisable conceptual umbrella. And because of that, it seems, whenever one talked about cosmopolitanism or the like, it became inevitable to trace it back to a Greek origin and Kantian philosophy—

Julian: The *polis* itself.

Zairong: Exactly. But at the same time, when you put the "cosmo" with the "politricks," it does not give up the "cosmos" part, the macro, majoritarian, collective—the premise and promise of cosmopolitanisms, especially at the moment, now that we have this increasing nationalism and divisive politics of bordering. So, to turn your concept into a question: how does the "minor" or the minoritised do the trick to the cosmopolitan?

Julian: I suppose the "trick" that it does is to keep itself in terms of what constitutes cosmopolitanism in the Global South. There's a practical cosmopolitanism in the Global South which of course originates in the Black Atlantic, in the slave trade that brought Africans—enslaved Africans—to the New World, particularly the Caribbean.

In a way, Jamaicans have always been traveling people. Jamaicans who traveled to Panama to build the Panama Canal; Jamaicans who, among others, traveled to Cuba to work on the farms and the sugar estates there. So there has been a tradition of migration that continued, to Britain in the fifties and sixties with the so-called "Windrush" (which is, by the way, a misnomer), and to North America, to the United States and, more particularly, to Canada. That's a way in which the idea of cosmopolitanism is sort of reviewed as an actual migration necessity to follow the wealth that had been extracted from the Global South. One of the principal, undeniable wealth-generating machines that literally fueled the entire industrial revolution, according to C. L. R. James and many others, was that of the plantations and the sugar plantations in the Caribbeans. So there's been these, if you like, movements of people and that's one way in which cosmopolitanism is embodied, not in the way it perhaps is thought of but in a way of necessity, of economic migration and enforced migration.

There's also another kind of movement which is an aspirational movement. It is in the Rastafarian-inspired lyrics of Bob Marley and many others in terms of the *exodus*, the movement of God's people. It's the idea of escape to a better place which, for Jamaicans whose ancestors came from West Africa, is often connected to a kind of "back to Africa" theme; it's celebrated almost like a new Jerusalem in the Christian sense, a state of Zion, a redemptive state. So we have a practical migrating as well as aspirational migrating to a better place going on; in the experience of the Global South, specifically through Jamaica, there's a lot of movement. This destabilises the idea of cosmopolitanism—basically, as it's been described, this is a cosmopolitanism from below, as opposed to the cosmopolitanism only for those with the freedom to move; the cosmopolitanism of the European middle classes, the global middle classes, who have the resources to be able to pick and choose where they invest their property money, where they travel for holidays, and so on and so forth. I think it's important that we don't let the middle classes, the elite, have a monopoly on the idea of cosmopolitanism. So that answers your question a bit.

Zairong: Wonderful! So, more on the trick: one of the very, kind of, universal tricks that one can find in many cultures and, as we discussed last time, in Jamaica as well, is the figure of "the one who does the trick," the figure of the trickster. The trickster kind of gives the title of our current conversation, right? "Mumbo-jumbo" and "jiggery-pokery." Could you say a little about mumbo-jumbo and relate it to the kind of cosmopolitanism from below that you were just invoking? Also, what does jiggery-pokery mean in this context?

Julian: Basically, we have to go via the figure of the trickster, which is a very universal figure, a very global kind of figure. In the Jamaican context, it comes from West Africa and the folklore figure of the spider. It's a male spider and he is called "Anansi." He figures in children's stories; he's comparable to a fairy tale character in the European tradition, like Little Red Riding Hood or Rumpelstiltskin. Anyway, the idea of the trickster is very, very widespread in many cultures, as the one that critiques authority. You haven't got power as minor cosmopolitan, sort of, "masked armies," but you've got your wits. "David and Goliath," that would be another way of putting it. The trickster is someone who can fool a bigger power into contradicting themselves or tripping themselves up; I see the trickster as a figure who is using the power of the bigger opponent against themselves, in a way of putting them off-balance. Even though I've got no practical experience, I'm thinking in terms of martial arts here, where you're using your opponent's weight and power against them; that's a sort of choreographic expression of "trickster-ism." From Jamaica, you've got, as I said, the folklore character of Anansi who goes back to Oshun Eleggua in West African cultures. He's a trickster character who sits at the crossroads and is in a position to deflect you one way or the other—to misguide you.

Let me jump continents back to America, and the south of the United States for a moment. There we have Robert Johnson, a famous banjo player who, in Me and the Devil Blues, claims to have sold his soul to the devil at a crossroads; that's a famous trope of blues music. The musician gets magical powers—the power to seduce, the power to entice, the power to charm—at the cost of selling his soul to the devil; he's a trickster character who will give you this gift for the price of your soul. The trickster character is also present in ancient Greek culture in the figure of Hermes. He's the thief, the sheep stealer. The idea of someone with less power using their wits is a very broadly shared kind of cultural trope.

Henry Louis Gates, of course, picks that up in the idea of signifying and playing double. It's the rhyming, it's the cleverness. This, of course, is one of the roots for things like toasting, where your prowess is expressed in a lyrical fashion. Here, we've got verbal trickery. Verbal trickery. That's another important root for it.

Where was I going with that? Oh yes! The other important thing in terms of the literature is W. E. B. Du Bois and his idea of double consciousness in a minor role in a major situation—that's to say African-Americans in America; the idea that we inhabit multiple selves, that we have a self for ourselves and a self for "the Man," for the system. That, to be two people at the same time, always, encourages, if you like, a sort of mental agility. Of course, this also continues into the carnivalesque, the carnival tradition, where, for a limited number of days per year, the social order is allowed to be upturned, the collective effervescence; the license to basically subvert for a limited period of days. Another aspect that plays into this, and another aspect of tricksterism in general, is that of mimicry. So carnivalism is truly where tricksterism has its métier.

The mumbo-jumbo was picked up and used as a title for one of Ishmael Reed's novels (he is tragically overlooked). What he was talking about there, was a form of expression and a way of being and a form of knowing which was completely dismissed. Mumbo-jumbo is the major cosmopolitan's interpretation of the minor cosmopolitan's forms of expression, but more deeply than that, forms of knowledge. These are "subjugated knowledges," in Michel Foucault's terms, which are very powerful but need to be disavowed and denied for the dominance of the major cosmopolitan knowledge system, that is, the epistemic knowledge systems of the book and the word; so they are put in the powerful category of "nonsense": they are not sense, they're non-sense. If you're trying to understand resources that we have, that the Global South has, that the subaltern has, it's very important to reconfigure these knowledge systems, disparaged though they are. Another example would be, you know, how the Enlightenment basically needed to create "witches" as the "other" knowledge system that the rationalists (that term's quite the joke isn't it?) need to totally disparage and deny as having any validity at all. The jiggery-pokery is, again, a way of dismissing something, it's something that's done by trickery. It's something that is designed to deceive you into thinking that which is not in fact true. Jiggery-pokery is all about disguise, about magic, it's about (to use another English phrase) pulling the wool over your eyes so you don't see what's really happening. These are just strategies, discursive and epistemological strategies for dismissing the subaltern as being stupid rather than clever and being deceitful rather than truthful; they're very, very powerful strategies in maintaining the major/minor power dynamic.

Zairong: To go back to the figure of Anansi, the spider man, which is a figure from West Africa and now found prominently in the Caribbean, especially Jamaica; this brings us to the tricksters as located in colonialism and anticolonial resistance. You have been saying something like "the trickster (for example Anansi) sitting at the crossroads and deceiving you." "You" can include the powerful and also the subaltern, right? So the trickster is not that moral, so to speak.

Julian: No, he is amoral—not immoral, a-moral. And, basically, he just likes to make fun. He likes to laugh at authority. It's about "The Emperor's New Clothes"—it's like exposing the dominant order as being a fabrication and an imagination. That's what's so powerful about this kind of destabilising. Because, basically, the more brutal the system (slavery being the horrific example), the more clever you have to be to survive. I mean, there are lots of examples whereby martial arts, arts of fighting, are reimagined or disguised as dance—something that can be portrayed as purely entertainment is a way of actually practicing your fight moves. Capoeira is a classic example of that in Brazil. It's not from West Africa, but rather from Angola. Another example is a particular kind of drum which the Maroons use; Maroons were previously escaped slaves in Jamaica, well, not just Jamaica but also in the Caribbean in general, in Latin America, and South of the States. You had these semi-independent communities. There, something that basically looked like a stool that you sit on, a low seat, but in actual fact, you'd just stick two little pegs in it and it turned into a drum. It was disguised so that the masters wouldn't recognise a musical instrument when it was right in front of them (because drumming was forbidden on the estates). So this whole idea of the necessity of deception is very prevalent and very important and that's part of tricksterism.

Zairong: So, if I get it right, the trickster only does jokes to the powerful.

Julian: Yes.

Zairong: So the figure is very interesting, in that he sits on a crossroads and only does tricks to those who have the privilege of traveling.

Julian: Well, that's … Yeah that would be one interpretation. But the crossroads is, you know, the crossroads of life, it's where you make your decisions.

Zairong: So this "you" can be anyone?

Julian: Yeah, that can be anyone.

Zairong: So who is more susceptible to …

Julian: To tricksterism? Well, I haven't thought about it like that, but basically the more you've got to lose, the more susceptible you are to tricksterism, right?

Zairong: That's a good point, yeah.

Julian: There's another Jamaican phrase, which I really like when we're talking about north/south and power and subaltern. It's basically: "those who have it all are those that think they have it all."

Zairong: That's very true.

Julian: That's one way of characterising the major/minor relationship.

Zairong: So now let's move to something that is a bit tricky, since we've been talking about tricksters. So the trickster is featured in this kind of collective unconsciousness, a Jungian archetype of sorts.

Julian: Yeah, absolutely.

Zairong: Is he, though? In my own work on mythology and mythological theories, I've come to resist the idea of archetypal clichés, such as the famous "fertility myth" and so on. I see these explications more as a kind of modern/colonial imposition. So my question is: how can colonial tricksters, such as Anansi, do the trick to trickster archetypes? That's on the one hand. On the other hand, this question is going towards the idea of queering and queerness, queer as this fleeting concept. It's another concept where we don't really know what its interiorities are or if it has an interiority at all. So maybe, could you say something on that?

Julian: I think that's really interesting. In one sense, it's self-deceiving; if you say: "How can the trickster destabilise itself?" the answer would be by, if you like, tricking itself. I think that's a perfectly kind of reasonable way to understand it. Basically, what the trickster is doing is not respecting boundaries. He (because it is gendered) is not respecting the boundaries of authority and so one could extrapolate—and it would be an extrapolation, because I can't think of historical examples or cultural examples where this is happening, where the trickster tricks himself. It's like the famous Cretan philosopher from ancient Crete who said: "All

Cretans are liars," you know. So there's a way in which the aporia, the gap, is identified. You could say self-tricking and self-deception is one way of understanding the Freudian unconscious or that consciousness doesn't have dominion over who we actually are. I'd be open to exploring how that would work, and that destruction of archetypes, which may or may not be helpful; but the point is, it does, if not "set things in stone," create expectations as you undermine, and they are always going to be co-opted by the powerful. So the tricksterism, to call it that, can be a way of undermining, well—what we are really trying to undermine (and that does take us to queering) is the idea of fixity, the idea whereby your self is defined from inside rather than as relational, in terms of relationships.

Zairong: Related to fixity, I have a question that is going back to the concept of cosmopolitricks. In a way, cosmopolitricks is the doing. It's the practice and the tricks, not really the trickster as a quasi-heroic and individualised or singular figure of resistance. This brings me to the actual practices that you talked about at the event; reggae music, street sound system and also the practices of counterfeit. I am thinking about *shanzhai* in China, *Jugaad* in India, and *gambiarra* in Brazil. In your talk, you said something very lucid, you said: "Well, these are an honest fix, a utilitarian fix. They kind of serve a utilitarian function."

Julian: Yes, exactly.

Zairong: But the trickster doesn't! Sometimes it just makes fun.

Julian: Yeah, sometimes it makes fun, but I think tricksterism has a very important material function: it enables survival. It's not just to make fun. I mean, it does make fun but that's ... We know humor, in terms of political critique, is very important, so it's basically helping to make a world that is one where we, in terms of the subaltern, have power; one in which we can survive. It's one in which we have skills, one in which we can be valued, one by the other. And that's very important.

Zairong: It doesn't have material value.

Julian: Well, the major does not have the upper hand. The "lower hand" is holding the whole amount and the whole set of resources. And if you haven't got anything, you've got your wits, you know, you've got your cleverness. Mental dexterity is shown in the lyrics, in the chatting, in all the musical forms, which are so important for the culture. It's sort of making a world where change is possible. Nobody wants to stay on the bottom of the pyramid. The trickster offers a way of imagining the world differently. The power of imagination is an important form of intelligence which, in medieval and ancient philosophy, was totally recognised.

These were predecessors through the idea of fixity, formulated most powerfully, one could say, in the idea of René Descartes' Cartesian *cogito*.

It's an essentialist, internalist thing—we are not defined by what's inside, we're defined by the relationships outside, and I use it in terms of the Nguni Bantu term, *Ubuntu*: "I am because we are." That's a way of recognising the essential sociality of ourselves. So one can explore (not only through tricksterism) our ways of being relationally, which gets it out of the fixity of the *cogito*. But then you can also explore it in terms of porosities and gradience; not boundaries, but a different variety of intensities. That's taking us into territory where I use it—again, I'm not so much an expert on queer theory—queer space and queer time, where you've got a way of understanding what were, in a major sense, put as absolute, *de facto*, *a priori* categories, which basically need to be broken down. It's a very short move from tricksterism, as the breaking down of authority, to breaking down the authority of the self as it is defined in a dominant ideology, and to be able to redefine it from underneath and from the idea of change. Basically, those who think they have it all, the one thing they don't want is change.

Zairong: Well said. So, just some thoughts and I'll bring this to a close with two related questions. Octavio Paz has this interesting poem in which he talks about the "we" and "I" and how the "I" can only be a "we." This is very similar to Ubuntu—I am because we are.

Julian: And you get it also in Mikhail Bakhtin, the dialogical; you get it in Valentin Voloshinov, he talks about language as an ideological construct that we cannot have as an individual; it has to be part of an apparatus. Arthur Rimbaud as well!

Zairong: Ah yes! "Je est un autre!" "We within the I" brings me to think of this very interesting translation of "reggae" into Chinese as 雷鬼, that is, "Thunder Ghost." So the ghostly, hauntological, is basically what the trickster attaches to the dominant system, right?

Julian: Yeah, that's a beautiful way of saying it. In a way, ghosting is a way of destabilising the idea of linear time of past, present and future—this idea of the ancestors being present. The Western idea is very materialistic, as you'd expect, and the dead do not have a presence in the way that they do in most belief systems around the world from the beginning of history. This idea of ghosting is, of course, exemplified to a great degree in reggae dub music. It all works on echo and reverberation; in certain ways, it's extending time, it's drawing it out. It's literally giving time its own space and its own time (because they have to be seen as an integrated dynamic, a whole). I just find that very powerful, that the destabilising actually has found a very beautiful and very shareable global cultural form of expression that people can get into, not least in Japan—there are many top-rate sound systems in Japan, Mighty Crown is one that, back in the nineties, won the reggae world clash.

One thing I haven't mentioned in trickster is of course the idea of "mimicry." This could bring us back to the Hegelian idea of master-slave relationship, where the slave always knows the master better than the master knows himself.

Zairong: The last question brings us back to the first question of nomenclature. You mentioned mimicry, lyrics and so on, and I think language plays a very important role in this whole enterprise. And of course naming something else has always been, since the biblical narrative, the core of colonial practices. I think in your work you have invented some kind of new concepts, like *alternational* or *overstanding*.

Julian: But these are not my concepts. I have no authorship of these concepts; they all come from the Rastafari tradition. But the idea of naming is, precisely, a colonial trick. One of my favourite poets from St. Lucia in the Caribbean is Derek Walcott and he has a poem called "Green Night" and in that, he says something along the lines of: "God gave Adam the task of giving things their name."[1] So the idea of naming as a power is very useful in the colonial context—as it is also the power of dismissing something, of saying that it's "mumbo-jumbo" or "jiggery-pokery." So in terms of language, there is also the denial of the power of language. A typical colonial thing to do is to use a particular form of power and then deny it.

Zairong: Can you explain that a little further?

Julian: Yes, of course. It is often said that the most effective ideology is that which appears as common sense. So when you have a cultural or political ideology called "change," what you're doing is shifting the center of gravity of what's considered possible or desirable; that's how authoritarian populism and even progressive politics is trying to shift the ground, trying to shift the idea of common sense. But the power of language and words, which is expressed through tricksterism and doubles and the figure of the signifying monkey (who is a trickster if ever there was one), is the ancient power of magic—the idea that saying something actually made it happen. You get that, for example, in the term "abracadabra," which is the fairy tale version of a magic spell. You say something—it comes out of your mouth, you *spell* it out—and you change reality. That is an absolute testament to the power of words. It shows a much deeper root to what language and verbal expression are than if you take the accepted idea of a language system and the Western tradition of it reflecting reality—it's actually transforming reality. Language is a transformative power. The magic in abracadabra is an example of that. The power that is expressed in the tricksterism—the making jokes and making fun—is indicating a deeper power. It's not a language to describe the world, it's a language for upturning it.

Zairong: So we could conclude by saying "minor cosmopolitanism" is a joke?

Julian: You could say that, but it may be a bit disparaging. It's the joke for changing the world.

1 Editor's note: the line referred to is "We were blest with a virginal, unpainted world/with Adam's task of giving things their names" from the poem *Another Life* (1973). *Green Night* refers to the collection of poems *In a Green Night* (1962).

S CONSTELLATIONS CONSTELLATIONS CONSTELLATIONS
TELLATIONS CONSTELLATIONS CONSTELLATIONS CONSTEL
LATIONS CONSTELLATIONS CONSTELLATIONS CONSTELLAT
S CONSTELLATIONS CONSTELLATIONS CONSTELLATIONS
TELLATIONS CONSTELLATIONS CONSTELLATIONS CONSTEL
LATIONS CONSTELLATIONS CONSTELLATIONS CONSTELLAT
S CONSTELLATIONS CONSTELLATIONS CONSTELLATIONS
TELLATIONS CONSTELLATIONS CONSTELLATIONS CONSTEL
LATIONS CONSTELLATIONS CONSTELLATIONS CONSTELLAT
S CONSTELLATIONS CONSTELLATIONS CONSTELLATIONS
TELLATIONS CONSTELLATIONS CONSTELLATIONS CONSTEL
LATIONS CONSTELLATIONS CONSTELLATIONS CONSTELLAT
S CONSTELLATIONS CONSTELLATIONS CONSTELLATIONS
TELLATIONS CONSTELLATIONS CONSTELLATIONS CONSTEL
LATIONS CONSTELLATIONS CONSTELLATIONS CONSTELLAT
S CONSTELLATIONS CONSTELLATIONS CONSTELLATIONS
TELLATIONS CONSTELLATIONS CONSTELLATIONS CONSTEL

MARIYA NIKOLOVA

pinecones

minor cosmopolitanisms sent me to australia I smuggled a pinecone there and it didn't even matter to the trees one burns. I had picked up the pinecone in bulgaria, like I picked up my grandparents' tradition of hugging trees eyes closed in exchange for energy much love is radioactive nowadays. I did not declare it as one doesn't declare history. My grandparents had done it, their grandparents too—hike in partisan woods, part myth, part masochism, you never follow a path, you always sing. Then, they saw the tree that belonged to each of them, separately, a different tree so they saw with something other than eyes—and went, in silence, embraced it, in full darkness, and true or not, became stronger. A genealogy of strength, that's how my mother raised me, their daughter, mountain for a heart, in some love relation to a tree that is meant to be mine. And we have all done it, her daughters, ran the woods, and found that particular tree which is never the same, and hugged it all the same—the closest thing to historical legitimacy the way one breathes when they see nothing.

Now, if by some odd chain of events, I have hugged the same tree my grandfather had—I might come closer to understanding the way I hug chainsaw the trees necrologies are made from and up bulgarian walls one hangs necrologies when no one is looking because it is a kind of shame when your people is dead people and nothing grows but they hang on cheap sellotape and isn't that what necrologies are for. I might as well have come to australia to find out places are impossible. I spent many years in germany, thirteen if one counts, quite stubbornly but I had always dragged big branches from the nearby park and placed them in the flat in whatever corner and constellation first allowed itself. Escape has coordinates. I line up and dream on linen sheets stuff a pinecone in my suitcase place it on a stranger's desk my desk and pretend none of it matters. Souvenir, we are all tourists, the fingers on my left hand touch my right wrist, I am five, communist, and waste love and paper and daughters I don't birth will hug trees all the same I smile from a necrology which will be my ticket back. You can love and you cannot love and print as many genealogies of strength as many people you become but then words are lines of full darkness mean nothing. I am stretched here and tighten. The places we carry we leave we never get to words bunch at the same walk between trees, I say a name, unknowable, stamp, what it means to be part of the placewherenotreesgrow, I carry a pinecone with me as if it is the closest thing под леда поточе чисто плачело като насън. This is a quiet way of love open your arms the edges old paper. We are random. This might declare us meaningful, a reiteration of strength a reiteration of strength is a bulgarian pinecone landing as random australian appear on land or bulgarian in german woods—where history is strong is dying. One way or the other, we will all hug the same tree necrologies are made from but the other children jump from burning tar to a burning page and I find it dangerous I have nothing to declare but silently walk past security and hope no one dies this time around.

jumpcut

minor cosmopolitanisms wanted me to finish my sentences they said I have something to give and I didn't sleep many nights in need. If you know words they are red and birth and burst and birds that scare when they see us which means I was finding a way to give in acceptable phrases read and re-read are professors and mentors and street hustlers and poetry in other shapes and one jumps from academic English to spare change to revolution in just three seconds. I kept insisting on writing the dissertation in jump cuts, the way one lives, impaired by loneliness. The thesis should look like the suit jacket, at least five different people complimented me on it, at conferences. *I did well*. The suit jacket was weighed with a bunch of other clothes, in bulgaria you have these second-hand shops which sell by the kilo. Something like five euro for a kilo of clothes. I am standing there, in my red suit jacket, and I want to explain to my four different supervisors and an audience of giants that the thesis should look like my mother's hands going through someone else' clothes she touches the fabric and she must know something my words could never convey. You want to press knowledge like that offer it to a child who will shine in the eyes of at least five different people and an audience of giants. It should never matter how we dress and so I stopped midsentence and said thank you and went home. The format is dangerous. I have thought long about how my sentences should move never find anything new lovingly choose embraces your child will know the meaning of and the thesis should sound like that disagreement not of minds but of colours and texture. You never know whom they belong to. I kept insisting on writing five different lives at once and on keeping them tight together misfits missing all signs to a closure. Distrust grammar how deep run deer inserted in veins when your hands are the only choices you get to make red is a colour I return to my mother wants the same one image you get to see and draw enjoyment from. I give and disagree. The other night I dreamt it is possible to have them all gather jump from the one to the next no one losing face their skin reddish in woods where a child picks pinecones and trees are gigantic. Distrust images. Or what you do well or how it appears. The thesis should weigh thirty-five grams, well ironed, in full consciousness and should not weigh at all. She touches the fabric and knows something my words could never convey and I say no to the image of her in stillness.

HEINRICH WILKE

silences

Silence is a complex thing. With its structure as intricate as its meanings multifaceted, silence is a fundamental feature of communication, and consequently deserves a central place in literary and historical analysis. It is variously act and fact. Seen as an act, silence always responds to a previous utterance or an already existing entity or facticity: it is a remaining silent *about something*. For instance, to write or invoke the history of the European working classes without reference to female and nonwhite workers is a distortion that disavows complex frictions and minor cosmopolitan solidarities. Similarly, to imagine Europe (or "the West," for that matter) as a homogenous whole exercising, in its entirety, power over the rest of the world is to disregard its numerous internal hierarchies, from regional power differentials to racism; this view effectively buys into the conservative supposition that society is, essentially at least, a harmonious body. The two examples indicate that silence can be an eminently political issue, instantiating power relations and bearing on the self-image of collective identities. Here, remaining silent means denigrating or concealing undesirable actors and inconvenient complexities. These matters are at the heart of Michel-Rolph Trouillot's *Silencing the Past* (1995). He posits that power is constitutive of historical narrative,[1] where it translates into silencing.

But if, according to Trouillot, "any historical narrative is a particular bundle of silences,"[2] then silence does not necessarily mark conscious political manipulation. Indeed, silence is created alongside every historical fact,[3] making the former—acknowledged or otherwise—a ubiquitous part of historical discourse. The import of silence does not end there. Every utterance necessarily implies a non-utterance: I cannot say something without thereby not saying other things. The act of not saying certain things is not itself acknowledged, that is, I do not say that I omit certain things. Silence is therefore constitutive of any utterance, oral and written, including literature.[4] Here, silence is a fact rather than an act. However, giving this much room to silence—accepting it as an omnipresent, ineluctable aspect of any text whatsoever—runs the risk of trivializing it. Since silence is everywhere anyway, one might think, why bother with its specific meaning? Indeed, can it have a particular meaning if it is, precisely, universal? And where has the political significance of silence gone all of a sudden?

The more fundamental question here is: which methodology follows from—or applies, if you prefer—the insight into the constitutive importance of silence? For Pierre Macherey, the interesting matter is not that every utterance points to, or presupposes, silence. In this case, all the critic can hope to do is transition mechanically from the said to the unsaid. This is an exercise in supplanting one meaning with another;[5] in this scenario, the utterance is always relegated to the status of a preliminary layer, soon to be discarded for the silence that the interpreter is really after. Rather, says Macherey, the more interesting task for criticism is to trace the said in the unsaid, the utterance in the silence. Instead of dispelling the explicit meaning by revealing the implicit one, here "the meaning is in the *relation* of the explicit to the implicit, and not on one or the other side of the fence."[6] The challenge is to interpret what the silence signifies, to see which meaning(s) it carries. However, this can only be achieved by paying close attention to the particulars of the text. The "what" and the "how" of a text lend specific contours to it; the reverse of these contours is its silence, which is therefore equally specific to the text. If interpreting silence means going beyond the text, this is so only because the particulars of the text itself suggest the direction to venture into.[7]

In Macherey's conception, the silence that matters is not simply something that the text does not say, or refuses to say. The critic is rather called upon to trace what the text "*cannot say*": a determinate silence.[8] From this perspective, it is possible to see my two examples of silence as a political issue in a different light. Perhaps the hypothetical speakers or writers do not efface female and nonwhite workers and intra-European hierarchies so deliberately, after all; rather than employing ideological mystifications, they might betray ignorance of these matters—an ignorance occasioned by their historically specific positionality. Silence here signifies, among other things, white ignorance.[9] Cases where silence stems from ignorance present complex entanglements of silence as an act and silence as a fact; though political issues easily bear on such cases, the force of intention and agency may not be immediately apparent. One of the silences Trouillot discusses is the absence of the Haitian Revolution in much historical scholarship and public memory in the West.[10] Trouillot claims that this absence stems from the fact that the mass uprising of blacks, and the independent black state in which it eventuated, is an "unthinkable history" to societies which have enslaved and marginalized black subjects for centuries. In this example, what is the relative weight of ideological mystification, global power dynamics, white ignorance, propaganda, the prosaic incomprehension of history, and the inability to imagine? Here, silence emerges in all its indeterminacy.

With good reason, then, silence has become a central category in several literary and historical analyses, not least those concerned with colonial contexts. Silence is arguably a key aspect of the unreliability of colonial archives.[11] In fact, the very ubiquity of certain images and comments can serve to shroud their object in silence. Marisa Fuentes has argued that the numerous representations of tortured black women in eighteenth- and nineteenth-century antislavery propaganda significantly contributed to the silencing of their subjectivity.[12] Suzanne Césaire has even divested silence of exclusively human significance: in her view, the lush tropical nature of the Caribbean silences historical and contemporary plight. Analyses like these hammer home the complexity of silences—and the need to make them speak.

[1] Michel-Rolph Trouillot, *Silencing the Past: Power and the Production of History* (Boston: Beacon, 1995), 28.

[2] Trouillot, *Silencing the Past*, 27.

[3] Trouillot, *Silencing the Past*, 29.

[4] Pierre Macherey, *Pour une théorie de la production littéraire* (Lyon: ENS Éditions, 2014), 82ff., esp. 85.

[5] Macherey, *Pour une théorie de la production littéraire*, 86.

[6] Macherey, *Pour une théorie*, 86; original emphasis; translation mine.

[7] Macherey, *Pour une théorie*, 93.

[8] Macherey, *Pour une théorie*, 86; original emphasis; translation mine.

[9] Charles W. Mills, "White Ignorance," in *Agnotology: The Making and Unmaking of Ignorance*, ed. Robert N. Proctor and Londa Schiebinger (Stanford: Stanford University Press,

2008), 230-49.

[10] Trouillot, *Silencing the Past*, 70-107.

[11] Myra Jehlen, *Readings at the Edge of Literature* (Chicago: The University of Chicago Press, 2002), 9.

[12] Marisa J. Fuentes, *Dispossessed Lives: Enslaved Women, Violence, and the Archive* (Philadelphia: University of Pennsylvania Press, 2016), 124-43.

[13] Suzanne Césaire, *Le grand camouflage : écrits de dissidence, 1941–1945* (Paris: Éditions du Seuil, 2015), 84-94.

ANOUK MADÖRIN

techne

After the Second World War, when the contours of the Anthropocene, the nuclear age, and the sixth extinction became more tangible, the domination of technology (techne) over the natural (physis) became a central narrative of critique. The Greek etymological meaning conceptualizes techne as both craft/art and the systematic knowledge and experience that underlies it. Differing from its conceptional twin, episteme, techne is concerned with applied expertise (making or doing something) as opposed to passive understanding or musing. For Aristotle, technology was a supplement to the natural and radically opposed to the non-natural (para physin), either imitating the natural or supplementing/perfecting what nature is deemed unable to. Opposing this relationship of exteriority, and understanding the natural and technics not in opposition to each other, we might see life as haunted by technology, as "from the very first there is instrumentalization [dès l'origine il y a de l'instrumentalisation]."[1] Not only is techne always already entangled with what is thought of as exterior. It is also, if we look at one of its genealogical traces, modeled after its enduring archetype of the pre-modern era: magic, or, the practice of conforming an environment to a set of rules. The "para," or that which is "beyond" nature, defining the relationship between the human and the thing made as a craft or inscription onto nature, thus also relates to non- or ir-rational capacities of transforming the world. To anchor techne's multiple genealogical strands onto a current political setting, such as the European border crisis, we might have to span the field of analysis: from the passport as a prosthetic technology to the shared knowledge practices of circumventing borders. Similar to the relationship between law and technology, citizenship is thought of as prosthetic, as attached to the body from outside, from where it then sanctions or authorizes a body to move across borders. In this scenario, for example, the passport becomes a crutch, or a tool that, conceived of in proper ableist fashion, complements the body natural, that is, the mortal body with all its defects. There is, however, another techne at play before Europe's borders: alongside the refugee and activist networks using GPS to navigate the Mediterranean, some make use of the "gris-gris," a thing made of the skin of a black cat or a goat that is fastened to the pirogue of a boat and prevents it from appearing on radars; it "tricks FRONTEX [and] will skew their machine."[2] In order to add techne to the minor cosmopolitan vocabulary, we will have to stay in the contradictions between denouncing technology as the rational outside defeating physis and welcoming it as a craft that is passed on through shared knowledge practices.

[1] Jacques Derrida and Elizabeth Rottenberg, *Negotiations: Interventions and Interviews,* 1971–2001 (Palo Alto: Stanford University Press, 2002), 215.
[2] Brigitta Kuster, "Biometric Film Images. A New Mode of Audiovisual Records Affecting Reality?," *European Institute for Progressive Cultural Policies*, March 2018, http://eipcp.net/transversal/0318/kuster/en.html.

SARA MORAIS DOS SANTOS BRUSS

modulation

Given the increasing importance of digital technologies for cultural production, media and cultural theorists have revisited technological concepts in order to explore cultural formations. Because technologies have facilitated the global expansion of capital (material) and cultural forms, the relationship between technoscience and sociality has, according to Gilles Deleuze,[1] shifted the modes of governance from discipline to control. This includes shifts from representation to affect,[2] and from explicit to increasingly implicit and flexible modes of governance and subjugation. Within these shifts, modulation has become "a description of a cultural logic with economic dimensions"[3] and increasingly global reach. The systems of governance inherent to this logic are broached through data and information, and thus understood as born-digital: bodies become information, are treated as such, while bodies of information not only produce, but become the modalities of control. However, many of the theoretical considerations on the logics of computation remain caught in a presentism that deflects from the origins of modulation's impetus: defining population variation and regulation. Expanding its timeline sees modulation reframed to predate the digital age, coinciding instead with the very birth of racial capitalism in the colonial encounter. Rather than being distinctively new, modulation must thus be understood to create race as an "underlying fixity,"[4] through which normative information produces and segregates infrastructures, bodies, matter.

As a digital process, modulation amplifies a certain signal, such as music, language, data, in the process of which the carrier or transmitter of the signal is altered, but also invisibilized, as the signal becomes more present. Within a globalized cultural context, modulation both informs and creates social infrastructures through segregation, decontextualization, and the accentuating of difference. As a "social operating system," modulation describes the neoliberal spread of information across the globe, which marks departures from "white typicality,"[5] to amplify and at the same time occlude its foundational value as common sense. Bodies diverging from this typicality are identified and transported into the margins, while an illusion of inclusion and mobility persists on the surface.

The colonial encounter offered a more visible practice of creating types through racist sciences, such as eugenics and craniometry. But modulation today blackboxes the analytical framework between input and output, and thus naturalizes discriminatory practices by removing insights into their genealogies and proposing digitality as radically different instead.[6] Turning to the moment of emergence of race, and, with it, categories of class and sex/gender, modulation becomes the always-already operating system that classifies practices and modalities of being as inherently different. Here, race emerges as technology, in the sense of a practice or skill that is applied and can be replicated.[7] Fingerprinting, identification papers, and/or biological categorization of bodies not only serve to govern and control these bodies as divergent, but performatively produce this divergence as essential. Instead of these ascriptions disappearing in line with "more" knowledge, they seep into today's most miniscule categorizations and identifiers. In this way, any form of sociality is pre-empted, meaning that the outcome of datafied knowledge queries is already pre-inscribed into any automated negotiation of identities and spaces.

Not only are historical lineages of discrimination and oppression hidden within algorithmic code, but the individual appears as a singularity, without social or structural cohesion. Modulation thus delegitimizes group identities as historically discriminated against, while explicitly harnessing them to promote neoliberal identification. In this way, a tweet about the structural quality of toxic masculinity can elicit the (individualistically) defensive response of #notallmen, while the hashtag #menaretrash is seen as a racist and sexist generalization. But the effects of modulation do not remain within the level of representation. Modulation further informs the creation of infrastructures, laws, and resources and thus has harrowing material effects for communities historically marginalized. Today, simple quotidian practices invisibilise their historical lineages as they become automatized, while living in a certain neighbourhood, liking certain music or going to certain events translates into racialized and gendered categories that algorithms can call upon to produce digital identities they address as consumers. In the meantime, unexpected occurrences—such as rich brown teens checking into luxury hotels[8]—are dismissed as "dirty data."

Automatized through supposedly neutral algorithms, modulation is increasingly hidden behind trade-marked code and becomes a societal "backend" to a "frontend" or "interface" on which difference is scandalized. As global communication networks allow for transnational exchange, however, networks that critique the normalcy with which we encounter digital interfaces as white create moments of disruption. The conceptual definition of modulation allows for a recognition of how these affects—to paraphrase Sara Ahmed—are not innocent psychological states, but cultural practices of producing value.[9] In this way, identities are constantly decomposed and recomposed, shifting the claims as to who is an outsider according to a racialized matrix that influences and determines the other in increasingly flexible ways. But as modulation extends divergence beyond those that are historically anonymized and alienated, it includes more and more peoples, irrespective of their social position. Reflective of its colonial origins, new experts may arise, whose histories are marked by more explicit modes of modulation. These "anonymized global networks"[10] must identify and make porous the artificial boundaries and segregations normalized through modulation on the level of representation, resources and matter.

[1] Gilles Deleuze, "Postscript on the Societies of Control," *October* 59 (1992) 3-7.
[2] P. T. Clough, "Future Matters," *Social Text* 22, no. 3 (2004): 1-23.
[3] Kara Keeling, *Queer Times, Black Futures* (New York: New York University Press, 2019), 156.
[4] Steven Shaviro, in Keeling, *Queer Times*, 156.
[5] Simone Browne, "Digital Epidermalization: Race, Identity and Biometrics," *Critical Sociology* 36, no. 1 (2010): 131-50.
[6] Wendy Hui Kyong Chun, *Updating to Remain the Same: Habitual New Media* (Cambridge, MA: MIT Press, 2016); Tara McPherson, "Why are the digital humanities so white," *Debates in the Digital Humanities* (2012), http://dhdebates.gc.cuny.edu/debates/text/29.
[7] Beth Coleman, "Race as Technology," *Camera Obscura* 24, no. 1 (2009): 177-207.
[8] Hito Steyerl, "A Sea of Data: Apophenia and Pattern (Mis-)Recognition," *e-flux* 72, (April 2016).
[9] Sara Ahmed, *The Cultural Politics of Emotion* (Hoboken: Taylor and Francis, 2013), 125.
[10] Aria Dean, "Poor Meme, Rich Meme," *Real Life*, July 15, 2016, https://reallifemag.com/poor-meme-rich-meme/.

JENS TEMMEN

the imperial grammar of jurisdictional incongruence

The notion of the United States as a (and eventually *the* sole) global power of the twentieth and twenty-first centuries has become a shorthand that reconciles the United States' self-fashioned identity as an alleged vanguard of democracy, a proliferator of universal human rights, and an exceptional nation of liberty and peace, with the way that this identity is projected and affirmed via violent imperial campaigns and colonial practices across the globe. The fact that Thomas Jefferson encapsulated this paradoxical identity in his vision of the United States as an "empire of liberty" as early as the 1790s suggests a historical dimension that has shaped the present narrative of a global and benevolent US empire.[1] A thorough and critical reading of contemporary US imperialism needs to capture this historical dimension of the narrative of US imperialism.[2] This more complex narrative suggests that the United States' current globalized phase is connected both with its continental phase (ca. 1782–1890) and its overseas phase (1898–ca. 1945), through the continuity of an "anti-colonial" and exceptional character of US expansion—both in terms of the particular modes of US expansion, as well as in relation to other Euro-American projects of imperialism.[3] Simultaneously, this narrative insists on strictly demarcating these phases based on their individual modes of territorial incorporation and management—all of which are allegedly distinct, yet equally "anti-colonial."

At its very core, the structural integrity of this paradoxical framework draws on the model of the Westphalian nation-state, which, conversely, lays down the congruence of state sovereignty, jurisdiction and territory as the key characteristic of any modern nation-state. Within the framework of the narrative of US imperialism, strict adherence to this notion of "jurisdictional congruence" becomes a marker of anti-coloniality.[4] In other words, the notion of different phases of "anti-colonial" expansion relies on the argument that US territorial expansion never challenged the "jurisdictional congruence" of the US nation-state.[5] This convoluted narrative of a many-phased anti-colonial US imperialism works like a fire blanket: it buries underneath it the colonial relationship of the United States with Native Americans on the continent and with Indigenous peoples in its overseas territories (among others), and it covers up the use of a global network of military installations as a neo-colonial tool. Thereby, this narrative tries to suffocate past and present efforts for Indigenous enfranchisement within the framework of the US nation-state, decolonial movements for political independence, as well as accusations of colonialism leveled against the United States from basically any direction.

A critical approach to any phase of US imperialism that seeks to lift that fire blanket needs to focus on the legal discourses that legitimize the notion of a many-phased anti-colonial US expansion, in spite of the United States' well-documented history of colonialism. Such an approach against the grain of US imperialism has to include the colonized voices and perspectives directly disenfranchised by this discourse. These voices challenge the narrative of separate and distinct phases of anti-colonial expansion from different vantage points. They tell stories of the ways that US expansion relies on the strategic *in*congruence of the core vocabulary of the Westphalian nation-state—sovereignty, jurisdiction, and territory—in order to simultaneously exert control over various colonial spaces, while veiling the coloniality of this control.[6] In other words, they describe how flexibly disconnecting this vocabulary functions as one of the fundamental mechanisms of US imperialism—the *imperial* grammar of jurisdictional incongruence, to keep with the metaphor. This imperial grammar is, paradoxically, at odds with the model of the Westphalian nation-state on which the narrative of US expansion rests. The United States were therefore at no point in their history a Westphalian nation-state in the sense of the model, but claiming adherence to the model was and is fundamental for perpetuating a narrative of a sovereign, legitimate, exceptional, and essentially anti-colonial US expansion.[7] The imperial grammar of jurisdictional incongruence is the core continuity across all alleged phases of U.S. expansion.

[1] Brook Thomas, "A Constitution Led by the Flag: The Insular Cases and the Metaphor of Incorporation," in *Foreign in a Domestic Sense: Puerto Rico, American Expansion, and the Constitution*, eds. Christina Duffy Burnett and Burke Marshall (Durham: Duke University Press, 2001), 89.

[2] Amy Kaplan, "Where is Guantánamo?," *American Quarterly* 57, no. 3 (2005): 832-34.

[3] John Carlos Rowe, *Literary Culture and Imperialism from the Revolution to World War II*

(Oxford: Oxford University Press, 2002), 3; Alyosha Goldstein, "Toward a Genealogy of the U.S. Colonial Present," *Introduction, in Formations of United States Colonialism*, ed. Alyosha Goldstein (Durham: Duke University Press, 2014), 14-15.

[4] Kal Raustiala, "The evolution of territoriality: international relations and American law," *Territoriality and Conflict in an Era of Globalization*, eds. Miles Kahler and Barbara F. Walter (Cambridge: Cambridge University Press, 2006), 232.

[5] Miles Kahler, "Territoriality and conflict in an era of globalization," in *Territoriality and Conflict in an Era of Globalization*, eds. Miles Kahler and Barbara F. Walter (Cambridge: Cambridge University Press, 2006), 5; Raustiala, "Territoriality," 219.

[6] Mark Rifkin, "Indigenizing Agamben: Rethinking Sovereignty in Light of the 'Peculiar' Status of Native Peoples," *Cultural Critique* 73 (2009): 89-90; Kevin Bruyneel, *The Third Space of Sovereignty* (Minneapolis: Minnesota University Press, 2007); Mary L. Dudziak and Leti Volpp, "Introduction: Legal Borderlands: Law and Construction of American Borders," *American Quarterly* 57, no. 3 (2005): 4; Jens Temmen, "'So it happens that we are relegated to the condition of the aborigines of the American continent': Disavowing and Reclaiming Sovereignty in Liliuokalani's Hawaii's Story by Hawaii's Queen and the Congressional Morgan Report," *Postcolonial Justice*, eds. Anke Bartels, Lars Eckstein, Nicole Waller and Dirk Wiemann (Amsterdam: Brill Rodopi, 2017), 3-4.

[7] Rowe, *Literary Culture*, 3; Goldstein, "Genealogy," 14.

ANNA VON RATH

convivial scholarship

Convivial scholarship refers to an ethical and political way of doing academic work. The concept was first introduced by Francis Nyamnjoh, Professor of Anthropology at the University of Cape Town in South Africa.[1] I suggest applying Nyamnjoh's notion of convivial scholarship as a minor cosmopolitan methodology. In the following, I will outline what this methodology comprises.

Convivial scholarship as a minor cosmopolitan methodology is especially relevant for cultural studies projects globally. The particular ethics and politics that pertain to this discipline resemble the underlying ideas of convivial scholarship. Ien Ang points out that cultural studies depends on "the claimed productivity of dialogue across disciplinary, geographical and cultural boundaries, on a committed desire to reach out to 'the other,' and on a refusal to homogenize plurality and heterogeneity as a way to resist, subvert or evade hegemonic forms of power."[2] Similarly, convivial scholarship emphasizes collectivity and the exchange of ideas between people who likely identify with different socio-political positions. Nyamnjoh argues that "convivial scholarship recognizes the deep power of collective imagination and the importance of interconnections."[3]

To enable collective imagination and interconnection, I suggest including conversations over a drink with a number of people involved in the field of interest into one's research method. These encounters between researchers, artists, activists, social critics or anyone who relates to the topic create a collective, foster the exchange of ideas and allow for insights into different perspectives and lived realities.

Doing research on topics that engage with power dynamics may make the convivial encounters challenging because conversation partners are likely to position themselves differently. This challenge is where the drink—be it water, coffee or a glass of wine—comes in handy: in a meeting over a drink, one has to expect clashes of difference and recognitions of sameness, which sometimes create distance or suspicion, and other times allow for a curious mutual interest in each other. Often, it seems impossible to enable eye-level conversations in which all partners feel comfortable enough to talk freely (the researcher included). The researcher, who is likely to be in a position of power, can momentarily become "minor" to a certain extent. Sharing a drink may reduce the potential awkwardness of these encounters because the drink gives each conversation partner something to hold on to and may make the meeting last at least as long as the drink. A written reflection on these conversations as an essential part of the research sheds light on otherwise often invisible power dynamics.

In a conversation over a drink, researchers clearly show interest in others by lending an ear to someone else. However, there is an interpretative element inherent to such a research endeavor. Most of the times, in addition to all the works cited, the researcher will reconstruct what people told them and organize it according to their own research questions. But convivial scholarship seeks to address this disparity. Convivial scholarship adamantly tries to avoid oversimplification by expressing awareness of "the hierarchies and power relations at play at both the micro and the macro level of being and becoming."[4] In practice, researchers acknowledge several layers of power within their academic work. Choosing sources, reading and listening are not passive or innocent acts but contain and are enabled by political and cultural capital. Therefore, a "reading alongside" of several sources proves valuable in order to refrain from falling into the trap of reproducing simplistic notions of any given research topic. Each of the sources offers a different angle on a specific issue. A contextualization of the cultural texts illuminates the different positions within the field of interest.

The next layer of power refers to context and socio-political positions of the fictional or real people with whom the researcher engages. Clearly, the researcher meets people and not simplistic categorizations. While categories—especially self-definitions—matter, someone who pursues conviviality within scholarship asks how people present themselves. What are their stories or the narratives they subscribe to? Convivial encounters with others thus gesture towards possibilities instead of insurmountable differences, which rule out any chance for dialogue.

Finally, the researcher's own position matters because it has an impact on their understanding and presentation of the research topic and related conversations. Implicitly, any writing that is invested in convivial scholarship as a minor cosmopolitan methodology is always concerned with the ways in which the researcher's position enhances or restricts their view on the topic. Within such a research endeavor, there are no pre-set rules to follow, only a reminder to stay open-minded, to reflect and to repeatedly adapt one's way of communication. Nyamnjoh points out that there are no permanent answers, that friends, enemies and alliances tend to shift, but that an interest in complexity and nuance can be used to challenge inequalities.[5]

[1] Francis Nyamnjoh, "Incompleteness: Frontier Africa and the Currency of Conviviality," *Journal of Asian and African Studies* 52, no. 3 (2015): 253-70.
[2] Ien Ang, *On Not Speaking Chinese: Living between Asia and the West* (London: Routledge, 2001), 163
[3] Nyamnjoh, "Incompleteness," 268.
[4] Nyamnjoh, "Incompleteness," 268.
[5] Nyamnjoh, "Incompleteness."

About the authors

Saima Akhtar

Saima Akhtar is a postdoctoral associate at Yale University, where she works on digital humanities projects that aid in the documentation, study and preservation of the built environment. She is an urban historian and architect by training with a research focus on the relationship between labor immigration, planning, and the rise of industry in early twentieth century US cities—in particular, Detroit.

Arjun Appadurai

Arjun Appadurai is a professor of Media, Culture and Communication at New York University and a Senior Professor at the Hertie School in Berlin. He is an authority on cultural globalization, violence, cities, and media, with a special interest in South Asia. His books, *Modernity at Large* (Minneapolis: University of Minnesota Press, 1996) and *The Future as Cultural Fact* (London: Verso, 2013) have contributed ground-breaking ideas on the dynamics and effects of cultural globalization. His most recent book, co-authored with Neta Alexander, is *Failure* (London: Polity Press, 2019).

Hinemoana Baker

Hinemona Baker is a New Zealand poet, performer, and writer currently living and working in Berlin. She writes and performs in Māori, English, and German where she traces her ancestry from several Māori tribes, England, and Oberammergau. Many cultures converge and challenge each other in her work—most obviously, her parents' Māori and Pākehā ancestries, but also her takatāpuitanga, her sexuality, which she defines as "indigenous queerness". The need to belong to the extended and nuclear group, the whānau as well as the family, is at odds with the equally pressing need to be an individual in the world. Hinemoana has travelled and performed extensively in the last 20 years, has published three poetry collections, edited several more, and produced five albums of her original music and poetry. Her stage shows pivot around sonic art, collaged language, lyric poetry and family storytelling—as well as what she calls "bad jokes and good times".

Sarnath Banerjee

Sarnath Banerjee has written five books of graphic fiction. *Corridor*, *The Barn*

Owl's Wonderous Capers, The Harappa Files, All Quiet in Vikaspuri and *Doabdil*. Through these books he has explored the nature of the Indian middle-class and its transformation from Nehruvian socialism to full-fledged neoliberalism. As part of his ongoing project involving collaboration with historians, Banerjee has produced Liquid History of Vasco Da Gama for the Kochi Biennial, 2014, and The Poona Circle, a series of vandalised history textbooks, for the Pune Bienale, 2017. During the same year, for Frans-Hals museum, Harlem, he produced I Got Ginger, 2017; a series of drawings and text that proposes the making of an 'insubordinate' children's book on Dutch colonialism.

His billboard series, Gallery of Losers, commissioned by Frieze Projects East, for the 2012 London Olympics, was widely displayed in East London. He has been a fellow of Akademie Schloss Solitude, Stuttgart, Indian Foundation for the Arts, Bangalore and the MacArthur foundation, Chicago. In 2019, Sarnath received the Bellknap fellowship from the history department at Princeton University.

Rosa Barotsi

Rosa Barotsi is a Marie Curie fellow based at the Catholic University of the Sacred Heart in Milan, Italy. She has previously held a postdoctoral position at the ICI Berlin Institute for Cultural Inquiry, where she developed a project on Slow cinema and debt. Along with Saima Akhtar and Clio Nicastro, she co-founded the In Front of the Factory research project in 2016. Rosa is a film scholar trained at the University of Cambridge, where she received her PhD in 2014. Her research focuses on the intersections between film, gender and work, with an emphasis on Italian and Greek cinema. She is currently developing a project on women filmmakers in Italy in the period 1965-2015.

Mario Bellatin

Mario Bellatin is a writer based in Mexico City. With over 40 books published, some translated into 15 languages, he is the recipient of the Xavier Villaurrutia, Barbara Gitiings Literature, Antonin Artaud, and José María Arguedas Awards. This year, he was awarded the Premio Iberoamericano de Letras José Donoso. In 2012, he was a curator and member of the Honorary Advisory Committee of the art exhibition dOCUMENTA (13) in Kassel. Apart from writing, he is the director of the Dynamic School of Writers and is directing a documentary called *Bola Negra: El Musical de Ciudad Juárez*.

James Burton

James Burton is a lecturer in Cultural Studies and Cultural History at Goldsmiths, University of London. His research concerns the philosophy and cultural politics of science fiction, memory, post-humanism, ecology and error. A former research fellow at the ICI Berlin Institute for Cultural Inquiry and postdoctoral researcher at the Ruhr University, Bochum, he is the author of *The Philosophy of Science Fiction: Henri Bergson and the Fabulations of Philip K. Dick* (London: Bloomsbury, 2015), and co-editor with Erich Hörl of *General Ecology: The New Ecological Paradigm* (London: Bloomsbury, 2017).

Marina Camargo

Marina Camargo is a Brazilian visual artist based in Berlin. She studied visual arts and holds a Diploma from Akademie der Bildenden Künste München (Germany), a Bachelor and a Master degree from Instituto de Artes / UFRGS, Porto Alegre (Brazil). She also studied Visual Culture at Universitat de Barcelona (Spain). In Camargo's work, the notion of displacement defines a modus operandi for dealing with an established order of World: whether as a physical displacement through space and places or by conceptual shifts. Cartographic and geographical references are often the basis of her projects.

Dong Bingfeng

Dong Bingfeng is a curator, producer, and research fellow in the School of Inter-Media Art of the China Academy of Art. Based in Beijing, he has curated the Guangdong Museum of Art and Ullens Center for Contemporary Art, and is the deputy director of the Iberia Center for Contemporary Art, Li Xianting's Film Fund, and of the OCAT Institute. Dong Bingfeng has been awarded the Chinese Contemporary Art Critic Award, the Yishu Award for Critical Writing on Contemporary Chinese Art, and the Robert H. N. Ho Family Foundation Greater China Research Grant.

Lucy Gasser

Lucy Gasser is currently lecturer in Anglophone literatures at the University of Potsdam. She completed her undergraduate and master's degrees at the University of Cape Town, South Africa, was a visiting researcher at Delhi University in 2017, and defended her doctoral dissertation at the University of Potsdam in 2019. Lucy has published on postcolonial studies and world literature, and has also taught at the University of Cape Town and the Free University of Berlin.

Julian Henriques

Julian Henriques is a professor of the Scriptwriting and Cultural Studies programmes at Goldsmiths, University of London, director of the Topology Research Unit, and a co-founder of the Sound System Outernational practice research group in the Department of Media and Communications. Prior to this, Henriques ran the film and television department at CARIMAC at the University of the West Indies, Kingston. His credits as a writer and director include the reggae musical feature film *Babymother* (Channel Four Films, 1998) and *We the Ragamuffin* (1992). Julian researches street cultures, music, and technologies and is interested in the uses of sound as a critical and creative tool. His sound sculptures include *Knots & Donuts* (2011) at Tate Modern and his books include *Changing the Subject: Psychology, Social Regulation and Subjectivity* (London: Routledge, 1998), *Sonic Bodies* (London: Bloomsbury, 2011) and *Sonic Media* (Durham: Duke University Press, 2018).

Anaïs Héraud-Louisadat

Anaïs Héraud-Louisadat is a performance and visual artist who lives and works in Berlin. Her work is currently focusing on the dimensions of sound, language, and voice in the transmission of knowledge and memory, as well as on the relationship between voice and body within the context of social and political activism.

Irene Hilden

Irene Hilden is a PhD fellow of the RTG minor cosmopolitanisms. She studied cultural history and theory, European ethnology, and German studies at Humboldt University of Berlin and Istanbul University. She has worked at the Berlin Sound Archive (Lautarchiv). Her research focuses on imperial knowledge production and its acoustic traces.

Tom Holert

Tom Holert is an art historian, writer, curator, and artist in Berlin who co-founded the Harun Farocki Institut. During the 1990s, he was an editor with Texte zur Kunst and a publisher of Spex magazine in Cologne. Since then, Holert has taught and conducted research at the Merz Akademie in Stuttgart, the Zurich University of the Arts, the Academy of Fine Arts in Vienna, and the Free University of Berlin, among others. Recent publications include *Knowledge Beside Itself. Contemporary Art's Epistemic Politics* (Berlin: Sternberg Press, 2020); *Marion von Osten: Once We Were Artists* (Utrecht: Valiz & BAK Utrecht, 2017), co-edited with Maria Hlavajova; *Troubling Research: Performing Knowledge in the Arts* (Berlin: Sternberg Press, 2014), with Johanna Schaffer and others; and *Übergriffe: Zustände und Zuständigkeiten der Gegenwartskunst* (Hamburg: Philo Fine Arts, 2014). In 2018, he curated (with Anselm Franke) the exhibition *Neolithic Childhood: Art in a False Present, c. 1930* at HKW, Berlin. Currently, Holert is working on the exhibition and research project *Education Shock. Learning, Politics, and Architecture in the 1960s and 1970s* at HKW (the opening is being rescheduled due to the Covid-19 crisis).

Huang Ya-Li

Huang Ya-Li is a filmmaker from Taiwan, director of the critically acclaimed film *Le Moulin* (2015). His artistic practices focus on image, sound and their interconnections and extensions. In recent years, he tries to establish dialogues between filmmaking and other disciplines and forms. With Sing Song-Yong and Iwaya Kunio, he curated the exhibition *Synchronic Constellation – Le Moulin Society and its Time* (National Taiwan Museum of Fine Arts).

Mary Jirmanus Saba

Mary Jirmanus Saba is a geographer who uses film and other media to explore the histories of the labor movement in the Arab world and its connections to Latin America, feminist internationalism, and new transformative possibilities. Her feature debut *A Feeling Greater Than Love* won the Critics Prize at the 2017 Berlinale Forum.

Liad Hussein Kantorowicz

Liad Hussein Kantorowicz is a performance artist, activist, and perpetual migrant. Her performances deal with de-exotifying and de-mystifying the positions of so-called sexual or political deviants. In them, the body is used as a tool to transgress the boundaries of the public space, and to call into question the public's 'democratic' limitations. She started co-ordinating street interventions and direct actions in the West Bank and performing in events in the formative years of Palestine-Israel's queer scene. After moving to Berlin she gradually placed her work on stage. Her works include: *Pussy. An Ongoing Performative Research* (2018), *No Democracy Here* (2017), *Queerhana: This is a Free Zone* (2017), *Terrorist Superstars* (2016). Her work has been presented at the 10th Berlin Biennale, Athens Museum of Queer Arts AMOQA, Kampnagel, Transmediale festival, among other institutions; she also performs in streets, social centers and queer bars in Europe and Palestine-Israel. Liad is a spokesperson for sex workers' rights and a founder of a Berlin peer project for migrant sex workers at Hydra e.V.

Liu Chuang

Liu Chuang is an artist. He lives and works in Shanghai. Major exhibitions include solo exhibitions at Antenna Space co Qiao Space (2019); Mother's Tankstation, London (2018); Magician Space, Beijing (2015); K11 Wuhan, Wuhan (2015); Taikang Art Space, Beijing (2014); Kunsthall Stavanger, Stavanger (2014); Salon 94 Freemans, New York (2014); Leo Xu Projects, Shanghai (2012). Major group exhibitions include: *Cosmopolis #2*, Centre Pompidou, Paris (2019); 5th Ural Industrial Biennial Of Contemporary Art, Ekaterinburg, Russia (2019); *Cosmopolis #1.5:*

Enlarged Intelligence, Centre Pompidou & Mao Jihong Arts Foundation, Chengdu, China (2018); *Long March Project: Building Code Violations 3 - Special Economic Zone*, Guangdong Times Museum, Guangzhou, China (2018); Foundation Louis Vuitton, Paris (2016); Para Site, Hong Kong (2016); Haus der Kulturen der Welt, Berlin (2016); 10th Shanghai Biennale curated by Anselm Frank, Shanghai (2014); 10th Gwangju Biennale, Gwangju (2014); Tampa Museum of Art, Tampa (2014); Rubell Family Collection, Miami (2013); UCCA, Beijing (2013); Whitechapel Gallery, London (2012); Minsheng Museum, Shanghai (2011); China Power Station, Pinacoteca Agnelli, Turin (2010); New Museum of Contemporary Art, New York (2009); and Astrup Fearnley Museum of Modern Art, Oslo (2007).

Anouk Madörin

Anouk Madörin is a lecturer at the University of Potsdam and former doctoral fellow of the RTG minor cosmopolitanisms. Her PhD project "Shadow archives" traces the colonial legacies of contemporary border and surveillance technologies from the colonies to the European refugee crisis. She was a visiting student at NYU's Graduate Center for Social and Cultural Analysis with a scholarship granted by the Alexander von Humboldt Foundation and a visiting scholar at the Department of Media, Music, Communication and Cultural Studies at Macquarie University in Sydney.

James Miller

James Miller is a professor of Humanities at Duke Kunshan University, China, where he co-directs the Humanities Research Center and the Planetary Ethics and Artificial Intelligence (PETAL) research laboratory. He is a worldwide renowned scholar of China's indigenous religion, Daoism, and has published six books relating to Chinese religions, most recently, *China's Green Religion: Daoism and the Quest for a Sustainable Future* (New York: Columbia University Press, 2017).

Sara Morais dos Santos Bruss

Sara Morais dos Santos Bruss is a postdoctoral researcher at the TU Dresden's GenderConceptGroup in the project Digital Gender. As a former member of the RTG minor cosmopolitanisms, she conducted her PhD on digital acts of solidarity, producing an analysis of feminist strategies to re-embody the digital. Her current research focuses on automated structures of inequality and identity in the digital, reviewing historical oppression and globalized cultures through feminist epistemologies of science, technology and society.

Clio Nicastro

Clio Nicastro teaches at Bard College Berlin and is currently affiliated with ICI

Berlin. She studied Philosophy at the University of Palermo (Italy) where she completed her PhD in Aesthetics and Theory of Arts with a thesis on the notion of Denkraum der Besonnenheit in Aby Warburg, which she is in the process of adapting into a book. In 2015 she moved to Berlin as a DAAD postdoctoral fellow working on the German filmmaker Harun Farocki. From 2016-2018 she was a postdoctoral fellow at ICI Berlin Institute for Cultural Inquiry. Her current research focuses on the cinematic representations of eating disorders as well as on cinema and labor, a project she has been carrying out together with Saima Akhtar and Rosa Barotsi since 2016.

Mariya Nikolova

Mariya Nikolova is a doctoral candidate at the RTG minor cosmopolitanisms with a joint PhD fellowship between Potsdam University and University of New South Wales (Australia). She received a Masters degree in Transnational Literature, Theatre and Film at the University of Bremen, and a Bachelor degree in English-Speaking Cultures and Political Science at the University of Bremen and Birmingham City University. Mariya has worked as an interpreter for women affected by HIV at the Bremer Public Health Department and as the coordinator for the Volunteer, English and Youth Zones Departments of the Bulgarian Youth and Children Parliament. Mariya's research revolves around Critical Theory and Experimental Literature. Her dissertation investigates tropes of futurity embedded in the American avant-garde canon. Mariya's non-academic engagements include performance art and photography.

Vivian Price

Vivian Price is a Professor at California State University, Dominguez Hills, in Interdisciplinary Studies and coordinates Labour Studies. She is active in community and labour issues focusing on social justice unionism and the struggle against environmental racism. Price is a filmmaker whose award winning work includes *Hammering It Out* (2000), *Transnational Tradeswomen* (2006) (both distributed by Women Make Movies), *Harvest of Loneliness* (2010) (distributed by Film and Media), and has published numerous peer-reviewed articles on gender, labour, visuality and pedagogy. She was a Spring 2018 Fulbright Scholar at the University of Liverpool teaching a class about and researching labour and climate change.

Anna von Rath

Anna von Rath lives in Berlin, where she works as a freelance cultural event organizer, and social justice and diversity trainer. She is one of the founding editors of poco. lit., an online platform for postcolonial literatures in the widest sense. In

2019, she submitted her doctoral thesis "Afropolitan Encounters: Literature and Activism in London and Berlin" as part of the RTG minor cosmopolitanisms at the University of Potsdam. Anna has published on Afropolitanism, postcolonial ecocriticism and travel narratives. She regularly writes for postcolonialpotsdam.org about Germany's colonial history and its contemporary repercussions.

Sundar Sarrukai

Sundar Sarukkai was, until 2019, a professor of philosophy at the National Institute of Advanced Studies. He was also the Founder-Director of the Manipal Centre for Philosophy and Humanities. His work is primarily in the philosophy of natural and social sciences. He is the author of the following books: *Translating the World: Science and Language* (Lanham: University Press of America, 2002); *Philosophy of Symmetry* (Shimia: Indian Institute of Advanced Study, 2004); *Indian Philosophy and Philosophy of Science* (New Delhi: Project of History of Indian Science, Philosophy and Culture, Centre for Studies in Civilizations, 2005); *What is Science?* (New Delhi: National Book Trust, India, 2012) and two books co-authored with Gopal Guru: *The Cracked Mirror: An Indian Debate on Experience and Theory* (New Delhi: Oxford University Press, 2012) and most recently *Experience, Caste and the Everyday Social* (New Delhi: Oxford University Press, 2019). His book titled *JRD Tata and the Ethics of Philanthropy* (London: Taylor & Francis, 2020) will be published this summer. He has also been active in outreach programs to take philosophy to different communities and places, including philosophy workshops for children, and that bring philosophy to the public, through his writing in the media and his initiative Barefoot Philosophers.

Sikho Siyotula

Sikho Siyotula is a doctoral fellow of the RTG minor cosmopolitanisms at the University of Potsdam, Germany and the University of Pretoria, South Africa. She is currently researching the visualisation of Southern African Later Iron Age Settlements in The Digital Age. Siyotula is informed by her training as a visual artist, practices of blackness in contemporary visual arts, as well as her research interests in intercultural relations. She is invested in practises of making—particularly the making of visual images—within academia.

Jens Temmen

Jens Temmen is a postdoctoral researcher at the Obama Institute for Transnational American Studies at the University of Mainz (Germany) and a member of the "Young Academy" of the Academy of Sciences and Literature in Mainz. As part of his PhD-fellowship with the RTG minor cosmopolitanisms at the University of

Potsdam, Jens wrote a thesis on "The Territorialities of U.S. Imperialism(s)," which was published with Universitätsverlag Winter (2020). His thesis analyzes conflicting discourses of sovereignty, jurisdiction, and territory negotiated in US legal and Indigenous life writing texts in the contexts of the North American continent and the Pacific. He is also co-editor of an anthology titled *Across Currents: Connections between Atlantic and (Trans)Pacific Studies* (London: Routledge, 2018) as well as co-editor of a special forum of the Journal of Transnational American Studies (JTAS) on American Territorialities. His postdoctoral research project employs an ecocritical and posthumanist lens to look at representations of the future of extraterrestrial human life in contemporary US literature and culture.

Heinrich Wilke

Heinrich Wilke studied English and Philosophy at the University of Tübingen and the University of Connecticut, graduating with a Staatsexamen (i.e., teaching degree) and an M.A. in English Literatures and Cultures. From 2016 to 2019, he was doctoral fellow in the DFG-funded RTG minor cosmopolitanisms at Potsdam University, where he is currently employed as a lecturer. In his dissertation, he researches the plantation system of the colonial Caribbean from around 1650 to 1800, under the supervision of Lars Eckstein and Marcus Boon (York University, Toronto). The project focuses on monoculture as a decidedly capitalist form of cultivation, inquiring into its economic and ecological presuppositions, such as enslaved labour and deforestation, as well as its sedimentation in the form of texts. To this end, he interprets anglophone and francophone writings of various genres, from plantation manuals and travel writing to letters, poetry, and political proclamations, from an eco-Marxist perspective.

Zairong Xiang

Zairong Xiang is the editor of this book and, until summer 2020, research fellow at Potsdam University with the RTG minor cosmopolitanisms. He joins the faculty of Duke Kunshan University as Assistant Professor of Comparative Literature and Associate Director of Art. He is author of *Queer Ancient Ways: A Decolonial Exploration* (Goleta: punctum books, 2018) and has co-edited the special issue "Hyperimage" for *New Arts: Journal of National Academy of Art* (32, 2018); and a special issue at *GLQ – A Journal of Lesbian and Gay Studies*: "The Ontology of the Couple" (25 no. 2, 2019). He curated the *minor cosmopolitan weekend* at HKW Haus der Kulturen der Welt in December 2018 and will co-curate the 2nd Guangzhou Image Triennial in 2021.

Acknowledgements

This book is supported by the DFG-funded Research Training Group minor cosmopolitanisms. I would like to thank my colleagues at the RTG for their support in the process of editing the book, especially Amina Balajo, who offered impeccable assistance with the editorial nitty-gritty at the early stage, and to Anke Bartels for her unconditional help throughout the whole process. The book would not have been possible without the commitment that the contributors to this volume have shown. Your engaged responses and timely submissions have made editing this book a huge pleasure.

My heartfelt thanks to Rosa Barotsi, whose thoughtful editing enhances the textual coherence of the project as a whole, while preserving the various texts' diversity in their respective styles, genres and contexts. Many thanks to Arthur Lang, whose beautiful design has further enriched the meaningful colors of this minor cosmos you hold in your hands. I am especially grateful to Marina Camargo for granting us the rights to use her marvelous artwork "Estudos sobre a noite" (2015–2018), which gently wraps around the covers of the book. A special thank you to Huang Ya-Li for giving me access to the rich image archive of the exhibition *Synchronic Constellations*. An earlier version of the chapter by Dong Bingfeng appeared as "Bio-Archiving: Shenyang Underground Music as History, Awareness of Life, and Art in Action" in the journal *Yishu: Journal of Contemporary Chinese Art* (16, no. 4, 2017), and is reprinted here with kind permission from the journal's chief editor, Zheng Shentian. I would also like to thank Tom Holert for putting me in contact with the editors at Diaphanes. Thank you Hendrik Rohlf and Michael Heitz for providing a wonderful home for this project.

The book is based on the *minor cosmopolitan weekend* I curated with the RTG minor cosmopolitanisms at HKW Haus der Kulturen der Welt in Berlin, in December 2018. I would like to thank all the participants, speakers, filmmakers, artists, performers, dancers, DJs, independent observers, technicians, caterers, cleaners, and volunteers for having jointly made the event possible; needless to say, all the core members of the organizing team: Lina Fricke, Monica Gutierrez, Joanna Louise Mackenthun, Farai von Pentz, Amina Balajo, Lars Eckstein, Dirk Wiemann, Anja Schwarz, Regina Römhild, Nicole Waller, and the interns Marie-Christin Hoffmann, Gracija Atanasovska, Francisco Bugmann Neto, Imge Turan, Joshua Pawli;

our collaborators at HKW, especially Olga Sievers, Stefan Aue, and Bernd Scherer, and our partner institution Zentrum für Gender- und Diversitätsforschung (ZGD) at Tübingen University, especially Gero Bauer and Ingrid Hotz-Davies; and all my other colleagues at the RTG: supervisors, coordinators, and fellows who have offered generous help: Judith Coffey, Sérgio Costa, Ina Kerner, Sina Rauschenbach, Marcus Boon, Rajni Palriwala, Satish Poduval, Ira Raja, Corinne Sandwith, Adam Haupt, Lize Kriel, Florian Schybilsky, Heinrich Wilke, Jens Temmen, Irene Hilde, Mariya Nikolova, Sikho Siyotula, Lucy Gasser, Yann Le Gall, Sara Morais dos Santos Bruss, Oduor Obura, Anna von Rath, Moses März, Anouk Madörin, Julia von Sigsfeld.

minor cosmopolitan
Thinking Art, Politics, and the Universe Together Otherwise
Edited by: Zairong Xiang

Contributions by Saima Akhtar, Arjun Appadurai, Hinemoana Baker, Sarnath Banerjee, Rosa Barotsi, Mario Bellatin, James Burton, Marina Camargo, Dong Bingfeng, Lucy Gasser, Julian Henriques, Anaïs Héraud-Louisadat, Irene Hilden, Tom Holert, Huang Ya-Li, Mary Jirmanus Saba, Liad Hussein Kantorowicz, Liu Chuang, Anouk Madörin, James Miller, Sara Morais dos Santos Bruss, Clio Nicastro, Mariya Nikolova, Vivian Price, Anna von Rath, Sundar Sarrukai, Sikho Siyotula, Jens Temmen, Heinrich Wilke, Zairong Xiang

Inside Cover Image “Estudos sobre a noite” (2015–2018) by Marina Camargo

Intermezzo “*minor cosmopolitan weekend* remembered”
illustrations by Nik Neves and photography by Camila Gonzatto

Proofreading and editing: Rosa Barotsi
Design: Arthur Lang
Printed by Printall AS in Estonia

ISBN 978-3-0358-0304-4

Publisher:
DIAPHANES
Zurich-Berlin-Paris 2020
www.diaphanes.net